THE RISING OF THE MOON

JONATHAN DOWNES AND NIGEL WRIGHT

Edited by Ronan Coghlan. Typeset by Jon Downes
Cover and internal design by Mark North for CFZ Communications
Using Microsoft Word 2000, Microsoft Publisher 2000,
Adobe Photoshop.

Photographs and Illustrations © 2005 CFZ

Revised edition 2005

Published by

XIPHOS BOOKS
1, HILLSIDE GARDENS, BANGOR
NORTHERN IRELAND
BT19 6SJ

All rights reserved. Without limiting the rights under copyright reserved above, no part of this publication may be reproduced, stored in or introduced into a retrieval system, or transmitted, in any form of by any means (electronic, mechanical, photocopying, recording or otherwise), without the prior written permission of both the copyright owners and the publishers of this book.

ISBN: 0-9544936-5-6

For Felinda and Sue

"Now, my own suspicion is that the universe is not only queerer than we suppose, but queerer than we can suppose. I have read and heard many attempts at a systematic account of it, from materialism and theosophy to the Christian system or that of Kant, and I have always felt that they were much too simple. I suspect that there are more things in heaven and earth than are dreamed of, or can be dreamed of, in any philosophy. That is the reason why I have no philosophy myself, and must be my excuse for dreaming."

J. B. S. Haldane

"In my mind's eye I'll light fires in your cities"

Charles Manson

"One of the reasons I took so long to become a magician was because of some of the people surrounding the occult scene. They have a yawning emotional gulf inside them and bolster it with all this gothic shit. There's a certain sort of Aleister Crowley-ite who's into a middle class view of evil: they're aso into Charles Manson and piercing. I've nothing against romanticism. But there's romanticism and acting like a spaz."

Alan Moore

AUTHORS' NOTE

Although this book is a joint project in every sense of the word it is unusual amongst books that have been co-authored in that it has been written by one author based largely upon the research of the other. Any errors, omissions or what would be vulgarly called `cock-ups` are therefore the joint responsibility of Jon and Nigel. The authors would like to thank the following people: Sue Wright, Graham Inglis, Richard Freeman, Mark North, Maxine Pearson, Jan Scarff, Richard Forsyth, Janet Kipling Roy Richardson, Nick Redfern, Nina Pendred, Sarah Moran, Marco Gianangelli and all at Devon News but for whom and all that.....

CONTENTS

INTRODUCTION TO THE 2005 EDITION 11

FOREWORD BY NICK REDFERN 13

INTRODUCTION 17

PART ONE: WHEN? 19

PART TWO: WHERE? 121

PART THREE: WHAT? 197

PART FOUR: WHY? 251

EPILOGUE 343

REFERENCES 345

APPENDIX 373

INDEX 379

PHOTOGRAPHS 188 – 196

INTRODUCTION
- TO THE -
2005 EDITION

This is a strange book, and sadly it is one that has been out of print for many years since I had a somewhat acrimonious parting of the ways with my old publisher. An awful lot has happened, and even more has changed in the intervening years.

The Centre for Fortean Zoology, which back in the halcyon days of 1997 when the events in this book took place, was a haphazard and anarchic bunch of people - basically "The Last Gang in Town" as Joe Strummer would have said. Now, we are the biggest and fastest growing cryptozoological organisation in the world and have been becoming ever more respectable as the years continue.

Toby the dog died in June 2000, and not a day goes by when I don't mourn the old chap.

Nick Redfern no longer lives in England, and furthermore longer believes in the Extraterrestrial Hypothesis - and indeed has recently published a book which in many people's eyes commits the ultimate act of UFOlogical apostasy by publishing a book which finally lays the story of a UFO crash at Roswell in July 1947 firmly to rest.

Nigel and I are still friends, but as I no longer live in Exeter, and he has more and more family commitments, our forays into the unknown together are becoming every more rare.

And finally. When I wrote this book, I was endeavouring to present the world with a `unified theory of everything`, a field theory which can encompass all fortean phenomena. It may be because then I was young, idealistic and naïve, and now I am older, and a more sober and less headstrong character, but now, although I think that the theory outlined in this book has its good points, I don't believe that *anything* as disparate and strange as the wide field of forteana can be explained by just one theory. Indeed, some years later, my friend and colleague Richard Freeman (who should really have been given greater credit in coming up with the theory in *this* book), came up with another theory which - we believe - fills even more of the gaps than does the one outlined in these pages. With Richard's permission, an excerpt from his book *Dragons: More than a Myth* (CFZ Press, 2005) is included as an appendix.

Why, you may ask, have I not done major rewrites to this edition? The answer is simple. There is a distressing tendency within fortean circles to present new editions of one's books as an excuse to revise and change what you originally wrote. In the same way as I heartily disapprove of musicians who re-issue their old records, having sanitised, remixed, and re-recorded them, I dislike the revisionist ethic in fortean publishing very much indeed.

Several on my favourite fortean books have been given this treatment in recent years, and I find this most distressing. Therefore - although I no longer believe that this is a unified theory of everything, I have made no revisions, apart from one passage which has been removed partly for legal reasons and partly because it subsequently turned out that it just wasn't true! A few spelling errors have been corrected, but otherwise this book is as I wrote it back during the autumn and winter of 1988 - a true and accurate portrayal of a strange and cathartic time of my life, together with our humble (and often bumbling) attempts to make sense of it all.

I would like to thank - in addition to those included in the acknowledgements - Ronan Coghlan, my father, and Corinna James for each doing their own inimitable thing in their own inimitable way.

Slainte

Jon Downes
Woolfardisworthy
North Devon
September 2006

FOREWORD

by
Nick Redfern

As someone who is a firm believer in the theory that some UFOs are extraterrestrial spacecraft, I have given much thought as to why I elected to write the foreword for *The Rising of the Moon* - a book that postulates so manifestly different a theory to explain the ever-present UFO mystery on our planet.

Primarily, there are three reasons:

- First, Jon is a good mate, and unlike so many other people I've come across in the UFO and paranormal fields, he has a fine sense of humour.

- Second, there was the lure of a copious amount of free alcohol and a selection of *Ramones* bootlegs from Jon's vast and varied record collection.

- And third (and, certainly, most important of all), his book is a damn fine read - at times funny, disturbing, tragic and ultimately cathartic.

But what can I say about this book without giving too much away to the unsuspecting reader? Well ... if you thought that you had spent your hard earned wages/giro (delete where applicable) on a straightforward "UFO Book", you would be very wrong. *The Rising of the Moon* is anything *but* a straightforward "UFO Book"! Rather, it is an intensely personal attempt of Jon's (and it should not be forgotten, Nigel's), attempt to get his head round - and make some sense of - that which in scientific terms, has come to be known collectively as "weird shit": UFOs, animal mutilations, lake monsters, crop circles, bigfoot, mystery big cats, and all manner of associated strangeness that plagues those of us engaged in the investigation of the incredible.

Of equal significance, however, is the fact that the writing of the book also played a part in Jon's - ultimately successful - attempts to exorcise his own personal demons; demons that took him to the very edge of sanity, and very nearly to the point of no return. Moreover, Jon is to be applauded for having the balls to reveal to one and all the stark facts surrounding this aspect of his life and writing career.

So, what does Jon's quest tell us? First and foremost, as anyone who knows Jon will be aware, he not only has a love of all things fortean, but he also has a vast knowledge of such matters too, and this shines throughout the text. What also shines through is Jon's dogged determination to check, recheck and cross-reference the evidence - something that is sadly lacking in much of today's paranormal research.

Jon and Nigel begin by acquainting us with the facts surrounding a spectacular wave of UFO encounters that occurred almost on their very doorstep during 1997, and go on in workmanlike fashion to chronicle the quite-literally astounding number of reports that subsequently followed; reports encompassing strange lights zipping round the Devon and Cornwall countryside; UFOs rising out of the sea at Otter Cove; "whale mutilations"; ghostly black dogs; and strange creatures seen roaming around the wilds of the Westcountry.

This - as you can imagine - was no standard "UFO wave". Rather, it turned out to be just one piece of a very large, and infinitely complex, jigsaw - a jigsaw which was to stretch Jon and Nigel's investigative skills to the limit, and that - finally - led them to propose an ingenious and highly plausible theory to explain that aforementioned collection of "weird shit".

As someone who writes primarily about government cover-ups surrounding the UFO issue, I was also intrigued to see that they had looked into a variety of rumours relating to British Government involvement in a number of purported UFO cases that Nigel had found, not just dating back to the 1940s and 1950s, but to the turn of the century when specific parts of the country were plagued by the so-called "Phantom Airship Mystery".

Again, Jon's ability to sort out the wheat from the chaff comes to the fore, and it is refreshing to find someone who is able to address such issues without allowing their personal prejudices to come into play.

The Rising of the Moon also takes us to the furthest depths of the human psyche, and gives us a disturbing and alarming look at the "mind monsters" that very possibly lurk within all of us - and, indeed, what can happen when they break free of their constraints and begin to …. Well, that's something for you to discover as you read the book.

Do I agree with all Jon's conclusions? No, of course not. But that is how it should be: In a field such as this, it is vital that we:

(a)   consider all manner of theories and beliefs; and
(b)   do not rule out those which we might contemplate as being too "out there".

Yes, I am an adherent of the theory that we do have - or at least *have had* - extraterrestrials among us, and I am also an adherent of the belief that the U.S Government has in its possession the remains of one or more retrieved alien spacecraft, as well as a variety of alien bodies held in suitably "cold storage". As Jon and Nigel rightly note in their book, however, there are accounts dating back centuries of strange bodies (many of the `mermaid` variety), rumoured to have been found in remote areas, only to disappear later, amid claims of cover-up and confabulation. The parallels between these accounts and that relating to the so-called `Roswell Incident` are plain to see. Those of us who do believe that in some government facility there exists prime evidence of UFO reality, would do well to recognise that such accounts are not solely the domain of late 1940s USA.

However, the "E.T Angle" is only one aspect of an infinitely broader mystery, and I feel confident in saying that when the full picture finally emerges into the public domain *The Rising of the Moon* will be judged as a prophetic and highly relevant piece of work.

So, if you enjoy reading about unidentified flying objects, fantastic beasts, strange lifeforms soaring amid the upper atmosphere, dark-robed figures creeping around in the dead of night, black-masses in ancient woods, and much more (including what is surely the epitome of all that is unholy -Toby the dog), then this book will not disappoint.

Indeed, it has something for everybody: The UFO devotees, the Charles Fort fanatic, the H.P.Lovecraft disciple, the Crowley crowd, and just about anyone else who has ever contemplated the mysteries of our planet.

In view of its contents, however, I suggest that you read *The Rising of the Moon* by candlelight on a dark and stormy winter's night - preferably in a suitably-spooky old house on the edge of some desolate and windswept moorland. Sit yourself down with a plentiful supply of mature scrumpy, and indulge in the black, disturbing and eye-opening ideas of a true visionary.

I thought about concluding my foreword in true *X Files* fashion by stating something like "The truth is in here", or "Trust no-one - except Jon Downes and Nigel Wright". Instead, I'll simply say: "Read and Enjoy; you will not be disappointed".

INTRODUCTION

"When the going gets weird the weird turn pro"
Dr Hunter S.Thompson

On the 28th July 1996 strange things were happening in the skies above East Devon. Mr Jerome Canvin of Heavitree, Exeter alerted his neighbours Sue and John Murphy at 2 a.m. Together they witnessed a bright, oval object shining in the clouds and flashing on and off irregularly. It shone powerful green rays of light in all directions. It then shone down on them and lit up the surrounding houses. They also saw more small ovals beaming light apparently randomly. The larger of the ovals completed a three quarters circle and rapidly `whizzed` off leaving the others which disappeared when a plane flew past. The display lasted twenty minutes. [1]

A middle aged couple, also from the Heavitree district of Exeter, were looking out of their bedroom window at about eleven thirty at night when they saw what they described as a glowing candelabra shape in the sky to the east. [2] They were only two of nearly a dozen witnesses who corroborated each other`s stories (as I later found out) to an amazing degree. At the same time as they were watching this glorious display of skyborne strangeness, another couple - this time much younger, were returning from an evening in a pub to their home on the outskirts of Exmouth. [3] As they were walking hand in hand up the narrow wooded drive to the house where the girl`s mother lived they saw an extraordinary animal cross the road only a few yards in front of them. They described it later as being a bizarre cross between a lynx and a dachshund but being far larger than a fox. About six miles to the west a complex crop circle (or to be more accurate a complex formation of circles) was appearing in a field of barley just north of Matford Roundabout. When investigators arrived on the scene the next day they were shocked to find the mutilated corpses of several pigeons strewn purposefully around the formations. [4]

Because of my high profile involvement in paranormal research across the West Country, the first thing that several of these witnesses did was to telephone me. However they were out of luck. The 28th July 1996 was also the day that my wife left me and the nervous breakdown which had been hovering over me like a baleful shadow for several years finally overtook me with a force that I had never been conditioned to expect. [5] As the witnesses of high strangeness across the region tried to contact me I was lying, semi-comatose with grief, whisky and valium on my sitting room floor gibbering with incoherent misery and pain as my friend and colleague Graham Inglis sat next to me, holding my hand and powerless to do anything to help me apart from making sure that I didn`t choke on my own vomit or carry out my repeated threats to kill myself. [6]

Over the next eighteen months the strangeness continued and a series of terrifying and bizarre events ensued. Slowly as I came to terms with both my loss and my mental illness I threw myself back into my work and together with a close knit band of friends and colleagues I investigated UFO reports, animal mutilations, crop circles and other incidences of high strangeness. We also uncovered some fascinating historical accounts which proved that whatever it is that has been happening in South East Devon over the past few years it is not a new phenomenon. It has been going on for aeons and shows no sign of going away. We discovered the prosaic truth behind some of these incidents and came up against a figurative brick wall surrounding many of the others.

As I slowly climbed back out of the black morass of psychosis, I became more aware of the intricacies of the fortean universe than I have ever been before. One horrifying conundrum remains, however - which are the more dreadful - the monsters which reputedly haunt the leafy Devon lanes or those which still exist inside my head?

I may never rid myself of the latter, but the nature of the former is now within my grasp and that of my band of friends and colleagues. This is my story, and their story...

PART ONE: WHEN?

"Now come tell me Sean O`Farrell tell me why you hurry so? Hush, a bhuachaill, hush and listen," and his cheeks were all aglow. I have orders from the captain, get you ready quick and soon for the pikes must be together at the rising of the moon"

Trad arr. **Shane McGowan**

I

I spent much of the first two weeks of August in a drunken stupor and unfortunately I missed hearing about one of the most exciting events to have been reported from the fortean universe in many years. It was actually the middle of October, several months (and a lot of pills and whisky) after the event that I heard about it. But using a mixture of detective work and hard core speculation we finally managed to piece together some semblance of what actually happened.

Several years before I had appeared in a number of episodes of a Westcountry TV series called *Mysterious West*. It was my TV debut and one which furthermore whetted my appetite for television work. As a somewhat unwanted side effect of my new found media exposure upon the small screen I was figuratively inundated with stories of high strangeness from across the region. It got to the stage that I was unable to go into a pub without a total stranger coming up to me and regaling me with stories of witchcraft, ghosts and things that went bump in the night. This was, as one can imagine, an invaluable source of new stories for me to investigate, and as part of my new found status as a bachelor Graham and I decided that we had to make use of this treasure trove of new source material.

We decided, one drunken night, that it would be a good idea if we were to start a generic research group for the Exeter area by which we could recruit new blood into our research team (which at the time only consisted really of the two of us). We also had a `covert agenda` (to steal someone`s phrase).

We had every hope that amongst the influx of keen eyed researchers that we fondly hoped would wend their way to our door in search of the answers to the great mysteries of the universe would be attractive young ladies who would find a grossly overweight (and soon to be divorced) fortean researcher to be a peerless companion for romance and wild adventures. Of course, it didn't work out like that.

I had known Graham for most of the previous decade. He had originally just been a friend, but after only a relatively short time of knowing him I discovered that he was somewhat of a wizard with a soldering iron, and furthermore he lived (at the time) in a murky and rather grubby basement where he was not only happy to allow an inept and very noisy rock band to practise, but he would also allow us to store the band's equipment in the corner of his abode. From being my friend, he soon became my roadie and over a period of three years or so he humped our gear and mixed the sound (as well as making videos) at the best part of a hundred gigs by my ensemble "Jon Downes and the Amphibians from Outer Space". [1] When my wife left me, he was the first person that I telephoned for aid and he spent much of the next month sitting (literally and figuratively) holding my hand and helping me through my first uncertain transition into bachelor status.

By default, he then became my business partner, and over a series of drunken brainstorming sessions we formulated the rough framework of our future activities. One of the first things that we started was the Exeter Strange Phenomena research group (our late night brainstorming sesh coming up with the initials E.S.P which we thought was an exceptionally funny pun - which over the next two years no-one ever seemed to understand). We announced the formation of the nascent group in the Exeter *Express and Echo* in early October, and, to our immense gratification we received a number of telephone calls from interested people who wanted to come and see us and discuss their experiences.

Unfortunately none of them were young nymphomaniacs with an irresistible attraction to overweight divorcees.

The first of our visitors introduced himself to us on the telephone as Peter Glastonbury and told us that he was in possession of some extraordinary video tape. He made an appointment to come and see us. We were convinced that a name such as "Peter Glastonbury" had to be a convenient nom-de-plume adopted by some hippy geezer in order to give himself some spurious new-age credibility. We were also convinced that the video that he was going to show us would be similarly inane new-age schlock. As is so often the case we were completely wrong. He turned out to be a leather jacketed, long haired hippyish bloke of uncertain age, but Glastonbury was his real name and the video he showed us and the story he told us was nothing short of extraordinary.

Wiltshire is still a strange and ancient land. In those few minutes just after sunrise, the shifting lights and desolately beautiful landscape can make the unwary visitor feel as if he's in another time. Just after sunrise on 11 August 1996 a student - we will call him John - was camping at Oliver's Castle, an ancient earthwork which, since a battle in the days of the Civil War, has been called after Oliver Cromwell. The night before, he had been drinking at The Barge, a pub at Alton Barnes, where he told his companions that he intended to spend the night watching the crops, hoping that, as on so many other occasions in previous years, an arcane symbol would be magickally imprinted into the corn. [2]

He was woken up by a distinctive humming sound. He reached for his Hi 8 video camera and ran towards the crest of the hill, filming as he went, and, more by luck than judgement, he captured what may be the most significant 19 seconds of video tape ever recorded. Within days the figurative echoes of this 19 seconds of video footage were to echo around the world, causing controversy, anger, awe, and disbelief - and, incidentally, making the poor cameraman's life almost untenable. This is why we have protected his identity, because, unlike some researchers in this field, we believe in the researcher's innate right to privacy.

What John saw and videotaped that day - not without precedent in the field of crop circle research (no pun intended!) - certainly captures a remarkable series of events.

He saw two lights swooping around like the Irish fairy birds *Éan Sí* [3] in one area of the field. He zoomed into the area of the field where the lights were most active; and, as the lights darted around the field only two feet above the ripened wheat crop, a complex pattern of 19 interlinked circles looking for all the world like a stylised snowflake appeared in front of the camera. The appearance of the formation took only four seconds. *"Oh, wow - that's amazing",* said John softly to himself, with the humility that only comes, when after many years of searching, one is confronted with a once in a lifetime experience. He videoed for a few minutes afterwards, but no more lights appeared.

In a daze, he packed up his tent. It was 6 a.m. As he prepared to leave the area, he saw a group of soldiers apparently on a training exercise. According to some reports, the sergeant hailed him cheerfully and asked, "Did you get what you came for?" John nodded dumbly and made his way to his car. We know nothing of his movements for the next six hours, until he entered The Barge pub, [4] at midday, looking for Peter Sorensen and Colin Andrews, two prominent crop circle researchers who had been staying at the pub. In a paradox worthy of Wessex's master of the contrived storyline, Thomas Hardy, as John was visiting the pub looking for them, they were visiting the crop circle. He turned up again in the evening and showed his footage to the people present through the viewfinder of the camera. However, because of the small display format, the people viewing the footage were unable to appreciate the significance of the video.

According to our sources, the video was shown on a TV screen later on, to a small group of researchers. Because it was so late in the crop circle season, however, most researchers had already left the area.

A week later, Peter Sorensen borrowed the master tape and took it to Lee Winterstone's video studio in Swindon, where copies were made. On John's request, the soundtrack was omitted from the copies because the original tape included his muttered profanities. John was already becoming apprehensive at the level of interest that had been engendered and with the innate paranoia which seems to be inherent in every researcher of the *X-Files* generation, he wanted the video to be distributed as widely as possible, so that the 'powers-that-be' would be unable to suppress the truth that he was certain was out there. He therefore waived his claim to copyright, putting his material into the public domain. [5]

His honesty and forthrightness were to be 'rewarded' when one of the leading figures in crop circle research hired a team of spectacularly private detectives to 'dish the dirt' on him. John promptly went to ground and although some reports have him working as a teacher in Bristol, other usually trustworthy sources have claimed that he's presently in the United States. Whichever is the case, his brush with notoriety frightened him so badly that he's never been heard from since - and it is doubtful if he will be camping in the Alton Barnes area in the next crop circle season!

A third-generation copy of the video reached Pete Glastonbury in September and, within weeks, he had taken it to us. Before seeing this video, we had been highly sceptical about the genesis of crop circles. Such things were, in our opinion, caused by merry pranksters with a head full of cider and a heart full of mischief.

The Oliver's Castle video, however, was to have a dramatic effect upon our world view. As Graham said in the December 1996 ESP Research Group newsletter, *"either we've seen a remarkably clever hoax, or we've seen the best evidence yet of life 'out there'."* [6]

The deterioration in quality when copying a video is easily compensated for with a fractal analyser and there is nothing on the original video that cannot be discerned on subsequent copies. Also, there is more information contained on a video tape than is evident on a normal TV. Hidden from normal view, video tape carries an extra line or strip of pixel codes. If a video sequence is manipulated in any way, the beginning and end of the sequence are both marked with a single pixel (dot).

In addition, every time a sequence is recopied, the type of video machine making the new copy is codified on the video tape by the addition of further pixels. Philip Head, of the Exeter University film and video department, who viewed the Oliver's Circle video, was able to determine the copying history of the video sequence - how many times the piece had been copied and on what types of video machine.

David K Wells of Westcountry TV has also studied the video and says that he can detect no trickery. With seven years' experience in special effects, he knows all the signs to look for. [7]

Although a colleague at a computer animation workshop in Bristol believes masking and morphing could have been used, there is no evidence that this actually occurred. He suggested that special software many have been written specifically for this type of fakery. We made a public appeal over Westcountry media challenging any wannabe video fakers to make a convincing fascimile. The only one we were sent was derisively bad.

The crop circle researcher who had hired the private investigators to investigate the hapless John vacillated between a cautious endorsement of the film for which it appears he claimed much of the credit on several transatlantic TV shows and a derisive dismissal of what he claimed was a crude hoax. He has claimed on a number of occasions that the whole affair is a conspiracy by unnamed government agencies (which governments is unclear) to discredit crop circle research in general and him in particular. He cites John's subsequent disappearance, hotly pursued by his hired gumshoes, as supportive evidence for his paranoid theorising. The most interesting aspect of the whole affair, however, are the balls of light. Pete Glastonbury has seen and photographed such phenomena in conjunction with crop circles on several occasions.

A few weeks after showing us the video Pete Glastonbury was approached by a mysterious man who claimed that he had a similar video taken in Wiltshire the previous year. The only difference was that this one was witnessed by police and other members of the security forces who were intent on stopping casual observers from viewing the events. Under circumstances of stringent secrecy Pete was taken to the man's house where he saw the video. Much to his surprise (and to the great joy of every X-Files conspiracy theorist to whom we have told this story), the video was just as had been described.

We are unwilling to accept the hypothesis that either crop formations or the glowing balls of light are extraterrestrial in origin. We also reject suggestions that they are somehow connected with military activities of one or more governments. We prefer to see them in terms of what we think of as "the Pan view of nature". As my friend and mentor Tony 'Doc' Shiels once said to us recently, on another but related subject, *"I don't know why you blasted forteans make such a fuss about all these things. They happen. It's just part of the way things are."* [8] And as Roy Harper (who coincidently went to school with Tony) once said, *"Everything is just everything, because everything just is."* [9]

Peter came up with a theory which astounded and intrigued us. European folklore is full of stories of fairy rings, and the concept has bewitched succesive generations. The generally accepted explanation for them is both dull and prosaic:

"Fairy rings usually appear in a lawn as circles or arcs of dark green, faster growing grass. A ring of thin, dead, or dormant grass may develop both inside and outside this circle or arc. They vary in size from a few inches to 50 feet or more in diameter, but most are 3-15 feet across. Fairy rings are caused by soil organisms that decay organic matter under the soil surface, i.e, tree stumps, large roots and buried construction lumber. The fungus spores grow and spread throughout the soil, sometimes to a depth of a foot or more, forming a dense, white, thread-like network which has a strong, musty odour.

In mild weather, following rains or heavy irrigation a large number of mushrooms or puffballs (the fruiting bodies of the fairy ring fungi) may suddenly appear in the circle or arc outlining the fairy ring. The lush, dark green grass of a fairy ring is due to the increased amount of nitrogen made available to the grass roots by the fungus as it breaks down organic matter in the soil. The ring of brown "dormant" grass is caused primarily by temporary exhaustion of soil moisture and possibly nutrients. The grass in this area may become so weakened that it succumbs to environmental stresses. It also may be killed by other diseases and invaded by weeds. The severity of the problem may vary from year to year". [10]

Like me, Peter had always thought this was a horribly prosaic explanation for such an emotive piece of quasi-folkloric iconography. How could a simple fungoid infection have inspired such glorious poetry as this

1641 piece by Dr Richard Corbett? [11]

"Farewell rewards and fairies"

Witness those rings and roundelays,
of theirs which remain.
Were footed in Queen Marys day
on many a grassy plain.
But since of late, Elizabeth,
and later, James came in,
they never danced on any heath
as when the time hath been.

By which we note the fairies,
were of the old profession.
Their songs were Ave-Maries,
their dances all procession.
But now, alas, they all are gone,
or fled beyond the seas,
or farther, for religions sake,
or else they take their ease.

This was, to me at least, the best indication yet, that far from being a relatively modern phenomenon, crop circles were something that had been around for many centuries. They were a manifestation of something gloriously strange and innately wonderful within the ambience of our planet and they were something far more important than the cider fuelled japes of a bevy of drunken students intent on inflicting their own quasi-artistic consciousness onto a hapless landscape. Surely the strange, beautiful and mysterious formations which appear year after year in farmers' fields across Wessex make far more convincing fairy rings than a mere outcropping of pernicious fungi?

Professor Robert Plot published a book entitled *A Natural History of Staffordshire* in 1686, in which he made passing reference to rings, circles and other shapes found in grassy fields. Much debate has ensued over Plot's observations; detailed as his notes were, some researchers still consider his evidence flimsy at best. They feel it more likely that Plot was describing "fairy rings" caused by common fungi. For many more, the jury is still out. [12]

But I knew nothing of this at the time - I had far more pressing matters to hand because the same day that the Oliver's Castle crop formation appeared the letter I had been dreading finally turned up. It was from my wife telling me that she wanted a divorce. [13]

Within days the people who had been our friends began to polarise into two armed camps: her friends and my friends. It was then that something cracked within my head and I entered a place that I had never been before; indeed a place that I never even knew existed. My perception of reality altered completely. In many ways it has never recovered.

As each day another one of my former friends would desert me I felt more and more alone. Graham and a few others stood by me, but slowly and inexorably my world fell apart and was replaced by a new and nightmarish landscape of unbelievable anguish. I found myself experiencing emotions which were so intense that there are no words to describe them, and even now I don't really know what they were. For the first time in my life I began to hallucinate without the aid of psychotropic chemicals and I saw visions and heard voices that are impossible to describe with any semblance of accuracy.

My true friends rallied around and each night. For a month one of them stayed in my house essentially on 'suicide watch'. By this time the constant security blanket of alcohol, valium and prozac was beginning to take effect and I went about my daily routine like a zombie. My nights, however, were horrific and my dreams were populated by monsters, daemons and the faces of friends of mine who had died many years before.

As I went through changes that even now, over two years later, I find hard to talk about strange things were afoot in the skies above me. According to an unreferenced Internet report two witnesses identified only as James and Clare saw *"a pale light in the sky. Not moving"* which *"disappeared after a few minutes"* in the skies above Dartmouth in South Devon on the night of the fourth of August. [14]

About sixty miles east of my house in Exeter is Maiden Castle - one of the finest Iron Age fortified villages in England. It was built on the site of a much earlier causewayed camp. Neolithic defences have been uncovered below the Iron Age ramparts. The Celts expanded Maiden Castle (Mai Dun) building the ramparts to a height of 60 feet. However this proved inadequate against the Roman 2nd Legion, who, under their commander Vespasian defeated the Durotriges in the 1st century AD. After using the site as a temporary military outpost the Romans founded the town of Durnovaria (Dorchester) and moved out. Maiden Castle was never occupied again, and has remained derelict for 2,000 years. [15] On the nights of the 17th and 18th August 1996 , David Kingston, an acquaintance of mine who is leader of the Dorchester CSETI Working Group, conducted a skywatch with very little success. Several days later, however, their efforts apparently reaped dividends:

"On the night of the 20th at 23.50hrs I received a telephone call from Dorset Police Headquarters relaying information over an alleged UFO sighting that had first been seen coming in from the direction of the sea near Portland (some ten miles from Maiden Castle) and then had headed over Maiden Castle before continuing on a northerly flight path to Shaftesbury. They had received quite a few calls from the public and asked if I minded my telephone number being given out if they received any further telephone calls on the subject.

I contacted two local military bases and a civilian airport, they all reported no air traffic that should not have been there on their radio. I decided as it was now a little late that I would make contact with the witnesses the following day. The main witnesses consisted of a family that had first seen a very bright "ball of light" as they were driving in their car from Sturminster Newton (North Dorset) towards Dorchester. The wife (driver or the car) saw it first and pointed it out to her husband. The three children in the rear or the car watched it and became very excited. It was described by them when they first saw it as being very bright and appeared to be a little smaller than a full moon looks on a clear night.

The wife and husband decided to try and follow the object (as they described it to me) which they did for some six miles around narrow and twisty country lanes before losing site of it. They eventually joined the A35 main road (dual carriage way) and continued towards Dorchester. They had not long been travelling along the main road when the children became very over excited shouting to their parents that there was a large craft (triangle shape and approx. 100 feet in length I discovered later when I obtained drawings from the children and parents separately) with lights on coming towards the car at about house roof top level.

It hovered above the car making no noise, but lit up the car on the inside through the sunlight roof vent. The wife explained that at this time she was feeling scared because if she drove fast the craft kept pace with her, if she slowed down it did the same. What she and her husband could not understand was that there were a lot of cars travelling along the same stretch of road, but did not take any notice of the craft. I discovered this was not true and interviewed another six motorists later in the week that had seen the triangle shaped craft and all when requested to draw the craft gave me sketches that looked very similar.

The craft followed the family for three miles before they turned of the main road to their house. All the family reported experiencing headaches which lasted a few days but no other effects, no loss of time etc. When the story broke in the local newspaper, I had interviewed eight witnesses by then, the story took an interesting turn. The local military base that reported they had nothing on radar for the area I had questioned them about put out a statement that there had been a night "Harrier" aircraft exercise on the night in question. I telephoned the base and asked if it would be possible for a Harrier with its jets in the downward thrust position to hover over a car at a height of fifty feet and not to be heard, let alone burn paint off the car. I was given a very short reply that they were not prepared to make any further comment on the incident.

All the witnesses that I interviewed, a priest, two policemen, a farmer and friends, a County Hall officer plus the family all stated that it could not have been a Harrier aircraft because there was firstly no noise, secondly it was a great deal larger and thirdly that the composition or the lights underneath were not consistent with that of a Harrier when I showed them photographs.

Did I instigate the UFO to appear after the Sky Watch? Was it Maiden Castle drawing it in - it has been the site for many UFO's over the years, both "balls of light" and during the last four years, the triangle ones?

This is something I'll never know." [16]

This report was far from being the only one from West Country skies during the summer of 1996. A few weeks earlier at the end of July, Steve Meller and his sister had been on holiday in North Devon. He later wrote:

"Whilst on holiday one night my sister and I noticed in the sky what looked like two bright stars but then they started darting around the sky and stopping for a few seconds, then darting to another point in the sky and stopping for another few seconds this whole thing lasted about five minutes then they disappeared. The next day in the local paper the main headline stated that a ufo was sighted in the sky so this was something a lot of people had obviously seen." [17]

It was obvious that something strange was going on, but at the time I was still too numb with grief and benzodiaepines to have done anything about it even if I had been aware of these reports. However, the human psyche is, despite what generations of poets and lovelorn romantics would have had us believe, a very resilient thing, and as the summer dragged on, and as I slowly began to put my life back together again I got back to work. My first `public appearance` as it were, was at the Zoologica exhibition in Sussex, at the end of August [18][19] and much to my surprise (and pleasure) I had coped with the stresses and strains of a long drive and forty eight hours of exposure to the general public and furthermore enjoyed the experience immensely. There were, I decided, two things that I could do. I could either carry on wallowing in a pit of despair and tranquilisers or I could shake myself down and get on with my life.

I decided to do the latter.

I also had to come to terms with the fact that I was mentally ill, but that clinical depression was not necessarily the end of the world. I was therefore determined to be the most productive neurotic in the business. Unfortunately, however, I discovered that the system was not geared up for someone who actually wanted to come to terms with his illness and to try and make something of himself despite it all. As the summer faded into autumn and as the long winter nights began to draw in I was shunted from one department to another as the Exeter City Mental Health professionals decided what to do with me. [20]

My Doctor had always been a source of strength to me and did his best to help and encourage me in my ongoing fight both with the darker side of my psyche and with the serried ranks of psychiatric officialdom who seemed determined to do whatever they could not to give me any treatment whatsoever. It was something like four months after I had originally turned up in my G.P`s surgery, incoherent with rage and grief that he and I finally got me a regular placement with a therapist at the local drop-in centre. By this time, although I was working again, my life had got significantly stranger - because more by luck than by judgement I had found myself embroiled in the first of a series of unpleasant, short lived and ultimately self-destructive relationships with young women who (with the benefit of hindsight at least) I can see were just as much in need of psychiatric help as I was.

By the end of October I was sharing my house with a young woman from Ireland who was not only barking mad, but an intractable alcoholic. Our relationship, such as it was, was stormy (to say the least) and finally fell apart when, early one morning she staggered drunkenly up to my front door and attempted to demolish it with the steel toecaps of her army boots. When I remonstrated with her for this unsociable behaviour she threatened to kill me, and by the time the police finally turned up to remove her she was screaming abuse at me and brandishing a kitchen knife in my general direction. I only mention this slightly unsavoury episode in my life because, about a week before the final parting of the ways we were sitting up in bed watching television when we heard the following piece of news (precised here by the CSETI web site): [21]

"1996 October 26 - Isle of Lewis, Scotland. A massive sea search was launched on Saturday 26th of October after reports of explosions and objects falling into the sea off the west coast of Scotland. At around 17.00hrs eye witnesses reported seeing the explosion in the sky off the Butt of Lewis. The area is the exact point where transatlantic flights enter British airspace. The RAF could not rule out an air collision and mounted a full search which cost £200,000, but they found nothing, or so the official line says. One eye witness reported a large aircraft and a smaller one collide. Another heard a couple of loud bangs and saw debris falling from the sky. But Air Traffic Control at Prestwick said they had no reports of planes missing.

A RAF spokesman from Kinross said, "We have a special unit investigating the matter. One of the things we are looking into is that it is space debris. But we are also searching through all the radar tapes around the time of the incident to see if there is any trace of aircraft.

Stornoway Coastguard initially mounted a helicopter sea search but as reports increased a RAF Sea King and a Nimrod joined in. Lochinvar Lifeboat was launched and all the shipping alerted in the area. A French fishing boat, at the time off Lewis also headed for the area as did the Port Salvo which usually operated in the Minch. Police and ambulance crews were also standing by at Ness, in case of survivors.

Witnesses reported a large pall of smoke out to sea. Another shocked resident said, "It lit up the sky and then fell to the sea. It was like a scene from the X-Files." Norman MacDonald of Skigersta Road said, "When I heard it at first, I thought it was a firework because its not long to Guy Fawkes night. Then I saw a trail of smoke. I saw three flashes in total and heard a further two bangs."

"I rushed into the local shop, and took the staff and customers out. They also saw the dense smoke trail going into the sea."

The top secret RAF tracking station of Flyingdales in Yorkshire was asked for any information that they may have picked up, but they said they had detected nothing. Flyingdales is equipped with highly sensitive tracking devices which gives warning of any nuclear missile attack on

Britain.

American military scientists from Sandia National Laboratories, which operate spy satellites from their base in Albuquerque, New Mexico are also interested in the incident and have begun their own investigations. The involvement of the US military has sparked off rumours of the military somehow being involved in the incident although they deny all knowledge of it. Incidentally two days later the same area saw a NATO exercise involving thirty ships and eighty aircraft.

Professor Mark Bailey of the Armagh observatory in Northern Ireland admitted he was puzzled and said, "I am torn between this being caused by the military, such as target practice, and a natural phenomena such as a fireball."

The SNP claims it has information that a naval frigate was in the area shortly after the incident lifting wreckage from the sea and Margaret Ewing is being asked to raise the matter in the Commons.

Meanwhile Nick Pope [22] *has taken an interest in the incident and is carrying out his own investigations saying that he would not rule out the possibility of this being a UFO.* "[23]

It was this event, above any other, that re-awakened an interest in UFOs which had been dormant for many years and which, since my involvement with cryptozoology had gone from being an expensive hobby to being a reasonably lucrative career, had been left on the sidelines. Although I think that it is highly unlikely that whatever happened in the seas off Scotland that autumn day had anything to do with UFOs per se it not only rekindled my interest in the subject but also prompted questions, a year later, in the House of Lords:

"Questions in the House - 14 October 1997. Written Answers

Mid-Air Explosion, Isle of Lewis

LORD HILL NORTON asked Her Majesty's Government:

What was the military involvement in the search for the unidentified object that witnesses believe exploded in mid air, before crashing into the sea off the Isle of Lewis on 26 October 1996, and what liaison took place with the US authorities with regard to this incident?

LORD GILBERT: Following media reports of an explosion, initially at-

tributed to a mid-air collision north of the Butt of Lewis, an extensive search of the area was carried out by RAF and Coastguard Search and Rescue assets, but was later abandoned after it became clear that no aircraft had been reported overdue. HQ US 3rd Air Force were also approached at the time. They confirmed that there had been no US military activity in the area." [24]

A week later I was single again, reasonably sober and the inaugural meeting of the Exeter Strange Phenomena Research Group in a back street boozer had been somewhat of a success. Things were beginning to look up.

Although I would be a liar if I said that I never had any further lapses into drug and alcohol fuelled psychosis, or that I never ended up in bed with (as Peter Shelley said) *"somebody I shouldn't"* [25][26] I was certainly on the mend, and I was able to look forward to the new year and what it might bring with a gusto that had been unimaginable the previous summer. On New Year's Eve, another piece of the jigsaw puzzle that was to define my life over the next few years fell into piece when Graham and I met an old acquaintance of mine at Exeter bus station. His name was Richard Freeman - he had been a subscriber to my magazine *Animals & Men* for several years [27] and over the course of a number of meetings and innumerable telephone conversations we became friends. In a spirit of seasonal bonhomie we invited him down to Exeter to "see the New Year" in with us - an event which eventually led to him coming to live with us permanently as a full partner in the Centre for Fortean Zoology [28] during the summer of 1998.

While all this was going on in my life, unbeknownst to me, thirteen miles away, a taxi driver who was happily living with his wife-to-be in Exmouth was only a few months away from having his quiet, happy and uncomplicated life re-arranged forever!

Most of the players were now in place and the drama which was to unfold over the following nine months or so could now take place.

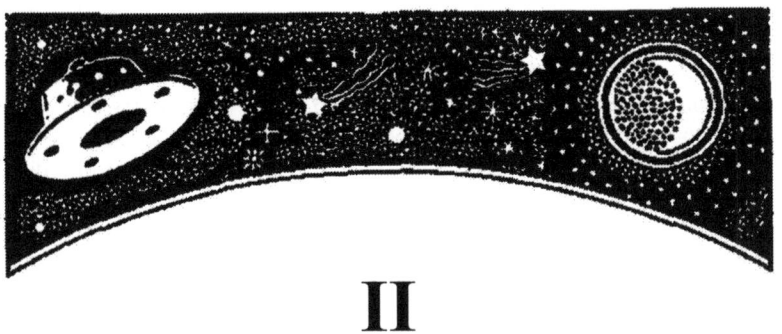

II

1997 started promisingly with a spate of UFO reports. On the 15th of January two witnesses reported seeing an object shoot past their car at it was stationary near Ottery St. Mary at 5.30 p.m. The object appeared bright green in colour and was emitting a glow about the size of a tennis ball. It shot up to a height of between one and two miles at a great speed. The witness cannot explain what happened that evening, but he is convinced that what he saw `was not of this earth`. [1]

This was just the beginning of an extraordinary eight months of UFO sightings, mostly in the East Budleigh, Woodbury, Exmouth and Ottery St Mary districts of East Devon. Something that had started off as a mild interest became a fascination, then an obsession and finally a full time job.

In January 1997 Graham and I were approached by a reporter from the local BBC Radio station who wanted to interview us in our capacity as founders of the Exeter Strange Phenomena Research Group about our involvement with paranormal research in the area. Always having an eye for the main chance we made a tentative enquiry about the possibility of us having a regular spot on the station. This is the sort of approach that we make all the time and so we were actually extremely surprised (as well as gratified) when, a week or so later, we had a telephone call from Janet Kipling - the host of the station`s weekday afternoon programme - asking us whether we would like to have a regular spot on her show. Would we? Of course we would, we replied joyfully jumping at the prospect of an unprecedented degree of access to the hearts, minds and wallets of the BBC Radio Devon listenership! So, early in February we made the first tentative broadcasts of our show "Weird about the West", which has now become a popular part of the station`s output!

What we didn't realise at the time, was quite how much credibility this new found position would actually give us. As representatives of the BBC (albeit unpaid and rather unconventional ones) we could open doors that had previously been closed to us and could have access to people who would previously never have bothered to listen to us. Because on the whole (apart from the cost of the license fee and the odd error of judgement vis a vis Michael Barrymore or an Australian Soap Opera) people trust the BBC, they trusted us and we soon became the repository for an unprecedented number of stories concerning UFO reports and other incidents of high strangeness in the area. Slowly, as we collated these reports on our various computer files a strange pattern began to emerge and we realised that these incidents were not, as we had originally thought, isolated occurences, but more a part of a greater and far more perplexing whole.

One night in April 1997 at about 11.00 p.m Yvonne Jackson was sitting in a car on the top of Haldon Hill with her boyfriend and another young man when they saw a semi-circular object with 3 rows of lights; approximately 20 lights of various colours flickering and rotating. It was at an elevation of approximately 50 or 60 degrees and seemed to be hovering in the sky over the Teignmouth Estuary. A few months later she described it to us with the picturesque phrase that it was *"bobbling around"* and when we spoke to her months later she could only say that *"It was bloody enormous..."* [2]

A friend of her boyfriend reported the sighting to the police, who said they'd had lots of reports of flickering lights. However, the police at Teignmouth were less helpful when we contacted them and could only say that reports of such incidents had to remain confidential. This is palpably untrue, because as we found out when contacting various other community policemen over the following months in most cases they were quite happy to give us information, although in many cases they preferred the information to be `off the record`.

This is mainly (as I have noted elsewhere), because at least in the West Country the pursuit of paranormal subjects has tended in the past to be the domain of a complex substratum of society whose most vociferous members tend to be either barking mad or the sort of folk that hapless members of the Devon and Cornwall Constabulary tend to think of as dangerous sociopaths (or more charitably) bedreadlocked weirdos. Having encountered a number of these people myself I am surprisingly in sympathy with the beleagured and underpaid representatives of Her Majestys Constabulary who are loth to be seen as collaborating with such socially undesirable elements! [3]

During May, Tracey Seymour of Exeter had a UFO experience of her own. Strangely, because we were, as can be seen from this book, very active in ufological circles across Devonshire at the time, we didn't hear about this particular sighting until over a year later when we were starting work on what was eventually to become this book. We found her report on The Internet:

" Date: 15.5.97 Time: 8.15pm
I was just going to bed and I was drawing the curtains. but as I was doing so I suddenly noticed a strange glow from beyond the street. This light appeared for about 20 minutes. During this time I made my way out the house towards the light. As I got nearer the glow got brighter. I could just about make out a shape from which this light was coming. The shape was squarish and was no aeroplane. I didn't hang around. I ran back to the house frightened. i would like to know if anyone saw this?"

We have done our best to contact her but to no avail and so her sighting must remain univestigated - at least by us.

At the end of May, Graham and I, in our official capacity as representatives of the British Broadcasting Corporation made three daily appearances at the Devon County Show. We were part of the BBC's "Roadshow" which was, like such events the world over primarily designed to provide cheap entertainment for the hoi polloi. There were Spice Girls look-alike contests where prepubescent girls were encouraged top perform high-kicks and pelvic thrusts to the soundtrack of inane pop music. There were vulgar party games featuring balloons and more inane pop music and there were chances for the aforementioned *hoi polloi* to win prizes consisting of mugs, T-Shirts and pens emblazoned with the logo of the aforementioned British Broadcasting Corporation.

There was also (feeling somewhat like the proverbial fish out of water) me, Graham and Toby the Dog doing a series of live question and answer sessions and providing a chance for the general public to talk about their experiences in the wacky world of the paranormal. Getting well and truly into the spirit of the thing Graham was wandering around the audience dressed as a `Grey` alien and I was giving away prizes donated by those terribly nice chaps at "Sightings" magazine (a UFO magazine - now deceased - that I was working for at the time).[5] A splendid time was had by all and much against my better judgement I was actually beginning to enjoy myself.

Several members of the public joined us up on the stage to tell us of their experiences which were mostly uninteresting in the extreme and our forty minutes were soon up. [6] Several interesting things, however, happened that day.

Firstly, as we were packing up our things and preparing to leave the County Showground an elderly farmer came sidling up to us with an embarrassed and rather sheepish look in his eye. He refused to tell us his name or give us any means of contacting him again, but he wanted, he informed us, to tell us his story. [7] [8]

He, apparently, owned a small farm in the east of the county (he was reluctant to tell us exactly where), and over the previous few weeks he had been experiencing some very strange things. A bachelor, he lived alone, but, or so he claimed, every night for some time, as he was lying in bed, he had heard the unmistakeable sounds of someone walking around on the flagstoned floor of his kitchen in what sounded like hob-nailed boots. His kitchen was directly below his bedroom and the sound, he said, was unmistakeable.

On several occasions he had gone down to investigate, and although on one occasion he had seen what he thought was a shadowy figure flitting away into the darkness he was not sure whether this had been the result of his imagination working overtime.

He had also seen strange lights hovering over a field of barley about a hundred yards from his farm, but a few nights before approaching us things had taken a sinister turn. In a scenario horribly reminiscent of one that Graham and I would encounter on the Caribbean island of Puerto Rico some eight months later, he visited his chicken run one morning to find about two thirds of his fowls dead with no apparent injury,

I pricked up my ears at this. *"Were any of the birds outside the coop?"* I asked him, wondering whether the attack (if indeed attack it was) would prove to have followed the scenario so familiar from having read accounts of chupacabras attacks in Central America. [9] *"How the hell did you know that?"* he muttered suspiciously and left. I gave him one of our business cards in the vain hope that he would get back in touch with us, but sufficient to say he has never done so.

We were slightly shaken by that so we made our way home feeling slightly chastened, On our way back we had to stop for petrol and in a spirit of slightly fortean *caprice* Graham dressed back in his alien costume and went to pay for the petrol and cigarettes in the guise of a Grey from Zeta Reticuli. [10] It says something about the times we live in, I think, that no-one paid him the slightest bit of notice.

The third main event of that momentous day took place when we got home. There waiting for us on the doorstep was a tall, thin chap with a big nose and greyish hair. I sent Graham on ahead to make sure that he was neither a debt collector or some hired lackey of my ex-wife's solicitors because at the time my divorce negotiations were entering a very sticky and unpleasant stage which was to culminate in her having a warrant issued for my arrest. [11] As I lurked sheepishly in the car-park Graham strode intrepidly ahead to see who this mysterious visitor was. I could see them conversing together but it was too far away for me to hear anything that they said. Then I could hear Graham starting to laugh. He then turned around and gave me a friendly thumbs up gesture. It was obviously OK to proceed.

As I walked up to my front door Graham introduced me to our sinister looking visitor. It was a bloke from Exmouth whose name was Nigel Wright. He had heard us on the radio and he had even bought one of our magazines in a local shop which is how he knew our address. He was, or so he claimed, a keen amateur researcher into UFOs and the paranormal. He had never seen a UFO (something that was to change over the course of the next three or four months), but as a child he had encountered a number of ghosts. He was willing to work for nothing and he wanted to join our investigative group. *"Yeah, why not?"* we said, and with this dull and rather inauspicious beginning a relationship was forged which would eventually lead to the writing of this book.

The events of the summer proper started on Wednesday the sixteenth of July when a well known Devonshire businessman and philanthropist who has asked to remain anonymous was sitting, with his wife on the balcony of his house at West Hill (an affluent suburb of the small market town of Ottery St Mary) at about 22.35 when they noticed a bright orange-white light to the south west. Around it were four smaller white lights that moved rather erratically. They watched it for a while before it flew off towards the north. [12]

The next evening an Exeter man who happens to be an acquaintaince of mine was looking east, towards Exmouth, out of the window of his flat in Alphington Road when he saw a similar light. He remarked to researchers later that it seemed not to cast a light or a shadow but to be complete in itself. He watched it for a few minutes before it sped off at a great speed. [13] His description of the object was remarkably similar to that given to me by one of the witnesses to the events which happened in Rendlesham Forest during the 1970's/1980s. [14]

A friend of mine [15] and I had only returned from Suffolk a few weeks before the man from Alphington Road told us of his experience, and she was so struck by the similarity between the two accounts - both featuring amorphous orange/white lights that appeared not to cast either shadows or reflections that she telephoned me immediately. Little did we know that just over a week later the floodgates would figuratively burst open, with a whole plethora of unidentified flying `objects`, one of which we would even see ourselves. [16]

A week later, on the 25th July, two hippies were travelling east along the A 30, at dusk, when they noticed a cigar shaped object in the sky over Woodbury Common, but it was two days later on Sunday 27th when the proverbial weird shit hit the equally proverbial fan. [17]

At lunchtime a Sea King helicopter was performing a mock air-sea rescue for the entertainment of the massed throngs of holidaymakers on the sea front. Amongst the enthralled audience was Dave Littlefield, an aviation expert and author, who was videotaping the excercise for his own archives. It was several days later that a friend of his pointed out that clearly visible behind the helicopter is a silver light which appears to be hanging motionless in the sky. The silver light was seen against the backdrop of a particularly distinctive bit of cloud, but when the helicopter returns to that bit of the sky, the light has vanished. It is useful to compare the light with the reflections off the shiny metallic bits of the helicopter itself. In appearance they are quite different and computer enhancement suggests that the object is either circular or disc shaped, although it is impossible to tell whether it is in fact metallic or whether it is acting as its own light source. [18] [19]

That evening Channel Four showed the Roswell Movie, [20] together with a documentary containing the disputed Ray Santilli `Alien Autopsy` movie. [21] Sceptics in the westcountry media blamed the veritable outpouring of sightings which took place over the next several nights as being influenced by this televisual treat. [22] The sheer volume of sightings, and the high degree of correlation between them, as well as the Exmouth video tape make this hypothesis unlikely. At random - a few of the sightings from that Sunday night: William Fraser-Jennings (a young man of 25 who doesn`t mind his name being used as long as we don`t do what a certain Westcountry newspaper did and quote his age as being 52!), [23] a telesales manager at Bushey Park, Budleigh Salterton, was with five friends on a hilltop near Budleigh Salterton, looking south to south east. They saw a bright white light which because of the height of the hill itself appeared at eye level, rose vertically then blinked out about four minutes later. They watched it through binoculars and described the shape as being elongated horizontally into what he later described to *The Exmouth Journal* [24] as being *"a dish-shaped object"*. [25]

Twenty minutes later they saw the same thing again for about four minutes. This time it moved northwards before disappearing.

At practically the same time (9.50 p.m) a retired person in Torquay who has demanded strict anonymity came out of a concert hall and saw a stationary bright yellowish `thing` in the north east - the direction of Exmouth across the Exe estuary. He described it as being the size of a thumb held at arm's length and at an elevation of 20°. He only observed for a few minutes before it disappeared. [26]

At about 10.00 the same evening, the mother of my best mate`s girlfriend was looking out of the window of her house at Beer in East Devon when to the west she saw a blueish-white light zig-zagging across the sky. It appeared to be over Exmouth/Woodbury. [27]

A few hours later, in the early hours of Monday morning an Exmouth businessman, who for reasons that are perfectly obvious would not tell me his name was in a parked car on Exmouth seafront with a lady who was not his wife. They saw a pair of bright blue lights over the sea zig-zagging around. [28]

At between four and five in the morning, about three hours after the events recounted to me by the philandering businessman a married couple who have asked NOT to be identified were looking out of their bedroom window which faced west towards the Royal Marine camp at Woodbury. At an elevation of about 45° they saw a bright white light (of burning magnesium intensity) which moved up and down relative to stars but which looked smaller than the moon would have been. She told us that they both felt scared because *"It felt close: I'd just never seen anything like it before"*. [29]

She telephoned our office on a number of occasions over the next few days. She seemed a likeable but very shy person who was more confused than anything else by her one and only excursion into what Dr Mike Dash [30] described as `The Borderlands`. [31] One of the most peculiar things about her experience is that her husband had a slightly different impression of the colour of the light that they had seen but their general reports coincided. The phenomenon of two witnesses of the same object describing different colours is a well known one within UFOlogy as a whole and is, indeed, one that I had encountered before. [32]

The next night at 22.04 p.m a young lady who has asked to be given the pseudonym of "Tracey Wilson" was looking out of her bedroom window in a house on the eastern edge of Tiverton. Her father is a vehement non-smoker, and she was having a crafty cigarette and so was sure of the time of her experience. She saw an orange and white light at an elevation of 30° moving northwards, the light was visible for about two minutes then flared brightly before going out.

The truth can now be told - well some of it anyway. We have never made any secret of the fact that "Tracey Wilson" is a pseudonuym. No names - no packdrill, but "Tracey" is actually the sister of one of the members of the Exeter Strange Phenomena Research Group, and she threatened her brother (who shall, of course, remain nameless) with all the sorts of cruel and unusual punishments that make me glad that I haven`t got a sister, if her identity was divulged. [33]

Her main, indeed as far as I can gather, her only reason for not wanting her identity divulged is so her father wouldn`t find out that she smoked cigarettes. [34]

Forty five minutes after "Tracey Wilson" was contravening her father`s wishes, a retired police officer was halfway down his garden path in the Redhills district of Exeter, facing his house (to the south), talking to his neighbour. The weather was clear, the temperature was in the mid 60's, it was dark and there was no visible moon. [35]

He saw a bright white flash over the roof, his neighbour, nearer his own house, was facing north and didn't see it. Two minutes later there was a second flash to the right of the last (approximately South-West); and the third flash (also seen by his neighbour) was even brighter in the west - towards Exmouth,

Each flash was half to three-quarters of a second; bigger (brighter) than Venus; each flash separated by about two minutes and was at an elevation of approximately 75-80°.

On the evening of Tuesday 29th July, Barry Payne, a plumber from Dawlish, was looking eastwards over the sea. He saw a bright orange and white light heading from south to north towards Exmouth. The flight was interspersed with zig-zag movements. Mr Payne is familiar with aircraft movements and is convinced that this was different. He watched it for about five minutes before it disappeared. [36]

Just before midnight on Friday 1st August someone identifying himself only as "Shane" who sounded particularly stoned telephoned me from an Exmouth `phone box to tell me that he had seen two bright lights zig-zagging around, up on Woodbury Beacon. [37] A few hours later, David Nelson was in the vicinity of Exeter Airport. He was looking north-east towards Exeter and saw an object at an elevation of 45°. It was cork-screwing (i.e moving left, right, up & down) and getting brighter; then it died out. His description of the colour was that it was initially white but that it died down to yellow. [38]

At about the same time an elderly Exmouth lady saw a strange whitish object to the south-east. It was triangular, and "misty round the edges, it didn't move, and it didn't twinkle". She watched it for about three minutes. [39]

On the 6th August between 11.30 p.m and midnight, five members of the Sanders family were having a barbecue in their back garden of Willa-combe, an estate in Tiverton, when the telephone rang. It was a neighbour who told them to quickly look up at the night sky. They saw two white lights horizontal to the horizon; one larger than the other - and with the smaller one "chasing it" east towards Cullompton direction. They were both circular in shape. [40] [41]

On the 7th August an acquaintaince of mine - a hippie living in Cornwall telephoned to tell me that there was a white glowing object hovering over her back garden and that she could see it out of her window as she was speaking to me. In the background I could hear her small son chattering excitedly about the "funny light in the sky", and whilst she is not necessarily the most credible witness in this book, I see no reason to exclude her from the narrative of events. [42] She also passed my name and telephone number onto a number of her friends within the `New-Age` Traveller`s community, and for several months I would receive the odd telephone call tellimng me of an ABC sighting, of a UFO encounter or from a hairy drug-addict trying to borrow a few quid off me until his giro arrived.

At 21.30 on the 11th August "Anna Epson" (a pseudonym, although we have her real name and telephone number on file) was driving along the South Zeal-Throwleigh road, on the edges of Dartmoor with her sister who was on holiday from London. They both saw a starlike whitish light moving steadily across the north of the sky in a westerly direction towards Lyme Bay. She told us *"If it hadn't been moving, I'd have thought it was just an average star"*. It was at an elevation of approximately 45°. They watched it through binoculars for several minutes and noted that there didn`t seem to be any change in the diameter of the object. They did note, however, that it moved in a zig zag motion which implied that whatever they were looking at, it wasn't a sattelite. [43]

One might well ask why so many local witnesses contacted me, rather than the local police or the South West Witness Support Group. I should point out that several local newspapers had run pieces on the sightings, and had quoted my telephone number as a contact point. At my request the specific details of what had been seen were kept to a minimum so that we could retain as much scientific objectivity as possible!

After the events of the 12th-14th August, however, this became impossible. The Exeter Strange Phenomena research group held a skywatch at various locations across Devonshire. Whilst Graham manned the Exeter location the rest of the core team, together with five other members of the group, and Janet Kipling, [44] from BBC Radio Devon were on Woodbury Common.

I arrived at about quarter past nine with a friend of mine. [45] It was in fact the first time that I had visited Woodbury Castle for many years [46] and I took the chance to look around. Dusk was falling as my dog and I wandered around the walls of the ancient earthwork. It was very quiet and very still. It was the sort of heavy summer night that one usually only experiences in the tropics and there was a distinct feel of thunder in the air. I climbed to the top of the ridge, and as Toby half-heartedly ambled after rabbits (who paid no attention to him whatsoever), I looked over towards the great mass of Haldon Hill on the other side of the Exe Estuary and wondered what the night ahead was going to bring.

The air was rich with the scent of gorse flowers and the little chirping sounds made by grasshoppers and other small insects. For a moment I allowed myself a brief daydream, mentally substituted the sound of English grasshoppers for the strident squeaks of crickets and tree-frogs, and it was like I was back in Hong Kong as a small boy. [47]

Just for a moment I could imagine that instead of the Exe estuary I was looking out over the myriad of tiny islands in the bay of Hong-Kong and that the lights from the town of Topsham way below me, were in fact the lights of dozens of little junks embarking on nocturnal fishing expeditions. For the first time in many months I felt happy and I drifted on a cloud of self indulgence until my reverie was shattered by the sound of approaching cars and the arrival of the other members of the team.

I called to Toby who had found something incredibly interesting to sniff at, and wandered purposefully back down to the car park. There were tiny pin-pricks of light on some of the bushes as I passed and I realised, much to my delight, that for the first time in nearly three decades I was seeing glow worms. [48]

The intrepid investigation team unloaded their equipment, mounted telescopes and video cameras onto their tripods, opened cans of beer and waited expectantly for something to happen.

Nothing did and it started to rain.

There was almost 100% cloud cover in North and West Devon and so our Bideford, Totnes and Tavistock groups decided to call it a night, but at Woodbury we still had about 40% visibility and so despite a light drizzle we struggled on. At about eleven (unfortunately just after Janet had concluded her interviews with us and gone home), all seven of us saw what seemed like a very dim blue-white star moving very erratically just within the burgeoning cloud cover. We watched it for several minutes, and then, as now, the best visual analogy that I can give is that it looked like a quasi-stellar version of the whirligig beetles [49] that whizz around on the surface of ponds and slow moving streams during hot summers.

Half an hour after our sighting, two young men, walking on Exmouth sea front saw two red lights behaving erratically. I met one of them at the BUFORA conference at Sheffield and he told me that they were "whizzing along just above sea level". His mate works for BAe, saw it in more depth, but refused to talk to our researchers even with confidentiality ensured because he works on government defense work. [50]

At midnight on the 12th-13th, DJ John Pierce said on *Gemini Radio* [51] that there were power cuts in the Budleigh area that SWEB couldn't explain. [52] I rang one of my contacts at Gemini the next day and they told me that one of the Torquay area transmitters had been struck by lightning. Although we can confirm that we saw thunder and lightning over Torbay on the previous night from our vantage point high up at Woodbury castle there does seem to be a minor mystery surrounding the whole affair. Graham rang SWEB on the 13th August at 19:45 and they denied that anything of the sort had happened happened. [53]

The `lightning strike` had occured at approximately the same time as we had seen the strange blue light in the sky, and at the same time another one of our group who was in the Torbay area, was trying to contact us on her mobline `phone and found that for some inexplicable reason that she was unable to get any reception. [54]

As we were at the skywatch itself, Jan Scarff was getting repeated interference on his car phone with which he was trying to maintain contact with the other groups carrying out their skywatches up and down the south coast of England. [55]

"Mark" (of Cowley Bridge, Exeter) works for British Rail and was on duty on the night of the 12th/13th. He refused to give any further information about himself and had used the 141 prefix on my telephone number in order to remain anonymous. He claims that if his employers heard about his experience they would accuse him of being drunk and sack him immediately. He was somewhere in the Exeter area on a train. At about 02:15 he saw two balls white light (with corona haze possibly due to fog) at an indeterminate distance with an elevation higher than 45° coming from East Devon towards Exeter. They were flying fairly fast - faster than aircraft using Exeter airport. The one in front was going slower than the following one, which was zig-zagging.

The balls of light *"appeared to be the size of an old half-pence piece."* [56]

Two days later Exmouth witnessed a night of high strangeness unprecedented in its history! At 9.00 p.m, Alan Gibbons was with friends in his garden facing north, and saw very large stationary flashing light at 60°. [57]

Half an hour later, two delivery people saw what was apparently the same object flying from north to south at an elevation of between 70° to 90°. They described it as *a "white, star-like object heading North"*

Over the next seventy five minutes six members of one family living on the Littleham Estate, Exmouth, all experienced different UFO phenomena. The following report is taken directly from Nigel Wright's log of the evening's activities.

"21:30 Mother saw bluey starlike object heading E to NE 45°, disappeared suddenly; reappeared and there were two; changed direction & headed N.

22:10 Took 16 yr old son out; both saw one object. They described it as *"a steady bluish-white light travelling slowly over the Estate at a fairly low altitude"*. It was reportedly coming in from the sea at Lyme Bay towards Woodbury Common.

22:30 Entire family (6) saw same object, but heading from N back to E.

23:15 Youngest son (15) with binocs saw expanding & contracting light 40° in N, green/red flashing lights on trailing edge of a *"left-handed-crescent shape."*

This last sighting was corroborated by an elderly lady from East Budleigh who reported looking out of her bedroom window when she saw what she described as *a "bright, elongated cigar-shaped craft with wing-like projections"* hanging vertically in the sky above her. She said that it then changed shape as if it had rotated and then headed out to sea over Lyme Bay. [58]

A few days later she wrote a detailed letter to Nigel, including a rough sketch of the object, in which she described her sighting in more detail and also told of another sighting, albeit a vague one, from earlier in the evening:

"I wonder if the `wings` are something being given off from the main object - but they have a shape. It is definitely something unusual. They look delicate like gold tracery.

I have also seen something flashing red when I went out at about ten p.m that moved quite quickly before it disappeared from my view but was not like a shooting star". [59]

By the time Nigel had been informed of these events other reports were flooding in from all over the town. An elderly couple rang in from a `phone box on the Estuary itself. They had seen an orange bright light 'low in the sky' travelling slowly from the estuary towards Haldon.

An anonymous Royal Marine (age 20) phoned in and reported a stationary orange object with green lights to each side which appeared and appeared to move backwards and forwards and then disappeared. He was facing east; and the object was at an elevation of approximately 45°.

Either Nigel, or Sue (his wife) were on the telephone to me at approximately half hourly intervals keeping me abreast of developments. It was then, I think, that I realised that Nigel was not just some geezer from the ESP group but someone with whom we could share more intense adventures and embark with on a career of extremely high strangeness.

The following night Nigel; who had been with the rest of the ESP group when we experienced our sighting on the 12th, saw a steady bluish-white light about the magnitude of Venus, but with a distinctly circular shape. It moved from the west to the south-east at a slow to medium pace (same sort of speed as a prop aircraft); before turning north and fading away. It was below the low cloud deck at an elevation of between 30-40°. His wife said to him that she was convinced that "That thing's watching us!" [60]

However, they weren't the only witnesses of a strange object that evening. The elderly lady from East Budleigh, who has, by the way, asked to remain anonymous although her name and address is on our files, telephoned Nigel excitedly to say that the same object had reappeared for a second night and that she had watched it for about twenty minutes. She had even managed to take a photograph of the mysterious "craft" (for this is what she is convinced that it was), but much to our collective disappointment, (although not greatly to our surprise), when the film was developed, the whole film (rather than merely the frames that she had attempted to take of the UFO) were blank. [61]

This is a syndrome which occurs over and over again in the annals of forteana and it is one that is most frustrating to the investigator. Again and again a potentially valuable piece of film doesn't come out, is over exposed, is double exposed, is stolen, or lost. Ted Holiday described, at some length a similar syndrome which besets monster hunters world wide:

"..........it was clear that the Morar monsters were acting in exactly the same curious way as the ones in Loch Ness. Either a camera was not available to record what was observed or, if it was available, circumstances frustrated the photographer. Almost everyone rejected such a notion because it introduced an element of irrationality. It also raised doubts about the true nature of dragons which those who were anxious to press the claim for an unknown animal chose not to encourage. Normal anirnals do not behave in such an inexplicable way because they cannot; therefore you had to conclude that the peculiarities were due to chance. This was the prevailing attitude amongst the investigators.

An explanation based on chance seemed to me most unsatisfactory. Chance is a random effect; it is just as likely to work in favour of the investigator as against hlm. If the ten years of intensive effort at Loch Ness which resulted in failure to get a detailed film was the result of chance then it was not a random effect and the expression became meanmgless. In that event, the explanation lay elsewhere." [62]

Over the next few years Holiday proceeded to collect a large number of *"examples of what appears to be some sort of a mental block in relation to the phenomena. There is a desire to minimize or dismiss what one has seen and this provides a brief interim in which the object escapes further observation."* [63]

This included testimony from such people as naturalist and author Gavin Maxwell, [64][65] and led him to believe that this syndrome was somehow part of the nature of what he was studying. When he had come to this realisation it was but a short step to another series of revelations:

"Even more marked than the above were the situations in which monster phenomena seemed to be actively evasive. The Loch Ness Investigation Bureau's camp at Achnahannet, for example, has maintained a watch over this part of the loch for six months of the year every season since 1965. But no major sighting has taken place in this area since the Bureau set up its 35 mm. cameras and 36 inch lenses. Yet in 1964 there were two authentic views of monsters from this spot by multiple witnesses which I have interviewed.

The apparent evasion of Bureau cameras by the phenomena is of long standing. An early case occurred in 1965 when a camera located on a platform near the Clansman Hotel was taken away for servicing. The next morning, the staff of the hotel had dramatic views of a hump moving about inshore. Over the years, quite a catalogue of such incidents built up!" [66]

The twin pitfalls of psychic backlash (see my books *Only Fools and Goatsuckers* [1999] and *The Owlman and Others* [1997,8]) [67] and this apparent inability to be captured on film have beset both monster hunters and UFOlogists for years.

I explained this to Nigel at the time, but he was new to the game, and back then tended to see the omniverse merely in terms of three dimensions, and I am sure that, although he nodded politely, he didn't really know what I was talking about and then, at least he couldn't really see the connection between lake monsters and UFOs, or between animal mutilations and crop circles.

A year or so later, I am sure that his mindset has changed considerably!

On two consecutive nights - over the weekend of the 16th and 17th August (Sat/Sun) Diane, from Colebrook, near Crediton was walking her dog aliong the Tumulus walk (between Spreyton and Colebrook) at 10 pm.. On both nights she saw a very bright starlike blue-white object in the north-west at an elevation of about 45° . She told us how she had watched it for about twenty minutes on each night, and whereas on the first evening it had just hovered in the sky before just `blinking out of existence`, the next evening she saw what appeared to be the same light zig-zagging erratically across the sky. [68]

The most important thing about this sighting, as far as I am concerned at least is that although it took place quite a long way outside the "Woodbury Triangle" it took place in a location which, though unjustifiably obscure, is one that if of great interest to fortean researchers.

In the 1920s Mrs Barbara Carbonell, travelled around this part of Devonshire in a quest to solve one of the greatest mysteries of Devonian forteana - the Celtic Black Dog. [69] This is one of the most widespread animal archetypes in the world and commonly takes the shape of a large black dog, the size of a calf, sometimes distinguished by one large eye in the centre of his forehead, and on a bad day dripping fire from his mouth. He is usually thought to be the harbinger of death, although occasionally he has appeared simply to accompany people on dark, lonely roads. It is found all over the world but is more widespread in the celtic lands.

Mrs Carbonell became interested in stories of the Black Dog found that many legends and sightings were clustered around a particular stretch of road that ran from Torrington to Copplestone, a distance of some twenty miles. Beginning at Copplestone, Mrs Carbonell was told by several local people that the Black Dog had often been seen near the Cross, actually a squared granite pillar some fourteen feet high, inscribed with Celtic symbols and known to date from before the sixth century. It is in the centre of a junction where three roads meet, and for many years has been both a centre for occult activity and UFO sightings. From Copplestone the road is accompanied by an ancient lane which runs into the cross-roads at the hill-top village of Down St Mary, where there is an ancient Saxon church.

Several people living in the village told Mrs Carbonnel *"how the Black Dog ran up the old lane on dark nights, past the smithy and between the church and the school. The dog was said to knock down the corner of the school, which juts out into the road, the noise of falling masonry being heard, but no damage was ever seen."* [70]

It is interesting how often sightings of these spectral animals occur in conjunction with UFO reports, and although there have not been any reports of black dog sightings along this stretch of road for many years, it is interesting, I think, that Dianne`s UFO experience took place at such a significant site.

One of the only non-celtic locations for a series of Black Dog sightings (and one that is even further outside the Woodbury Triangle/Lyme Bay area than Copplestone) is El Salvador, where a creature called a *Cadejo* follows lonely travellers at night. It neither barks nor whines, but wails. Those who hear the wails of the *Cadejo* nearby can be safe that he is far, far away. It is those who hear him in the distance who should be wary, for if you do you must not turn around lest you should find the beast staring you right in the face with cinder-red eyes. To gaze into the eyes of a *Cadejo* might cause the person to become frozen with fear.

The *Cadejo* stands about 3 feet at the shoulder and will often follow lone travellers for miles before giving up the chase. All the while ululating its spine-chilling wail, hoping perhaps, in its own malicious way to cause the person to turn around and face it or try to attack it; for if one does, the *Cadejo* swells up to the size of a bull and will trample and maul its victim. [71]

Those afflicted maybe found by the wayside, frozen in terror still, unable to utter a single word for weeks. Most often then not, the person recovers: such encounters are only occasionally fatal.

Back to the area covered by the main text of this book and we have what is, apart from the `Hound of the Baskervilles` of course, quite possibly the most famous black dog encounters in Devonian history. This account is taken from *Mystery Animals of Britain and Ireland* (1986) by Graham McEwan

"The lane which runs along the boundary between Devon and Dorset at Uplyme has long been reputed to be haunted by a black dog and was called Dog Lane because of this, the phantom also lending its name to an adjacent public house. One encounter with the beast occurred in 1856. The witnesses were a local couple and the woman described the incident as follows:

As I was returning to Lyme one night with my husband down Dog Lane, as we reached the middle of it, I saw an animal about the size of a dog meeting us. 'What's that?' I said to my husband. 'What?' he said, 'I see nothing.' I was so frightened I could say no more then, for the animal was within two or three yards of us and had become as large as a young calf, but had the appearance of a black, shaggy dog with fiery eyes, just like the description I had heard of the 'black dog'. He passed close by me, and made the air cold and dank as he passed along. Though I was afraid to speak, I could not help turning round to look after him, and I saw him growing bigger and bigger as he went along, till he was as high as the trees by the roadside, and then seeming to swell into a large cloud, he vanished in the air. As soon as I could speak, I asked my husband to look at his watch, and it was then five minutes past twelve. My husband said he saw nothing but a vapour or fog coming up from the sea." [72]

In view of the plethora of reports of UFO activity and other episodes of high strangeness reported from Lyme Bay over the years (as many as possible of which we have included in this book) it is hard not to draw the conclusion that all these phenomena are, in some intangible and complex way, all inter-related.

However, enough of speculation. We should return to the summer of 1997 where at the ESP HQ in Exeter things were really beginning to get out of hand.

One afternoon, a group of us including Nigel, Graham, and I decided that enough was enough and that we really should try to collate the enormous amount of information that we had gathered and we spent a laborious afternoon trying to do so. Even as we typed and telephoned witnesses to confirm the salient points of their experiences more reports were coming in. That afternoon alone we had five telephone calls from eye witnesses and the situation was rapidly getting out of hand.

Mrs Turner an elderly lady from Topsham, (the other side of the Exe Estuary) saw glowing balls of light nearly every night for over a week. They always appeared between 22.15 p.m and 23.45 pm and she described them as *"bright starlike objects with a pillar on top and a smaller star-like object on top of that",* (a description somewhat reminiscent of that of the witness from East Budleigh who had seen, and attempted to photograph an object in the sky a few days before). Mrs Turner said that they "wobbled as they moved" and furthermore she was convinced that they were trying to contact her, and she was not alone in her supposition. When Sue, the wife of my co-author, who was initially at least a complete sceptic about all matters even slightly fortean, had her own sighting towards the end of August, she insisted to Nigel: *"that thing's watching us!"* [73]

A UFO flap would not have been a UFO flap without a supposed Government conspiracy and/or cover up, and this one was no exception. For those of you expecting some juicy titbit of a westcountry Roswell, however, this particular conspiracy is of a much more minor nature.

As I wrote at the time in *Sightings* magazine:

"An elderly resident of Woodbury Salterton has seen these lights on a number of occasions and is convinced that what he has seen are parachute flares dropped by Royal Marines during exercises on the common. Despite claims by the authorities that such pyrotechnics had been forbidden this summer due to the almost unprecedented heat wave he is convinced that "The military don't always do as they're told by Clinton Devon Estates of East Budleigh who administer the common".

He is convinced that the stranger manifestations could be caused by a spiralling motion which happens if the parachute doesn't open properly. It is a nice theory, but even if someone in the military IS breaking the rules, such activity can't account for more than ten percent of the sightings which we have logged since July!" [74]

We spoke to him again at the end of August to see whether he had seen any more anomalous lights. He had, and was again adamant about their source, although he told us that he *"wasn't sure exactly who was responsible. It could be the Marines, it could be Territorials or even conceivably the police..."* [75] [76]

He was a very sensible if slightly stolid witness and we are as convinced as we can be that his interpretation of events is almost certainly correct. What he saw on so many occasions was a multi flare. This, however, goes no further towards explaining the main body of the sightings in the Woodbury/Exmouth area.

His report is only included for the sake of completeness, and because as I have mentioned it in writing elsewhere it should be covered in this narrative, as, indeed should the next event.

According to various sources on The Internet, I was quoted extensively in an article for the *Western Daily Press* (August 12th, 1997). The interesting thing here is that I don't remember speaking to them, nor did I say anything about flight paths to and from South Wales: [77]

"A mysterious series of West sightings has excited UFO experts after 17 separate incidents in six days. John Downes, head of the Exeter Strange Phenomenon Research Group, has been inundated with calls reporting strange bright lights that hover or zig-zag in the sky. Six people saw them on Sunday July 27, three people on Monday 28, and at least two more every day until Friday August 1. All the incidents occurred between Budleigh Salterton and Tiverton in East Devon.

Tracey Wilson, an accountant in Exeter, saw the lights from her bedroom window in Tiverton at 10pm on Monday. She said "I went to open the window and saw these bright orange and white lights moving across the sky. They glowed for about two minutes, flared brightly and then disappeared. My first instincts were that they belonged to an aircraft, but that doesn't account for the way they flared.

They were much brighter than normal aeroplane lights." Most of the 17 witnesses said the lights burned as brightly as magnesium, but some saw only one colour and others more. Barry Payne from Dawlish, near Exmouth, saw a light at 10.30pm on Tuesday while he was out walking his dog. He said "I saw a bright orange and white light flying slowly above me. It seemed to zig-zag a little and I remember thinking it was heading north towards Exmouth.

"It definitely wasn't an aeroplane and after a few minutes it seemed to disappear." William Frazer-Jennings of Budleigh Salterton reported seeing a bright rectangular light at 9.30pm on Sunday. "It just appeared and rose slowly" he said. "I rushed in to get my binoculars and saw it hover for about four minutes and then blink out. Because my house is on a hill I had a pretty good view."

Ufologist Mr. Downes, aged 37, traced the sightings on a map and found a clear line which, if carried forward, went across the Bristol Channel and into South Wales. He said:"Its incredible. The phone just kept ringing. There have been previous sightings in all these areas. We are taking this very seriously."

Although it seemed that most of the UFO activity in Britain was centred upon one little corner of the westcountry, other parts of the country were experiencing more than their faeir share of weirdness. On the 10th August, [78] a newspaper not known for unbiased and quality reporting wrote:

"ALIENS are being blamed for the slaughter of hundreds of animals in the beautiful countryside where the TV hit Heartbeat is being filmed. Farmers in North Yorkshire are gripped with fear after a series of bizarre deaths on open moorland.

In the latest, nine sheep were found with their stomachs ripped out in the village of Snainton. And deer were found with holes in their head and drained of blood in the Dalby Forest area. Over a three-year period, similar strange deaths have been reported all over the North York Moors. Former police sergeant Tony Dodd, now a UFO expert, says all the evidence points to aliens. "There have even been reports of the dead *animals falling from the sky, often coinciding with UFO sightings." he says.*

"Without doubt, there is something very sinister going on."

In America, UFO experts believe aliens caused the death of up to 10,000 cattle, found with heads and necks as skeletons but the rest of their corpses intact.

Similar strange cases are still unexplained in the Scottish Highlands and, in October 1995, along the Ulster border."

This series of incidents caused widespread controversy within the UFOlogical and fortean community. Kevin McClure a veteran fortean writer and researcher for whom I have a lot of respect has long stated his antagonism towards animal mutilation research as a branch of forteana. For reasons that are given later in this book I do not necessarily agree with what he has to say, but his reasoning, if not his conclusions, are sound.

He is editor of *Abduction Watch* a monthly newsletter whose remit is to combat the hysterical nonsense that so many commentators within the UFOlogical community have spread, especially on the subjects of abduction research and animal mutilation.

In issue two he wrote:

"Underlying the specific themes there seems to be something nastier, and more pernicious. The abduction mythos feeds on the fear of those who are convinced of its truth, and the unifying factor of all the 'Unnamed Soldier' material is fear and helplessness. Fear of governments, of the Americans, of NATO, of all things military, of black helicopters and flying triangles, of underground bases and implants and alien technology, and of the burning and cutting, and coring and the removal of skin - of humans and animals - that is at the heart of the mutilation rumours. This is the stuff that drives the real crackpots in American ufology, and not only them, but the militias, the fascists, and the bombers, too. Someone, it seems, has decided that it's Britain's turn to suffer this madness.

As for a culprit, or culprits, I really don't know. But I do have to bear in mind just how long the crop circle hoax - for barring certain small, rough, simple circles, hoax it certainly is - has persisted. It has gone on for years, taking substantial planning, investigation, information gathering, secrecy, deceit, and an unimpressive willingness to manipulate, confuse and mislead a considerable number of people, many of whom have changed their lives and futures because of the beliefs that they have been encouraged to hold. I don't believe that ongoing circle hoaxing has any 'government' links whatever, but it certainly establishes the extent to which intelligent, organised and sustained hoaxing can be taken." [79]

I cannot help but agree with him. As an avid reader, and especially as someone who is regularly sent books on fortean subjects generally and UFO related subjects specifically, I will be the first to admit that a good deal of what is written and published on the subject is arrant nonsense.

As will be seen later in this book, much of what has been written on the subject of animal mutilations and abductions is not just arrant nonsense but unpleasant nonsense as well. Where Kevin and I differ, is that I believe, as will be shown in the concluding chapters of this present book, that in some instances of animal mutilation and abduction at least, there is a genuine case to investigate.

Where I differ from most commentators on the subject is that I think that the interpretations usually put on the phenomena by UFO researchers are both childish and facile. On this subject, at least, Kevin McClure and I are *ad idem*. Writing in *Abduction Watch #3* Kevin McClure complains with some justification that:

"I'm trying to make sense of the proposition that, from the bodies of dead animals, it's possible to draw a logical conclusion that they're dead because they've been killed by alien beings. Dr Dolittle aside, there is no evidence of coherent two-way communication with live animals, let alone with dead ones, yet their deaths have been made into a key element of the abduction mythos, and a justification for believing that the abduction of animals supports the arguments for the abduction of humans." [80]

Unfortunately the scenario that "aliens" from "another planet" are visiting "us" in order to "mutilate" our animals and "abduct" our deluded hippy women for "purposes" of their own is a highly widespread belief. Like Kevin McClure, I believe that it is also nonsense.

Kevin McClure has been unafraid to point the finger at people whom he believes are proliferating this unviable belief system. Also in issue three of *Abduction Watch* he writes:

"Tony Dodd, a former police sergeant turned UFO researcher, has amassed a large number of mutilation reports in Britain. Many of his cases show much the same hallmarks as those reported in the US and other countries - bloodless wounds; the 'surgical removal' of organs,

eyes and tongues; the rectum 'cored out' and the jawbone stripped of flesh. Since the early 1990s, Dodd claims, incidents of mutilation have involved wild animals such as foxes, deer, badgers, seals and wild birds, as well as livestock."

Illustrating this piece is a colour photo of a dead fox with a hole in its forehead, and this photo also appears in two very similar articles by Dodd in the July/August 1995 and March/April 1997 issues of UFO Magazine. *In the earlier article, the picture is captioned "A fatally wounded fox discovered on a moor at Staintondale, North Yorkshire, in 1993. The hole seen on the top of the head is not a bullet wound. The brain was removed."*

In the later article, there are also colour photos of a dead lamb, two dead deer, and a dead hedgehog. The page where they appear is noted "All photographs copyright Quest Picture Library/Anthony Dodd", and the caption reads, "Numerous types of animals both large and small have been mutilated since 1993. This small selection forms just part of a major file currently under investigation by Tony Dodd. The fox, deers, and lamb were discovered in a forest in North Yorkshire between 1993-95. The tiny hedgehog was found in West Yorkshire".

Some of the cases presented in both articles appear to just come from local papers, and the absurdly over-hyped Bratton White Horse makes an appearance. This is the nature of mutilations - the alien link rests substantially on a couple of old hypnotic regressions publicised by Linda Moulton Howe, and meaningful, physical, on-site investigation is rare. However, Dodd states that, possibly (presumably?) in relation to the animals in the photos,

"In the smaller animals (sheep, deer, foxes etc) the rectum had been cored out and each had a neat hole bored into the head - through which the brain and spinal cord had been totally removed. In every case blood had disappeared without any spillage on the ground."

Sadly, the later article also presents a photo of a 'mutilated' human - I'll try to deal with this aspect in a month or two - but if we are to establish what actually caused the deaths of these animals, we need to know something about the investigation that has actually taken place. Dodd says he wrote about mutilations to the Ministry of Agriculture, Fisheries and Food (MAFF), the National Farmers Union, and the National Veterinary College, but that "The replies were basically the same, 'We are unaware of any cases of this nature'. This reminded me of the old saying: 'If in doubt, deny everything'."

Dodd writes - without specifying any dates or places - that

"During this time Intelligence Investigators from MAFF turned up at the farms, but strangely refused to enter into any detailed discussions about the incidents. These shadowy figures arrived and quickly departed, not wishing to disclose their involvement or interest. On many occasions animal carcasses were speedily removed from the scene before public interest could be aroused".

He says he has
"evidence that shows creatures as small as mice have been killed and their rectums cored out. They also have holes in their heads. In nearly all the cases previously mentioned, several common factors have emerged: The identical nature of the injuries - the perpetrators are never seen and have never been caught - the total blood loss in every case - the strange glowing objects seen performing aerobatics in the area"

He does not mention whether he has reported these mutilations to the police, the RSPCA, the NFU, or the National Veterinary College. I presume that a professional veterinary autopsy would be vital to establish that "the brain and spinal cord had been removed" through "a neat hole bored into the head", but no vet is mentioned, or autopsy report quoted. Dodd is, however, very specific about MAFF

"Regardless of the cause, strange and patently horrific animal mutilations are occurring, yet nobody associated with the Ministry wants to talk about it. I keep asking: 'What the hell is going on and why are you (Ministry of Agriculture and Fisheries) afraid to talk about it?'

Their findings are now firmly embedded in a department similar to that seen in the X-Files. We have not seen the last of this phenomenon."

Well, MAFF in North Yorkshire isn't entirely unwilling to talk about the subject, because they wrote to me recently. I'd sent them Dodd's later article, including the photos of dead animals allegedly found in North and West Yorkshire. I asked them what they knew about these animals and, particularly, whether Dodd had notified MAFF of these deaths, or asked them to become involved in investigating how those deaths occurred. MAFF replied

"I have made some enquiries locally but have failed to identify anybody within the Ministry who has any knowledge of the incidents described in the article. The Ministry does not have a team of intelligence investiga-

tors employed to investigate the sorts of incidents which have been described, although it is possible that, if the police became aware of animals dying in unusual circumstances, they would turn to our Veterinary Laboratory Agency for advice or assistance. I have checked with the nearest laboratory and also the veterinary field staff responsible for this region and they have had no such enquiries.

I am sorry I cannot be more helpful, but I am as confused as you are by Mr Dodd's reference to "shadowy figures" from the Ministry."

Before we consider drawing conclusions, or even speculating more than is reasonable without the full story, there's some serious questions to be asked here. They have to be serious because, unless some sick fool is tampering with the corpses of animals that are already dead, mammals which feel pain just the same as you or I are being killed and mutilated by something - or somebody - for no acceptable reason; if such a reason could exist. I have no doubt at all that such killing and mutilation is likely to be a criminal act.

I'll be sending copies of this issue of AW to Graham Birdsall (Editor of UFO Magazine - "Factual reporting, factual research) and to Dodd himself, and I'll publish any sensible response next issue. The simple questions are factual, though they may lead to more: were the deaths and mutilations of the specific animals in the photos ever reported to MAFF, to the police, to the RSPCA, or even to a competent veterinary surgeon for autopsy, while the bodies were still available for examination, or the locations for investigation. If not, why not? And if so, bearing MAFF's response in mind, when, to whom, and what evidence is available to establish that those reports were made? Has MAFF, deliberately or inadvertently, provided me with incomplete or inaccurate information

The more complex questions are these. If there's no proof that these animals were ever taken or touched by alien beings, how did their photos come to appear in UFO Magazine? How did they come to be copyrighted to the Quest Picture Library/Anthony Dodd? How did Dodd find out about these dead animals? And, most important, how did they get the neat holes in their heads? How did they die? And why did they die? It is notable that Tony Dodd appears to be the only person in this country who knows, at first hand, about these horrible and extraordinary mutilations, so it is inevitably to him that these questions must be addressed. I'm really looking forward to bringing you the answers to what, for some living creatures, may be questions of life and death." [81]

In the fourth issue of his newsletter he attacked Tony Dodd`s findings as

described in the aforementioned story in *The Sunday People*. Not prepared to pull any punches, he wrote:

"......Meanwhile, it seems that the Sunday People for 10.8.97 reported "strange deaths all over the North Yorks Moors", "Over a three-year period". It appears that "Farmers in North Yorkshire are gripped with fear after a series of bizarre deaths on open moorland". Dodd is quoted as saying that "all the evidence points to aliens", and that "There have even been reports of the dead animals falling from the sky often coinciding with UFO sightings". I was sorry not to have the chance to debate the issue publicly with Dodd at the BEAMS do, but maybe I'll have my chance at Solihull next year, where, at the 'Secrets Unlocked' Conference (the advert says), "Former North Yorkshire police officer Anthony Dodd (UK) discloses disturbing evidence that a rash of mysterious animal deaths is being deliberately kept hidden from the general public and media". With a title like 'Secrets Unlocked', and the "disturbing evidence . . being deliberately kept hidden", it's nice to know what a fine sense of irony the UFO Magazine team still has." (82)

One gets the impression that he was merely `baiting` certain sectors of the UFO Establishment here, because it wasn`t until the next issue that he really went in for the kill by providing not only a detailed analysis of the events but also producing some new evidence of his own:

"When it comes to revealing information about claims of the mysterious mutilation of animals in the UK, official and national bodies are putting up a much better show than UFO Magazine and Quest International. After the earlier reply from MAFF, a few weeks ago I wrote to the RSPCA in North Yorkshire, enclosing the 'Phantom Killers' article from UFO Magazine (see AW3 & 4 etc), and asking what they knew about the reports in that article. I also asked a more specific question

"I have enclosed a copy of an advertisement for a 'UFO Conference' in Solihull next year. Mr Dodd will, it seems, be speaking there to disclose "disturbing evidence that a rash of mysterious animal deaths is being deliberately kept hidden from the general public and media". It seems likely that the supposed 'Yorkshire' cases will be at the heart of his presentation. It would be most helpful to know whether the RSPCA - surely the organisation that should be most aware of "a rash of mysterious animal deaths" in the UK - considers that Mr Dodd's allegation is in any way true?"

To my surprise the helpful reply came not from North Yorkshire, but from "Chief Inspector A G Foxcroft, Staff Officer to the COI", at the RSPCA

Headquarters in Horsham. He wrote

"I am still awaiting details from our ten Regions, covering England and Wales, on animal mutilation cases that may have come to their attention over recent years. However, I do know that none have been previously reported to these Headquarters which would suggest that few, if any, cases of this type have been reported to the RSPCA.

As you point out in your letter, in most instances of animal abuse, the RSPCA is the first point of contact hence the 1.3 million telephone calls we receive each year. These calls result in 110,000 complaints of animal cruelty being investigated by our 307 Inspectors.

One of our officers has an interest in 'Ufology' and will continue to monitor media reports that suggest alien mutilation. If, on the other hand, we receive a complaint and evidence is available, I can assure you that we will conduct a thorough investigation and attempt to bring any person, responsible for an animal suffering, to justice."

I will leave you, for now, to draw your own conclusions from this, but I suggest that rather than saving his "disturbing evidence" of "a rash of mysterious animal deaths" for a UFO Conference in Solihull, Tony Dodd should pass it all, immediately, to the RSPCA. It can then be professionally investigated in the hope that such cruelty will not recur in future. I would be most grateful for news of any further report of this kind in the UK: I promise that I will pass it straight to the RSPCA myself. I've said before that people are more important than ufology. That goes for animals, too." [83]

The news of the unpleasant incidents in Yorkshire left somewhat of a bad feeling in our mouths. However the UFO sightings in south Devon continued and we continued to investigate them.

In this chapter there is only really room for one more, but, it is, we believe, a strangely significant one. This report was taken from an Internet News Group:

*"From: Steve Yarwood
Source: Unknown UK newspaper (scanned report)
Date: August 1997*

UFO leaves couple with 'horrible feeling'...

..after a UFO experience on the road from Hope Cove to Galmpton at

10. 30 last Thursday evening. The husband and wife, who have asked for their names not to be revealed for fear of being considered cranks, were walking up the road towards Galmpton after playing a game of bowls at Galmpton Village Hall.

They were about 300 yards from their home when from the Bolberry Down direction on their right flashed a tea plate size white object. It came to a sudden stop in their path and instantly switched off.

The woman gave her description: "it came to us at such speed. It was like a shooting star, only much closer to earth. There were no flashing lights or anything like that, just a simple white disk."

"When the object stopped in front of us it was as if a light went out. It was a strange, strange feeling, like we were still being watched.

"I didn't say anything because I thought it might just be me who saw it, but then my husband shouted "what the heck was that?"

"I think he was more affected by it than me. He can't stop talking about it.

"It has left us both with a horrible feeling, especially as we are beginning to think we were the only people who saw it."

She reckoned the whole incident lasted only about a second." [85]

We have included that particular incident in the book, even though it comes from a geographical area away from that which we were researching. This is mainly because of the graphic description of the feelings of unease and paranoia reported by the unnamed witnesses.

Later in this book we shall discover similar reports, and, indeed, we believe that for the first time we are able to present a hypothesis which goes some way at least towards explaining them.

We have always disliked the sort of UFO book that is nothing more than a long list of reports and when we started to write this book we were determined that this would not be one of those books. We have, however, given every report up until the end of August in this chapter for two reasons. Firstly, to try and give an indication of the sheer scale of the events with which we were inextricably involved, and secondly to give an overview of the diversity of experiences that were reported to us. This, I think, we have done.

Now it is time to stop.

The reports continued unabated until the third week of September when they fizzled out. However there is no point in listing them all in excruciating detail. [86] The time has come to examine some of the other strange occurences of that long, hot, summer.

III

By this time, partly because of his association with us, and partly because of his own entrepreneurial skills, Nigel Wright had his own column in the *Exmouth Journal* and he reported a bizarre sighting from the first of September, which again corresponded with one of the sightings reported by the elderly lady from East Budleigh:

"At approximately 10.30 p.m the gentleman was standing on the corner of Asleigh Road and Chichester Close. He observed, at very low level, a flashing red light coming from Exeter which moved erratically. It flashed three times then remained constant. It then moved towards Haldon. Behind this light came a conventional aircraft showing ordinary navigation lights. This aircraft appeared to be following the red light as it continued over the estuary towards Haldon Hill. The informant commented `It was like the plane was chasing the weird light`". [1]

This witness, who has asked to be identified only as "Andy" is a personal friend of Nigel's and they have known each other for over a decade. Nigel describes him as a *"down to earth type not given to fantasy"* [2] and assured me, both then and now, that any testimony he gives can be trusted wholeheartedly. He had been a serving Life-boat man and his observational skills are unquestionable. Two days previously, however, he had reported another strange experience which Nigel reported faithfully in his newspaper column:

"The current wave of UFO activity over the East Devon area has taken a rather unusual twist over recent weeks with the Exeter Strange Phenomena Research Group now receiving reports of red lights both very fast and still low down over the waters off both Exmouth and Brixham-Berry Head area.

These strange events started a few weeks ago when two gentlemen saw two very bright red lights again moving fast at sea level off Exmouth in the early hours of the morning. Now in a separate incident, we have a report from a local man of certain radio traffic relating to a not dissimilar event, only this time in the Brixham-Berry Head part of the coastline.

For rather obvious reasons, the man concerned wishes to remain anonymous, mainly because the radio channel involved (Marine Band zero) is a restricted one used by the emergency services, e.g. lifeboat, coastguard etc. What happened on the night of August 28 on this channel can now be revealed for the first time.

RED LIGHTS AND HELICOPTERS

A member of the public reports a 'red light' resembling a flare over the sea at 1.00 p.m. He views this from Brixham Marina ~ He reports the fact to the coastguard who from their Brixham radio base, call out the Berry Head Mobile Unit, The Brixham Mobile Unit, and alert the Berry Head Lookout. Also the Brixham Lifeboat is launched.

It was then that Portland Coastguards called on the assistance of Rescue Helicopter `Whisky Bravo` from Portland to aid in the search for the mystery red light. The informant was listening to this radio traffic high up on Foxhills Hill in Exmouth. The night was clear and this person could look right across the bay up to and beyond Berry Head. Because of his keen radio listening and former lifeboat duties, he was aware that `Whisky Bravo` would fly along the coast and up the River Exe to Exeter Airport for refueling. However, this night it did not"..... [3]

This, as Nigel sagely pointed out whilst we were engaged in a pointless attempt to convert the newspaper cutting to computer-friendly text by means of a scanner with OCR Software, (and failing dismally), beggars the question. Where did the helicopter go that night? It didn't follow the usual flightpath but it obviously went somewhere. The helicopter was, according to the intercepted radio message at least, ordered to search the sea off Brixham/Berry Head but if it had done so, "Andy" would have been able to see it clearly from his vantage point high on the hills on the outskirts of Exmouth. It was a clear night, but he didn't see anything.

His original report in the *Exmouth Journal* confirms, however, that the search for the source of the anomalous red lights was continuing apace:

..."The Brixham lifeboat was searching by visual and radar means. The lifeboat picked up four radar targets and investigated them. They proved

to be two marker buoys on fishing nets and two yachts - neither of which were in distress. Berry Head lookout reported that they saw a helicopter with a red flashing light underneath it on the Brixham side of Berry Head. Unusually this was also not visible to my informant on Foxholes Hill". [4]

Mystery solved, I thought, and said as much to Nigel who gestured rudely to me and continued dictating from his original report:

"... Brixham Coastguard contacted Air Traffic Control to see if any helicopters were in the area. According to the Air Traffic Controller there was no civilian traffic in that area at all. The police helicopter `Oscar 9-9` was not airborne and the only military helicopters in that area were three sea kings based at RNAS Yeovilton which were undergoing coastal navigation training at that time, but these were supposedly flying in close formation. Brixham tried to contact these helicopters but to no avail.

During all this time the informant reported a strange code-like language unlike anything he had ever heard before on this channel being used occasionally. Finally Berry Head Mobile reported that the light was heading up the River Dart and the search was called off". [5]

The thing that makes this incident so interesting is the experience of the witness himself. As an ex-lifeboatman he was *au fait* with the operating procedures of lifeboat stations and he informed us that it would normally be unheard of for a search on this scale to be mobilised, purely because of reports of a red light. Although the practice is strictly illegal he had been using a scanner to monitor radio traffic for at least the previous decade and he had never heard anything like this strange `code` before. The `code` was a conglomeration of words and phrases IN ENGLISH which made no sense at all. This is actually a well known `scenario` within UFOlogy: [6]

One famous case where UFO reports were linked to radio messages containing a mixture of decipherable words and garbled gibberish comes from a paper called *CIA's Role in the Study of UFOs, 1947-90 by* Gerald K. Haines [7]

"The Agency was also involved with Davidson and Keyhoe in two rather famous UFO cases in the 1950s, which helped contribute to a growing sense of public distrust of CIA with regard to UFOs. One focused on what was reported to have been a tape recording of a radio signal from a flying saucer; the other on reported photographs of a flying saucer. The

"radio code" incident began innocently enough in 1955, when two elderly sisters in Chicago, Mildred and Marie Maier, reported in the Journal of Space Flight their experiences with UFOs, including the recording of a radio program in which an unidentified code was reportedly heard. The sisters taped the program and other ham radio operators also claimed to have heard the "space message." OSI became interested and asked the Scientific Contact Branch to obtain a copy of the recording.

Field officers from the Contact Division (CD), one of whom was Dewelt Walker, made contact with the Maier sisters, who were "thrilled that the government was interested," and set up a time to meet with them. In trying to secure the tape recording, the Agency officers reported that they had stumbled upon a scene from Arsenic and Old Lace. "The only thing lacking was the elderberry wine," Walker cabled Headquarters. After reviewing the sisters' scrapbook of clippings from their days on the stage, the officers secured a copy of the recording. OSI analyzed the tape and found it was nothing more than Morse code from a US radio station.

The matter rested there until UFOlogist Leon Davidson talked with the Maier sisters in 1957. The sisters remembered they had talked with a Mr. Walker who said he was from the US Air Force. Davidson then wrote to a Mr. Walker, believing him to be a US Air Force Intelligence Officer from Wright-Patterson, to ask if the tape had been analyzed at ATIC. Dewelt Walker replied to Davidson that the tape had been forwarded to proper authorities for evaluation, and no information was available concerning the results. Not satisfied, and suspecting that Walker was really a CIA officer, Davidson next wrote DCI Allen Dulles demanding to learn what the coded message revealed and who Mr. Walker was. The Agency, wanting to keep Walker's identity as a CIA employee secret, replied that another agency of the government had analyzed the tape in question and that Davidson would be hearing from the Air Force. On 5 August, the Air Force wrote Davidson saying that Walker "was and is an Air Force Officer" and that the tape "was analyzed by another government organization." The Air Force letter confirmed that the recording contained only identifiable Morse code which came from a known US-licensed radio station.

Davidson wrote Dulles again. This time he wanted to know the identity of the Morse operator and of the agency that had conducted the analysis. CIA and the Air Force were now in a quandary. The Agency had previously denied that it had actually analyzed the tape. The Air Force had also denied analyzing the tape and claimed that Walker was an Air Force officer. CIA officers, under cover, contacted Davidson in Chicago *and promised to get the code translation and the identification of the transmitter, if possible.*

In another attempt to pacify Davidson, a CIA officer, again under cover and wearing his Air Force uniform, contacted Davidson in New York City. The CIA officer explained that there was no super agency involved and that Air Force policy was not to disclose who was doing what."

Before we leave the subject, it should be noted that another spate of similar reports the following year provoked a very rational and reasoned response from the powers that be, as reported by the newspaper most likely to be read by their wives:

"A spectacular meteor shower sent hundreds of anxious onlookers scurrying to phone the emergency services, convinced aliens were about to land. Police and coastguards were inundated with calls when the skies above Southern Britain lit up with stunning flashes and smoke trails and echoed to rumbling explosions.

Many mistook the shooting stars for distress flares from a ship in trouble, while others believed they were seeing UFOs. In fact, the light show signalled the return of a group of meteoroids called Virginids, which reach the Earth every Spring. Experts say they will be around for weeks. Sunday night's display was particularly spectacular because of the nearly full moon and crystal-clear skies.

Emergency services across the South and West said yesterday they had taken hundreds of calls. Police were also alerted, but soon learned the lights were shooting stars after checking with weather experts. The Brixham Coastguard in South Devon said it took up to 30 calls reporting red distress flares in an area from Exmouth to beyond Plymouth.

"It was obviously quite a severe meteorite shower," a spokesman said. "We actually saw one over our own coastguard station. There was a bright flash of white light with a bang and some smoke. It was like a very big, very high firework. Meteorologist Dr Richard Porter, from Kingsbridge, South Devon, told how he saw a trail of light across the sky.

"It was like a rocket which broke up into five or six pieces and disappeared but there was a smoke cloud which remained for ten minutes. I also heard bangs and rumblings for two or three minutes. "I believe it was a meteor a foot or so across at about 18 to 30 miles up in the sky. This is comparatively low in our atmosphere and the lowest I have seen. It may have been a piece of space debris and not a true meteorite."

Gerald White, secretary of the Norman Lockyer Observatory in Sidmouth, Devon, said the meteors varied from the size of sand to a pea or even a cricket ball.

Tens of thousands of these lumps of rock and iron head towards Earth every year, but only 100 or so are large enough to survive their fiery descent and reach the ground. When they float through space they are known as meteoroids. When they burn up in the atmosphere they become meteors and if they crash into the ground they are meteorites. Meteoroids hit the atmosphere at up to 45 miles a second. Friction with the air turns them white hot and they appear as streaks of bright light. Mr White said reports of smoke were explained by vapour.

Most are the size of grains of sand and disintegrate at least 50 miles up. But larger meteoroids, travelling at five times the speed of sound, can produce sonic booms as they approach the ground. They are created when asteroids collide in space, although some are debris from comets.

Meteor showers occur when the Earth passes through orbiting clusters of rocks. Some return annually, others every few decades." [8]

However, we must leave the subject of mystery red lights and garbled radio signals and move on to another extraordinary incident in the collective lives of the Exeter Strange Phenomena Research Group - one which has nothing to do with the former, but a little to do with the latter.

One of the more bizarre episodes which happened to us during the long hot summer and autumn of 1997 was what my friend and colleague Jan Scarff dubbed "The Case of the Weird Warbling Whatsit of the Westcountry". [9]

Graham was on holiday in Cornwall with his Mum during the last week of September, and therefore missed all of the excitement. I feel sure that had we had him available with his level of technical expertise, the situation which eventually arose would never have happened.

He was on holiday and so I did the *Weird about the West* radio show accompanied by Jan Scarff. Our guest was a zoologist who was talking about strange and anomalous appearances of animals in the British countryside. This was an area with which, in my capacity as Director of the Centre for Fortean Zoology, I am very familiar. We managed to conduct a pleasant if unremarkable show and then went back to my house to drink tea, smoke cigarettes and listen to a new CD that I had just bought by

Scott Walker - an artist of whom we are both inordinately fond. (10)

I can't really remember how Jan became part of the ESP investigation team. I think that he just heard us on the radio one day and then turned up at one of the meetings. Her certainly predated Nigel as a regular in the ESP camp, but unlike Nigel he has a job in London much of the time and is thus unable to spend anything like the amount of time working with us on ESP investigations as I suspect that he would have liked to. (11)

It so happened, however, that he was working relatively civilised hours on a job in south Devon during the spring and summer of 1997 and was therefore, for a few months at least, able to be part of the fun and games that were afoot. It is lucky (if, indeed there is any such thing as 'luck' which I personally doubt), that he was available to join in the events of that summer because with hindsight I doubt if we would have managed without him.

We were sitting at home with Toby the Dog, relaxing and listening to Scott Walker's inordinately glorious voice when the telephone rang. It was the bloke who had been our guest on the afternoon's show and he had a peculiar incident that he wanted to share with us. It appears that just after we had finished the broadcast one of the people who had been listening to us telephoned the BBC studios, not realising that our guests habitually join in the show by telephone, and asked to speak to him. (12)

More by luck than for any other reason she managed to get hold of his telephone number and rang him to tell him a most peculiar story. The lady lived at Clyst St Mary (a little village just outside Exeter) who had been hearing strange bird calls outside her window in the middle of the night, every night for the previous five weeks. (13)

He was convinced that the matter was a strictly paranormal one, and outside his remit which was purely zoological in nature and so he passed the case over to us, wished us luck and rang off. We immediately rang the old lady in Clyst St Mary..(14)

Luckily for us, it transpired that she had managed to make a cassette recording of one of these episodes of strange bird calls, and she played it, first to Jan and then to me, down the telephone. It sounded like nothing else I had ever heard before, although it was mildly reminiscent of the weird call of an Albatross, but even though Albatrosses have been known to venture into the Northern Hemisphere on odd occasions (15)(16)(17)(18) the chances of one alighting outside a lady's bedroom window at precisely the same time each night and issuing forth unearthly cries for a precise number of times before dissappearing every night for six weeks was so unlikely as to be statistically impossible.

We decided to visit the scene of these events, and in the words of the characters from a dozen third rate US TV cop shows "stake out the joint". This we did on the night of the following Friday, accompanied by Dave Hopkins - a keen ornithologist, [19] whom we brought along not just because he is good fun, but because we thought is it WAS some strange bird making these noises then he would be the person in our team most likely to know what sort of bird it was.

According to our witness these noises always occurred at four minutes past two in the morning, and so we began a long and lonely vigil in the car park of the boozer opposite her house. [20] curious, the pub landlord stood outside with us giving us coffee and telling us ghost stories. Apparently a bar manager several years before had hung himself and ever since there had been a string over poltergeist reports and even the occasional sighting. Some of the more superstitious bar staff refused to work after hours alone.

Although we started the evening in high spirits and an atmosphere of hilarity had prevailed, by the time two o'clock approached we were actually getting quite scared, and when all the owls in the area started to hoot and screech we were quite un-nerved, [21] but unfortunately we heard nothing even approaching the noises that had been played to us. Feeling somewhat deflated we all went home, but the next day Jan telephoned me to tell me that much to his surprise, the lady had reported hearing the same noises as usual on the previous night, and had even been watching us wandering around the garden at the same time as she had heard them. This was getting very strange indeed and when, on the next two nights (Saturday and Sunday) she produced tape recordings of what was apparently the same sound, we decided that there was only one thing that we could sensibly do - we had to go to her house, at four minutes past two, wait in her bedroom and see what happened.

Understandably she was loth to have a whole bunch of quasi-fortean weirdos trampelling around her boudoir and therefore it was only Jan who visited her laden with paranormal investigating equipment the following night. As the hour of two approached the atmosphere in the house became strained and tense, and by two o'clock you could, (in Jan's words) "cut the atmosphere with a knife". [22]

Four minutes later the unearthly sounds started. Jan, together with the lady's son Paul, rampaged around her bedroom and eventually found the source of the noise .... it was a novelty Japanese watch with an alarm consisting of the electronically generated sound of a cock crowing. [23]

The mystery was solved, but there is an object lesson here for us all. During the days before we knew what had actually caused these sounds I appeared on the BBC Radio [24] and played the tape, voicing my opinion that here MIGHT be a genuine paranormal occurence. As it was, it was nothing of the kind, but if I had not come public here in this column with the truth of the matter "The Case of the Weird Warbling Whatsit of the Westcountry" could well have passed into the canon of fortean literature as a genuine unsolved mystery.

One wonders how many other well known cases have equally prosaic explanations?

The really important thing here, however, isn't the fact that we solved a minor fortean mystery and in doing so managed to get a couple of figurative feathers in our collective cap, because, let's face it, whatever kudos we might have gained from doing that was lost by playing the recordings of a novelty Japanese Alarm Clock to a hapless reporter from BBC Radio 4's *Today* programme in the guise of being evidence of a genuine paranormal phenomenon.

No, the real importance of this episode is that it is a great indication of our collective mindset at the time. By the time that we became embroiled into this particular adventure we had been in the middle of a UFO flap of epic proportions for nearly two months. Then - at the end of September it all stopped.

In the closing sequence of the 1969 film *The Battle of Britain* [25] the fighter pilots, who for about six weeks had been engaged in a titanic struggle against the overwhelming odds of serried ranks of incoming Luftwaffe aircraft, are sitting outside the Nissan huts of their airdromes on the south coast of England waiting for an onslaught that never came. The pilots were tired, pale and drawn, and could not really believe that The Battle of Britain was over.

On a personal level, one Tuesday morning at the end of September 1997 I knew how they felt. For weeks I and my gallant (if slightly eccentric) investigation team had been receiving nightly reports of UFO activity in the East Devon area. Nigel, Graham and I, in particular had been averaging three hours of sleep a night, and I had been resorting to tranquilisers to get me to sleep during the few times when the telephone was not actually ringing. As I slowly woke up - my head still fuzzy from Valium, and with cramp in my left foot, from where my dog Toby had been lying asleep on it, I slowly began to realise that the telephone hadn't rung since the previous day, and that I had been asleep for nearly fourteen hours. For the time being, at least, the East Devon UFO flap seemed to be over. I stretched, yawned and went back to sleep.

That afternoon Jan and I went on BBC Radio Devon to present a fairly uninteresting show about out of place animals, and the rest is as they say `history`.

During the four months leading up to the end of September we logged about forty different incidents involving anomalous aerial activity, involving a total of one hundred and twenty six witnesses, but the greatest concentration of this acticity was between Sunday 27th July and Friday the 15th August during which at least fifty individuals saw a variety of different objects in the sky, and suddenly it was over. We are all relatively sober and level headed infivduals and I would not like to say that we were clutching at straws but on one level at least I am sure that we were.

It was a time of immense change for all of us. At the time the Exeter Strange Phenomena Research Group was the largest and most active that it had ever been and there were half a dozen people working with it who have not been named in the text, not because I want to denigrate their contribution towards our research but because they have since drifted away, and we have lost contact. Being (usually at least) a relatively ethical writer I do not want to be in the position of dragging people who would probably not want it into the glare of publicity just for sake of a complete narrative.

The fact that so many of the people who were working so hard together during the summer and autumn of 1997 are no longer in contact with each other is actually, I believe, quite important. We were like old army buddies who had fought a long campaign together and who, after demobilisation would never see each other again.

The affair of the `Weird warbling Whatsit` was like the final skirmish before the cessation of hostilities.

I know, or at least I THINK that I know, that these events were an enormous psychological watershed in all of our lives. The members of the team who usually had normal and fairly mundane existences were actually quite worried at the imminent end to this brief period of excitement in their lives. For two months they had been giving and receiving tele-

phone calls at all hours of the night, camping out at Woodbury Castle to watch the sky, and collating evidence that we all believed was going to lead to something fantastic. As it turned out we were right but not in the way that we all thought!

I am certain that for these people, the idea of returning to a normal suburban existence was too much to bear and that this is why we leapt on the idea of the `Weird Warbling Whatsit` with such gusto.

For me, however, there was a whole different range of stresses which were making the imminent end of the excitement of the summer seem like an insurmountable obstacle. By this time my divorce had come through, but, although on paper I was a free man, the reality of the situation was something else entirely. This is not the time or place for recriminations, but sufficient to say that the emotional strain of the divorce and the resulting pain that it had caused to me and my family was too much to bear. There were complex financial settlements to consider and it so happened that with what some people would no doubt refer to as life`s little ironies and others would call the gods of chaos playing silly buggers with me, for the first time in many years I was beginning to make some money with my writing. At the time that my wife and I separated I was earning practically nothing and we had mounting debts. I was therefore faced with the very real possibiltiy that my new found success as a fortean spokesman and writer would be negated by the perfectly legal fact that the woman I was not living with was entitled to half my new found income.

Things started to get very nasty and at one time I was even threatened with imprisonment if I did not comply with certain requests that I felt to be unreasonable. This was too much for me to deal with and I slipped very quickly back into the dark morass of psychosis.

I didn`t want to admit it to anyone but I was hallucinating nearly every day. Each night the voices in my head got louder and more insistent and again I found myself facing an abyss that was so unlike anything I had ever been prepared to deal with before that I really didn`t know what to do. My only life-line was my involvement in the incredible events of the summer, and the thought that they were rapidly coming to an end which would leave me with nothing in my life apart from writing to earn money that I probably wouldn`t be allowed to keep was a horrific prospect.

After well over a year of waiting I had finally been accepted for a twelve month course of psychotherapy at Wonford House psychiatric hospital in Exeter. Everybody warned me that this was likely to be extremely har-

rowing and although at that time I would have done anything to get rid of the crushing weight of despair and the mocking voices and visions which tormented every waking and sleeping moment I was not looking forward to it. The idea of life without any excitement, cameraderie or fun was a daunting and abominable prospect.

So for all of us, I think that the fact that, for a while at least, we were taken in by the peculiar case of the `Weird Warbling Whatsit of the Westcountry` is quite understandable, even justified. The important thing is that this should really be seen as an object lesson for all wannabe forteans. We had a bloody good team of reasonably hard nosed investigators who are not prone to jumping to conclusions. But we did; and if it can happen to us it can happen to anyone!

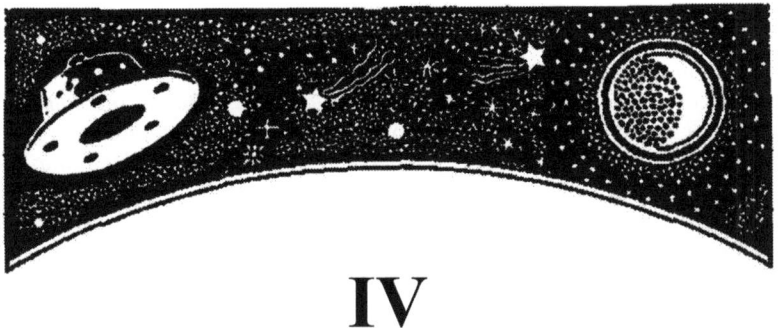

IV

As I have noted elsewhere one of the most peculiar aspects of contemporary culture is the way that whenever a mainstream movie from one of the Hollywood studios is a box office success a number of things invariably happen. People start to identify with the main characters of the film in a way that one would not normally imagine. They name their dogs after them. They name their children after them. They even try to dress like them. One of the most bizarre (and little known) aspects of the contemporary film industry concerns a small company in Santa Monica who, whenever a film is a hit at the Box Office, immediately rush out a pornographic version of it. The results are usually highly silly and completely unerotic but sell by the bucketload and include such masterpieces as *"Edward Penishands"*, *"Jurassic Poke"* and my all time favourite - the sensitive retelling of the story of Cyrano de Bergerac which didn`t feature sensitive and acclaimed French Actor Gerard Depardieu but did feature a bloke who couldn`t act with a large and unconvincing plastic penis gaffer taped to the tip of his nose. [1]

When I finally managed to afford to go on the Internet I discovered that there was a similar, if less commercial operation being carried out in cyberspace. There is, I discovered, a highly organised library of pornographic (and semi pornographic) stories based around well known films and television programmes. These include S&M versions of the Hanna Barbera cartoon "Scooby Doo", Sub/Dom versions of "Star Trek" and a series of stories which claim that the main reason that the two protagonists in "The X Files" have not developed a personal as well as a professional relationship is that Special Agent Scully is a devotee of what some of the author`s fiondly refer to as "Girl on Girl". Much to my surprise, some of these stories are not just an outlet for the fevered (and usually unpleasant) sexuality of the author but contain clues that the author is not just a pervert but a fortean one to boot. (3)

For example:
"Scully was freezing; that didn't even begin to describe it. She couldn't ever remember being so cold, not even on their last arctic adventure. She was in Barrow, Alaska, with Mulder investigating some whale mutilations. She couldn't believe that she let him talk her into this one. Sure, he was technically her superior but she was sure she could have convinced Skinner that this one was over the edge, even for Mulder. All they had seen, in her opinion, was a very sick attempt to cover up the poaching of some pilot whales. Mulder, on the other hand, opted once again for the little green men theory. He claimed that poachers would not leave all of that good blubber, she countered that they did it knowing some moron would think it was an extraterrestrial incident and they would be free to poach again. They were dropped off by an Air Force supply transport and were not scheduled to be picked up for another three days. They had already spent two days on the ice." (4)

Proving that life, on occasion at least, DOES imitate art this report is from Nigel back when he was merely **(merely?),** the Exmouth Representative of the ESP Research Group and is dated October the first!
"Approximately three weeks ago two young men were swimming in Otter Cove. As darkness drew in they decided to make for the shore and change to go home. As they got changed, one of them looked out to sea. He saw what he described as a `greenish` light, under the surface. He called to the other young man and they both watched as this light `rose` to the surface of the water. The next thing they knew there was a very bright light shining into their faces. They turned and fled the scene". (5)
On the cliffs above, the mother of one of the young men was waiting to collect them in her car. Frightened, they told her of their experience, only to be told that she, too, had experienced something strange that evening. Driving towards Otter Cove about ten minutes before she had seen a strange animal like an enormous cat which she described as being "all lit up inside itself". The strangeness doesn`t end here, however. (6)

The next day a dead pilot whale was washed up on the beach nearby.

The following report from Nigel is taken from the files of the Exeter Strange Phenomena Research Group:

"To see any of God's noble creatures come to a painful, and sad end, is never a nice thing. However, sometimes we can learn from the way in which the animal met its end. This may very well be the case is this instance. One of the largest of all the worlds creatures, dead, and

without any apparent cause for its fate

It was about 6.30 p.m. when I got to hear of a dead pilot whale, which was washed ashore at Otter Cove. Now, not being a zoologist, I decided to phone Jon, to obtain his advice on how to treat this news. He asked me to go straight down to the cove and try to obtain some photos of the creature, along with some samples. I must admit that the very idea of being so close to this dead leviathan of the ocean was not really something that I was looking forward to. For a start, I had heard of the really quite disgusting smell, that was supposed to emit from such things. Take it from me, this much is true, my nose can testify to this fact. Also, I am quite a sentimental man, and to look at this mammal, as it lay sadly still and yet so complete, on that cooling summer beach, was a sight that almost brought me to tears.

The first thing that stuck me, as I looked on at this scene, was how perfect the carcass was. There was no decay or huge chunks torn from it. Then, as I wandered around it I noticed that there was only one external wound, in the area of the genitals a large round incision, the size of a large dinner plate, was cut right into the internal organs of the mammal. The sides of this incision were perfectly formed, as if some giant apple corer had been inserted and twisted around. From the wound hung some of the internal organs. I quizzed the official from English Heritage, who is responsible for the disposal of the carcass, he informed me that no natural predator, or boat strike, would have caused this wound. As I looked at this sight, the first thing that came into my mind was how this looked just like the cattle mutilation cases of recent times. Could this be just a coincidence, I was not certain at that time, I decided to phone Jon again, so I rushed off to find the nearest phone box!

Have you ever noticed a funny thing about persons who have a great knowledge of their particular subject. They have a knack of sounding very calm and collected, even when you are tiring to tell them something that is, to you, so very exciting. This is the position I found myself in, that night, as I stood in that phone box. Jon remained very calm and collected as I recounted the details of the strange wound, that I had seen on the creature. In the quiet, restrained tones of a college professor, he just said, "Um! Rather interesting". That was it, no outpouring of wild excitement, or ranting at the top of his voice, praising my having found the lost conclusive proof of alien involvement. No, just three little words. However, little was I to know, that this was indeed, a significant moment in our investigations into the mysteries that surround this part of our coastline.

Later that week, we had the photos back from the lab, we compared these phtos to the ones of classic cases from the U.S., of cattle mutilation. As if to confirm my initial thoughts, the type of wounds were very similar. This similarity remained just an oddity, in what was up to then, a very odd year. Then, early in 1998, I attended a UFO conference, at this, I was informed of another set of events, which in themselves, which was strange enough, but when placed with this sad case, was enough to ring alarm bells in Jon and my minds." [7][8]

There were no signs of injury to the beast except for a circular hole, apparently incising its genitals and anus. [9] As many UFOlogists know such injuries have been reported on domestic and wild animals, often in conjunction with flaps of UFO activity. [10] It is important to note that the zoologist from 'English Nature' who examined the creature was at a loss to explain such peculiar injuries. [11][12] The fact that a marine mammal exhibiting such injuries is found in conjunction with USO activity, is, we believe, at least partly significant!

What compounds the strangeness of this episode is that ten years before, almost to the day, another whale was stranded in the area. This time at Otter Cove itself. The *Exmouth Herald* for September 25th 1987 reported:

"Please could we have our whale teeth back

Callous looters hacked off the lower jaw of a rare whale washed up near Exmouth to steal its two front teeth. After the 20-ft long Cuvier`s beaked whale was found dead at Otter Cove on monday, Exeter's Royal Albert Museum and the British Museum in London sent experts to retrieve it for research. But during Tuesday night, the whale floated back out into Lyme Bay because nobody had secured it. In the meantime, Customs officers who had arrived to take charge of the carcase on Tuesday mornmg found that the teeth which are Government property were missing.

Mr. Kelvin Boot, from the Royal Albert Museum in Exeter, said: "This whale is one of the rarest as far as beaching goes. There are no records of one being stranded in Britain this century. There was a sightng in the 1960's, but that is not like having the actual whale to investigate. It is a very significant find. Perhaps we should have chained it to make sure it didn't float away, but I am confident that it will turn up again on a beach along the coast. The Marines are on stand-by to tow it oft as soon as it is sighted.

We will then dissect the whale, taking samples of various organs to check for heavy metal pollution in the sea and to discover what it has been feeding on. So little is known about this particular beaked whale. I just hope we can get it back. We may never get the chance again.

Fortunately for the scientists the whale obliged on Thursday morning, when it was washed up at Budleigh Salterton. Mr. Keith Green, an Exmouth-based Customs and Excise officer, said:"We would like to hear from anyone who has any information on the whereabouts of its teeth - they are still the property of the crown. All whales, porpoises and dolphins stranded on the British coast are the property of the Receiver of Wrecks, a department of the Customs and Excise service.

Under its rules, the mammals' teeth have to be removed and sent to the British Museum to establish the age and sex of the whale."

Here, we would like to note that whereas the newspaper's conclusion that the lower jaw was hacked off by souvenir hunters is probably correct, this IS remarkably reminiscent of another scenario commonly reported in UFO related animal mutilations. The coincidence between the locations and the timing (as we shall see there were UFO reports in 1987 as well) is worth remarking upon.

As Nigel pointed out, they would have, made spectacularly uninteresting souvenirs and having come face to face as it were with another suppurating cetacean ten years later, he feels it unlikely that any but the most psychotic of curio hunters would have summoned up the intestinal fortitude to hack the jaw off the great beast. I have to agree with him, and would add that the task would have been a particularly onerous and time-consuming one, and would also add that Otter Cove is a particularly isolated spot that can only be reached by driving through the grounds of a local holiday camp. [14][15]

If the mutilation was carried out at night (which it would have to have been in order to escape the prying eyes of gleeful holiday makers) it would seem almost impossible (having visited the location) that:

a. The operation (which would have needed a chainsaw to complete) could have been carried out without attracting attention.

b. That the perpetrators (whoever they were) could have taken the immense jaw up the treacherous cliff path without having incurred an unreasonable degree of danger.

or

c. Anyone would have bothered.

A refutation of the `callous souvenir hunter` scenario can be found in this folllowing account of the species:

**"Cuvier's Beaked Whale. Order Cetacea : Family Ziphiidae :
Ziphius cavirostris
G. Cuvier**

Cuvier's Beaked Whale (Ziphius cavirostris) Description. A moderately small beaked whale with upperparts ranging in color from dark brown to lead gray or blackish in color; underparts paler, but not whitish; occasionally head and upper back whitish; beak moderately prominent and the forehead rising rather sharply; lower jaw longer than upper; pectoral fin relatively small and the dorsal fin placed on posterior third of body; prominent keel extends from dorsal fin to tail; skull with length of rostrum less than twice its breadth at notch; lower jaw of males with one large tooth (about 7 cm in length and 4 cm in diameter) at the tip; in females the teeth are small and seldom break through the gums so that the animal appears to be toothless; two converging grooves on throat. Total length of adults, 5-7 m. Weight, 2.5-4.5 metric tons.

Distribution in Texas. Sparsely distributed throughout tropical and subtropical waters of the world. In the western North Atlantic, these whales are found from Massachusetts to Florida and the Gulf of Mexico.

Habits. Little is known of this whale beyond information revealed by stranded specimens. They are often observed in groups of 10-25. These whales are deep divers and may remain below water for 30 minutes or longer. They are known to eat squid, fish, crabs, and starfish.

The reproductive habits are almost unknown. There does not seem to be a distinct breeding season as calves are born year round. Calves are about 2.1 m long at birth. The length of gestation is unknown." [16]

D.J.Coffey (1977) also notes that:

"...the male has a pair of teeth at the point of the lower jaw. In the female these do not erupt" [17]

As every report on this particular stranding has stated the animal was a female. This satisfactorily refutes any allegations that it would have been mutilated by souvenir hunters even if they had had the time, the opportu-

nity or the motive, which is very questionable.

Another story in the *Exmouth Herald* a week later proclaimed:

"Hankies out for whale

Exmouth foiled out a carpet of polythene to bring ashore its most unusual visitor. a rare Cuvier's beaked whale on Friday morning. The 20ft. whale had been washed up dead on rocks at Otter Cove near Exmouth, and became a television celebrity overnight. But before experts from the Royal Albert Museum in Exeter could begin examining the five-ton female whale, thieves sawed off part of her lower law and two front teeth.

The whale was then washed away on the tide but found again in the estuary of the River Otter, at Budleigh Salutation. On Friday's high tide, Royal Marines from Limestone Camp secured lines around the whale and towed her out to sea as staff from the Exmouth Dock Company laid out a polythene carpet down Mamhead slipway on the pierheard.

As the whale was brought alongside by the Marines a line was thrown ashore to waiting dockers. A crowd of more than 100 watched the whale being pulled up the polythene carpet until the line broke. It was then a case of the one that got away as the whale drifted out to sea before the Marines nudged her back on to the slipway with inflatable boats. A new line was attached to the whale, which was pulled slowly up the sllpway and on to the road.

Several people reached for their handkerchiefs as the whale was lifted on to a waiting lorry - not to wipe away a tear, but to cover their noses. The carcass was then taken to a knacker's yard at Newton Abbot where staff from the museum began the task of stripping off the flesh. Mr. David Bolton. one of the museum team, said.' "We now know that the whale had a number of broken ribs and there was evidence of internal bleeding. This points to it having been hit by a ship or thrown across some rocks. "The whale had a punctured lung and a more detailed examination of the skeleton will provide some idea of her age. " [18]

The Ziphiidae, the family to which Cuvier's beaked whale belongs is poorly known and full of so many zoological surprises that it has excited cryptozoologists as well as their brethren in the more mainstream branches of the narural sciences for many years.

Bernard Heuvelmans, the Belgian zoologist known universally as "The father of Cryptozoology" [19] waxed lyrical on the subject in 1968:

"No family of whales is so mysterious as the Ziphiidae, or 'Beaked Whales', which are really dolphins. Hyperoodon is the only one of its five genera which is at all common and the only one which has been known since the beginning of the last century. There seem to be several different species of Hyperoodon, or Bottlenose, reaching a length of about 30 feet, but the one most unlike the others is known almost entirely from skulls washed up in the Southern Hemisphere. Yet Hyperoodon has been caught only in the North Atlantic.

Cuvier's Whale (Ziphius) was first thought to be extinct when Georges Cuvier described in 1823 a partly petrified skull that had been washed up in the Mediterranean in 1804. Nearly half a century after the first stranding another was washed up in the same place. Later a whole specimen with an identical skeleton was found in New Zealand. Oddly enough in old specimens the skull is almost petrified, fossilised before its time, and in other respects it seems designed to fool the naturalist, for it is light above and dark below, thus breaking all the rules of animal coloration.

Mesoplodon is perhaps the most puzzling genus of all. It was first known from a carcase washed up at Elgin in Scotland and examined by Sowerby. It was brown and had a strangely curved lower jaw with only two teeth. In 1825 a similar beast, but with no teeth at all, was stranded alive at Le Havre. It lived for two days, and sightseers who had odd ideas about cetacean's diet-tried to feed it on bread soaked in water. Henri Ducrotay de Blainville studied it and christened it Aodon dalei on account of its absence of teeth, but subsequent scientists have said that it was just a Sowerby's Whale that had lost its teeth with age. It could well have been a female, for they are often found to be toothless. In 1850 Paul Gervais gave the species the name Mesoplodon bidens, which it has kept ever since. Meanwhile several different species of Mesoplodon have been reported, but their descriptions are based on so little evidence that it is hard to say whether there are ten or fifteen of them. One of the rarest is Gervais's Whale (Mesoplodon europaeus) of which only six specimens are known. The first was found floating in the English Channel in 1840; but the next three were washed up on the coast of New Jersey in 1889, 1933 and '935, and the last two, a mother and child, in Jamaica in 1953, which was rather unfortunate for a supposedly 'European' animal. Blainville's Whale (M densirostris) has an even more bizarre distribution. Only seven specimens have been found, but they could hardly have been farther apart: in the Seychelles, on Lord Howe Island, south of Africa, near Massachusetts, in Madeira and New Jersey. M stejnegeri is known only from two specimens from the Pacific coast of North America, and M. hectori from two specimens in New Zealand. The description of M bowdoini is also based on two New Zealand specimens, but as they were only skeletons we still know nothing about their external appearance. And I need hardly say that we know absolutely nothing about the habits of the various Mesoplodons, which are sometimes more than 15 feet long.

We hardly know more about the two species of Berardius, Arnoux's and Baird's Whales, which were first described in 1851 and 1883, and which may be over 40 feet long. The second has teeth which no mammalogist would have believed in had they been described by a layman, for they are embedded in cartilaginous sacs, and it seems that they can be erected at will. New species of Ziphiidae continue to be discovered. As recently as 1937 Oliver had to create a new genus, Tasmacetus, after three Beaked Whales of a hitherto unknown type were stranded in New Zealand. They were between 23 and 29 feet long; yet people still say that the sea cannot hold any large unknown animals." [20]

In the thirty years since Heuvelmans wrote the above passage, the Ziphiidae have given up a few of their secrets and presented us with many more. Even if it were not for the undoubtedly interesting fact that:

A. The Beaked whale was washed up on the same beach as the USO sightings.
B. Both whales exhibited apparently inexplicable mutilations
C. The whales were washed up ten years apart and according to David Bolton at the Royal Albert Museum in Exeter, apart from two small dolphins there are no other records of cetacea strandings from Lyme Bay.
D. Both strandings coincide with other episodes of high strangeness.

The stranding would have been interesting anyway. The combination of all these factors is an irresistible one!

It should be noted that as Nigel stated above, at the Dorchester UFO Conference in April 1998, we were told about a series of `mutilated dolphins` from Brittany, at, apparently the same time as the Otter Cove incident. However despite the impressive reputation of our informant we have not been able to obtain any more details and so there, for the moment at least, the matter must rest.

A mutilated roebuck was found at a nature reserve on Wooodbury Common during the height of the UFO activity in August. Interestingly, although the animal was too decomposed for any thorough examination of its wounds, it had been dismembered and both its legs and head were detached from its body. There were, however, no teeth marks as one would expect from predation by `normal` carnivores, nor were there the marks of knives which would have been found on the bones if the animal had been butchered by a human. Again, although the evidence is not conclusive, and indeed the investigation has not yet been concluded, it appears that this unfortunate beast may have been a genuine UFO related animal mutilation! [21][22]

As we have already seen, British fortean researcher Kevin McClure [23] has, on occasion described the study of such things as the most `tasteless` form of `paranormal phenomena`. He considers, with some justification, that these attacks on hapless domestic creatures are the work of perverted human individuals rather than having any genuine fortean significance. Although he feels that the subject should not be given any credence, and furthermore, that by doing so, fortean researchers are merely encouraging such activity, I have shown elsewhere, that on some occasions at least, there is enough evidence to suggest that these incidents warrant further investigation.

Ufology is, on the whole, a fringe science, and thus largely the preserve of the keen amateur rather than of the accepted scientific institution. It mildly annoys me, therefore when `amateur` writers adopt the status of `officialdom` in a vain attempt to boost their own credibility. In many cases this tends to detract from what would otherwise be a sober and well thought out piece of research, such as this piece, which explains in some depth why both the fortean and the UFO researcher should be interested in these attacks on domestic livestock.

Writing in *Operation Mutilation: The Official Report* Jon Elliston described the genesis of UFO related animal mutilation. [24]

"For decades a mysterious phenomenon has baffled ranchers, law enforcement officers and the general public. Somebody or something has removed selected body parts from dead livestock, leaving gruesome carcasses and troubling questions. How do the animals die? What accounts for their missing parts? Are the mutilations a sign of some sinister plan, executed by government agents, cultists, or extraterrestrials? These theories and more have emerged in attempts to explain the fate of hacked-up horses and butchered bovines.

The origin of the mutilations saga is generally traced to September 1967, when a horse in Colorado by the name of Lady was found dead and missing suspicious amounts of skin and other body tissues. In mutilations lore, Lady is known as "Snippy," a tongue-in-cheek reference to the animal's apparently chopped-up condition. The horse's owners said they believed there was a UFO connection, kicking off decades of allegations that aliens were to blame. The Snippy story achieved almost mythical status. Further reports of "mutes" occurred in the years that followed, and by the mid-1970s, there was a full-fledged epidemic underway, at least in terms of public attention focused on the issue. In several western states, rumors of evil agendas behind mutilations spread like a prairie fire.

The "classic mutilation," as it came to be called, usually involved the discovery of a cow corpse with some or all of the following characteristics: the absence of organs such as the tongue, the genitals, the anus and at least one eye, all of which had apparently been "surgically removed"; a body drained of all its blood; internal organs that had turned to a mushy consistency "like peanut butter"; and the presence of dead flies on the body.

Observers and investigators floated an array of explanations for the mutilations. Some "mutologists" said the strange slayings were the result of secret military biological warfare research. Often the incidents were reported in concert with UFO sightings in the area of the mutilation, giving rise to the theory that the sinister snipping was the product of alien animal abductions. In some cases, there were reports of unmarked helicopters in the region. Others believed that Satanic cults were responsible.

Waves of mutilations filled the headlines of cattle-town newspapers and gave rise to mute newsletters, books and documentaries. For the ranchers searching for an explanation of their lost livestock, the mute mystery became more maddening with every new theory. Cattle associations offered thousands of dollars in reward money for information on the perpetrators, and ranchers began forming vigilante patrols to catch a mutilator in the act. Despite these measures, no suspect was ever identified or apprehended."

The affair of the dead whale, the USOs and the animal that was, in the words of both the eye-witness, and the late lamented Commander Woodruffe, (at the Grande Review of the Fleet at Spithead to celebrate the Coronation of George V), "all lit up" [25] [26] was not the only anomalous occurrence to take place in Lyme Bay during the September of 1997. In early October, the financial problems caused by full time UFO investigation and the imminent advent of a new baby forced Nigel back into taxi driving for a few weeks. One morning at about 10.00 he was driving a trawler captain from the docks to his home on the outskirts of Exmouth, when, to his surprise he heard another bizarre story.

Again, he reported it for his column in the *Exmouth Journal*:

"Unfortunately no precise date can be given for the evening when a fishing boat encountered a strange light over Lyme Bay, but since this was told to me by the skipper of the vessel concerned I can vouch for its authenticity. The vessel in question was five miles off Budleigh Salterton. The crew became aware of a bright, white-blue light which hovered some distance from the boat. At first they thought that it was a helicopter but they heard no engine sounds, nor saw any navigation lights...." [27]

The Captain told Nigel that it had been a bright, clear night, and that if the object, whatever it was, had, indeed made any sound, it would have been audible for miles. he also confirmed that his crew were experienced seamen who would have easily been able to recognise a helicopter if, indeed such a rara avis as a helicopter that could hover silently above the calm waters of Lyme Bay did indeed exist. [28] Nigel's original report continued:

"The light remained stationary for about one and a half hours. Judging by the mast of their vessel, which is twenty-eight feet high, the crew estimated that the light was not much higher than that". [29]

Nigel confirmed that the crew had used the mast as a reference point for confirmation of the elevation of the object and that their estimate of the altitude of the object is likely to have been largely correct! [30]

Nigel's newspaper report concluded:

"It then very suddenly disappeared". [31]

An unreferenced Internet article provides a useful overview of the subject of 'Unidentified Submarine Objects' (USOs:):

"There is one clue in the behavior of UFOs which suggests strongly that their origin lies beyond our solar system. It is their attitude toward water. As far as we know, Earth is the most watery of planets in our particular system. Perhaps in some form water lies in or under the clouds of Venus or in the gaseous layers of the outer planets. To a small degree it is almost certainly present on Mars.

But large deep bodies of water such as ours seem definitely unique in our solar system. Presumably, therefore, if our space visitors came from a

neighboring planet, they would approach our lakes and oceans with wary respect. Without such watery expanses of their own, they would never feel at ease on or in ours, no matter how advanced their technical development.

But the striking fact is that, where water is concerned, UFOs appear far more at home even than ourselves. They seem to regard it as an element barely distinguishable from air and, except for an apparent interest in sampling it (ref. May-June issue), they treat it with indifference. They have been seen flying into it and emerging from it at full speed. Observations of strange subsurface luminous discs suggest they may even live under it. " [32]

These objects (if indeed objects they are) have been reported from all over the world, but seem to have a particular predilection for Scandinavian waters as this extract from a paper called *Observations of Unidentified Submarine Objects in Norway* by Ole Jonny Brænne indicated:

"Let us first go back in time to some early reports.

On Thursday, July 18, 1946, a "ghost rocket" crashed into Lake Mjøsa (in southeastern Norway). Between 12 and 12:30 p.m., several witnesses observed a V1-like object coming in low from the west, at about 50 meters' height. The witnesses first heard a strong whistling sound, not exactly like that associated with known aircraft. The object flew so low as to cause the trees to sway. It impacted in Lake Mjøsa, about two kilometers from the western shore and seven kilometers from Minnesund, where the depth is 300-400 meters. It was cigar-shaped, about 2.5 meters long, with about one-meter-long wings placed one meter behind the nose. The front and back parts were shining like metal, but the middle section including the wings was dark. The wings seemed to flap a little, as if made of fabric. No fire, exhaust, or light was seen.

When it hit the lake, the water splashed several meters into the air. There was no explosion. The sky was clear, and the water quickly calmed. Some winesses thought they saw two objects, one in front of the other. The Norwegian Defense High Command conducted an investigation, according to press reports of the period, but the documents have never been recovered. There is a distinct possibility that all documents on the 1946 ghost-rocket wave have been destroyed. If so, this is a disaster for UFO historians, who will be left with only newspaper accounts as source material.

Shortly before 7 a.m. one Thursday in October 1952, Johannes Nordlien was waiting for coworkers when he suddenly heard a howling, jetlike sound. A moment later a saucer-shaped object, four meters in diameter, came at high speed from the west and passed by him 100 meters away. It impacted with a violent splash in the river Lågen. The object was white as snow, and Nordlien clearly observed its flat and round shape as it hit the water. When his fellow workers showed up, the water was still boiling. The loud howling sound vanished as soon as he saw the object.

At 11:55 a.m. on Sunday, June 1, 1958, a silent "unknown aircraft" with no identifying markers crashed into the Alta fjord. At the impact site, 70 meters deep, a column of water rose up. The aircraft resembled a twin-engine delta-winged jet. The witnesses were Bjørn Taraldsen, Nils M. Turi, Kate Julsen, and Rasmus Hykkerud. When others arrived half an hour later, all they found were a number of dead fish. The frigate KNM Arendal and the submarine KNM Sarpen, along with divers, searched for the aircraft friutlessly for over a week. The Arendal, however, did get sonar reading of a mobile object.

At 10 one evening just before Christmas 1959, Lorentz Johnsen saw a dark, silent object - which he described as looking like a small bus with a number of windows along its side - fly slowly by at an altitude of 150 meters. It was heading in the direction of the Namsen fjord. It descended to about 50 meters, grew fiery red, then exploded with an ear-splitting crash. According to Johnsen, "It looked like sort of a cover was torn off the object in one piece. This, along with a number of other things, fell into the water. I especially noticed three black 'columns,' about two meters long and one-half meter in diameter. The cover itself was torn off in one piece and reminded med of a curved sheet of metal. This was fiery red at first but grew black before reaching the water." [33]

As we have seen again and again in this book it is impossible to view any quasi-fortean phenoemnon in isolation. A splendid example of this, which is indeed of the most striking pieces of evidence for a link between UFOs and other phenomena comes from this 1952 report of a USO from Kelowna in British Columbia:

" We were living at Summerland on Lake Okanagan at the time," Stewart said, " and Dorothy and Gordon had just arrived from Vancouver to visit us for a while. As it was her first trip to the Okanagan since leaving her home in England, we had set out on a motor trip for the day to see some of the country.

"It was a clear bright morning in September and when we reached the ferry slip to cross over to Kelowna we realized we would have to wait a bit because we could see the ferry still on the other side. And then about half a mile north of the ferry we noticed this other thing. I remember pointing it out and saying what a beautiful white boat it was," Dorothy S. added. " It was moving around so gracefully and, though we still couldn't make it out very well at that distance, it seemed to have a smooth round design we had never seen before."

As the three watched from their car in admiring curiosity, they noticed the strange craft had started to move across the lake in their direction. By that time cars for the ferry were beginning to line up behind them, so they were also in a position to observe what happened next.

"We could see the wash coming out from either side, yet somehow the boat, as we thought it was, didn't seem to be moving very fast," Stewart said. (Dorothy compared it to a line from Dante, "Hasten slowly.") "As it came closer we still thought it must be some unusual kind of modern boat. It looked like a round hard hat sitting on a platter. But there was something about that was that looked different and that started us wondering."

Although neither could explain precisely what the difference was, possibly it was caused by the circular shape of the craft moving lightly on the surface, like a flatly thrown stone.

"Then suddenly it really surprised us," Stewart continued. "It was a few hundred yards away when all at once the wake disappeared and we realized the thing was in the air. It changed direction to the right so that it came straight toward the ferry dock and then it stopped dead, less than 100 feet in front of us and about 50 feet above the water."

Despite the 17 years that had since elapsed, Stewart's memory of that experience was obviously still very much with him. He shook his head in amazement as he spoke of it and seemed to live the whole experience over again.

His cousin, on the other hand, said she had not thought of it for a long while, though she was sufficiently impressed at the time to make a note of it in her diary.

"We sat in the car spellbound," she said. "We couldn't believe what was happening and afterwards, for some reason, we had no desire to talk about it. It was as if we had been told not to."

The witnesses described the object as about 30 feet in diameter and having a haziness which made the outline indistinct. Also it had a translucent quality which gave them the impression that anyone inside could have seen them without being seen in return. (A description of translucence often occurs in sighting reports in which the UFO is dome shaped, such as this one.)

"It stayed there, absolutely silent, for a minute or so," Stewart said. "and we definitely had a feeling it was watching us. Then it started back across the lake. By this time I was out of the car to get a better look and I told the others I wished I had a pair of binoculars. An American tourist in the car behind heard me and said, 'Here take mine. I've seen enough.' He looked as if it had scared him."

Through the binoculars Stewart watched the object reach the opposite shore, just over two miles away, in five or six minutes, giving it a leisurely speed of about 20 mph. Then it seemed to fly parallel to a trail bordering the lake before it shot up and disappeared.

After a moment Stewart handed the binoculars back to their owner and he remembers how they stared silently at each other in disbelief.

"I guess I looked just as shocked as he did," Stewart said, "and it must have affected the others the same way. We were a pretty quiet bunch going across on the ferry."

Having seen and been examined by craft that may have come from a world light years away, it was no wonder." [34]

I would question that they were indeed "*seen and been examined by craft that may have come from a world light years away*", [35] [36] but it is interesting that their experience should have happened in that particular location for Lake Okanagan is perhaps better known as the home of another well known quasi-fortean phenomenon, a lake `Monster` known by the charming, if slightly annoyimng appelation of `Ogopogo`.

Ogopogo is not an Indian name for the world-famous, friendliest inland sea monster. The name is derived from a music hall song that was popular in the 1920's.

The Ogopogo Funny Foxtrot

I`m searching for the Ogopopo
the funny little Ogopogo
his mother was an earwig
his father was a whale

> *I'm gonna put a little bit of salt on his tail*
> *I'm searching for the Ogopogo*
> *as he's playing on his old Banjo.*
> *The Lord Mayor of London*
> *The Lord Mayor of London*
> *The Lord Mayor of London's*
> *gonna put him in the Lord Mayor's show* [37] [38]

Interestingly enough, despite claims to the contrary in books like *In Search of Lake Monsters* by Peter Costello, [39] the animal described in the song and pictured on the front cover of the sheet music isn't at all reminiscent of the animal reported from the lake. Rather than beimng a water dwelling leviathan, it is a small humanoid creature with antennae like those of a bumble bee. [40]

The main protagonist of the song is *"a funny little man"* from *"the hills of Hindustan"* who wears plus fours and whose modus operandi whilst chasing the elusive Ogopogo is to use an Elephant Gun as well as the tried and tested method of putting *"a little salt on his tail"*. [41]

In light of this evidence it is tempting to theorise that the appellation was granted to the lake monster because the sophisticated settlers of European origin DIDN'T believe in the monster, and felt that it was as amorphic and ridiculous a creature as the one described in the song, rather than because of any supposed physical resemblance between the two beasties.

Indians referred to Ogopogo as N'HA-A-ITK which when translated means "Lake Demon". Legend explains that the creature was actually a demon-possessed man who had murdered a local known as Old Kan-He-K. (Lake Okanagan was named in his honor). As punishment, the native gods turned the murderer into the giant sea serpent so he would remain at the scene of the crime for all eternity. Hence Ogopogo's longevity. To appease the monster N'HA-A-ITK (Ogopogo), the Indians offered small animals at it's legendary lair/submarine caves off Squally Point near Rattlesnake Island. Ogopogo frequents the waters between his favorite island and Mission Valley and has made journeys to both ends of the lake. Recorded sightings date as far back as the early 1800's. In 1860, John McDougal lost his team of horses when they were pulled under as he was swimming them across the lake in a canoe....never to be seen again.

Ogopogo is dark green in colour, estimated at one to two feet in diameter with a length ranging between 15 to 50 feet. Ogopogo has been mistaken for a log, boat wake, large sturgeon and other floating mysteries.

The government in 1926 announced that the new ferry being built for travel across the Okanagan Lake would also be equipped with special "monster repelling devices". Since the construction of the floating bridge, it is assumed that the bridge has enough support and strength to withstand any nuzzling or advances of Ogopogo. Travellers safety while crossing the floating bridge is assured as maintenance crews are often checking for and repairing any damage.

Ogopogo has been sighted by many individuals who have remained firm in their belief despite the ridicule from legions of nonbelievers. Both sides in debate seem to be divided into equal camps. The majority of sightings have been consistently similar. The "fearsome thing" is generally described as having a snake-like body about 20 feet long, dark green skin, with a bearded horse or goat shaped head. [42]

We shall see more connections between UFO activity and lake monsters (and indeed between UFO activity and practically everything else within the gamut of fortean experience) later in this book. Meanwhile we must return to the long, hot summer of 1997 where my co-author is still faithfully scribbling stories for the *Exmouth Journal.*

In the same column that he had described the USO, [43] Nigel mentioned another anomalous object, which, although its precise identity was not in the least open to question, did provide a possible explanation for some of the unusual things that had been reported in the skies of the area:

"I have also had rather vague reports of a brightly lit airship seen over Lympstone at night"....

Here, we should perhaps mention that Lympstone is the site of the Royal Marines Training Centre. The original Camp was built in 1939 for the training of Reservists on the expansion of the Corps before the Second World War. It was called the Royal Marines Reserve Depot (RM RD), Exton.

In 1940 most 'Hostilities Only' recruits were trained at Lympstone, whilst regular recruits and 'H0s' destined for sea service were trained at the Divisions. Towards the end of the war the Commando School at Achnacarry closed down and re-opened as the Royal Marines Training Group (Wales) at Towyn. During the immediate post war years, the Officers' and NC0s' Schools were also moved to Lympstone, as was more recently all Commando and Specialist Training. [44]

Consequently, the majority of the Corps Military and Specialist Training is now concentrated at the one establishment, finally re-named the Commando Training Centre Royal Marines in 1970. However, despite such a glorious career, it has been most well known, nay - notorious, in recent years for reports of bullying of new recruits which has led on several occasions to their suicide, for the ignominious end to Prince Edward's military career, which took place here and for the persistent rumours that some unsavoury video featuring the late Diana, Princess of Wales and an unnamed Marine Officer is circulating around the camp. None of this has any direct (or indeed indirect) relevance to the story at hand, but it does establish that the military installation at Lympstone is important enough for the Royal Family to send its youngest scions to it and, as Nigel's account implies, it is also important enough to be used by the British Government for other purposes:

"I suspect this to be the rather poorly kept 'secret research airship' being evaluated by the Armed Forces over the area and last seen by many witnesses including myself in broad daylight whilst hovering over Lympstone village". [45]

This 'airship' was supposedly radar invisible and was allegedly part of new experiments into 'Stealth Technology', which does seem mildly amusing when one considers that large sections of the populace in South Devon actually *saw* the thing in broad daylight.

There were even more mysterious happenings in Lyme Bay, however, albeit not until the following year, because in October 1997 Roy Richardson, of Littleham wrote to the *Exmouth Journal* in response to Nigel's reports on undersea lights:

His letter read:

"I refer to UFO sightings, an article by Nigel Wright which I read with great interest concerning strange events in this area, and published in the Journal of October 16th. May I first of all bring to the attention of your readers that UFO does not automatically refer to alien or extraterrestrial life forms viewing our planet. In brief, it refers to any item that we see, but cannot at the time identify. For instance, these days cats and dogs wear reflective collars and discs etc so when a bright light is seen shooting across a road or field, then please keep an open mind. With regard to the very interesting stories that Mr Wright feels free to report on, may I try to solve the bright light that appeared from the sea which I have, myself, often seen.

On a regular basis, and due to a health problem, I often sit out all through the night." [46]

Here I feel that we should point out that Mr Richardson suffers from severe Tinnitus [47] and so it is only during the relative peace and quiet of the night-time that he can get a modicum of tranquility. He therefore spends long periods of time sitting quietly on Exmouth Sea Front at night.

That little mystery having been cleared up, his narrative continues:

"The first time that I witnessed this event, I thought I had viewed a strange encounter, but as the very, very bright light came nearer to me, I thought that I would challenge whatever it was and stare it out.

As the so-called `alien` approached me, it was wearing a wet suit and armed with a harpoon gun to which a number of large skate fish were hooked. The person concerned was a skin diver who goes out at all hours to make his catch as it were..." [48]

Here, we should point out that the underwater currents at Otter Cove are extremely dangerous and that it is extremely unlikely that any experienced skin diver would venture near the place. Secondly, although skate can grow in excess of seven feet, they can and do fall prey to passing spear fishermen. However not even the most psychopathic skin diver can be accused of causing the death of a twenty foot pilot whale by rectal coring. Thirdly, and perhaps most importantly, the incident desrcibed by Mr Richardson took place in the relative civilisation of Exmouth Sea Front not in the seclusion of Otter Cove two miles to the east. [49]

Mr Richardson`s letter continues:

"On one occasion I did see a small boat appear from within the distance, (sic), which threw an object into the water, with a kind of greenish dim light affixed to it." [50]

Again we feel constrained to point out that not only have none of the USO reports concerned "greenish dim" lights but also that experienced fishermen, like those who witnessed the second event are unlikely to be fooled by an anomalous sighting of a luminescent fishing net marker light! We have also found it impossible to explain how either an errant skin diver or an anomalous fishing buoy could hover in the air, twenty feet above the surface of the sea and then blink into non-existence. But perhapse we are nit-picking! [51]

Mr Richardson's letter ended amusingly with the comment that:

"Whilst walking along the sea front in the very late hours, I have often seen `aliens` of this town filling up sacks with sand from our beaches to take back to their planet in their clapped out UFO trailers!" (52)

Nigel went to see Mr Richardson, who turned out to be a repository of local folklore and they endedb up the best of friends.

There has been a long history of high strangeness in Lyme Bay. An advertisement in the London *Daily Post* of January 23rd 1738 read:

"To be Seen, next door to the Crown Tavern in Threadneedle Street, behind the Royal Exchange, at One Shilling each, the Surprising Fish or Maremaid, taken by eight Fishermen on Friday the 9th of September last, at Topsham Bar, near Exeter, and has been shewn to several Gentlemen, and those of the Faculty, in the Cities of Exeter, Bath, and Bristol, who declare never to have seen the like, so remarkable is this Curiosity amongst the Wonders of Creation. This uncommon Species of Nature represents from the Collarbone down the Body what the Antients called a Maremaid, has a Wing to each Shoulder like those of a Cherubim mentioned in History, with regular Ribs, Breasts, Thighs, and Feet, the Joints thereto having their proper Motions, and to each Thigh a Fin; the Tail resembles a Dolphin's, which turns up to the Shoulders, the forepart of the Body very smooth, but the skin of the Back rough; the back part of the head like a Lyon, has a large mouth, sharp teeth, two eyes, spout holes, nostrils and a thick neck.

The Topsham mermaid, apart from being another illustration of the historical gamut of high strangeness from the Lyme Bay region, does present us with an interesting fortean zoological if not cryptozoological conundrum.

The nearest animal that one can find to the 1738 description of the Topsham creature is a manatee, a dugong or one of the other members of the *sirenia*.

"Sirenians, which are sometimes called sea cows, are large mammals that spend their entire lives in water. Their forelimbs are modified to form flippers, their hindlimbs are reduced to nothing more than a vestigial pelvis, and their tail is enlarged and flattened horizontally to form a fluke or paddle. Sirenians are massive, sometimes weighing over 1150 kg. Their body is streamlined and mostly nearly hairless. Their ears have

no pinnae. Their eyes lack obvious eyelids, but are closed by a sphincter-like mechanism. Their bones are unusually dense, a condition called pachyostosis; the extra mass probably helps them remain suspended at or below the surface of the water. Their nostrils are located on top of their snouts and closed by valves. The lips are large and mobile, and they are covered with stiff bristles." [91]

They are peculiar creatures, but with the exception of the (probably) extinct Steller's Sea Cow they are exclusively tropical beasts which never venture far from land and which unlike other rare marine visitors from the tropics would not be able to durvive in British waters.

Steller's Sea Cow, however is another kettle of pseudo-fish. Writing in 1886, a hundred and forty years after the animal was first discovered, and a hundred and eighteen years after the species was almost certainly hunted into ignominios extinction A.E.Nordenskjold wrote:

"Steller's sea cow held in a way the place of the cloven-footed animals among the marine mammalia. The sea cow was of a dark-brown color, sometimes varied with white spots or streaks. The thick leathery skin was covered with hair which grew together so as to form an exterior skin, which was full of vermin and resembled the bark of an old oak. The full grown animal was from twenty-eight to thirty-five English feet in length, and weighed about sixty-seven cwt. The head was small in proportion to the large thick body, the neck short, the body diminishing rapidly behind the short fore-leg terminated abruptly without fingers or nails, but was overgrown with a number of short thickly placed brush-hairs; the hind-leg was replaced by a tail-fin resembling a whale's. The animal wanted teeth, but was instead provided with two masticating plates, one in the gum, the other in the under jaw. The udders of the female, which abounded in milk, were placed between the fore-limbs. The flesh and milk resembled those of horned cattle, indeed in Steller's opinion surpassed them. The sea cows were almost constantly employed in pasturing on the seaweed which grew luxuriantly over the coast, moving the head and neck while so doing much in the same way as an ox. While they pastured they showed great voracity, and did not allow themselves to be disturbed in the least by the presence of man. One might even touch them without their being frightened or disturbed. They entertained great attachment to each other, and when one was harpooned the others made incredible attempts to rescue it." [92] [93]

Readers of my other writings will be aware that in many ways I carry a torch for the writings of Rudyard Kipling

Born in British India in 1865, Rudyard Kipling was educated in England before returning to India in 1882, where his father was a museum director and authority on Indian arts and crafts. Thus Kipling was thoroughly immersed in Indian culture: by 1890 he had published in English about 80 stories and ballads previously unknown outside India. As a result of financial misfortune, from 1892-96 he and his wife, the daughter of an American publisher, lived in Vermont, where he wrote the two Jungle Books. After returning to England, he published "The White Man's Burden" in 1899, an appeal to the United States to assume the task of developing the Philippines, recently won in the Spanish-American War. As a writer, Kipling perhaps lived too long: by the time of his death in 1936, he had come to be reviled as the poet of British imperialism, though being regarded as a beloved children's book author. Today he might yet gain appreciation as a transmitter of Indian culture to the West. [94]

It was from the works of Kipling, most notably his book *Puck of Pook's Hill* (1902) [95] that I extrapolated much of the material that later became an integral part of my Theory of De-Deification with regards to zooform and zoomorphic phenomena as discussed in *The Owlman and Others* (1997, 1998) [96] and indeed I draw heavily upon Kipling for much of my forthcoming book *The Mystery Animals of Hong Kong.* [97]

Unfortunately, Kipling is best known these days through the twee Disneyfication of his work by the full-length cartoon *The Jungle Book* which effectively not only trivialised Kipling's gloriously fortean prose but emasculated it as well. However in the original text version of *The Jungle Book* published in 1894 was a story called *The White Seal* [98] which not only addressed ecological and 'green' issues a century before they became the fashionable stock in trade of everyone from pop stars to politicians, but included a glorious description of a 'sea cow' which I had to include in this book:

"'By the Great Combers of Magellan!' he said, beneath his moustache. 'Who in the Deep Sea are these people? They were like no walrus, sea-lion, seal, bear, whale, shark, fish, squid, or scallop that Kotick had ever seen before. They were between twenty and thirty feet long, and they had no hind flippers, but a shovel-like tail that looked as if it had been whittled out of wet leather. Their heads were the most foolish looking things you ever saw, and they balanced on the ends of their tails in deep water when they weren't grazing, bowing solemnly to one another and waving their front flippers as a fat man waves his arm."

The story of the discovery, and extinction twenty seven years later of *Rhytina stelleri* is one of the most despicable episodes in man's shamefull co-existence with his environment. It is probably for this reason, rather than because of any real body of hard evidence, that scientists and dreamers alike have concocted absurd theories to suggest that against all the odds the species may have survived to the present day. Similar theories have been advanced for the putative survival of other victims of humanity's inhumanity - it has been suggested that the dodo, the Carolina parakeet and even the passenger pigeon still exist in small numbers in the wilder parts of what would once have been their range but on the whole there is little evidence to support these claims. [99]

In the case of Steller's Sea cow some sightings *have* been made since 1768. According to Roy P.Mackal:

"Russian scientists A. A. Berzin, E. A. Tikhomirov, and V. I. Troinin published a report of what may have been a whole herd of sea cows in the Russian journal Priroda in 1963. The episode involved the whaler Buran in the vicinity of Cape Navarin, south of the Gulf of Anadyr. Early on a July day in 1962 a small number of strange animals, neither seals nor whales, were observed close in-shore. These observers were experienced hunters and whalers making observations at less than 100 meters (a hundred yards); certainly they were likely to identify known marine life. The same kinds of animals were seen again the following day in a shallow lagoon where plenty of aquatic vegetable matter, including the known types of seaweed and sea cabbage favoured by Steller's sea cow, was flourishing. The lagoon did not freeze over even in winter and therefore would be a likely place for sea cows to find food and shelter. According to the report of the crew of the Buran, the animals were 6 meters (twenty feet) to 8 meters (twenty-six feet) in length, dark in color, with a small head. They appeared to have a harelip, and their heads were differentiated from the bodies or necks. The tail resembled the bilobate tail of Steller's sea cow and sprouted a sort of fringe along the edge. The animals moved about slowly, submerging and surfacing regularly" [100]

but even he will admit that:

"Most of these reports have been dismissed as mistaken identification of a narwhal as Steller's sea cow. That sea cows are no longer present around Bering and Copper islands cannot be disputed." [101]

One has to use a certain amount of logic here. Even if a small population of these shy and retiring beasts have survived in the wilder parts of the Arctic Ocean, then the chances of one of them having swum thousands of miles only to be ignominiously caught in the sea off the Exe Estuary is so absurd as to be risible.

This account of the `Topsham Mermaid` would, therefore be just another anomalous one-off occurrence if it were not for the fact that the mysterious waters of Lyme Bay delivered forth a similar creature over two and a half centuries earlier.

In August 1995, Martin Ball was walking along Chesil Beach at Portland when he saw what he described as a strange creature "some twelve feet high, half fish and half giant seahorese". After some research he equated the creature that he had sighted with an ancient sea creature known as Veasta. As he wrote in an article for *Dorset Life* magazine: [102]

"Veasta is a rather nice name for a monster. The root of the word stems from old Dorsetshire dialect, meaning a feast - the olden-day beach gathering that was held on warm summer evenings on the neatly shelved banks of Portland's Chesil Beach. This area once had well-established trade links with Spain. Depending upon the pronunciation, Veasta sometimes sounded like 'vista', that is the Spanish for 'sighting'. And so Veasta has been sighted, several times now, off the Isle of Portland on summer nights - sighted in all her splendour, bathing off the hidden shores of this mystical coastline."

Ball then deicides to wax lyrical for a while on the subject of Portland`s prehistoric past, theorising that Veasta has a more complex relationship with the local ecosystem than being merely a survivor from prehistory...

"Portland's Jurassic landscape lives in a cycle of submergence and emergence revealing its pre-historic existence. This isle traces the evolution of life ~ quarried stone denudes petrified ammonites and trilobites locked in the fossils of the moment. Mammoths and sabre-toothed tigers once roamed their their kingdom now greatly reduced in scope by natural convulsion. At the Portland Race, tides from the east and west converge, drawing upon the forces of the sun and moon to reflect raw energies to the ocean depths. Unimaginable power is unleashed as fathom upon fathom of dense, green Sea collide unrelentlingly against unyielding tides.

The isle has always fed the Chesil Bank as its seemingly inexhaustible waste debris falls carelessly into the seas and nourishes the beach by perpetual 'attrition. These are the seas that organise and rank those cohorts of brightly coloured calcareous, quartz and jasper pebbles on Portland's ancient beach, whose shields of armour dazzle in the sunlight. It is these shores, which have defended England's southerly coastline against the ravages of storm and tide, which hold the secret of

Veasta." ⁽¹⁰²⁾

It is, however, the historical sightings of this semi-mythical creature that are of most interest. The first account of an anomalous creature from the Portland region of Lyme Bay comes from the *Chronicles of England, Scotland, and Ireland,* by Ralph Holinshed (1577). ⁽¹⁰³⁾

When this book was first published in 1577, it was the most impressive British history England had ever seen. While the book is often referred to as *Holinshed's Chronicles,* Raphael Holinshed was not its sole author. An English printer, R. Wolfe, started the project and employed Holinshed to organize the compilation of the history (after Wolfe's death, another set of printers took over the financing of the chronicles). Holinshed wrote the histories of England and Scotland, William Harrison supplied a description of England and Scotland, and Richard Stanyhurst supplied a description of Ireland. The text provided a geographical description of each region, and an account of its past, traced back to prehistorical and legendary origins and continuing up through the sixteenth century. The Chronicles' sources are multiple, including old and contemporary histories, eye-witness accounts, documents, and anecdotes. Each history is organized as a sequence of monarchs, including the name of the king or queen and the year of his or her reign. ⁽¹⁰⁴⁾

The Veasta is not the only semi mythical creature that it has described. A section oft quoted by cryptozoologists says:

"Lions, we have had very many in the north parts of Scotland and those with manes of no less force than those of Mauretania, but how and when they were destroyed I do not yet read" ⁽¹⁰⁵⁾

This passage has been subjected to analysis by a number of different authors but no firm conclusions have ever been reached. A less well known account from his writings concerns a monstrous cockerel which was seen by the entire population of Portland in November 1457. It was seen, rising up, with the mass of four or five men and standing on the waves. It was then described as crowing to each of the cardinal points of the compass before disappearing back into the waves.

According to Martin Ball:

"It would seem that Veasta has visited the shores off Portland over a period spanning five centuries. She was first sighted in 1457, then in 1757, then in 1965 and most recently in August 1995...as far as is known." ⁽¹⁰⁶⁾

I have always wondered whether Holinshed's description of the chicken of the western world should be taken literally. Not, I hasten to add, because I believe in the literal existence of a giant cockerel four or five times the size of a man, but because of the possibility that what Holinshed described as the entire population of `Ile of Portland', had been suffering from a mass hallucination, possibly caused by the ingestion of bread made from grain tainted with ergot.

Ergot poisoning, sometimes known as ergotism is one of the most common form of fungal poisoning and its cause has been known since the end of the 18th century, although its effects have been noted and feared for centuries before that. It is caused by the consumption of the sclerotium - the food storage structure that can be found in some fungi - of the fungus *Claviceps purpurea*, which is a member of the Ascomycota. Family. The symptoms of ergotism can be divided into two categories: gangrenous and convulsive. In gangrenous ergotism, the victim may lose toes, fingers, hands, feet, arms, legs or ears, due to gangrene caused by the constriction of arteries and veins from the ergot. The constriction of the arteries and veins restrict the amount of blood to the extremities of the body thereby causing gangrene. Convulsive ergotism is characterized by nervous dysfunction, such as writhing, tremors and wry neck due to muscle spasms as well as confusion, delusions and hallucinations. The fungus is a natural parasite of rye *Secale cereale*.

Rye was originally a weed grain and occurred wherever wheat was cultivated. Often it became the dominant plant when wheat fields were abandoned. Thus, in a way, where ever civilization became established, rye would follow it there. However, it was not cultivated for food until some time, in the early Middle Ages (around the 5th. Century), in what is now eastern Europe and western Russia. It was during the Middle Ages that the symptoms (but not the knowledge of what caused the symptoms) from consumption of ergot was well documented. It was also at this time that it came to be called holy fire or St. Anthony's fire. Holy fire because it caused burning sensations at the extremities from gangrenous ergotism, and St. Anthony's fire because hospitals were set up, which were dedicated to Saint Anthony, to take care of patients with the disease. The cause of this disease was unknown. Unlike other disease that were common, there were a number of characteristics of this disease which was not consistent with other types of diseases. It was generally not common in urban areas, but rather in rural areas among the poor. It did not seem to be contagious since it might strike only one member of a family or an entire family without infecting neighbours. Children and feeble people were more susceptible than others and nursing mothers might see the symptoms in their babies. [108]

Although there is no doubt that ergotism occurred in the Middle Ages, because medicine was at a very primitive state at this time, and some of the symptoms of ergot can be caused by other problems, the outbreaks of ergotism couldn't always be confirmed. However, it seems rather certain that it, at least occurred sporadicallly during the Middle Ages. From the year 900 AD, when records evidently became common in many regions of France and Germany, to around 1300 AD, there were severe epidemics of ergotism over large areas every five to ten years. [109]

The alkaloid present in the ergot fungus has been synthesised and used as the basis for several recreational hallucinogenic drugs. However, the theory that the Portland sighting (and indeed other similar episodes) are due to mass hallucinations caused by the active alkaloid in ergot is an unworkable one, mostly because hallucinations don`t work that way.

My experiments with hallucinogenic drugs were many years ago and neither remarkable or many in number. For a while Graham Inglis was much more *au fait* with the hallucinogenic affects of lysergic acid diethalymide 25 than I ever have been, and so we asked him for his comments upon chemically-induced mass hallucinations:

The Hairy Wallpaper

"LSD and psilocybin mushrooms are called hallucinogens, and many people do see things that aren't there, either when they close their eyes and experience visions or dream-like sequences or patterns, or perhaps, when their eyes are open, experiencing distortion of their visual perception.

In 1977 I swallowed a handful of "magic mushrooms" at a rather interesting party. The effects of the psilocybin mushroom are similar to those of LSD ("acid") and such "trips" are not something to be casually or lightly undertaken. Over the next four years I experienced quite a few trips and was interested to find that the effects varied considerably from one session to the next, and even more variably from person to person. Such relative unpredictability is of course one of the potential problems when dabbling with such substances.

Most of my hallucinatory experiences occurred with my eyes shut - perhaps in the manner of sensory deprivation. With them open, I was mainly aware of persistence of vision, creating the bizarre effect of trail-backs. (Older video cameras suffer the same effect when aimed at a light source and the light leaves a distinct trail on the video tube that takes several seconds to fade away.) But people differ: some people mainly experience conceptual stimulation (imaginative ideas, say) rather than basic psychedelic effects.

The notion of mass-hallucination is a recurring one, but I have never heard of any significant example of such a thing. Sure. when a group of people are tripping, an external stimulation, such as a noisy passing vehicle, can modify everyone's trip simultaneously - perhaps with a bit of a jolt; but the direction in which everyone's trips proceed from that point depends very much on the individual person. In general, if the group is being interactive - talking, rather than just lying back and self-indulgently drifting to the sounds of Gong or Hawkwind! - then the trips are more likely to be similar to one another, yet rather less likely to be hallucinatory. Basically, everyone's more tuned in to each other, rather than all off on their own individual planets.

However, distortions of perception can always pop up... We (ie me and some pals) once went on a bizarre excursion to a pub, which had carpeting on the walls. After consuming magic mushrooms, we sat around, enjoying watching the patterns wiggle on what we termed the 'hairy wallpaper'. The locals seemed rather bemused by the way we sat around a pub wall and paid rapt attention to it, as if it were a television programme - we were even passing comments on it from time to time and pointing things out. Then we finished our lagers and went off for a walk.

Shared visual 'disturbances' can certainly occur but I have never heard of anything more advanced than this occurring. " [110]

Having disposed of the hallucinogenic interpretation of events we must return to Martin Ball who has proposed another, and less exciting interpretation:

"The earliest sighting of Veasta was misunderstood, because in the 15th-century, imagery of the cockerel and the pheasant was used to describe the unknown in terms of the known to a rural audience. It is easy to ridicule this 'hallucination' as pre-Age of Enlightenment delusion. Yet it is clear from Holinshed's Chronicles that 15th-century man could distinguish between whales, dolphins and sea-cows. However, Holinshed also tells us that a creature was seen in 1457 'in the isle of Portland'.

Veasta is sometimes portrayed as a mermaid.... " [111]

In Holinshed's time it was popularly believed that the oceans were populated with monsters and merfolk, and indeed these entities would have been seen by Holinshed and his contemporaries as being as `real` as whales, sharks and dolphins. Perhaps they were?

In *The Owlman and Others* (1997, 8) [112] I have shown that the archetype of the winged humanoid is one that is repeated in every culture on the the globe. The same can be said about merfolk.

* THE BABYLONIANS worshiped a sea-god called Oannes, or Ea. Oannes was reputed to have risen from the Erythrean Sea and taught to man the arts and sciences. A Greek priest called Berossus writing in *Babylonian History* described the Oannes thus:

'The whole body of the animal was like that of a fish; and it had under a fish's head another head, and also feet below, similar to those of a man, subjoined to the fish's tail. His voice, too, and language, were articulate and human; and a representation of him is preserved even to this day... When the sun set, it was the custom of this Being to plunge again into the sea, and abide all night in the deep; for he was amphibious.' [113]

* THE SYRIANS AND THE PHILISTINES were also known to have worshipped a Semitic mermaid moon-goddess. The Syrians called her Atargatis while the Philistines knew her as Derceto. It is not unusual or surprising that this moon-goddess was depicted as a mermaid as the tides ebbed and flowed with the moon then as it does now and this was incorporated into the god-like personifications that we find in their art and the ancient literature. Atargatis is one of the first recorded mermaids and the legend says that her child Semiramis was a normal human and because of this Atargatis was ashamed and killed her lover. Abandoning the infant she became wholly a fish. [114]

Atagarsis was also said to have been born from an `egg` that dropped from heaven into the River Euphrates. [115]

There are many links between these ancient amphibious sea gods and modern UFO reports mostly because of a book called *The Sirius Mystery* by Robert Temple in which he claims that the Dogon people of Mali in West Africa worship the memory of extra terrestrial amphibious beings from Sirius that landed in the Persian Gulf concurrently with the dawn of civilisation. He claims that deities such as Oannes and Atargatis and the `Nommos` of Dogon mythology are all one and the same and merely fabulous interpretations of these extra terrestrial visitors. [116] [117]

* THE INDIANS, amongst their many gods, worshipped one group of water-gods known as the Apsaras, who were celestial flute-playing wa-

ter-nymphs. We have already delved briefly into some ancient Indian texts which the `ancient astronaut` school of UFOlogy claim are conclusive proofs of their theory, much as they have also claimed the ancient folk tales of the Dogon for their own. We make no such claims, and refuse to be drawn into the discussion at all, and have included these accounts in this book merely for the sake of completeness. [118]

* IN JAPANESE AND CHINESE legends there were not only mermaids but also sea-dragons and the dragon-wives. The Japanese mermaid known as Ningyo was depicted as a fish with only a human head. [119]

* POLYNESIAN mythology includes a creator named Vatea who was depicted as half-human form and half-porpoise. [120]

* GREEK AND ROMAN MYTHOLOGY is often placed together as the two are very similar and it is in the literature from these cultures that one finds the first literary description of the mermaid, and indeed the mermen. Homer mentions the Sirens during the voyage of Odysseus but he fails to give a physical description. Poseidon and Neptune were often depicted as half-man and half-fish but the most popular motif of the ancient world that depicts mermen was the representations of the tritons, Triton being the son of the powerful sea-god. The Nereids, who were the daughters of Nereus and the Oceanides, who were associated with Ocean and the Naiads who lived in the fresh waters of the ancient world, while being water creatures were depicted as humans and not merpeople. [121]

Martin Ball continues:

"The Age of Enlightenment may be considered to have begun in the year 1700. Veasta was sighted in June 1757 by no less than the Reverend John Hutchins, famous historian of Dorset. Not only was the monster seen but the corpse was washed ashore at Burton Bradstock. What happened to it?" [122]

The scenario whereby a carcasse of potential importance to cryptozoology has just disappeared is a common one. We have already discussed the saga of the Minnesota Iceman, and in *The Owlman and Others* I describe the twenty year hunt for the vanished skull of a putative sea serpent that turned out to be nothing more than a pilot whale. [123] [124]

Mermaid reports still occur today. Whilst in Cornwall researching *The Owlman and Others* in 1995/6 I met a young woman (now sadly died) whose mother told me of a sightings she had experienced in the mid 1970s. [125]

She had been on a school trip from her home near Falmouth to the Scilly Isles and they were passing (she thought) Wolf Rock and she was looking over the side of the boat when she saw a human figure sitting on the rock. It appeared to be naked, and had long brown hair. She did not notice any fishy lower portions to the person's body, not any secondary sexual characteristics by which she could diagnose the sex of the `merperson`. She stared at it for several seconds before it slipped into the sea and disappeared.

She was adamant that she hadn't seen any boats within miles, and they were a long way from land, and that as the `merperson` was naked it was highly unlikely that she/he was merely a human swimmer. Mermaid reports from Hong Kong, however seem likely to be more prosaic in origin. A dugong was harpooned by local fishermen in 1941 and its carcass was brought in triumph back to Hong Kong. [126]

These magnificently primitive marine mammals are not supposed to exist in the South China Sea, but at least one specimen obviously did. It has been speculated that sightings of these grotesquely human-looking creatures are responsible for the reports of mermaids which have been made for centuries by fishermen in the South China Sea. Only a few years ago a Hong Kong fisherman reported by radio having caught a `mermaid` in his nets. A vast crowd turned up on the quay waiting for his return, but no-one turned up. The rumours quickly went around that the fisherman's boat had capsized under mysterious circumstances. It is tempting to suggest that this could be circumstantial evidence for the Chinese superstition that catching a mermaid is bad luck, but it is more likely that it was a hoax. [127]

During the writing of this book the following report from South Africa winged its way to my computer through cyberspace, through the good offices of Loren Coleman:

SUN TIMES --
SEPTEMBER 13, 1998

Something fishy in San art baffles the experts Images of mermaids in San paintings have sparked a new round of debate.

IT'S an unlikely place for mermaids. Half-human, half-fish - the strange rock paintings in the mountains around Meiringspoort in the Karoo have baffled scientists for generations. Though there is little doubt about the artists - San hunter-gatherers who lived and

painted in the area for thousands of years - everyone still wonders about the mermaids. Are they for real, drug-induced, or merely figments of hunter-gatherer imagination? The recent discovery of even more fish-like figures in Ezeljachtpoort in the Karoo has sparked fresh debate.
Real or not, the fact is that a lot of people believe in mermaids. So much so that the last time anyone said the M-word near Meiringspoort they had to call the police.

That was in 1996, during the Oudtshoorn floods, when a radio DJ joked about a mermaid who had been washed up and taken to a freshwater tank in the local museum for safekeeping. Hundreds of people demanded her release. "We even had the police here," said cultural historian Anita Holtzhausen of the C P Nel Museum in Oudtshoorn. "They said if we didn't put her back where she came from there would be an even bigger flood. I couldn't believe what I was hearing. "People in the binneland feel strongly about mermaids. In Afrikaans we call them *wateranties* or *watermeids*."

Mermaids are among the numerous strange figures that feature in San rock art, a treasure trove of paintings and engravings etched into dolerite boulders. There are thousands of open-air galleries, a jigsaw puzzle of earthy folk- tales, each a potential clue to unravelling the little-known history of South Africa's earliest inhabitants. New paintings are still being found, astonishing international rock-art experts who consider San art a vital window into a Stone Age past that has almost completely disappeared.

"Paintings provide a dimension that one can seldom get, even from archaeological excavations," said Professor Tim Maggs, a Cape archaeologist. "No doubt we've already made huge strides in piecing evidence together, and will continue to do so. It will always be controversial because interpretations of paintings can seldom be proved in a conclusive way,"Maggs said.

Then there is the monster "zigzag" man who appears on a rock face in KwaZulu-Natal, and several other monster figures, often half-man, half-beast. The famous Wit Vrou van die Brandberg in Namibia has also raised quite a few eyebrows in its time: a black lower body with a white upper body, whatever that means. Some people claim to have found paintings depicting Phoenician sailing ships or UFOs, though these are often smudged or faint, looking more like Rorschach tests than ancient artwork.

There's even talk of a massive "Last Supper" engraving somewhere on the banks of the Orange River, though to date it has not been found. That's not to say that interpreting paintings is all guesswork. Far from it. Several experts spend their time recording artworks around the country, sometimes trekking to remote sites that have never been publicised. The Wits University-based Rock Art Research Institute sends field worker far and wide to document paintings. There is particular interest in a 12,000-page San ethnography written in the 1870s which comprises a series of comprehensive interviews with /Xam clansmen from the Northern Cape, offering valuable insight into the San heritage. Though the /Xam did not paint or engrave, they believed their grandparents probably did.

"Those texts are extensive and internationally recognised as very important," said University of Cape Town art historian Pippa Skotnes. The texts are irreplaceable - and help to explain the significance of painting in San society. The problem is that nobody went into too much detail about mermaids, leaving experts happily flinging explanations at one another at slide shows and conferences around the country.

One school of thought is that the mermaid or monster-like figures represent the hallucinogenic experiences of the San people's shamans, who did most of the painting. Others feel the figures represent the departed spirits that regularly intervened in San society. "The debate about mermaids in the art derives from comments by an elderly San man last century, who said they represented 'water-maidens'," said rock-art expert Anne Solomon.

"I believe the 'water-maidens' relate to female initiation. /Xam stories describe disobedient initiates abducted by the Rain [deity] and drowned, but still seen at the water hole in various forms such as flowers, stars or frogs," she said. Perhaps, as an elderly San hunter once told a foreign journalist, the present can never completely understand the past - a period he described simply as the time when things happened that no longer happen today.

Then again, there is still talk of mermaids popping up in picturesque Meiringspoort, a place of deep pools scoured out by age-old waterfalls. "We've had a couple of people who've claimed they've seen mermaids there," Holtzhausen said. "Not so long ago a car crashed there and overturned into a deep pool, drowning everyone inside. One woman later said she saw a mermaid sitting at the edge of the pool, staring into the water. Who knows?"

{Note The Sun Times is South Africa's largest circulation weekly newspaper with a readership of more than 2.2 million, for Gauteng (Johannesburg), Cape Town and Durban.} [128]

Mermaid carcasses are also oddly elusive...

Cryptozoologist and fortean author Dr Karl Shuker notes one particularly interesting case in *The Unexplained* (1996)

"As documented in volume two of Alexander Carmicheal's treatise `Carmina Gadelica` (1900), in or around the year 1830 some people were gathering seaweed at Sgeir na duchadh in Grimnis, on the Outer Hebridean island of Benbecula, when a strange woman-like entity began frolicking nearby in the sea. After fruitless attempts to catch the creature, a boy threw a stone that struck it heavily. The creature sank beneath the waves. A few days later its dead body was found washed ashore 3km away at Cuile in Nunton.

According to the detailed description given in `Carmina Gadelica` the creature's upper portion was about the size of a well fed three-four year old child but with an abnormally developed breast. Its lower body was like a salmon in shape, but lacked scale~ Its skin was white, soft and tender, and its long hair was dark and glossy. Not surprisingly, such a remarkable sight drew great crowds, who gazed at it closely and even touched it, and everyone went away convinced that this was truly a mermaid. Indeed, it was so human in form that Duncan Shaw, factor for Clanranald, (baron-bailie and sheriff of the district), ordered a coffin and shroud to be made, and its body was formally buried a short distance above the shore from where it had been found - a unique funeral attended by many people. If this had been nothing more than a dead seal or a beached whale, it is highly unlikely that eyewitnesses as knowledgeable about maritime matters as the seafaring inhabitants of Benbecula would have mistaken it for a mermaid or accorded it a ceremonious funeral." [130]

All attempts by cryptozoologists and fortean researchers to locate the grave of the poor mermaid have failed miserably and at the moment the story, well documented though it is, languishes in that grey area between fact and folklore where so much of the material contained in this and other books has perforce had to be consigned.

It should also, perhaps, be noted that a second `carcasse` of dubious provenance has also been reported from the same location.

A number of photographs were published in national newspapers in 1996, but they had been taken nearly sixteen years earlier.

Louise Whitts, a nanny from Bedlington, England, took the pictures during a vacation in Scotland when she was 16. She and her family were mystified by the 12-foot anomaly covered by sand and seaweed, which they believed might be the corpse of a sea monster.

"It had what appeared to be a head at one end, a curved back and seemed to be covered with eaten-away flesh or even a furry skin and was about 12 feet long. And it smelt absolutely disgusting! But the weird thing was that it had all these shapes like fins along its back -- like a dinosaur or something. We didn't know what it was, although we laughed about it being the Loch Ness Monster." [131]

As newspapers noted at the time:

"Two incidental factors elevate the intrigue of this situation to an even more sensational level. First, the stretch of Benbecula where Whitts made her discovery had an interesting neighbour. "It was beside some land owned by the Ministry of Defence and there were big notices all over the place saying that if people found anything on the beach they were not to touch it," Whitts recalls. "But they must have been thinking of the bits of metal and propellers and things there were laying about, not a monster like this!"

Additionally, Benbecula was reportedly irradiated heavily by fallout from Chernobyl. A high rate of cancer cases on the island has been attributed to the 1986 nuclear disaster, although medical experts have disputed any likely causal relationship. Could this mean Whitts stumbled across secret genetic experimentation by the British military? Or perhaps a radiation-spawned Godzilla mutant?" [132]

It has to be said, as well, that the object in the photographs makes a very unconvincing 'monster'. Firstly, Louise Whitts is actually pictured *sitting* on it, which implies that unless she had very peculiar tastes it was unlikely to be a putrefying mass of flesh and animal tissue. It also should be noted that it looks very much like a sculpted sand castle rather than the remains of any animate object. [133]

Other mystery carcasses are equally problematical.

In the 2nd Century AD, a 'pickled triton' was exhibited at Tanagra in

Southern Greece. The historian and traveller Pausanias described it thoroughly:

'Tritons are certainly a sight; the hair on their heads is like the frogs in stagnant water: not only in its froggy colour, but so sleek you could never separate one hair from the next: and the rest of their bodies are bristling with very fine scales like a rough-skinned shark. They have gills behind the ears and a human nose, but a very big mouth and the teeth of a wild beast. I thought the eyes were greenish-grey, and they have their hands and fingers and finger-nails crusted like sea-shells. From the breast and belly downwards they have a dolphin's tail instead of feet.' (134) (135)

Disappearing evidence is a common scenario within all avenues of fortean research. The fragments of a crashed UFO, which only days later were replaced by bits of a USAAF weather balloon is perhaps the most widely known account, but there are many others. The negative of one of `Doc` Shiels` 1977 photographs of the Loch Ness Monster disappeared under mysterious circumstances whilst in the post to a colleague of his in the United States, (136) (137) and specimens of apports produced during spates of poltergeist activity have also vanished as mysteriously as they appeared. (138)

It is common knowledge that in the second half of the eighteenth century visits to the sea-side became popular amongst the middle and upper classes, due in great part to the popular scientific belief in the curative properties of salt water. The Prince Regent was an early convert to this way of thinking and where the arbiter of fashion led, the rest of the country (or at least those that could afford to) followed.

It is surprising how the social infrastructure of an area can be so radically changed by such an apparently insignificant series of events. The effect of this new social trend upon Exmouth and Littleham will be discussed later in this book, but for the moment, we should merely consider the effect that it had on one tiny Sussex sea-side fishing village.

In 1085 the fishing village of Bristemestune was referred to, in the Domesday Book, as being worth £12 and paying the rent of 4000 herrings. The Anglo Saxon name of Brythelmyston was the forerunner of Brighthelmstone which held fast until the first years of the 19th century, when it became fashionably known as Brighton. (139)

The early history of the town was spectacularly unremarkable. This account is taken from a Web-Site containing much information of interest on the history of Brighton and the surrounding areas:

"By the early years of the 14th century the town was prosperous enough to support a market despite over 40 acres of land being claimed by the sea between the years of 1260 and 1340. When Henry VIII was fighting Louis XII in 1554 Brighthelmstone was burned but beacon fires on the Downs played an historical part in rescuing the town from complete destruction. In Tudor times Queen Elizabeth was instrumental in the granting of land for the erection of sea defences and when the Armada sailed up the channel in 1588 no Spaniard set foot on the shore.

As early as 1635 Brighthelmstone was suffering from a depression in the fishing industry because attacks at sea and on land were frequent and the town found it increasingly more difficult to recover. At this stage Brighthelmstone was still only contained within a square - The Lanes - as we know it today, with the boundaries being West Street, East Street and North Street with South Street already having succumbed to the sea.

For centuries the area between West Street and Black Lion Street consisted of open fields called The Hempshares, and these open plots grew hemp for the rope used in the fishing trade.

In 1651 The Lanes played a large part in the escape of Charles II when he came to the town looking for a ship to take him to Normandy - see Street by Street history of Ship Street. The devastation of the sea and the French onslaughts had reduced Brighton to its lowest population of 1000 by 1740 and it was thought then that it would be completely depopulated. In his Tour Through Great Britain, Daniel Defoe wrote of the great storm of 1703 that destroyed most of the town as a "dreadful tempest" and that its affect on Brighthelmstone rendered it "not worth saving". The destruction of the town over the centuries explains the paucity of anything older than the mid-sixteenth century.

Yet even in those days when the people of Brighton seemed depressed beyond the hope of recovery there were those who were aware of the beauties that have attracted visitors to the place ever since. As a community of fishermen and farmers living in relative isolation Brighton underwent little essential change until the middle of the 18th century.

The beach had serviced the fishermen for centuries, but from 1750 bathing wagons were introduced and they then became characteristic of Brighton beach. Fashionable women were "dipped" and the men were "bathed" in segregated areas of the beach and the "dippers" were headed by the celebrated Martha Gunn who was a favourite of the Prince Re-

gent. Dr. Richard Russell was to bring about the most celebrated change to the town. He moved from Lewes and purchased land on the site of the Royal Albion Hotel in Old Steine, and sent his first patients to Brighton in 1753 for a sea water cure. He administered to the Prince of Wales who appeared to suffer from swelling of the thyroid gland, which was probably the reason he sported the high collar and cravats, which rapidly became a fashion of the time, to hide the swelling. The English Seaside was popularised by Dr. Russell when the curative powers of sea bathing and seaside air were acknowledged by royalty through to local tradesmen. The recovery of the town in general can be attributed to the arrival of the Prince Regent and to Dr. Russell because in 1761 there were still only six principal streets in Brighton. By 1787 the first version of the Royal Pavilion had been completed. During this time 62 new houses had been built in North Street; a two pair coach journey from London was 16/- and by May 1791 the first Royal Mail coach was established and the journey took 12 hours from London. In 1823 alone, 12,000 loads of sand were removed from the shore to assist in Brighton's building boom and the enormous growth of the town necessitated important improvements in the layout of the main streets." [140]

Almost overnight, Brighton had changed from an obscure fishing village to a fashionable watering place and the social infrastructure of the area was changed completely.

As I have shown in *The Owlman and Others* (1997,8) [141] it seems apparent that when the social or physical infrastructure of a place has changed, what I call the psychic infrastructure - that is the inate *spiritus loci* of the area changes also. In the case of Mawnan Smith I noted that:

The Church was re-consecrated in the 15th Century and that a series of radical extensions to the Churchyard at Mawnan Old Church resulted in some ancient earthworks being demolished. [142]

If I am correct and that "paranormal" (the quotation marks are intentional) occurrences are somehow linked to damage in the `psychic infrastructure` of a location, then could not a radical change in that psychic infrastructure have much the same effect?

We shall return to this subject in parts three and four of this present book. In the meantime however, we should return to Martin Ball, who explains what effect this new found popularity of seaside resorts had upon Weymouth and its particular `monster`.

"In the mid-1740s, important figures in the town of Weymouth, including

Sir George Bubb Dodington, 'Portland-based' Edward Tucker Esq and the former Mayor of Bath, Ralph Allen, formed an alliance. They were aware of the potential to transform the town. They had all recognised that tastes and fashion were changing and leaning towards a return to Roman traditions for good health and long life, which advocated the consumption of sea-water (together with a portion of wine for good measure). There was more than one case of occasional visitors, 'come to drink up the sea, finding their primeval instincts aroused by that curvaceous bay. The 1757 sighting came as unwelcome news to the 'dealers in saltwater' who had committed vast sums of their personal wealth to the success of the resort of Weymouth. They feared the genteel visitors' disgust and revulsion at the prospect of a monster creature sharing their bathing area and contaminating local supplies of sea-water by its very presence. Although there is clear evidence of the 1757 sighting, the fact that it is not documented in more detail suggests that a plan was hatched to destroy all documentation relating to the sighting of Veasta and to have all witnesses to the monster's corpse silenced." [143]

This must be almost unique in the annals of cryptozoology and its allied disciplines. The history of these subjects is full of accounts of situations where the people responsible for the local tourist industry inflate the reputation of a local 'monster' in order to boost the reputation of the area in terms of holiday receipts and the tourist industry but this must be one of the first, if not the only, time in history where exactly the opposite took place in a scenario amusingly reminiscent of that described by Peter Benchley in his best selling novel *Jaws!* [144] [145]

Luckily, for the beleagured fortean zoologist and for the reputation of the monster alike, help was at hand in the unlikely form of a local antiquarian. As Martin Ball explains:

"........unknown to the Weymouth men at that time, a communication had reached the Dorset historian, John Hutchins, who had been afforded the time to research his work thoroughly and had been able to view and document the evidence. This surviving report appeared in the first two editions of his great History and Antiquities of Dorset but was suppressed m the third. It was trivialised and lampooned by Sir Frederick Treves in his Highways & Byways in Dorset. It is by no means the only example of the history of 'Weymouth and Portland being re-written for the convenience of powerful vested interests." [146]

So many accounts of episodic sightings of creatures like this tend to fizzle out a couple of hundred years ago, and it is very refreshing to find an almost unknown cryptid whose appearances have continued until the present day. Martin Ball again:

"At that time, then, Veasta was a monster that should be seen but not heard of. Yet there have been two sightings during the last 30 years: not only in 1995 but at Church Ope Cove on Portland in 1965 by two reliable witnesses. This sighting was mocked in cartoons which portrayed the creature as blonde, buxom and wedded to the tail-end of a fish. Are there other creatures of the same species as the one washed ashore in 1757, lurking off Portland's shores? Will the plan to illuminate Chesil Beach between the watering-places of the Ferry-bridge Inn and the Cove Inn this summer make it impossible to ignore Veasta, Portland's own sea-monster, any longer?" [147]

We would agree with Mr Ball. It is impossible to ignore this strange phenomenon any longer. It is generally believed by many fortean researchers that there is a definite correlation between monster reports and those of UFO activity. One of the first researchers to draw this conclusion was Ted Holiday who wrote as far back as 1973:

"People of the Magdalenian Culture of between 12,000- 15,000 years ago observed the same or very similar U.F.O. phenomena to those described by recent witnesses. We can be confident about this because the Magdalenians were without equal as artists in the world of prehistory as is proved by their superb coloured murals. When they sketched a Flying Disc, therefore - and hundreds are depicted in cave-art - it seems obvious that they actually observed such objects just as they observed the horses depicted at Lascaux and the mammoths at Rouffignac. Discs are particularly plentiful in one of the most famous caves of the period - Altamira. These people painted not only bison, bears and other wildlife but also 'flying saucers'.

From a somewhat later period emerges a device which can lay claim to being the most ancient religious symbol on record. Scratched on a Mesolithic stag-antler are a series of zigzag undulations leading up to a Disc. There is little doubt that these undulations represent the humps of a dragon because the same symbol, rendered much more clearly, has survived into modern times. There is a good example on a cross in the churchyard at Clonmacnois, Co. Offaly in Ireland. This symbolism brings the dragon and the Disc into juxtaposition for the first time. How the idea developed and continues to develop - we will examine later.

For at least 150 centuries, therefore, people have not only been aware of the existence of dragons and U.F.O.s but have related them symbolically in a distinctive way. The vigour of the concept seems unique in human thought. No other idea has such an enormously long pedigree. Entire civilisations were constructed around it as we will see. Outliving the decline of paganism, the concept flourished in carved stone throughout the cathedrals and churches of Christendom. Today, we seem to be encountering a new variation of the message - something observable by scientist and layman alike. If the foregoing is substantially true then it is time to think about supporting evidence. A flimsy framework is not enough; the evidential structure must be massive if it is to carry the necessary degree of impact. Moreover, it must be available for scientific inspection.

I believe such a structure exists. And the testing has already begun.

Various mistaken science attitudes are discussed in these pages; yet science is basically not at fault. It has a duty to be cautious. Nevertheless, the dragon and the Disc are both currently under investigation by scientists of repute. But so low is the research priority for this work that progress is painfully slow. This is the case even though a measure of wisdom concerning these mysteries might well result in a spiritual reappraisal for the whole world with a corresponding diminution of the numerous evils we see festering in society all around us. There is no proof of this but it seems a real possibility. The first problem is to recognise something that mankind knew about for millennia but which has been forgotten. The second problem is to do something effective about it. It is against this background that the evidence is presented." [148]

Whilst his evidence may be flawed in parts, it has been suggested with some justification we feel, that many of these `discs` that he claims are depicted in the ancient cave paintings are in fact nothing of the sort. Similar claims by the likes of Erik Von Daniken have also been widely refuted. There is nothing, however, wrong with his reasoning, because there is a long history of correlation between these two types of phenomena. In a book published in 1980, Janet and Colin Bord coined the phrase BHM (Big Hairy Men), to describe anomalous man beasts and beast-men sighted worldwide. [149] There is a burgeoning amount of evidence linking these zooform BHM phenomena with UFO sightings.

One of the most significant events of this type took place in Uniontown, Pennsylvania on October 25th 1973. It was researched by psychiatrist Berthold Eric Schwarz who recounted his findings in *The Flying Saucer Review Vol. 20 #1* (1974). The incident began at about nine p.m when 'Stephen Pulaski' (a pseudonym chosen by Schwarz) together with about fifteen other witnesses observed a red light hovering above a field just outside the town. For reasons that (as far as I know) have never been disclosed he collected two ten-year old twin boys and went to investigate.

As they approached the headlights of their car dimmed mysteriously and the UFO slowly started to descend. It was dome shaped *"like a big bubble (....) making a sound like a lawn mower"* and the three witnesses, who by this time had got out of their car and were gazing at the apparition in awe, strange screaming sounds could be heard. [150] [151]

Suddenly two strange creatures were revealed in the pulsating light given off by the strange object. Pulaski and his two companions thought that they were bears. The North American Black Bear *(Eurarctos americanus)* is certainly found in the area [152] but are considerably smaller than the animals described by Pulaski and his friends. According to veteran fortean researchers Loren Coleman and Jerry Clark:

"Both had long dark gray hair, and arms that almost reached the ground. The taller one, about eight feet in height, was running its left hand along the fence. The shorter, which stood slightly over seven feet tall, seemed to be hurrying along to keep up with its companion. Both were making a whining sound, like a baby crying, and apparently were communicating with each other via this strange noise." [153]

The witnesses later asserted that these 'creatures' were definitely ape-like rather than bear-like. One of the young boys fled the scene in terror and Pulaski, showing a charmingly investigative attitude, shot at the larger of the creatures with his rifle. The animal made a whining noise and reached out towards its companion. The UFO vanished leaving a phosphorescent glowing area bright enough *"to read a newspaper by"* and the two animals retreated, apparently unharmed into the woods. [154]

Interestingly enough, although these animals do not resemble the aforementioned North American Black Bears, according to Richard Freeman, from The Centre for Fortean Zoology, *"they do not resemble standard Sasquatch reports either. Reconstructions of the animals from witness accounts endow them with long, wolf-like ears, fangs and claws. This makes them look rather more like the popular notion of a werewolf".* [155]

We will find this bizarre mixture of primate and canid again and again during our search for the truth behind the worldwide zooform BHM phenomena.

There seems to be no doubt that these animals were closely related in some way to the UFO. There is a long history of both UFO sightings and 'Bigfoot' reports in Pennsylvania. Indeed the Pennsylvania Centre for UFO Research publishes a newsletter The Creature Research Journal which chronicles 'Bigfoot' reports in the locality. In number 16 (Fall

1994) the Editors published a chart showing the breakdown of 'Bigfoot' reports over the previous ten years. They comment that:

"The results clearly show that like UFO sightings, creature encounters fluctuate periodically" in a pattern totally unlike any records of living, breathing animals. [156]

PART TWO: WHERE?

"And come tell me Sean O'Farrell where the gathering is to be. At the old spot by the river quite well known to you and me. And by way of signal token whistle loud the marching tune, With your pike across your shoulder at the rising of the moon"

***Trad arr* Shane McGowan**

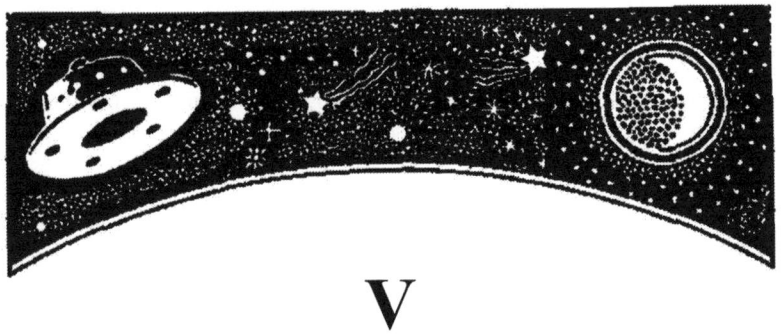

V

Woodbury Common, the epicentre of many of the UFO reports and other events discussed in this book is an ancient and weird place. It has a long history of strange, anomalous and unpleasant events, and both Nigel and I are convinced that there is some arcane connection between this history of high strangeness and the UFO reports which are, after all the main subject of this book.

We cannot do better as an introduction to Woodbury Common than quote an undated report from C.Keeling-Basford to the Devonshire Historical Research Association:

THE GEOLOGY OF WOODBURY COMMON. EAST DEVON

The sedimentary Igneous and Metamorphic rocks on the Common', generally speaking, are not Metallic, yet, tons of imported hard core, were used during the last 100 years, by the Army (N.O.D.) for making pathways and it is possible to find Metallic substances amongst them. The basic local rocks found in this part of the South West, are Limestone, Granite, Metamorphic Killas, Quartz, Serpentine, Baryte, Pyrite, Tourmaline, Prypsom, Fluorite, Calcite, Sandstone, and Flint. The best way to observe the Geological structure of Woodbury, is to position yourself at the Hill Fort Castle, which stands 560 feet above sea level. This spot gives a wonderful view, embracing the whole of the New Red Sandstone Landscape around the Exe estuary. The formation of the scarpe (Pebble Beds) are best seen from the B3179 (Knowle-Four Firs Road). It is worth noting the gravel pit workings on route.

The DIP SLOPES (Heaths/conifers) follow the Scarpe Face to the Pebble Bed Sand and Marl Beds due to hillwash." [1]

This may seem rather a dry and uncompromising document, but the *genus loci* of Woodbury Common is such that even Keeling-Basford had to comment upon it:

"This undulating, rather sparse countryside, with its Neolithic Burial Mounds, gives an air of antiquity and even, to some people, a feeling of depression.

It is recorded, that there are Dead Spots, or areas of bad signal reception. Perhaps this is caused by the Marl Beds, enclosed by sharpes and woodland It is interesting to note that the question of Ley Lines, crop up time and tirne again. This is a completely different form of Scientific Analysis, and should be kept seperate from the factual information as submitted.........." [2]

This is neither the only account of the peculiar feeling of otherworldliness which can be experienced in the Woodbury/Budleigh area, nor indeed, the only time that it has been linked with ley lines. In November 1982, the *Exmouth Journal* printed a rather unconvincing photograph, purporting to be that of a UFO, under the headline "A Close Encounter". The picture looks to us like a photographic anomaly caused by a drop of moisture on the lens of the camera, but could be identified as a similar `plasma ball` to those which were filmed in conjunction with the formation of the Oliver`s castle crop formation in August 1996. The newspaper account is interesting, not because of the incident itself, but because of the interpretations that were put on it:

"An expert in the subject of Unidentified Flying Objects, this week released what he called photographic evidence of strange phenomena at Pulhayes Farm, East Budleigh. The picture is thought to support the claim of a holidaymaker that he was kidnapped by aliens and held for two hours on April 20th, 1981. A mysterious circle appears at the foot of the row of trees in the photograph, taken during an exploratory trip by Eric Morris, chairman of the Plymouth U.F.O. Investigation Centre.

He was accompanied by "Trevor," a 35-year-old bachelor from Kingston-upon-Thames, who says he was felled by an invisible force after seeing strange lights at this spot 14 months ago.

Mr. Morris explained: "The unusual feature on this photograph is the light, outlined, uneven circle. "I do not know if it is solid or just a ball of charged electricity. It was not visible at the time I took the picture.

Trevor was with me when I took the photo. At the time, I had an ultra violet lens-cover on my camera. It was not raining. The lens was perfectly clean. This I checked, as when taking photographs during a U.F.O. 'investigation we try to 'obtain the best quality results".

Trevor's full name is not being revealed by Mr. Morris who says he wishes to remain I unidentified to avoid ridicule.

Another explanation for the events has come from Mr. George Shutter, an expert on the ancient history of Exmouth and Budleigh Salterton. Mr. Shutter, who lives at 3, Ryllcourt Drive, Exmouth, believes that Trevor experienced a strong force from the local ley line, an ancient power which is believed by some to control, among other things, bird migration and physical progresses.

The ley line, he says, originates from a burial barrow on Budleigh Salterton golf course. close to the house where Mrs. Juliet Rowe was murdered in September last year.

Mr. Shutter thinks the ley line is connected with both Mrs. Rowe's death and the disappearance of Genette Tate four years ago. He said: "If you are sensitive, you can feel it. I've felt the power twice in Exmouth. It's a force that absolutely impels. It makes you feel disorientated. Your brain doesn't work properly.

"This is what may have happened to the man who said he saw a flying saucer. His head was full of reading about U.F.O.'s. He'd probably been watching them on television or reading science fiction paperbacks. What happened was all inside his head. Nothing came from outside, except the force."

Mr. Shutter added:

"There must be hundreds of people in Exmouth who have felt the force of the ley line.
They don't say anything because friends and relatives would think they were bonkers." [3] [4]

Unfortunately, we have been unable to discover anything else about the alleged abduction investigated by Mr Morris. There are, however some other aspects of the above story which are of interest. There seems to be very little evidence to suggest any occult link to the murder of Mrs Juliet Rowe, although it has to be admitted that a certain amount of mystery still surrounds the case. A local one-time small businessman named

Keith Rose was convicted of Mrs Rowe's abduction and murder and although he has appealed, unsuccesfullyl against the charge there seems no doubt that the guilty verdict that was returned was the correct one. [5]

Mr Shutter's comments are particularly interesting from a number of viewpoints. Not only do they endorse the report quoted above from Mr Keeling-Basford but they mirror Nigel's and my feeling that the strange phenomena that have been reported from the area over the years are all somehow interlinked.

Mrs Rowe's murder was not the only one on Woodbury Common that year which could be lioned with anomalous phenomena or quasi-occult activity.

"Satanists may have held a black mass on Woodbury Common close to the scene of the double murder of thirty-eight year old Michael Brooke and 16 year old Tina Ellacott.

A horrified teenager saw the eerie ceremony in the early hours of Sunday, two days before the two bodies were found. The spot is 200 yards from the place where Tina was shot dead

The young man, who has asked not to be named, saw two figures dressed in light coloured robes. Their faces were covered by ~ hoods their robes were lit up by the glow from a fire.

He heard the sound of a bell and looked round to See the two hooded figures. One was holding out his hood and looking Into the fire, but his face was hidden.

The man aged 19, was walking home towards Colaton Raleigh at 2.20 a. m. when he witnessed the ceremony. He hed been vislting his girl friend in Exmouth.

*He told the Herald: 'The figures were in a clearing but I could not see exactly how many people **were** there because more were behind the trees. I must have been looking at them for a minute before I took off. I ran like the clappers past Boarden Barn, and then I turned round to see if anyone was following me. I kept praying all the time. As I was running, I could hear a rhythmic beat. It carried on when I stopped. I went down to Yettington, where I could still hear it.*

*It was a dark and silent night. I **was** really frightened. Normally the dark does not bother me, but anyone seeing that on thelr own would have been scared. I told my parents about it when I arrived home and they told* *me to ring the police straight away. Apparently the police saw lights on the common as well..........* " [6]

We should examine these claims in more detail. The term `Black Mass` is a much overused and misinterpreted one. According to the Encarta Encyclopaedia:

"Black Mass, legendary parody of a Roman Catholic mass involving the worship of Satan. Accounts of this mass describe a number of rituals that include suspending a crucifix upside down and reciting prayers backward. The legend probably originated during the Middle Ages. Some scholars believe that the modern image of the black mass developed in the 1600s, when many people in Europe and the American colonies were executed as witches." [7]

American occultist Anton LaVey wrote:

"The Black Mass is a valid Satanic ceremony only if one feels the need to perform it. Historically, there is no ritual more closely linked with Satanism than the Black Mass. It has long been considered the principal elective of Satanists, who were assumed never to tire of trampling on crosses and stealing unbaptised infants. If a Satanist had nothing else to do, and was independently wealthy, newer and more blasphemous versions of the Messe Noir would be invented in order to nourish the jaded existence, the theory went. Though a titillating concept to many, it is without validity, and as devoid of logic as the assumption that Christians celebrate Good Friday every Wednesday afternoon." [8]

Anton LaVey wrote a number of black masses which owe as much to showbusiness as to genuine occult practises, and at the risk of attracting negative responses from any of his followers who are reading this, it is tempting to suggest that his `First Church of Satan` has more to do with self aggraindisment and a desire to be part of the Hollywood glitterati than any real desire for occult advancement. His black masses are full of details which tell us a lot about his sexual proclivities but very little else, and it should be noted as well that he played the part of Satan in Roman Polanksi's 1968 film *"Rosemary's Baby"* [9] [10] was a professional organist. He committed the ultimate crime against good taste by being photographed for the cover of a West-Coast country rock band's LP. [11]

Although an awful lot is talked about Satanism (mostly by people who don't have much of an idea what it really means), there is not much evidence for an organised Satanic Cult in the United Kingdom. The Church of Satan, which LaVey founded in 1966 (declaring himself `Black Pope` and instituting 1966 as Year One of Satan's Reign), [12] seems to be a mostly American institution, and one with little following outside California. The much touted link between 'Satanism' and rock-music seems to go little further than lyrical content, and although there are some Scandinavian musicians whose involvement in the subject is notorious, it seems probable that the involvement of most of their followers in the dark arts goes little further than wearing the T.Shirt. [13]

Unfortunately, most people who write about the subject know very little about it, and make a number of elementary mistakes, such as confusing witchcraft and Satanism.

A wiccan website notes this common practise and does its best to set the record straight in a sober and non-judgemental fashion:

"SATANISM. Often confused with witchcraft is the worship of Satan. Satanism logically is a denial of Christianity rather than arising out of its own context. It involves a rejection of the Christian God in favor of all that is opposite. In belief and ritual it uses Christian forms and reverses their meaning. The most famous element used by Satanists is the Black Mass. Satanists operate from the world-view of magic. There are both public Satanic churches and hidden, secret organizations. Some groups worship Satan as a god while others use the idea of Satan as a historical figure representing philosophical principles. Any discussion of Satanism leads to heated accusations making it difficult to determine where reality truly lies. Much written in opposition to Satanism has merely been used as text material for those interested in following some of their practices. Satanists do share a number of symbols (and ritual practices) in common with all magical religions, but several are unique and distinctive. The inverted pentagram, the five-pointed star with the single point down, is the most frequently used. The Horned God in the form of the goat of Mendes is common. The pentagram is often stamped upon the goat's forehead. A black inverted cross is sometimes used. In recent times the Black Mass is not practiced by most groups. Satanism can be an attraction for those who are often called "sickies" even by avowed public Satanists. They may form groups using Satan worship to cover a variety of sexual, sado-masochistic, clandestine, psychopathic, and illegal activities. From these groups come grave-robberies, sexual assaults and blood letting (both animal and human). These groups are characterized by a lack of theology, short life, and informality of meetings. On the other hand are the public groups which take Satanism as a religion seriously. Their systems closely resemble liberal Christian theologies with the addition of a powerful cultural symbol (Satan) which is radically redefined." [14]

Many people died in the witch scare that gripped Europe in the sixteenth and seventeenth centuries. There were claims of widespread Satanism, and those practicing old forms of pagan religions were often misidentified as Satanists, as well as those having nothing to do with witchcraft at all. The most famous incident was the Black Mass scandal in the court of Louis XIV and led to the arrest of more than 300 persons. In the 1670's, Madame LaVoisin, one of Louis XIV's mistresses, suspected she was losing Louis' affection and hired a priest to say Black Masses. Some of the masses included the killing of babies and the use of Madame LaVoisin's nude body as an altar. Louis imprisoned or banished the participants.

According to several authorities, the oft quoted Biblical line "thou shalt not suffer a witch to live" (Exodus 22.v.18) is actually the result of an unfortunate mistranslation. The original passage went "thou shalt not suffer a POISONER to live", and the line became perverted during the translation process from Greek to Roman about 1600 years ago. One wonders how many friendless and lonely old women were tortured to death due to this simple, and horribly easy mistake. [15] [16] [17]

Although I am essentially a Roman Catholic, I have many friends who are witches and I have partaken with them in some of their rituals, and they have all stressed to me that modern witches try to separate themselves from any connection with Satanism. They identify with ancient European pagan beliefs.

Wicca is polytheistic. The prime deities are the Goddess and God, usually represented as the Triple Goddess and Horned God. The triple aspects of the Goddess are maiden, mother, and crone. Psychic abilities are prized and effort is made to develop them. Trances are used both for spells and for a sense of contact with the gods.

"The two essential books of the witch are the grimoire and the book of shadows. The grimoire is the book of spells and magical procedures. The book of shadows is the traditional book of rituals. According to custom, it is copied by hand by each individual witch, and thus no two copies are alike.

The basic organization of witches is the coven, though there is also an affiliation between covens of like belief and practice, especially where one coven has broken off from another and sees it as the parent group. The coven is often made up of 13 people but the number may vary widely. The regular meeting of the coven is called an esbat; but eight times a year there are seasonal festivals called sabbats. The most famous festival is October 31, Halloween. Others include Candlemas (February 2), May Eve or Beltane (April 30), August Eve or Lammas (August 1), and the lesser sabbats—the two solstices (June 22 and December 22) and the equinoxes (March 21 and September 21).

Most covens have both a basic initiation and higher initiations which are reserved for the coven leaders, priests, priestesses, and candidates for those positions.

Work within the coven is done within a magic circle drawn on the ground. Within the circle are placed the various magical items, often including the athame (ritual knife), chalice, and sword. Some covens worship "skyclad" (naked) but others use ritual robes, often bound with a colored cord similar to a cincture.

There is a belief in reincarnation and the power of spells. Spells may be cast for healing, for some positive result, or against someone else." [18]

With few exceptions, covens in both Britain and the United States date from the 1960s or later. Most are based on the writings of Gerald B. Gardner. Gardner was born in 1884, and spent most of his working adult life in Malaya. He retired, and returned to the UK in 1936. He joined the Folklore Society, and in June 1938, also joined the newly opened Rosicrucian Theatre at Christchurch where it is said he met Old Dorothy Clutterbuck whom, he claimed inducted him into practising coven of the Old Religion, that met in the New Forest area of Britain. [19]

In his own words

"I realised that I had stumbled upon something interesting; but I was half-initiated before the word, "Wica" which they used hit me like a thunderbolt, and I knew where I was, and that the Old Religion still existed. And so I found myself in the Circle, and there took the usual oath of secrecy, which bound me not to reveal certain things." [20]

During World War II, Gardner claimed to have participated in the efforts of British Witches, led by Dorothy Clutterbuck, to turn back Germany's invasion troops. Gardner was active in the Craft and published a fictional novel about medieval Witchcraft in 1949. He started a Museum of witchcraft on the Isle of Man after the 1951 repeal of the last anti-witchcraft law in England. Coming out publicly as a Witch in 1954, he published "Witchcraft Today". [22]

At that time, he believed the Craft was dying out-most of the members were older and few young members were being initiated. Gardner strongly believed not only in reincarnation, but that he would be reborn to the craft. If it died out, this could not be, and so he dedicated himself to reviving the Craft. Unable to directly reveal much of his coven's workings, he developed a system that was a synthesis of various elements from Masonic ritual, ceremonial magick, French Mediterranean Craft and the teachings of his coven. Gardner and later Doreen Valiente, re wrote some of the ritual, improving its poetic qualities and adding yet another dimension. As generations of Witches, they became the basis of Gardnerianism, and those who practised these rituals as handed down (not as published) became known as Gardnerians. He wrote of his witchcraft experiences and attempted to describe the practices, understandings, and prayers of the group. Later covens often used his work as a basis and came to be called collectively Gardnerian groups. A later charge was that, rather than presenting the practices of Wicca, he in effect created a religion out of bits and pieces from other groups. [23]

Other comtemporary occultists describe themselves as Neopagans:

"Neopagan groups differ primarily from witchcraft groups by their rejection of the designation of witch. They will also occasionally vary by their use of some term other than coven to designate groups (nest, grove, etc.) or by their adoption of a particular pre-Christian tradition (Druidic, Norse, Egyptian) from which to draw the inspiration and the symbols of their ritual life." [24]

The Alexandrian tradition of Wicca was established in the 1960s by Alex Sanders, and his wife Maxine. Originally he claimed to have been initiated by his grandmother when he was seven years old (reference, The King of the Witches by June Johns), but later admitted that this was untrue. In fact, he was initiated into a regular Gardnerian coven, by one of Patricia and Arnold Crowther's initiates, a lady by the name of Pat Kopanski. [25]

When Sanders began to publicise Wicca, he encountered strong opposition from more traditional members of the Craft. Some saw it as nothing more than a bid by Alex for personal notoriety; others that he was profaning a mystery. Whatever his motivation, the publicity certainly made people aware of his existence; he and Maxine initiated a great many people in the 1960s and 1970s, including Stewart Farrar and Janet Owen authors of. *What Witches Do* (1971) which remains the best guide to the way in which a typical Alexandrian coven operates. Rare, but perhaps still available in second hand shops, is a record of Janet's initiation, narrated by Stewart, called A Witch is Born, which also sheds some light on the traditional Alexandrian coven. [26]

It is, of course, hard to quantify just what makes the essential "Alexandrian Tradition", as covens vary considerably, even within the same culture. Generally though, Alexandrian covens focus strongly upon training, which includes areas more generally associated with ceremonial magic, such as Qabalah, Angelic Magic, and Enochian. The typical Alexandrian coven has a hierarchical structure, and generally meets weekly, or at least on Full Moons, New Moons and Festivals.

Most Alexandrian covens will allow non-initiates to attend circles, usually as a "neophyte", who undergoes basic training in circle craft, and completes a number of projects, prior to being accepted by the coven for initiation to 1st degree. Some, though not all, Alexandrian covens will also welcome non-initiated "guests" at certain meetings.

Alexandrian Wicca uses essentially the same tools and rituals as Gardnerian Wicca, though in some cases, the tools are used differently, and the rituals have been adapted. Another frequent change is to be found in the names of deities and guardians of the quarters. In some ways these differences are merely cosmetic, but in others, there are fundamental differences in philosophy.

That said, over the last thirty years, the two traditions have moved slowly towards each other, and the differences which marked lines of demarcation are slowly fading away. Individual covens certainly continue to maintain different styles and working practices, but it is possible to speak today of "Wicca" encompassing both traditions.

I have met and worked with witches from both traditions and have attended a number of rituals involving *"figures dressed in light coloured robes"* and I have to say that there is nothing that the un-named teenager described that leads me to believe that anything apart from a harmless wiccan ceremony was in progress.

There is also no evidence whatsoever that there is any occult link to the tragic murders of Tina Ellacott and Michael Brook. Two local men, Graham Gilliard and Stephen King were jailed for the killings, and Gilliard's wife was jailed for conspiracy to pervert the course of justice and conspiring to murder. Gilliard alleges that he was framed, but as in the case of the Juliet Rowe murder there is actually little doubt that the British justice system convicted the right malefactors. [28]

However, there do seem to be an inordinate number of murders on Woodbury Common.. As we have already seen several commentators have alluded to the depressing and strange *genius loci* of the area and it is perhaps significant that the defendants in an armed robbery case from the early 1980s claimed that they had been inspired to commit the crime after 'feeling weird' whilst on Woodbury Common. It was a spectacularly unsuccesful defence gambit, but another indication that Woodbury Common and the surrounding environs are some of the most peculiar places that one is ever likely to discover. (29)

There have also been a large number of suicides from Woodbury Common - nearly all of them from the car park at Four Firs near Woodbury Castle. According to an informant of ours who would like to remain anonymous, but who worked for many years, for a local firm of undertakers there were eight or nine suicides by exhaust fumes from this one car park alone and from another car park on the other side of the road (now closed down) two suicides by the extremely unpleasant method of self-immolation. This was, the way, the same car park where Tina Ellacott and Michael Brook were murdered. (30)

We should now discuss the most famous mystery to be associated with Woodbury Common. It is one about which I have been interested for a long time, because I have several personal links to it. It is also one about which an inordinate amount of rubbish has been written over the years, and this book is as good a place as any to try and put tome of the record straight!

As briefly alluded to by Mr Shutter, on Saturday afternoon, 19 August 1978, thirteen-year old Genette Louise Tate set out on her newspaper round from Barton Farm Cottage, her home in the village of Aylesbeare on the fringes of Woodbury Common. The paper round was never finished. Genette was last seen just before 3.30 p.m. Minutes later, her bicycle was found lying on its side in the country lane that she had been cycling along, with newspapers strewn all around it. Genette Tate is still missing and the events of that hot, afternoon remain shrouded in mystery.
(31)

I took an interest in the case for three reasons. The first reason is that one of the major suspects in the case was found guilty in 1981 for the brutal a savage murder of a teenage girl from Tiverton College. Her best friend was a girlfriend of mine for a while and I was, and to a certain extent still am, touched by the level of her grief. The second reason for me taking an interest in the case is that the sister of my oldest friend was Genette's best friend until her disappearance and the third reason is that for a short time I was actually a police-suspect in the case and, although I was soon eliminated from their enquiries, I have a vested interest in trying to find the true culprit.

When child-killer Robert Black was finally arrested and convicted of the Caroline Hogg and Susan Maxwell killings a few years ago I breathed an audible sigh of relief. Soon after the murders the police released an identikit photograph of the killer. The picture was a very good likeness of Black, who eventually was caught *in flagrante delecto* as it were, but also looked rather like I did at the time and during the summer of 1983 I was actually questioned on a number of occasions about my whereabouts at the time of the crimes. Black has also been questioned about the Genette Tate disappearance, and although he has always denied his involvement he remains, in many people's eyes at least, the prime suspect.
(32)

Eighteen years after Genette's disappearance, and (one must suppose) her death, Graham and I became involved with the case when,. under particularly peculiar circumstances we took part in a hunt for her grave.

I have a wide collection of strange acquaintainces with a wide variety of arcane powers and abilities. One of these is Phil Johnston; a bass player, a spiritual healer and a psychic detective. I have worked with him on a number of cases and in tests he has shown himself to be about 65% accurate as a psychic. One night as we were involved in a remote viewing exercise involving something completely different he mentioned, almost in passing, that he had a definite and very promising lead on the Genette Tate case. I was immediately interested and asked for more details. In 1996 was kind enough to give me a photocopy of the relevant pages from his `case book`, and I am quoting excerpts from them here with his permission:

"About a year ago I attempted to get to the bottom of this mystery. I had no preconceptions of what I might find, and expected to get no further than those psychics who had tried in the past. (....) While map dowsing a large area surrounding Ayelsbeare I kept on getting drawn to the same area again and again. Doubtful of my readings I turned the map face down and tried again in an attempt to confirm my findings. I pushed a drawing pin into the map at the appropriate place, turned it over and was amazed to find that it was marking the same location that I had been drawn to already.

I decided to go to bed. No sooner had I tucked myself in when an apparition of a man appeared in front of me. He was in his late thirties with blonde hair and he had a big smirk on his face. He was wearing a three piece suit, shirt, tie and shoes. They were all white, and he looked uncannily like Marty Hopkirk, the ghostly detective from the 1960's TV series 'Randall and Hopkirk (Deceased)'. I tried to question him but he was either unwilling or unable to answer me". [33]

Phil was convinced that this apparition was something to do with Genette Tate's disappearance. The vision returned later in the evening and he confonted it, accusing 'him' of being the murderer of the litle girl. Five weeks later he encountered the man 'in the flesh'.

Phil is a mobile mechanic. He was called to a repair job at a remote farm in the middle of Woodbury Common. It was very close to the spot in the woods that he had located on the Ordinance Survey map.

"As I was packing up, a pick up truck pulled up and out got a man. I looked at him in disbelief. We locked eyes and stared at each other in silence for what seemed like ages. He looked like the man whose 'spirit' had visited me in my bedroom, but aged about twenty years. We said nothing but I was convinced that he recognised me".. [34]

I was fascinated by this story. Not necessarily because it was true but because of Phil's obvious belief in its veracity. We decided to visit the woodland where, by now, Phil was convinced that Genette was buried. We drove there the following afternoon, and I watched in awe as Phil paced over the ground with a divining rod in each hand. There was an enormous reaction as he approached a spot between two small trees. We repeated the experiment, but this time Phil dangled a pendulum in front of him. Again it began to swing wildly - but only over the same spot; a spot about the same size as a child's grave. My dog Toby refused to go near the place and sat on his haunches, whimpering until we put him back in the car. It was the middle of winter and the ground was frozen so we resisted the temptation to dig and see if this was indeed the final resting place of the tragic girl.

The next day we went to the police who treated us with polite scepticism as we handed over our documents on the case together with our photographs and maps. They thanked us courteously but we got the impression that they didn't believe us and thought that we were just another bunch of well meaning nutters intent on gaining our little morsel of vicarious fame. Since then we have heard nothing, although the case has recently been in the news again with her father appealing for information at a well publicised press conference.

I have no idea whether she is buried there or not. As a concerned citizen, however, I am appalled that the Devon and Cornwall Police have not followed up every possible lead - no matter how unlikely it may seem - in an attempt to finally solve this mystery and set her grieving parent's minds at rest once and for all. Maybe now the story has appeared on the international stage they will finally be forced into doing something about it! [35]

This is neither the time nor the place to examine the veracity of psychic detective work. The important thing, as with so much of the material presented in this book, is not whether Phil (and others like him) actually *do* have the power to do what they claim and believe, but iyt is the belief system which is behind these claims. We would not be doing our job as researchers and (to a lesser extent) chroniclers of the high strangeness of the region were we to ignore these undeniably fascinating vignettes. [36]

The claims of Phil and other psychics are not the only ones that have been made surrounding the disappearance of Genette Tate.

Mystery Cat researcher Di Francis mentioned Gennette's disappearance in her book *The Beast of Exmoor* (1993):

"I broke through to the open hillside and looked down. My line of vision went precisely down to the two gates at the point in the lane where Genette's bicycle was found. Had I been a hunting big cat, I would almost certainly have left the wood at about that point and I would have looked directly across the open hillside to the field on the other side of the lane where sheep were grazing. If I was viewing the sheep as potential prey, then I would have run in a straight line down the slope, leapt over the gate at that exact point, crossed the lane in a single bound, sprung over the opposite gate and been in the field of sheep in seconds, once again hidden from the road.

I sat down on the grass and tried to visualise the scene two years previously. What if a hunting cat had been passing through and had stood on the hillside that afternoon, eyeing the sheep hungrily? What if it had decided to make an attack, had bounded down the hill towards the obvious crossing point, when suddenly an animal had appeared moving up the lane? Not a walking, upright human of the sort the cat had learnt to avoid, but an animal the size of a deer or a sheep, travelling on all fours, its head bent forward, its sloping back an inviting target? Yet not a sheep or a deer but a young girl, bent forward, riding her bike? A swift leap over the gate, a grab, a second leap over the opposite gate carrying its prey and away? No sound, no voices raised, no car, no body. Just a bicycle lying tumbled in the road, its wheels still spinning, papers scattered for her friends to find.

There is no way in which to prove that such an attack took place. Any physical evidence would have vanished long ago, rotted, removed by scavengers, or blown on the wind. Only the discovery of Genette's whereabouts, or the finding of her killer, could prove that it had not. But the hypothesis made sense of the known facts.

The area was ideal for an attack by a wild animal but it was not a likely spot for a human attacker to choose, especially overlooked by houses..........." [37]

As a character in one of Pete Loveday's wonderful *Big bang* comics once said,. "This ain't just bullshit, it's revolting bullshit! [38]"

There are, however, some undoubted quasi-fortean aspects to the case, and, whilst we refute most of the tasteless, hurtful and revolting nonsense that has been talked about her disappearance, we feel that we should make some reference. Much of the material printed here, has, we believe, never been presented in a fortean context before.

Writing a few years for an Orbis Publications part-work called *Unsolved*, Barry Smith listed the better known fortean aspects of the case:

"Was she spirited away?

The disappearance of a child is always the cue for eccentrics of every kind to offer their services. During the first few months of the Genette Tate inquiry, police received over 1400 leads from psychics alone. In an inquiry where there are next to no clues, the evidence of the occult detectives - UFO enthusiasts, diviners and mediums - is likely to gain the attention of parents and even of the police.

The newspaper that Genette was delivering when she vanished contained a front-page report of a local UFO sighting. The same evening, there was a temporary interruption in the electricity supply caused by a fire at the sub-station. And shortly afterwards some burn marks - probably due to a fertiliser - were discovered in a nearby field. Many people concluded that Genette had been spirited away in a UFO

This was the theory of one young man who visited the Tates in the November following Genette's disappearance. He claimed to be the descendent of a 5000-year-old eastern god and to have calculated that the Venusians who had taken Genette away would return her in the middle of the night on 4 or 5 November. Partly because it was conceivable that he genuinely knew where Genette was, and might have devised a bizarre means of returning her, John Tate joined him in an all-night vigil outside. The following night, the guru sat outside alone, holding Genette's teddy bear. The Tates never saw him again.

In the same month, a 'psychic research unit, moved in to Aylesbeare; mediums came and went. Police frogmen searched a three-mile (five-kilometre) stretch of the River Clyst following a lead from the famous Dutch medium Gerard Croiset. On another occasion, the police went hunting in the grounds of Castle Drogo following another paranormal lead..............." [39]

Whilst we would heartily scoff at any suggestions that the unfortunate girl was abucted by aliens, indeed for the most part at least, we heartily scoff at the Extra Terrestrial Hypothesis - at least the more sensationalist and ridiculous aspects of it, there is no doubt at all that her disappearance coincided with a wave of UFO activity over the Exe Estuary. Indeed the front page of the *Exeter Express and Echo* for the day that she disappeared did carry a UFO story, but the main gist of it was merely that one of their staff photographers had snapped a glowing light above Cathedral Close in Exeter on the previous night, we shall not quote it again here. [40]

What is undeniable, however is that her disappearance closely mirrors that of another little girl sixty years before almost to the day. The *Exmouth Journal* of Saturday August 25th 1917 reads:

"Exmouth Sensation: Little Girl's Mysterious Disappearance

A girl, 'Emily Bamsey`, aged 12, has disappeared from 1, Castle Cottages. Littleham where she was staying with her mother and Aunt. On Saturday morning last she left the house about 11.30 to go picking blackberries and from then up to the time of writing no trace has been found of her. She is an attractive well build girl, with full, fresh face, and dark brown curly hair hanging down her back. On leaving home she was dressed in a blue serge skirt and pink blouse, wearing black boots and stockings, and carrying a brown waterproof cape with hood. She had no hat, and was carrying in her hand an enamel cup. On her disappearance being made known, Sgt Fishleigh of Exmouth organised a search party of civilians and members of the Volunteer Corps, who searched until late that evening and again on Sunday.

The search was resumed on Monday morning but no trace has been found of the girl. The parents at one time lived at Exmouth and the mother and the daughter were on a visit to Littleham. The father is at present serving in the Navy. The girl was by no means a stranger top Littleham, she and, her parents being natives, Mother and daughter have made frequent visits to their relatives in the village. The girl was very bright and intelligent, with an excellent school record and knew the district quite well. The search made on Sunday was most thorough and systematic in every detail, for, in addition to the police and the many members of the Volunteer Corps, nearly all the villagers assisted in scouring almost every inch of the woods and fields in the neighbourhood, as well as the cliffs and the beach in the opposite direction to that in which the little girl was believed to have set out in. The gamekeepers, who knew the ground well, acted as guides all over the ground searched. The woods are not of any great extent and are in the most unlikely places in which anyone could be lost, at least, for so long a period as has elapsed.

The suggestion was made that it was too early in the season for blackberry gathering and that it was a mistake for the girl to have started out on such a quest. But, although early, several pounds of the fruit were gathered in the district last week. Various theories have been put forward to account for the girl's disappearance.

Had the girl gone in the direction of Budleigh Salterton and proceeded straight along the road, she would have reached the main road between Exmouth and Budleigh Salterton, near Knowle Hill. With that idea, search was made of the woods in the vicinity of Bystock and the common near Withycombe and Woodbury. These would be off the roads and lanes and are traversed by tracks, the following of which would puzzle any but those who know the common well. There are several claypits in the neighbourhood and these have been duly examined.

Diligent searches throughout the week have proved of no avail, and up to the time of writing yesterday, the police were without the slightest trace of the girl's present whereabouts". [42]

As far as we have been able to ascertain, neither Emily Bamsey nor her body have ever been found and her disappearance remains a mystery. The one thing that we would like to point out, before leaving this case, and indeed this entire subject, for the time being is that Emily Bamsey disappeared in the same location as Mrs Juliet Rowe was shot seven decades later. [43]

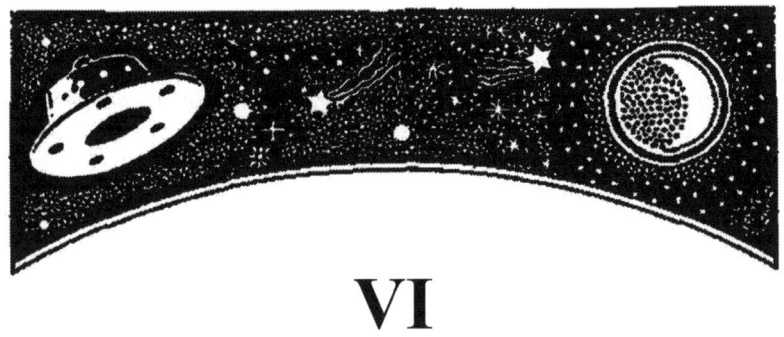

VI

A nineteenth century Devonshire folklorist, A.J.Davy submitted the following account of an ancient Devon legend to *The Transactions of the Devonshire Association* in 1899:

"THE MAN WHO MALTREATED A GHOST; OR THE LEGEND OF LITTLEHAM.

The following has been condensed from the pages of **The Western Miscellany** *for 1849 (a very scarce publication, which only lived twelve months), and makes one Captain Izaaks, of Exeter, the introducer of tobacco-smoking into Devonshire in 1550.*

"It is well known in all the country east of the River Exe that the ancient church of St. John's in the Wilderness, in the parish of Wythycombe Rawleigh, has been long deserted by the parishoners, from the crowds of spirits and bogies which frequent that desolate building and its adjoining cemetery. The inhabitants, in consequence, about a century ago, built the chapel where they now attend Divine service. All attempts to remove the ancient structure having failed for many years, they have long been discontinued. The dreadful disasters which befell all persons attempting demolition, at length deterred them from such sacrilege, so the grey old tower, with its venerable but humble shrine below, still braves the elements, unrepaired indeed by mortal hand, hut protected from decay by unseen artificers. About the end of the fifteenth century Sir Roger de Whalinglham held this manor of Wythycombe Rawleigh; the neighbouring estate of Littleham being in the possession of Sir Hugh de Creveldt, a knight of German extraction who used our language in common conversation with ease, but swore, and that very largely, in the German tongue.

These two gentlemen were neighbours, but not friends. Many things constantly transpired to place them in enmity with each other. Their tenants and dependants constantly encroached on each other's rightful district of raking for cockles and other shell-fish in the estuary of the Exe. Again, in the case of a wreck of a Genevese galliot, Sir Roger's men, who were first on the spot, secured a rich cargo of velvets for their master's use; while Sir Hugh had obtained little else than sixteen jars of caviar, which, as it displeased his palate,
had caused him to discharge his whole vocabulary of German invective on all around him. Many other things occurred year after year to add to their hatred, until at length Sir Hugh, in an altercation with his neighbour, was so heated with passion, as to speak that in plain English which he had often before cast against him in German, and to call him 'the foul fiend of ghosts and goblins,' 'the Wythycombe bogie feeder,' and many other dreadful appellations. This was indeed to wound his enemy to the quick. Even in these rougher times there was the delicacy not to insult the de Whalinghams with a calamity known to accrue to their family-that of a nightly visit from the inhabitant of the neighbouring churchyard, to demand the performance of seven musical requiems for their souls, in which the apparitions themselves would join. The mournful tunes were nightly borne down the gale to the valley of the Exe; and the village of Kenton, or Ken-tone, still retains a name derived from the inhabitants listening to the sound.

Sir Roger sank into the deepest gloom at this illiberal sarcasm of his enemy; his feelings were too deep for mild expressions of reproach. At length, eyeing his tormentor with a keen and cutting glance, he said, 'See to thyself, de Creveldt, that when my spirit leaves this body it visits thee not in the fair domain of Little ham ! It shall sit by thee in the hall ! It shall meet thee in thy walks! It shall draw the curtains of thy bed 'till thou shalt pray for the immortal minstrels of Wythycombe to sing their requiem to its disturbed and wandering nature.'

"*Years rolled on. The neighbours rarely met. A frown or a scowl alone marked any accidental rencontre, for no words ever passed between them while in this mortal state. It was on a wild and gloomy evening in December that Sir Hugh, sitting in a doze, at ten at night, after the fatigues of a day's otter hunting, heard three deep and distinct tolls from the church bell at Wythycombe Rawleigh, a mile and a half from Littleham. To hear the bell of St. John's in the Wilderness was nothing new, but it fell more deep and melancholy on his ear than ever before. Now, this bell of St. John's was a strange and mystical bell, as Sir Hugh knew. It had been taken to Italy, and there christened by the Pope himself; it* was the only bell in Europe, excepting the famous one in the Cathedral of Saragossa, which tolled the knell for the departing spirit without having been moved by mortal hand. For, as the far-famed bell of Arragon tolled out by its deep note, only once uttered, the death of a monarch of Spain, so the Wythycombe Minster informed the afrighted peasant that de Whalingham was no more; and hence the ancient rhyme-"The bells of Wythycombe they say spontanaeous tells the fatal day."

Sir Hugh in his doze had been dreaming of the promise of his neighbour when released from the flesh, and the bell had informed him that the release had taken place. A little recovered from his first surprise he listened, hoping to catch the sound of more strokes, for if the number exceeded three it might be tolled by human hands for some departed parishioner. But all was silent. He turned to throw himself into his chair, when, to his horror and dismay, he saw it occupied by his ancient foe, with a cap of rich Genoa velvet on his bead. Sir Hugh was too horrified to speak. No conversation passed, and after a visit of about an hour the spirit left him, vanishing with a slight musical sound, which a ghost utters at the compression necessary to pass through a key hole. For a month, three times in every twenty-four hours, the visits were repeated; for one hour in his walks, one hour in the night, and one at meals; and in this latter case only was the conduct of the ghost very oppressive and officiating, for it stood on such occasions always at his elbow. Whatever was put before the knight it instantly removed, and replaced it by a plate of caviar. In vain was the whole store of that delicacy drowned in the Exe; the ghost always had plenty at his command. A settled gloom hung over Littleham. The knight pined away in spite of his old huntsman's attempt to entice him with the otter hounds, or his daughter, the Lady Amabel, trying to soothe his sorrows with her lute.

"So matters continued until an Exeter trading vessel arrived from Cadiz (in 1550 it was) and anchored in the river. It was commanded by Captain Izaaks, who was well known to Sir Hugh. The knight told his tale of woe. The sailor meditated deeply, and at length exclaimed, 'I have it, Sir Knight, I have it! By St. Nicholas, I would smoke him out!' 'Smoke him out!' said the knight. 'Why, lhe himself is mere smoke, air, vapour, what you will.' 'So much the better,' quoth the captain, 'for the adage hath it that two of a trade can never agree.' The sailor then described the nature and properties of the American weed, which, for the first time, had been brought to Europe by some of the companions of Columbus and. of which he had brought a considerable sample, in his own vessel, from Cadiz. The plan was laid and settled, and no sooner had the apparition taken leave after its morning visitation than the captain proceeded, as he called it, to caulk the room, to close every hole and cranny for the double *purpose of confining the vapour and preventing the egress of the spirit. The door was left a little on the jar. The spectre entered as usual.*

The rich curlew pie was served for supper, but was instantly removed and the daily allowance of caviar substituted for it. Supper was removed, and the door closed, when the apparition discovered there was no avenue by which fresh air entered the room. (Spectres breathe only pure oxygen, without azote, while mortals are compelled to inhale the mixed elements.) Two tubes were produced, the Indian weed ignited, and the whole room was soon enveloped in a dense atmosphere. The spirit soon became invisible, but a rustling of velvets, accompanied by deep and unearthly sternutations and sneezes, were perceived. It was indeed an awful night, but Captain Izaaks persisted in smoking. At length a hollow groan was heard, and a voice succeeded it, 'If thou wilt once open the door, Sir Knight, I will haunt thee no more; destroy me thou canst not. The poisonous vapour may affect my aerial substance; it cannot annihilate me.' A parley ensued, by which Sir Hugh de Creveldt obtained remission from the sufferings he so long endured.

"So runs the story. It is further said that Sir Walter Raleigh, who came from a neighbouring village (which after the death of the last of the de Whalinghams became the property of his family), was so excited in his infancy by this story, that one of the first acts of his life was to bring a quantity of this weed from Virginia to England, and to him has consequently been attributed the first introduction of it amongst us." [1]

The places mentioned in the story still exist. *Wythycombe Rawleigh* is now known as Withycombe Raleigh and the Church of St. John's in the Wilderness not only still exists but still has a fearsome reputation amongst the local people.

It has a long and chequered history, as this account from 1948 testifies:

"ST. JOHN'S-IN-THE-WILDERNESS.

There is complete evidence that a church has stood on the same site from very early times, and was rebuilt in stone in the twelfth and fifteenth centuries. The present tower is all that remains of the fifteenth century building. It was a chapel under the jurisdiction of East Budleigh, but was undoubtedly used as a Parish Church by the Withycombe parishioners from the fifteenth to the seventeenth century

It seems that about 1114, when the inhabitants petitioned the Pope for a new chapel and burial ground, it was stated that :- "the chapel of St.

John the Baptist was a mile and a half from the parish church of All Saints, Boddeleyg, and a mile from the parish church of St. Andrew (Littleham) Furthermore, the flooding of the area is so bad in the winter that the dead cannot be borne to the said chapel for burial."

Many suggestions have been made as to the reason for its isolated position, and it would seem that the most likely is that offered by the late Miss Williams, who advances the theory that when William de Clavill founded his Manor House in Withycombe about 1254, he was unwilling to sacrifice valuable ploughing land for a church and churchyard, and so built it on the " waste land" higher up.

St. John's had a chequered history, for in 1788 it was stated to be in a very bad condition and but little used, and the Vicar of East Budleigh made an attempt to have it pulled down. A commission of inquiry was appointed and as a result demolition proceeded and only the Tower and North Aisle were left standing. The lead from the roof was sold and two of the three bells were disposed of to an Exeter ironmonger for £74 18s. 6d. The only remaining bell to-day bears the date " 1655."

The fine old church then remained derelict for many years and the tower was covered with a mass of ivy. There was a famous yew tree growing close to the church which, as far back as 1840, a visitor noted that "a yew tree growing close to the church takes fifteen paces to encompass." Meanwhile, efforts were being made to separate Withycombe from East Budleigh parish, and this was finally accomplished in 1850. In 1895 some attempt was made to raise funds to clean the tower of ivy, but the scheme was not carried out until 1910, when there were quite a few protests to the Vicar (the Rev. M.S. Shaw) against the removal of this "mark of antiquity."

In 1922, an appeal was launched by prominent Withycombe Church workers to restore all that remained of the, church, and regular Sunday services commenced there. As the congregation increased and additional accommodation was required, a further restoration scheme was commenced in 1926 and completed in 1937. Messrs. F. J. C. Hunter and Frank Cheesman were the leaders in the project. During the work, many interesting discoveries were made, providing valuable data for those interested. The Royal Arms, bearing the date " 1693," were placed in the church during the reign of William and Mary, and there are monuments in the church associating it with the two famous families of Drake and Raleigh, the former family being owners of the Bystock Estate until 1712.

A boss in the ceiling is one of the few church memorials in the country, to the short reign of the uncrowned king, Edward VIII, during which, this part of the restoration was carried out. There are many people of distinction buried in the churchyard, the only one displaying Arms on the tomb, however, is that of Count de Vismes, whose interesting family history is dealt with in detail in the Memorials of Withycombe mentioned above. Francis Danby, the painter, is also buried at St. John's. On July 18th, 1421, Bishop Lacey gave a license to Sir John Tryvet, Vicar of East Budleigh, to have service in the Chapel of St. Michael's Church (Withycombe Village), St. James's (Dalditch) and St. Margaret's (Exmouth). St Margaret's Chapel was right on the Parish Boundary, and Messrs. Webber's butcher's shop on the corner of Margaret Street and Chapel Street, is to-day probably the oldest house in Exmouth, and as such it should be carefully ~estored and preserved. In the front wall is the holy water stoup of St. Margaret's.

In 1724 Polwhele states that St. Margaret's was converted into a dwelling house. St. Michael's at Withycombe was rebuilt in 1722, chiefly at the expense of Sir John Colleton, of Rill, who was a great benefactor of the Parish and of whom mention has previously been made in this volume. He was buried at St. Michael's in 1754, and the memorial stone with his Coat of Arms can still be seen." [2]

Nigel`s first wife used to claim that no local resident would go near the church on All Hallow`s Eve. This is because of a widespread local belief that this was the night when the dead would rise from their graves in the churchyard. [3][4] Other local residents have confirmed this story, but unfortunately for the "X Factor" of this book, we have no reports of anyone actually encountering the spirits of their ancestors on the night of Samhain. [5]

Probably the most famous series of hauntings that have been reported from Littleham are those which took place over about a century in a house in Bicton Street. Like so much in forteana, the story is muddled and even the true name of one of the principal characters/victims is unclear. Theo Brown, the doyenne of Devonshire folklore for so many years, named him as Fontelautus Dennis, [6] making quite a `meal` of the fact that he had such a peculiar name. Peter Underwood, veteran ghost hunter and President of The Ghost Club namkes him as Dennis Fontelautus (a somewhat more believable appelation), and it is his account that is quoted here in full:

"According to S. Baring-Gould's Devonshire Characters and Strange Events (1908) and Devon and Cornwall Notes and Queries (1956-8) there is a house in Bicton Street that is said to have been haunted for

over a 100 years. The curious genesis of the haunting is generally regarded as having been the appearance of what seems to have been a headless child. This frightening apparition is said to have been seen by the cook of the family resident at Belmont House at the time, a family named Fontelautus. The cook maintained to her dying day that she was sitting quietly in the kitchen one morning in May, 1826, when the silent form entered through the open door and disappeared into the pantry.

Less than a month later, on 1 June, little Dennis Fontelautus, the younger son of the family, died before reaching the age of two. An autopsy was performed, during the course of which it was necessary to decapitate the body, and the conclusion was that little Dennis had died of water on the brain following a fall. The little body lay in its coffin in the attic for three days before the funeral and during those days and nights the pleading voice of the dead little boy was heard by the child's nursemaid, his mother and his sister Maria, apparently emanating from the attic. After the funeral the voice was still heard and Maria also saw her brother's little hand stretching out, pleadingly, from the window of the attic when she was outside the house.

In spite of the decapitation taking place during the course of the autopsy, the family, worried by what they had seen and heard, became convinced that the boy was still alive and, in fact, after the body had been buried it was subsequently exhumed and re-buried in the garden. Mr Fontelautus, a vicar, according to Sabine Baring-Gould, writing on the case in 1908, maintained that the events were due to 'demoniacal activity'. Be that as it may the house is said to have been haunted for many, many years afterwards. In 1986, I spent several hours making enquiries and looking for Belmont House, Bicton Street, but it has either been re-named or the information I have is incorrect." [7]

Many of the residents who live along the side of the disused railway line which runs through the middle of Littleham housing estate have claimed to have heard the steady mechanical thudding of what they believe is a phantom railway train. The line has been disused since the predations of Beeching in 1963 and ran between Exmouth station and Budleigh Salterton. This sound is always heard in the middle of the night, and lasts for several minutes. [8]

One Littleham resident whom Nigel questioned told him that she believed that it was the sounds of the Devil`s footsteps. [9]

As Nigel points out, it is interesting that these should be reported in one of the same locations as the 1851 "Great Devon Mystery", but he wonders whether this is a genuine piece of local folk belief or just the individual witnesses interpretation of events. Nigel's wife, who is Littleham born and bred heard it on several occasions as a child and was always told that this was a ghostly railway train. Interestingly enough this would have been around about the time that the line was destroyed, suggesting that the legend is older than one would otherwise expect and almost certainly has little or nothing to do with Dr Beeching's economic restructuring of the British railway system. [10]

The concept of the ghostly train is a common one in literature but it is surprising how few actual accounts there are of what appear to be genuine ghostly railway trains. One interesting one that sounds surprisingly similar to the Littleham ghostly railway was described by a teenage boy from Sweden:

"This thing happened about 3-4 years ago when I was 12. I had my room on the first floor (now I have it in the basement). One night, it was 11.45pm exactly (I remember that) and I was half-awake. I looked at the clock to see what the time was. The clock was standing on my table in the front of my window. Exactly when the clock showed 11.45pm I heard a train coming (we are living in a big valley with lots off houses, and the nearest railway is about 1-2 miles away).

I froze and couldn't move with fear as I heard the train coming closer. Suddenly I heard the train on the little road which you could see from my window, I turned my head slowly to the window and through the curtains I saw some kind of strange light which disappeared with the train sound. It faded away like it came. I was so frightened that I didn't move or say anything until 00.35am (exactly). Well I didn't say anything then either, I screamed!!.

The next morning I thought about what happened to me and then I realized that it was not a modern train. It was the sound of an old train (maybe a steam train - such as you would see in one of the old Western movies). I told my parents about the train and they did not believe me, my mother said that I just heard a train on the railway 1 mile away. So I looked at the timetable for the train in my town. The last train that went through the station was at 10.40pm.

I never heard the train again. And I really want to know what sort of train this was, I would like to contact other people with the same experience." [11]

Local folklorist Roy Richardson, whom we have already met, has a sadly prosaic explanation for the Littleham Ghost Train, however, and believes that the vibrations are due to the sound of a local water pumping station. [12]

Nigel, however, who lives adjacent to the aforementioned water pumping station has questioned this interpretation of events as he has never heard either water pumping noises or a ghost railway and, because of his small children, he is often awake for the greater part of the night and would therefore have been in a perfect situation to hear anything should it have occured. [13]

Meanwhile, local residents are still reporting the strange noises to him on a regular basis.

The next story was given to us by Roy Richardson and is told in his own words:

"It was some two years ago and whilst I was out shopping within Exmouth, that having entered 'Fads' wallpaper shop in Rolle Street, I was soon in conversation with a young female assistant concerning decorating materials for my home.

How it came about I do not know, but we ended up in serious conversation with regard to the history of the town, to which ghosts and hauntings were soon to be the topic of our conversation. At this, the young lady seemed to leap into conversation with regard to a story that concerned her sister.

She gave the fullest of details to me concerning a ghost, haunting the house in which her sister lives with her children, the family home being situated in Dinan Way in Exmouth.

As she entered into conversation, she described a number of incidents that took place at the above address, one being that of a glass spinning round on its own on a table top, then moving to the edge before throwing itself onto the floor and smashing. In conversation with her I asked if their were any witnesses to this incident, to which she replied seriously, stating that it happened one evening when both herself and boyfriend were visiting her sister.

She went on to state that the children had also encountered sightings, one in particular being that of a ghost of a monk, who for some reason appeared from behind the television set in the lounge. At that time I began to feel somewhat apprehensive, thus asking did any other person or persons witnessed this, to which she replied instantly, 'Oh yes, and my sister used her camera to take a photograph of the apparition'.

Thinking that she would then become vague in her statement, I asked her if the photograph was still available. In all honesty I thought the reply would have drifted into the usual excuse of either the picture has been mislaid or lost, or even that when the picture was taken there was no film in the camera. However this was not to be so.

I was amazed and delighted to learn that in fact her sister still had the photograph, so I asked her if she could borrow the item from her sister for me to see and, that I would call back to the shop to view it. But I was told to call at her sister's house anytime and her sister would be more than happy to let me see the relevant photograph.

Therefore I left it some four weeks and, without any appointment or any communication with either the young girl or her sister I called on spec, as it were, to the house. On my arrival I explained my interest in a photograph that her sister at 'Fads' had told me about.

Immediately I was made most welcome and asked to enter the house, where I was greeted by her children, who, when questioned separately and more importantly did not know that I would be calling, told the very same story about the monk appearing from behind the television, then on request I was given the actual photograph to hold and view.

Before I glanced down at the picture, I expected to see something that could not be clearly identifiable, but was greatly impressed to see a clearly identified face in the vicinity of the television screen, and yes, I have to admit it did without any doubt resemble that of a hooded monk.

The photograph matched the location of the television set and surrounding decor, so it had been taken in the same lounge of the above stated property. It was whilst the mother was making me a cup of tea, that I got up from my seat and went over to the television set, to examine the surrounding area to which I put out my hand and arm to feel the atmosphere. As my hand passed to the rear of the television set, I gained a tingling feeling of my fingers and skin and there was to me a different temperature much colder than the rest of the lounge. I would have expected completely the opposite really, as the television was switched on and had been for some two hours before I called at the house.

I felt the television set, especially the back panel, which was quite warm due to the length of time it had been in operation and built up generated radiation, so why should the area that I investigated be the coolest part of the room, more so, why did my arm and hand immediately gain that of a tingling sensation?

Due to my research, I feel that something is evident, but nothing could possibly have been planned in the circumstances. as the family did not know of my identity, or that I was calling to see them on the day in question. The tenant of the property did not in any way appear to show signs of making up or inventing such a story, she was very open in her conversation.

She made a concluding statement, that she had approached the Press before about the monk, but there seemed to be a lack of belief as to the story she told, to which she told me she did not care if the press did not believe her, as she had the photograph to prove her story and, that is all that mattered to her, she knew she was not imagining the situation neither were her children.

To this very day the whole story remains a complete mystery." [15]

Roy Richardson also investigated a number of reports of poltergeist activity in Littleham. The first account is particularly interesting because it involved reports of a ghostly cat being seen at the same time as the normal accounts of strange noises and mysteriously moving objects. This cat was seen on a number of occasions "walking along the ceiling" of the front room. The lady who called Roy in to investigate these occurences was having marital difficulties at the time, and she blamed them on the *genius loci* of the house. She said that it had always had a "weird atmosphere".

Even Nigel has reported what appears to be poltergeist activity in his flat. When he, his wife and children, and all the household pets are in one room, strange sounds are heard from other rooms in the house, and a nuimber of objects have been moved apparently of their own volition.

Another series of reports from a house in Nelson Drive reportedly involved another dysfunctional family whose children reported being "lifted" out of their beds at night in a scenario very reminiscent of the most famous British poltergeist episodes from Enfield, Middlesex in 1977.

"In late August of 1977, Mrs Peggy Harper, a divorcee in her mid-forties, had put two of her four children to bed. They were living in a semi-detached council house in Enfield, North London, that had three

bedrooms. Late at night, Janet, aged eleven and her brother Pete, aged ten, complained that their beds were "jolting up and down and going all funny". As soon as Mrs Harper got to the room the movements had stopped - as far as she was concerned her kids were making it all up.

The following night at 9.30 pm, Peggy was called to Janet and Pete's room when they complained something was making a shuffling noise. Janet said it sounded like one of the chairs moving, so Peggy took the chair out of the bedroom to put their minds at ease. Saying goodnight to the children once more and turning off the light, she too heard the shuffling noise. As though somebody was "shuffling across the floor in their slippers". She turned the light on to see the furniture as normal and the children under their covers. Turning the lights off again, the noise started once more.

They then heard four loud knocks on the partitioning wall of the house and Mrs Harper was astonished to see a heavy chest of drawers moving about 18 inches across the floor, well beyond the children's reach. As soon as it stopped, Mrs Harper pushed it back against the wall, but as she turned her back, it moved once more to its former position. This time she found it impossible to move. Mrs Harper recalls shaking with fear, yelling at the children to get out of their beds and to go downstairs - she was convinced that something unexplainable was going on. Seeing that their neighbour's lights were on, the Harpers, still in their night clothes, ran next door for help.

The neighbours searched the house and garden but found no one. Soon they also heard the knocks on the walls which continued at spaced out intervals. At 11pm they called the police, who heard the knocks, one officer even saw a chair inexplicably move across the floor and later signed a written statement to confirm the events.

The following day, the events continued with small plastic bricks and marbles being hurled around house - when picked up, they were found to be hot. This 'attack' continued for three days by which time they sought help again, not only from the police, but a local vicar and local medium. But no-one seemed to be able to stop the escalation of events. The Harpers eventually turned to the press and the Daily Mirror sent out a reporter, Douglas Bence, with a photographer, Graham Morris, who stayed in the house for several hours. Nothing happened and the reporters decided to leave - they were almost in their car when the 'flying bricks' promptly resumed. They were called back and a toy lego brick flew across the room hitting the photographer on the forehead as he attempted to take a picture. Later, as the photographer developed his negative he noticed that it had an inexplicable hole in it and that the flying *brick could not be seen. Senior reporter at the* Daily Mail, *George Fallows, was so impressed by his colleagues experience that he followed up the story himself. He suggested that the Harpers call in the SPR (Society for Psychical Research) which in turn contacted Maurice Grosse, a member and resident of North London.*

Grosse arrived at the Harpers on September 5th, a week after the disturbances had begun. For the next few days nothing out of the ordinary occurred. Then, on September 8th, whilst Grosse and a journalists from the Daily Mirror *were keeping vigil, between 10 pm and 11 pm, they heard a crash in Janet's bedroom. They discovered that her bedside chair had been thrown about four feet across the room where it was lying on it's side. Janet was asleep at the time and no one saw the chair move. But when it happened an hour later, the photographer Morris was ready and captured the event on film.*

Grosse claims that then he experienced the strange happenings - first a marble was thrown at him from an unseen hand, he saw doors open and close by themselves, and claimed to feel a sudden breeze that seemed to move up from his feet to his head.

On 10th September, the Enfield case made the front page of the Daily Mirror, then the story was picked up by LBC radio (a London based station) and that evening, Grosse, Mrs Harper and her neighbour took part in a two and a half hour NIGHT LINE programme.

The phenomena continued - there was interference with electrical systems in the house, electrical faults and mechanical equipment failure, as soon as camera flashes were recharged they were quickly drained of power, an infra red sensitive television camera was brought in to do remote monitoring of the bedroom, but as soon as it began filming the tape would. The same thing happening to the BBC Radio reporters tapes when tape cassettes were found to be damaged, often the recordings erased, the metal inside some of the machines would be found bent, and even some of the tape decks would disappear reappearing several hours later.

Grosse was soon joined in his investigation by writer Guy Lyon Playfair and the two men spent the next two years studying the case until it finally ceased.

The knocking on walls and floors became an almost nightly occurrence, furniture slid across the floor and was thrown down the stairs, drawers were wrenched out of dressing tables. Toys and other objects would fly across the room, bedclothes would be pulled off, water was found in mysterious puddles on the floors, there were outbreaks of fire followed by their inexplicable extinguishing, curtains blowing and twisting in the wind when all windows and doors were closed, even accounts of human levitation - Janet claimed to have been picked up and flung about her room by an unseen entity (witnessed by neighbours passing by and looking up into the girls' bedroom). Both girls claimed that they were being pulled out of their beds by an invisible force and Janet claimed that the curtain beside her bed twisted several times in a tight spiral and attempted to wrap itself around her neck trying to strangle her. This was backed up by her mother who had witnessed this more than once...." [16] [17]

Poltergeists (from the German, "noisy ghosts") usually manifest as strange electrical effects and unexplained movement of objects. At one time, these phenomena were thought to be due to ghosts, but after decades of investigations by researchers, notably by William G. Roll, the evidence now suggests that poltergeists are PK effects produced by one or more individuals, usually troubled adolescents. The term "RSPK," meaning "Recurrent Spontaneous PK," was coined to describe this concept. Parapsychologists A. Gauld & A. D. Cornell collated recorded information about poltergeist activity from 1800 up until the late 1970s. They identified 63 different characteristics regarding poltergeists in which 64% were associated with the movement of objects. [18]

It seems certain that whatever poltergeists are, they are NOT the spirits of the dead, or even ghosts *per se*. I explored the connection between poltergeist activity and traumas associated with adolescent girls in *The Owlman and Others* (1997,8), and I also noted a number of poltergeist and quasi-poltergeist episodes that I have been involved in. [19] However, whilst researching material for this book I came across a radical new theory which, in many ways has overturned my preconceptions of this type of parapsychological activity.

Albert Budden, B.Ed., is an investigator specialising in the scientific study of the paranormal as well as electromagnetics and health and he has extrapolated an electromagnetic cause for the `noisy ghosts` and whilst not rejecting the causative link between emotionally disturbed adolescents and poltergeist activity he has gone a long way towards indicating the method by which these manifestations seem to operate. He has shown how a long list of the most commonly reported symptoms of poltergeist activity can be explained by using electromagnetic terms of reference rather than phenomenological ones:

"1. Light bulbs constantly 'pop'.

A power surge will supply power to a circuit through the atmosphere and through the glass of a bulb, subjecting the tungsten filament to increased levels of electricity. These repeated 'boosts' to a filament will create a small movement each time, especially when the filament is hot and more flexible when the bulb is on. It will not be long before this repeated movement induces metal fatigue, and soon, when the light is switched on, the filament will break with that familiar 'ping'.

2. The video machine malfunctions on some occasions but works on others.

A magnetic field can affect the electronic circuitry, causing it to malfunction by inducing what are known as magnetostrictive effects. That is to say, a magnetic field will cause the microscopic ferrite components to deform so that critical contacts are lost&emdashin turn, inducing the circuitry to fail. When the field drops, the ferrite components resume their normal dimensions, contacts are regained and the circuitry functions normally.

3. Loud snapping 'clicks' and heavy, plodding footsteps are heard.

When iron or steel is magnetised by a field which then abruptly drops, an auditory sound wave is produced by a mechanism called magnetostrictive acoustics, also known as the Page Effect. Deep-sounding 'thuds' or high-pitched 'cracks' will be heard depending on the thickness and length of the metal and how it is held in place in a building. For example, thick metal girders embedded along a floor will produce a series of progressive 'thuds' as the field moves along them, giving the impression of footsteps, whereas a thin iron conduit carrying wiring embedded in a wall will produce a sharp 'snap'.

So far, these phenomena can be understood by identifying them in the Jandbook of Magnetic Phenomena *by Harry E. Burke.1 The fires inside matchboxes which are inside drawers could certainly be ignited by the thermal effects of microwaves, and I have personally seen flash-bulbs blown at a distance by the diathermy effect induced by a microwave field. The chiming doorbells could easily be induced by power surges activating the circuitry, just as car alarms can be set off in this way. One would not have thought that taps could be turned by magnetic fields because of the levels of mechanical force needed, but it was pointed out to me that a whole range of seemingly mysterious events, including doors locking, windows flying open and taps turning, can be typical indicators of immi-*

nent Earth tremors. Such reports are collected by seismologists and are known as "diagnostics". These revelations have shown me that not everything can be understood from a commonsense, everyday logic point of view and that 'hidden knowledge' can be found through a disciplined tradition of repeated mental exercises, commonly known as education!

However, as we work our way down the list of 'poltergeist' phenomena, it becomes clear that there is a point where the laws of physics cannot help us and we venture into the realms of the unknown, the unclassified and the purely experimental. How do objects, some of them quite heavy, levitate when they are not made of iron or have any iron content? (The heavy table must have moved for it to have overturned.) How does stone and/or concrete shatter and/or catch fire? How does mirror-glass crack? And how did electromagnetic fields make my coffee turn into a miniwhirlpool before my eyes? I had a problem. I knew that poltergeist activity took place in electromagnetic hot-spots, but what were the physical mechanisms involved in generating these effects?"* [20]

Budden then cites the experimental work of Canadian electromagnetics expert John Hutchison, the electromagnetics pioneer who has, according to Budden, at least, made discoveries which show that poltergeist activity is electromagnetic in nature. Whilst not prepared to be quite as enthusiastic as Budden, we must admit to being impressed by his accounts of Hutchison's findings:

"Basically, what Hutchison did was cram into a single room a variety of devices which emit electromagnetic fields (such as Tesla coils, van de Graaff generators, RF transmitters, signal generators, etc.). He found that after they had been running for a while, effects began to occur that were identical to what have come to be regarded as poltergeist phenomena. Objects of any material levitated into the air and hovered there, or moved about and then fell; fires started in unlikely places around the building; a mirror smashed at a distance of 80 feet away; metal distorted and broke; water spontaneously swirled in containers; lights appeared in the air and then vanished; metal became white-hot but did not burn any surrounding materials; and so on.

Everything that psychical researchers have been documenting for decades as poltergeist activity, that priests have been called in to exorcise eventually turned up in the laboratory where John Hutchison's device operated. Although it was made up of different parts, it operated as a single entity, and phenomena occurred in the same unpredictable way as reported poltergeists: you could be there for days and nothing would happen, then suddenly coins would flip and fly, water would swirl and a transformer would blow. And this brings me to an unfortunate aspect of the device: it has a tendency to destroy itself. It is worth recalling at this point that psychical researchers have in fact dubbed poltergeist activity as "destructive haunting". "[19]

Two other accounts of weirdness from Littleham are in this report that Nigel submitted to the Exeter Strange Phenomena Research Group:

"For a small part of Great Britain, Littleham has more than its fair share of ghosts and strange tales! From children's tales of orchards where no one could roam, without fear of never being seen again, right up to terrifying rumours of old ladies roaming churchyards, abducting children, who disappear without a trace!. These yarns and tales have been, no doubt, embellished as the years have gone on. The main thing that interests me is where is the beginning of these quite frankly, disturbing stories.

I had heard these, to begin with, from my wife, Sue. She is a local girl, having been born and raised in the village itself. When I asked her where she had heard these stories, she replied that she had just been told these years ago. Obviously, these tales were very old, so I decided to try and track down the roots of these weird and frightening legends. To my surprise, there were no real events that I can quote to account for their existence. No matter how much I dug into the written history of the village, could I find any real event that had any tie-in to these tales? NO! So, what does all this mean? Is it just a case of children trying to frighten their friends with tales of old witches and strange enclosed plots of lands, where children may not enter, for fear of disappearing of the face of this planet. I don't think so! I think it far more likely that these tales have their roots far back in the mists of time. As for the case of the orchard where children may not enter, I feel that this one was a case of a previous owner, who, having a valuable crop of apples, or whatever, started a rumour of disappearing children, to scare and prevent lads and lasses from entering his property! He would,no doubt, be very pleased to discover that his plan had been so successful, that even today, many years later, children are still scared to enter his land.

Now to the case of the lady in the churchyard. This is a far more interesting one. If one enters any churchyard in this, or any other country, one will find elderly ladies tendering the graves of their dearly departed. It is not, for my mind, inconceivable that a lady had, many years ago, perhaps chased some youngsters out of this churchyard, for whatever reason. Over the space of time, this story has become the frightening tale of the weird lady, who makes kids disappear. How we English love our frightening stories........ ". [21]

It is interesting to note that although there *are* a number of Ghost Stories from other parts of the Exmouth area apart from Littleham, on the whole these are of much more recent provenance than many of the ones reported from Littleham itself, and indeed a number of them are directly connected with the great change in the social infrastructure of the area, which as noted in a previous chapter, happened when Exmouth changed from being an obscure fishing village to being a fashionable seaside resort. [22]

One of the earliest, and indeed the most famous inhabitants of Exmouth was Lady Nelson, the estranged wife of Britain's most renowned naval hero. When she separated from Admiral, Lord Nelson in 1801, her estranged husband gave her the sum of £1,200 a year to live on and she moved to Exmouth.

She died, and was buried in Littleham churchyard in 1831.

"........The inscription on the tomb is

Underneath are deposited the remains of
Frances Herbert Viscountess Nelson, Duchesse of Bronte,
who departed this life
on the 6th May 1831 aged 73 years.
And also, Her Son, Josiah Nesbit on the 14th July 1830
aged 50 years.
And also 4 of his children, Horatio Woollward, Herbert Josiah,
Sarah and Josiah, all of whoin died young.

Inside the church is a very fine tablet by P. Turnerelli, the famous sculptor, in memory of Lady Nelson and the Nesbits.

Josiah Nesbit was a captain in the Royal Navy and son of Lady Nelson by her first marriage. When she came to Exmouth to live, he accompanied her. Captain Nesbit and his children died in Paris and were buried there, but Lady Nelson had the bodies exhumed and employed a French vessel to bring them to Exmouth. The ship arrived at the Temple Steps earlier than expected, consequently no preparation had been made to receive the bodies. The Custom House officer rose to the occasion, however, and had them removed to the house of a Mr. Edmund Webber, then being built but not completed, on the sea-front where Alston Terrace now joins it. The bodies were re-interred in Littleham churchyard.

This house where the bodies were temporarily placed, was by reason of its circular shape to be called Beach Castle, but after this incident was known as Corpse Castle and of course, reputed thereafter to be haunted. The superstition must have been very real, for even when the house was completed nobody ever lived there.

As the building deteriorated and became the happy hunting ground of all the cats in the neighbourhood, its name, far from being sinister, was succeeded by the humorous one of Cats' Castle." [23]

Two final episodes, which whilst not being hauntings *per se* most definitely contributed to the reputation of Littleham as a whole are recounted in a 1948 book:

"An amusing episode happened at Littleham graveyard in which "Tally Jack," so named because he was an Italian, was concerned~elsewhere in this volume he is referred to in connection with the Ropewalk. On one occasion at the First and Last Inn somebody wagered Jack a quart of cider (price twopence), that he would not go to Littleham and lie in an open grave.

He immediately accepted the wager, and off he went, followed by those who had overheard the conversation. Arriving at Littleham, there was a partly dug grave into which without any hesitation whatsoever Jack jumped and promptly laid down. The man who had laid the wager immediately began to fill in the earth, and mid roars of laughter from the bystanders "Tally Jack "jumped out as quickly as he had jumped in, and chased the practical joker all the way back to Exmouth.

The older inhabitants of Littleham still laugh over a similar incident concerning Jack Franks, who literally saw "a spirit rise from the grave. It was his habit to walk across the churchyard on his way to work, and early one morning his gay whistle was cut short, for to his horror the head and shoulders of a man popped out of a newly dug grave asking "What's the time, Jack?" Poor Jack dropped his lunch basket and took to his heels, without so much as a backward glance. It was only on his return home that night that he learnt that a local character, Lionel Bradford, left The Plough late the night before and took a short cut home through the churchyard. He had been imbibing refreshment well but not wisely, and so failed to see the partially dug grave before he fell into it. It was some five feet deep, and unable to clamber out of it he made the best of things and curled up for the night. Jack must have woken him up with his whistle." [24]

Is seems clear that for some reason, the ghostly population of Exmouth seems to be mostly situated in Littleham and the surrounding regions. A pattern is beginning to emerge, and we shall be returning to it in order to study the matter in greater depth in the concluding chapters of this book..

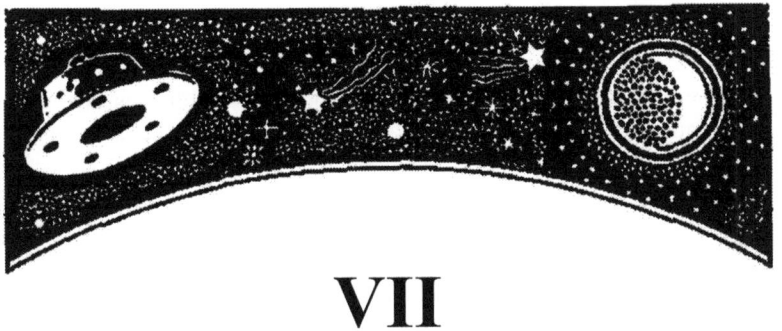

VII

At the same time as the plethora of UFO reports that took up most of our time during the long, hot summer of 1997, we also received a number of reports of strange animals in the area. In our capacity as the Centre for Fortean Zoology, this is not unusual. On average, we receive three or four reports of sightings of mystery cats and other anomalous beasties from various parts of the English countryside each week, but these reports were different from the norm. This is not just because they appeared at the same time as the UFO activity, but because on one occasion at least they happened to the same people.

Stuart is a young teacher who lives in a mobile home facing onto a field on the outskirts of Exmouth at Higher Hallam Road. His mobile home is situated on a smallholding owned by his landlady, a genial woman in middle age. One morning in May 1997 he looked out of his window to see a disturbance. The field contained a flock of sheep which, as he watched, all started to look down the field. Suddenly he saw a large, cat like creature about the length of Alsatian (German shepherd) but with much longer legs crossing the end of the field. [1]

I asked him how far away he was from this animal and he gestured vaguely to me and estimated that it was about the length of a football pitch. He described the animal as having an upswept tail, longer than half the length of the body. He said that it was black in colour and had a small head with pointed ears. *"I noticed that in particular because it seemed to have the body of a puma and the head of a lynx"*, he told me when I eventually met him about six weeks after the sighting. He told me in a calm and considered voice how he had watched it for over two minutes.

"It came out of the hedge, scared the sheep, scared me. I didn't even think of going in to get my camera and said `Wow`. It then went back

through the hedge into another field below".

So far this appears to be a normal sighting of an alien big cat, but three days later whilst Stuart was in Bristol, one of his landlady's dogs was apparently attacked by the animal late one night. It had what appeared to be claw marks on its belly.

The vet told the landlady that these marks looked like those which would have been made by the predations of a big cat and that there had been more cases brought in to the surgery.

This is highly unlikely because as I have noted in *Mystery Animals of the Westcountry* (1999) [2][3][4] and elsewhere, both pumas and leopards are particularly partial to the flesh of domestic cats and furthermore a domestic cat unlucky enough to have encountered one of their larger 'cousins' would be highly unlikely to have survived the experience. When I visited Stuart at his home, I examined the cat in question, and it did indeed have a peculiar ridge of scar tissue along the underside of its neck. This pattern of wounding is one that I have never come across before, and furthermore, is one that if, as the vet claimed, has been repeated on a number of occasions, is definitely deserving of further attention.

These encounters are neither the only ones from the district, nor the only ones that had happened to Stuart or his landlady. Further down the road, almost down at the bottom of the field where Stuart saw the big cat lives an old gentleman who has, apparently seen them on a number of occasions. [5]

Two years ago, however, Stuart was lying in bed and heard the hedge rustling behind the caravan. He told me that the next moment, *"I could hear the dogs in the house going mad the way they do if they see someone they know walking past or if someone pulls up in a car".* He then thought *"That's weird, It can't be the dogs .... it pushed itself under my caravan and I could feel it push up the chipboard floor of my caravan so hard that I could feel it moving my bed. My landlady then let her dogs out and I could hear them chasing something which pushed past my caravan and back through the hedge again. My landlady said that she saw 'something with a swept up tail' run from the top garden up towards my caravan".* [6]

I telephoned his landlady who has, since we originally investigated these events become seriously 'spooked' and has refused either to be identified or to have anything further to do with us or our investigation. She told me of another occasion that summer in which one of her animals was attacked by a mysterious creature.

"It was about 11.00 at night. I let my four dogs out to have a `wee` as usual, and of course I went out into the garden with them. The two younger ones went up to the top of the garden and disappeared. Suddenly I heard the most dreadful noise, which was more of a squeal than anything else, and the dog came running in"... [7]

The noise was so loud that people living on the other side of the field could hear it. The next morning she went out and saw signs of a struggle but no hair, fur or footprints. [8]

I examined the dog and found the scar tissue from what appeared to be three claw marks underneath the body running from the back of the animal's legs to its tummy, and what appeared to be three bite marks on its belly. She told us of other sightings that had been experienced by members of her household... [9]

"At the beginning of June a young couple who were staying with me were walking home at about 2 a.m. when they saw what they swore was a lynx crossing the drive in front of them" [10]

and then finally, as she summoned up enough courage, she told me of her own encounter with the creature...

"I've only seen it clearly once. About two years ago it was coming out every night. I saw it coming out from behind the caravan. It had a big bushy tail coming up over its back and it was about three foot long not counting tail, and about 18 inches to two feet high. The tail was longer than half the length of the body. It was dark coloured, but I couldn't tell you any markings because it was the middle of the night. It had a surprisingly small head in comparison with rest of the body, but I couldn't see the shape of its ears" [11]

Sufficient to say that whereas the descriptions given to me by the other members of her household corresponded in part at least to those of known species of exotic animal which could, in theory at least, be escapees from private collections which are now living wild on Woodbury Common and the woodlands on the outskirts of Exmouth, the animal that she encountered corresponds with no species known to science. I interviewed her on a number of occasions and she was (and presumably still is) adamant about the facts of her encounter.

On August 14th, the same night as what seemed to us at the time to be half of Exmouth were reporting UFO sightings to Nigel and his hapless wife, she also saw what she described as a huge glowing disc spinning silently in the sky above the veranda of her house. Surely, as if we needed any other proof, strange things were afoot that summer! [12]

These were not isolated incidents:

"Pet owners at Woodbury are troubled by the thought that a mystery animal which killed a gentle old Labrador could strike again. The Labrador, named Champagne, is pictured with a Jack Russell which was her constant companion. The big dog, just 13 years old, died this week from deep neck wounds inflicted a month ago by the unknown animal. Her flesh had been torn to the bone in a savage attack close to her home at Marlee Cottles Lane, Woodbury, which is on the edge of open country where any large and unusual predator could escape unseen.

Champagne's owner, Mrs. Joyce Poole, said: "She had been out only ten minutes when I heard her barking at the back of the house. I knew immediately something was wrong because her bark was so different. "When I rushed out to see what was wrong, I found she had been bitten all around her neck."

Mrs. Poole's brother and neighbour, Mr. Peter Ingleheart, tried to help Champagne, but, he said:

"Whatever it was, it meant to kill her. She did not just have skin wounds - her flesh was ripped right down to the bone. "And it must have been something quite big to attack her, because Champagne, although she was gentle, was a fully grown labrador.

"Some people have said it was a badger or perhaps a fox, but I don't think so."

Many people have missed Champagne, a familiar and well-loved character in Cottles Lane, where she used to take the Jack Russell for a daily walk. Mrs. Poole said: "She was a lovely dog. Everyone knew her. She was very good-natured. She never even barked at anybody."

Mr. Ingleheart added: "She had grown into a graceful old lady." [13]

There have been other hints that mysterious animals are on the loose in the Exmouth area for many years. Strange sounds have often been heard in the area at night. The following report appeared in the *Exmouth Journal* during 1983:

"Big cat on the loose?

An eerie high-pitched cry has mystified residents of the Marley Gardens Estate, in Exmouth. They are now wondering if the so-called big cats of Dartmoor have prowled into new territory. The cry has so intrigued one resident of Maple Drive he has attemped to record it in the hope that someone will be able to offer a simple explanation. The sound began last week and went on for three nights and lasting for about ten minutes time.

But since Mr. John Hannaford set up his tape recorder in readiness in the window of his home, the cry has not been heard. A neighbour, who has heard a recording of the cry of the cats of Dartmoor, believes they are one and the same.

Said Mr. Hannaford: "The more I think about it, the more I am inclined to believe it is a big cat. "It's an awful noise. Very hard to describe. It's certainly not a mechanical noise." The cry is coming from the undeveloped building land between the new housing estate and Knappe Cross.

If anyone else has hard it or can offer an explanation, please call as at the Herald." [14]

The "a recording of the cry of the cats of Dartmoor" referred to in the text is probably nothing of the sort. It is most likely that it is the recording referred to in this excerpt from *Cat Country* by Di Francis (1983): [15]

"On my arrival back to civilisation I had been greeted with, 'Have you heard about the ocelot sightings in Wales?' Of course, I hadn't, having been cut off from all news for a few days. I telephoned Ian Tillitson in Tregaron, mid-Wales, to see if he'd heard anything. He hadn't, but promised to check it out. I then settled down with a cup of coffee and turned on the television. It was 'John Craven's Newsround' and behind him flashed up a picture of an ocelot. I was suddenly all attention as I grabbed for my tape recorder. Apparently a man in Wales had photographed and recorded such an animal. I managed to record the catlike scream as it was played over the air. 'The photographs', said Mr Craven, 'have been sent to be processed and should be back on Thursday'; he moved on to another item, but I was already on the telephone to Broadcasting House in London. Within minutes I was speaking to the 'Newsround' team. No, they had no more information, the item had come from BBC Cardiff. Cardiff were helpful. They hadn't a name or telephone number for the man in the Neath area who took the photographs. However their contact was a Mr Howell Britton. Would I like his number?

Would I!"

At the time Di Francis was living in Devonshire and had been engaged in a long and relatively fruitless search for evidence that a hitherto unknown species of British big cat was lurking undetected in the murkiest wilds of the westcountry. Whilst there is no doubt that they live here - I have seen one myself - there is also no doubt whatsoever that Ms Francis` conclusions - that the animals are not descendents of those released from captivity in the wake of the 1976 Dangerous Wild Animals Act but rather a new species of large endemic British felid are highly erroneous. [16] [17]

However, I digress.

At the time, with the possible exception of Trevor "Beast of Exmouth" Beer, [18] Di Francis was the westcountry's most well known mystery animal hunter. At the time I was merely a callow youth whose rank amateur status had not yet been compromised and, whilst I read the accounts with interest, did not take an active role in the investigations. I remember, however, that in the wake of the aforementioned book, Ms Francis appeared on local television on a number of occasions and when she did so, I believe that she did indeed play a tape recording of a cat noise - presumably the one remembered by Mr Hannaford from Exmouth.

In the midst of our investigations during 1997 there were more reports of big cats seen on Woodbury Common itself.

John Cranmer from Newton Poppleford was driving through the village one Sunday morning in October when he saw "the most beautiful animal I have ever seen" leaping across his path from the right hand side of the road. He said that it was". ..."*about three to four feet long. It was stretched out as it crossed the road in bounds, and it had a fantastic head with black pointed ears and a wonderful tail that was curled up and then round again. Its colouring was creative - black on top (on the side I saw) and silky looking with a light gingery colour on the rest of it.*

It was an incredible experience. It was just feet in front of me and I had a split second view of it. I just wish someone had been with me to see it or had a camera. It was a wonderful picture.

I think it must have been a puma - it was very cat-like but was definitely not a domestic cat. It was not a fox either. It was quite light at that time of the morning. I have driven enough hundreds of miles to know a fox when I see one, and I have never seen anything like this. I have heard of people seeing beasts - but this was beautiful - not a beast!" [19]

The sheer wonder that he felt at his experience came over in the interview and even more when Nigel and I interviewed him in person. Like so many people in this book he was just an ordinary person to whom something extraordinary had happened for once in his life.

Sufficient to say, that despite his detailed description, the animal that he told us about was no puma. Like so many other of the creatures described in this chapter it really didn't fall into any category of felid known to science, and, for the moment at least, remains a mystery.

Another account, a month later, described what seems to be the same animal:

"It looked like a very large black cat but it was not puma-like because a puma is sleek. This was tubby and had every feature of a large black cat. It had a long furred, heavy tail and at first we thought that it might be a fox but it was too big. It was two or three times the size of a badger.

We were about 100-120 yards away and it was reasonable weather so we could see clearly. I think that this thing heard the hounds and it was running along in the opposite direction from them, lolloping along like a big cat.

It was black, although if anything there was a hint of a gingery tint to the edge of its fur"... [21]

As I have shown in *The Smaller Mystery Carnivores of the Westcountry* (1996) and elsewhere, there are a number of species of exotic felid presently living in a wild state across the moorlands of south-western England. [22]

Unfortunately, however, the general public at large do not know the scientific names and descriptions of many wild animals. Indeed, as a well known mystery cat hunter once remarked in the pages of *Animals & Men*, most people don't know the diference between a frog and an elephant. [23]

Of course, it's not actually that bad, but as far as ABC research is concerned, it is a well known fact that members of the public do tend to use the words `puma` and `panther` as if they were interchangeable, and think that `jungle cats` are cats that live in the jungle rather than a species in their own right. For the purposes of comparison, therefore, we have combed The Internet for brief thumbnail descriptions of four of the species of exotic felid thought, or known to exist in the Westcountry.

Puma *Panthera concolor* (Formerly *Felis concolor*)

The puma has a small broad head with dark, large, round eyes and rounded ears, an orange-red nose and its mouth is surrounded by white. Its coat is a tawny color with lighter under-parts and white on the chin and throat. It has a powerful body with long hind legs to jump over forty feet and a long tail which is 50-80 cm long (that is tipped with black) for gained balance. The puma is the second largest cat in the Americas and is a champion jumper among cats. Cougars vary in size and weight throughout their range. Adult males weight 1.4 times more then females.

The puma is the cat with many names. Puma, cougar, panther, mountain lion, night screamer, painter, deer tiger and catamount are all names for the same animal. They range from north-west Canada to south-west of South America, with a small population in Florida; there have been sightings of the puma in states such as Massachusetts and Vermont, which may mean there are still scarce populations along the east coast of North America. The puma lives in many different habitats including in mountainous forests up to 16,000 feet to lowland swamps, grasslands, and desert. The puma is very territorial and marks its territory, which can be over one hundred square miles (depending on the food supply) by spraying urine or scratching trees. [24]

Black panther (Panthera pardus)

'Black panthers' are actually leopards with a recessive melanistic gene. They are more common in areas with less light; out of all the big cats, leopards are the most likely to have melanistic coloration. The leopard may weigh anywhere from 60 to 210 lb. The male leopard is slightly larger than the female and size and weight vary through its geographical range. The leopard is five to eight feet in length and has a long tail which it uses for balance

Leopards are found in Africa below the Sahara desert and in southwest Asia in woodlands, lowland forests, and savannas. Its ability to live in many different habitats and feed on a larger source of prey has given it a better chance for survival then that of the cheetah or lion. The leopard favors areas where there are trees, and in the savanna leopards are often seen near one; they are amazing climbers. Territory is marked by scratches, feces, urine, and anal secretions. Male territories are larger than that of the female, and may overlap several female territories.

The leopard is a solitary hunter, and stalks its prey generally at night. After a catch is made, the leopard will carry it up a tree, even if the prey is three times its weight, showing tremendous strength and agility. In the open grasslands of the savannah, leopards prey on wildebeest, impala, *gazelle, and young eland, as well as hares, reptiles, and even insects. In woodland areas common prey includes small monkeys, duiker, and various rodents such as rats, porcupines, and squirrels.* [25]

Lynx *(L.lynx)*
In relation to its cousin, the Canadian lynx, the Eurasian (or northern) lynx is larger, the largest found in Siberia. This lynx has greyish fur and subdued spots with a short tail with a black tip. Long legs and big feet are adaptive to its cold environment; the lynx does not sink into the snow when it walks.

The northern lynx is found in rocky and/or forested areas away from cities in the northern parts of Eurasia. Much of the day is spent sleeping. A nocturnal hunter, the lynx hunts a variety of mammals, but prefers deer up to the size of small ungulates, unlike its cousin the Canadian lynx who prefers mostly hare. Using sight and sound, the lynx stalks its prey, being successful one out of every six tries. Feeding takes place in the evening.
[26]

Jungle cat *(Felis chaus)*
The body length of Felis chaus ranges from 56 to 94 cm, and its tail length varies from 20 to 31 cm. It stands 40-50 cm at the shoulder. Larger in body size than most members of the genus Felis, F. chaus has a relatively short tail, barely reaching its heels when the animal is standing. Its limbs are much longer than those of most other cats, and they are decorated with dark markings on the inside and back of the forelegs. The colour of the animal ranges from yellow-brown in the East to yellow-grey in the West. A young jungle cat has closely space blurry dark stripes on its body, which fade as it reaches adulthood. It retains a black tip and 3-4 black bars on the dorsal surface of its tail, as well as lacrimal face stripes. Its ears are also blackish, but with an ochre strip. Black animals are common. Felis chaus has a slender, pointed head; high, pointed ears with small brushes of hair; and a slender body. Some characteristics of the genus Felis include a fully ossified hyoid bone in the vocal apparatus, preventing roaring, a hairless strip along the front of the nose, and retractable claws with the sheath longer on the outer side. Felis chaus tends to be larger toward the western end of its range and displays strong sexual size dimorphism. The largest of the nine subspecis resides in the Nile Valley, while the smallest is found in Indochina. [27]

As can be seen, with the possible exception of a particularly unusually marked specimen of *F.chaus* there are none of the main contenders for the identity of the British Big Cat which even slightly resemble the creatures described above. This is a syndrome that one meets again and again when investigating accounts of mystery animals seen concurrently with other episodes of high strangeness. There are three possible explanations:

* That all the sightings are misidentifications of endemic British wildlife
* That all the sightings are misidentifications of one or other species of exotic felid
* That all the sightings are mistaken

Unfortunately for the peace of mind of those of us who like to lead a quiet life and who look for simple solutions to our problems none of these three explanations really holds water, at least not when one considers the sheer volume of sighting material available to us. Therefore, we have to look for a fourth solution!

One could well ask why I have bothered to discuss the matter of big cats in the Exmouth woodlands and on Woodbury Common at such length. After all, there is no doubt, as I have stated repeatedly, that putative populations of pumas, jungle cats, leopard-cats and quite possibly several other species are living, and indeed thriving, in the English countryside. The fact is that as someone or other once said *"at night all cats are grey"* to which the entirely (probably) mythical Lazarus Long replied that there were in fact an *"Endless Variety"*. [28] [29]

The fact is, that although there is no doubt that some of the animals reported are the aforementioned flesh and blood felids, and some more again are misidentifications of foxes, badgers and domestic dogs, there is a hard core of reports which appear to be something else entirely!

Fortean researchers have long noted the apparent connections between Alien Big Cat sightings and those of UFOs. In his book *Mysterious America* Loren Coleman writes that sightings of `Black Panthers` in the United States..

"may have some oblique connection with the UFO problem" [30]

He continues:

"The phantom felines are so oddly elusive that inevitably they remind one of Ivan Sanderson's dictum about Fortean phenomena: "We'll never catch them."

Witnesses have shot at them without apparent effect, set traps, conducted "safaris," and done everything possible to bring a specimen in for exami-

nation. Like UFOs, the mystery cats possess that weird tangible intangibility that makes understanding so difficult and investigation so frustrating. As a Toronto Star *editorial writer once expressed it, black panthers are the "flying saucers of the animal world." When talking about the supposed reports of "pumas" in New York in the 1950s, a State Conservationist called them "feline flying saucers." It is in the United States, as opposed to England or Africa or Australia, where I have been able to examine the subject the closest, and have come away the most perplexed. For in America, there are large cats - the puma or mountain lion - but in spite of this, the reports of phantom panthers float above the normal, and give notice to the world that something strange is taking place."* [31]

Although Janet and Colin Bord have drawn parallels between sightings of "Black Shuck" and other Celtic black dogs and UFO activity, most notably in *Alien Animals* [32] connections between alien big cats and UFO reports in the United Kingdom are less common. One that we did manage to find was from an unreferenced Internet report which dealt largely with mystery cat reports that can be dealt with through zoological terms of reference...

"Interestingly, around this time a local UFO group received a report of a strange alien creature alongside a road near Tewkesbury. The 'alien' was described as looking a little like a brown paper bag propped up on a stick. As the witness passed in his car the creature bounded off down the road. Robin Coles, the UFO investigator who questioned him, showed me a sketch which the witness interpreted as a creature with exceedingly large upright ears but which, to my eyes, looked surprisingly like the silhouette of a cat crouching beside the road with its haunches raised as if ready to spring.. While I would hesitate to assert that this was a misidentification of the Beast, it does illustrate how investigators tend to interpret evidence according to their own preconceived ideas or theories. It also suggests that many other similar cases lie hidden in other groups files, labelled as alien visitors, ghosts, pixies or indeed ABCs as determined by the prejudices of the interviewer." [33]

Kenneth Parsons, founder of the British Earth and Aerial Mysteries Society, who is best known as a crop circle researcher spent many years researching a number of quasi-fortean phenomena reported in the vicinity of a British Government Intelligence headquarters called 'Chicksands', located in Bedfordshire. In an undated article called *The Chicksands Enigma* for *The Truthseekers Review* he provided another link between these anomalous animal sightings, UFO reports and incidences of other paranormal/fortean activity:

> "Recently a black, big-cat type creature has been perceived by numerous credible witnesses, roaming both Chicksands woods and nearby Clophill, yet no physical evidence, such as track-marks, fur, droppings etc. has ever been discovered. Earliest reports date back to the 1940s, when locals went hunting for the beast armed with shotguns! (A point worth bearing in mind here is that apart from the aforementioned areas, the mysterious PUMA or PANTHER has now been seen in practically every county throughout the British Isles over the years; and what is more, sightings are on the increase!!)
>
> Chicksands Priory is undoubtedly haunted. Used, as it was, as the officers' mess after the end of WW2, a number of high-ranking British and American personnel who stayed there claim to have witnessed wraith like figures, including the form of a nun.
>
> Although there is officially no air traffic, either coming in, or leaving the base (remember, that Chicksands is primarily an eavesdropping station) still UFO's have been reported being observed above, and even landing within, the spy base... " [34]

Kenneth Arnold's UFO sighting in the summer of 1947 which almost singlehandedly ushered in the modern era of UFOlogy has been described many times. Indeed, we have even done so elsewhere in this book. This almost insignificant event has now assumed almost mythic proportions. What is less well known is the interpretation that Arnold put upon his sighting because according to noted zoologist Dr Karl Shuker, Arnold considered that what he had seen were not spaceships from an alien galaxy but living organisms "sort of like sky jellyfish". In many ways this theory makes far more sense than the far better known Extra Terrestrial Hypothesis, but, probably because it is less romantic and far more prosaic, it has been largely ignored. [35]

In 1978, UFO researcher and author Trevor James Constable published a remarkable book called *Sky Creatures* in which he suggested that many sightings reported as UFOs were actually of living creatures - highly-modified unicellular animals very reminiscent of amoebae. He describes them as possessing a metallic outer body surface and `vibrating` in the infra-red portion of the electromagnetic radiation spectrum which would make them usually undetectable by human eyes. Constable included photographs which he claimed to be of these `sky beasts` which he claims range in sizes from lengths of half a mile down to just a few inches. He referred to these organisms by the somewhat annoying term of `critters`. [36]

Constable notes several eye-witness accounts of what he believed were these `critters` including this one from Everest Mountaineer Hugh Ruttledge:

"The second phenomenon may or may not have been an optical illusion. Personally, I am convinced that it was not. I was still some two hundred feet above Camp 6 and a considerable distance from it when, chancing to glance in the direction of the north ridge, I saw two curious looking objects floating in the sky. They strongly resembled kite balloons in shape, but one possessed what appeared to be squat, underdeveloped wings and the other a protuberance suggestive of a beak. They hovered motionless, but seemed slowly to pulsate, a pulsation incidentally much slower than my which is of interest supposing it was an optical illusion.

The two were very dark in color, and were silhouetted sharply against the sky or possibly the background of a cloud. So interested was I that I stopped to observe them. My brain appeared to be working normally, and I deliberately put myself through a series of tests. First of all I glanced away. The objects did not follow my vision, but they were still there when I looked back again. Then I looked away again, and this time identified by name a number of peaks, valleys and glaciers by way of a mental test. But when I looked back again the objects still confronted me. At this I gave them up as a bad job, but just as I was starting to move away again, a mist suddenly drifted across. Gradually they disappeared behind it and when, a minute or two later it had drifted clear, exposing the whole north ridge once more, they had vanished as mysteriously as they had come.

It may be of interest to state that their position was roughly midway between the position of the 1924 Camp 6 and the North-East shoulder. Thus they were at a height of about 27,200 feet and as I was at about 27,600 feet when I saw them, a line connecting their approximate position with my position would not bring them against a background of sky, but against lower and distant mountains. It is conceivable, therefore, that it was some strange effect of mist and mountain magnified by imagination". (36)

Trevor James Constable again wrote about space animals in the 1970s, this time in more detail. He postulated that the UFO space animals *"...are amoebalike life-forms existing in the plasma state. They are not solid, liquid, or gas. Rather, they exist in the fourth state of matter - plasma - as living heat substance at the upper border of physical nature."* He also believed that they are of low intelligence and, because they remain in the infrared part of the electromagnetic spectrum, usually invisible. He concluded that they had *"...deeply confused UFO research."* [37]

Although Constable is perhaps the best known proponent of this theory he was neither the first, nor indeed the last to suggest it. Nearly twenty years earlier John M.Cage suggested that some UFOs were sentient lifeforms charged with `negative electricity`. He drew some interesting paralells between sightings of UFOs trailing aeroplanes to incidents involving dolphins following ships at sea. [38]

In an article for *American Astrology* (September 1955) Countess Zoe Wassilko-Serecki suggested that the upper atmosphere is inhabited by huge `energy eating` creatures like `giant bladders` which are spherical when stationary, but assume cigar like shapes when moving. Numerous UFO reports since then have indeed featured immense, cigar-shaped objects. [39]

The first to suggest this idea was Charles Fort, in his 1931 book *Lo!* where he speculated that unknown objects in the sky could be *"living things that occasionally come from somewhere else."* [40] A few days after Kenneth Arnold's sighting on June 24, 1947, John Philip Bessor wrote to the Air Force to tell it what the flying discs were: A *"form of space animal"* propelled by *"telekinetic energy."* These creatures might be carnivorous. "Many falls of flesh and blood from the sky in times past," he declared, could be the leftover remains of unfortunate persons eaten by hungry UFOs. Several reputable scientists have also discussed the possibility, lending considerable academic weight to what could otherwise appear to be just a nice but rather crackpot theory. [41]

Ivan T. Sanderson again addressed the question, and many others, in 1967, concluding that there *was "...nothing illogical, irrational, or even improbable about it. In fact, it is so probable that it must be given first rank in consideration of the question, 'What could UAO's [unexplained aereal objects] be?"* [42] That same year, Vincent H. Gaddis addressed the topic, attributing the original idea to a John P. Bessor, who had sent it to the Air Force the month following Arnold's classic 1947 sighting. Gaddis discussed the writings on the subject by Austrian Countess Zoe Wassilko-Serecki and John Cage, a New Jersey inventor, and concluded that *"...the time will come when one or more of these entities will be caught, weighed, measured, and exhibited."* [43]

In 1977, distinguished astronomer, author, and biologist Dr Carl Sagan collaborated with Cornell University astrophysicist Dr E.E. Salpeter in publishing a paper on the possibilities of life on Jupiter. They concluded that the swirling gasous clouds of the giant planet might have developed into an ecosystem with many paralells to the oceans of our own planet. Salpeter and Sagan hypothesised creatures filling filling a wide range of ecological roles and postulated that they would be enormous sac-like organisms, filled with helium, which would propel themselves through through the clouds by controlled expulsion of this gas from their bodies. They even suggested that the presence of such creatures in the atmosphere of the gas giant could actually explain the frequently perceived areas of red colouration. Other scientists with equal reputations have suggested that similar creatures might exist in the upper atmosphere of our own planet. [44]

`Sky Beasts` have also appeared widely in science fiction. In a story called `A Meeting With Medusa` published only a few years before Sagan and Salpeter postulated the existence of Jovian Gas-Beasts, Arthur C. Clarke presented the world with a very similar fictional entity, also living in the gas clouds of Jupiter. [45] One of the earliest fictional accounts of such creatures, however, comes from none other than the creator of Sherlock Holmes himself.

If James Brown is the `Godfather of Soul` [45] then Sir Arthur Conan-Doyle must hold a similar position within the world of paranormal and Ufological research. His dictum that "when one has eliimated the impossible whatever is left no matter how improbable must be the truth" has been quoted again and again by fortean writers deperate for a soundbyte. His stories forshadowed much of the methodology of modern cryptozoology in *The Lost World* [46] He also explored the worlds of spiritualism, faeries, and mysticism. He was also one of the first to postulate the concept of `earth as organism` in *The Day the Earth Screamed*, [47] a story which predicted many of the contemporary concepts of Gaia. In a 1913 story called `The Horror of the Heights` [48] he discussed the concept of sky-beasts, describing a plethora of insubstantial but terrifying entities living in the upper atmosphere. One has to remember that when this story was published in the Strand Magazine [49] it was only ten years after the Wright Brothers had first taken to the air, and aeroplanes were still very much a novelty. Conan-Doyles fictional aviator described:

`..the serpents of the outer air. These were long, thin, fantastic coils of vapour-like material, which turned and twisted with great speed, flying round and around at such a pace that the eyes could hardly follow them. Some of these ghost-like creatures were twenty or thirty feet long, but it was difficult to tell their girth, for their outline was so hazy that it seemed to fade away into the air around them.`. [50] [51]

Within a few years a writer identifying himself only as `A Philosophical Aviator`, claimed in an article for the *Occult Review*, that he had encountered very similar creatures in real life. (52)

The next pasage is taken verbatim from Dr Shuker's account in the 1996 CFZ Yearbook:

"The correspondent from whom the philosophical aviator had obtained his astounding account was described by him an being an experienced (but un-named) World War 1 airpilot, who had allegedly confronted at considerable altitude a weird apparition that he likened to acolourful dragonesque creature, floating through the air towards him at an appreciable speed - an unnerving event that, (not surprisingly) had persuaded him to descend to earth at once! As Watson suggests, he was most probably suffering from oxygen deficiency, a hazard when flying at great heights, and capable of engendering a wide range of optical hallucinations.

Needless to say, the conspicuous absence of names for both the airpilot and the `philosophical aviator` unavoidably turns thoughts towards the possibility that the entire report was nothing but a hoax (perhaps even inspired by the Doyle story), but even if this is true, how can we explain the many other reputed sightings of sky-serpents that have been reported over the years, and from numerous localities worldwide?

In `Curious Encounters` (1985), Fortean researcher Loren Coleman documented several such cases, which make strange reading indeed. Whatever a certain farmer in Bonham, Texas, expected to see when he looked up at the sky while working on his farm one day in June 1873, it certainly was not the gigantic, yellow-striped serpent, writhing and thrusting, that floated overhead! A hissing sky-snake was also reported during May 1888 in South Carolina's Darlington County, a Scandinavian equivalent was spied over southern Norway and Denmark in May 1935 and nine months later another one appeared over Brazil's Cruz Alta. Nor is Britain immune to overhead ophidians - the Devon town of Bideford was brightly illuminated by a twisting sky-serpent for six minutes on 5th December 1762." (53)

During the summer of 1997 whilst we were chasing UFO reports all across the heathlands of South-East Devon, David Spoor, a retired amateur photographer from Lowestoft was taking a series of fascinating video films of anomalous objects in the sky over Suffolk. One of these sequences of film shws two strange trangular objects swooping and darting like duelling butterflies in the sky over a disused MOD site in Suffolk. Many people who have seen this have commented on the organic appearance of these objects, and have speculated that they might indeed by examples of Trevor James Constable's `Critters` rather than being secret items of military hardware. [53] [54]

Writing in the *1996 CFZ Yearbook* Dr Karl Shuker noted a proliferation of Tudor Dragon reports including an example published in an Elizebethan book called `Contemplation of Mysteries`. In the year 1532 `flying dragons` were seen in various parts of the country and were described as ... *'flying by flocks or companies in the ayre, having swines' snowtes; and sometimes were there seene foure hundred flying togethir'*. The description of the`dragons` was an exacting one::

`The flying dragon is when a fume kindled apeereth bended, and is in the middle wrythed like the belly of a dragon, but in the fore part, for the narrownesse, it representeth the figure of the neck, from whence the sparkes are breathed or forced forth with the same breathing`. [55]

Unfortunately a writer named Blout, cited by Dr Shuker explained that these `dragons` were in fact metereological in nature:

`there is a fire sometimes seen flying in the night like a dragon; it is called a fire-drake. Common people think it is a spirit that keeps some treasure hid, but philosophers affirm it to be a great unequal exhalation inflamed between two clouds - the one hot, the other cold (which is the reason why it smokes), the middle part whereof, according to the proportion of the hot cloud, being greater than the rest, makes it seem like a belly, and both ends like a head and a tail`. [56]

And as Dr Shuker points out the manner in which the shape of the `dragon` is created was succinctly described in *The World of Wonders* (1882) edited by A.Taffs:

`When vapours of an inflammible kind collected in the air and ascended to a cold region, the vehement agitation thereby produced induced a flame. The highest part, being more subtle, assumed the singular form of what was presumed to be the dragon's neck, and then, having been made crooked by the repulse it received, formed the dragon's belly, while the hind part, turned upwards by the force of the same collision, represented the monsters tail. Then, with impetuous motion, it fled through the heavens - all ablaze, as it were - striking deadly terror into the hearts of the ignorant and superstitious`. [57]

However can this explain all accounts of `flying dragons`? We think not.

It so happens that I share a house with an expert on all things draconian. Richard Freeman is a Dragon Expert and I have drawn liberally upon his researches for this section of the book. When he was a child he heard the story of St George and the Dragon, and found himself firmly on the side of the dragon. He later became interested in dinosaurs and when he read Peter Dickinson's *The Flight of Dragons* [58] which suggested that dragons were in fact evolved descendents of dinosaurs it led him back full circle.

There are several different types of dragon as listed by Richard in *Animals & Men* #14:

"Of all legendary monsters, the dragon is both the most widespread and the most ancient. They flap and slither through almost every culture from the Mas D`A Zil Mesolithic cultures of twelve thousand years ago to contemporary tales of winged serpents in Africa.

Several species of dragon are spoken of, so before we delve into what may be behind the legends, it may be as well to examine these differing draconian types...

1. The Heraldic or 'True' Dragon

Also known as the 'Fire Drake', this was the most powerful of all dragons. A huge quadrupedal reptile, it had huge, bat-like wings. The heraldic dragon was armed with savage teeth and claws and had a mighty tail. Its most formidable weapon, however, was undoubtedly, the white-hot gusts of flame, it could spit at its victims. Heraldic dragons were the most magickal of beasts. They had many powers attributed to them including shape/form changing, self healing, invisibility and mind-reading. These dragons were almost impossible to kill being covered with scales harder than steel. They (like 'Smaug' in The Hobbit, by J. R. R. Tolkein) had one tiny spot of vulnerability, but the location of this 'spot' was never the same in two different dragons.

2. The Wyvern.

A very similar beast to the creature described above, but with only one pair of legs. It is also usually depicted as being somewhat smaller than the gigantic heraldic dragons. The wyvern bore a deadly barbed sting in its tail, and was believed to spread pestilence and disease in its wake.

3. The Guivre or Worme.

This is the commonest celtic dragon. The worm was a vast limbless serpent. It inhabited vast lakes, marshes and rivers. Worms killed by crushing their victims in their enveloping coils (like a constricting snake) and with their poisonous breath which they used in much the same way as the other species used their breath of fire. This poison had the ability to shrivel crops and choke both man and beast.

This type of dragon (as typified in its most famous example - 'The Lambton Worme" could rejoin itself together after having been hacked in two and ~ thus was extremely difficult to kill.

4. The Lindorm or Blind Worm.

This odd creature resembled the Guivre, except for possessing a pair of hind legs. It seems not to be as much linked to water as the preceding type and is mostly reported from Asia and Southern Europe.

5. The Amphiptere.

This was a limbless winged serpent generally reported from the Middle East and North Africa. Amphipteres are still reported today in the South East African country of Namibia. The Mexican God Quetzacoatl was an Amphiptere, with feathers instead of scales.

6. The Eastern Dragons.

Unlike their occidental counterparts, oriental dragons were portrayed as being beneficial in nature. They controlled the weather, the seas and the rivers. Interestingly, at different stages of their development, they seemed to resemble one or other of the standard western types of dragon.

Oriental Dragon eggs took a thousand years to hatch, and the young dragons resembled snakes. After five hundred years, they resembled giant snakes with the heads of carp. Five hundred more years and they developed a bearded reptilian head and four legs. A further five hundred years brought horns, and the final stage, after yet another five centuries, brought forth wings, with the final result looking like an ornate, but skinny analogue of the western Fire Drake.

Many scholars have argued about what lies at the root of this most uni-

versal of legends.

Fossilised dinosaur bones have been hypothesised as the remains of dragons in many areas. In China they are still known as "Dragon's Bones!" and are prized in powdered form within various types of folk medicine. Dragon legends, do, however, occur in places where no fossil bones have ever been found and, moreover, some legends speak specifically in terms of live dragons and their interactions with mankind, rather than just in terms of a pile of petrified bones." [59]

According to Ralph Whitlock, a:

"...dragon is supposed to haunt the two iron age hill forts of Dolbury Hill and Cadbury Hill, situated on opposite sides of the Exe Valley, just north of Exeter. Great treasures are hidden in one or both of these ancient castles and guarded by the dragon who flies from one to the other at night. Of the treasures, a local rhyme states:

*'If Cadbury Castle and Dolbury Hill delven were,
all England might plough with a golden share".* [60]

Richard Freeman notes a correlation between dragons and UFOs:

"Other ideas are even more esoteric. Many people have commentated on the parallels between modern alien abduction cases and the folk legends of people kidnapped by elves and taken to fairyland. Both have elements of missing time and memory. Both feature `implants` - high tech probes on the part of the `aliens`, and magic silver pins inserted by mischievous elves. They seem to be the same phenomena, adapting to, or filtered through, the collective subconscious fears of mankind. What were once elves and pixies were once bug-eyed aliens. Could this not be the same with dragons?

There seems to be some analogue between UFOs and dragons. Both are often seen near water and seem to be cross cultural. UFOs outpace planes and seem to defy all attempts to capture them "Roswell shenanigans" excluded. Early dragon legends portray them as beasts of God-like power and universal consequence. It was only later that the tales of more mortal dragons and dragon slayers emerged. These can be interpreted as allegorical tales of Christianity`s triumph over paganism (can anyone really believe that a puny knight on his `mouse` of a horse would really triumph over a mighty reptilian dragon?)" [61]

Richard Muirhead has also drawn parallels between UFO reports and historical sightings of a giant, glowing, flying-snake in Namibia:

"The snake is also reported to have a light on its head. This may be a reflective scale, a white spot, a lighting up stone, a lamp or a mirror depending on the perspective of the viewer on on the mythological context that we view the ``creature` within. The light only shines at night, but the only direct witness that we have to the light did not see the snake itself. Michael Oarum says:

"I saw a light coming out of the mountains, and just wondered whether it could be an aeroplane or something like that, but after a couple of minutes I thought; `but aeroplanes do have sounds. What kind of thing is this which doesn`t make any sounds?` That`s when I saw a big light in the clouds, and later on approaching slowly but surely `till I was spotted (?) (word indistinct on original recording), in the light. It was kind of blinding me, so I turned my back on it. Shortly afterwards something told me `its a big snake. Run for your life!` so I ran away".

This is not an eye-witness to a mystery snake, but there is, in the heat of the moment, a referral to a cultural belief linking a flying snake with a mysterious light. In the west we have a similar link between `foo fighters`, ball-lightning and mysterious lights in the sky. We shall return to the historical perceptive links between lights in the sky and `dragons` later.

To corroborate, Dr Sigrid Schmidt, of the Namibian Scientific Society during the 1970`s, says:

"Like the ghosts or UFO`s in Europe, these snakes are seen by people who believe in them, and people who do not believe in them do not see them. A teacher once sarcastically told me: If at night, people see the light of a motor-bike or a car where only one head-lamp is working, people say: `Oh there is that snake again!`"..

Given the paucity of concrete evidence that there is a real light/snake link, it seems that the sightings of mysterious lights have been `grafted` on to the stories of the mystery snake. Perhaps the snake, has become the explanation for some otherwise inexplicable lights. Our more technological society relates similar lights to hypothetical aerial craft manufactured by a civilisation with a superior level of technology. " [62]

It should be noted that it is undeniable that many of the 1997 UFO sightings in South-East follow the flight path given by Ralph Whitlock for the Devonshire Dragons. Coincidence. We think not.

But dragons and UFOs are not the only strange things that have been reported from the skies over Exmouth.

On the 19th June 1984, Fred and Elsie Down, both aged 80, of Halsdon Road, Exmouth, were settled down ready to watch *Crossroads* (which starts at 6.35) when they were startled by a crash which rocked their terrace home. A large block of ice crashed through the roof and into their tiny house. The report gave no estimated size or weight, but the hole in the ceiling is over 2ft by 1ft. Fred said: *"When we opened the bedroom door I could not believe my eyes. There was a terrible mess. You could see the sky through the roof. It smashed clean through the slates and broke a rafter. There were also lumps of ice the size of two men's fists lying on the bed."* [63] [64] [65]

Although anomalous falls of ice, which so fascinated Charles Fort, are often blamed (these days at least) on ice which formed on, and then became dislodged from the wings of flying aircraft - or more unpleasantly on the frozen sewage discharged from airline lavatories [66] - some anomalous objects which can and do fall from the sky are far less easy to explain.

During the summer of 1983, a year before Mr and Mrs Down had their unfortunate accident I was working in Exmouth. I was a student nurse on attachment to Stoke Lyne (a hospital for mentally handicapped children which has now been demolished). I became friends with one of my co-workers there, a Mrs Rowley, and I often used to visit her at her home in Littleham where I would stay for an evening meal with her and her two young daughters. One early evening in July the elder of the two girls, who must have been about twelve came running in, greatly excited to tell me that there were three "horrid snakes" in the garden. Replete from an excellent meal, her mother and I wandered out into the garden expecting to find that the girls had discovered a nest of slow-worms or perhaps grass-snakes. Much to our surprise, there, arranged neatly on the lawn in an almost perfect triangle were three dead, and very desiccated, pipe fish.

Several species of pipefish (peculiar creatures closely related to sea-horses) live in British waters and they are not particularly rare beasts, but they are one of the last things that one expects to find strewn neatly across someone's lawn in the midst of comfortable suburbia. Mysterious falls of living creatures (sometimes called fafrotskies) [67] [68] are a well known phenomenon and one which which was particularly dear to Charles Fort.

He had several bizarre and gloriously imaginative theories to explain such strange falls from the heavens. His most imaginative idea was the concept of what he called the 'Super-Sargasso Sea'. Just as the Sargasso Sea in the North Atlantic is supposed to be full of shipwrecks and all manner of objects caught up in its gulfweed, so the 'Super-Sargasso Sea' might be a repository for terrestrial and extra-terrestrial matter high above the earth's surface. Sometimes the sea would suck things up; at other times it would spew them back down to earth. [69][70] He also formulated the theory of 'teleportation' - a force capable of transporting objects and animals from place to place without traversing the intervening distance. This has been used to explain several anomalies including creature-falls and the anomalous appearance of various out-of-place animals which appear in places that logic and the accepted dicta of conventional zoology suggests that they should never be. [71][72]

Other explanations for such phenomena are numerous, but Dr Mike Dash calmly and logically manages to demolish the most widely accepted of them:

"........Another explanation is often advanced to account for the fall of frogs and fishes: the hapless animals were scooped up from a river or a pond by a passing waterspout, and deposited later some way off. This theory has something to recommend it: for one thing it has long been recognised that a number of falls really are caused by waterspouts. A whirlwind dropped fish at Quirindi, New South Wales, in November 1913, and fish fell from a waterspout in Louisiana in June 1921. Nevertheless, the waterspout hypothesis has weaknesses. There do not seem to be any accounts of rains of tadpoles, nor of smelly mud, broken bottles, old bicycles and the rest of the detritus that normally lurks in ponds alongside the frogs and the fish. And the theory cannot easily explain a number of the most peculiar cases. There are instances of extremely localised falls: at Mountain Ash, in south Wales, a large number of freshwater minnows and sticklebacks fell from the sky, in February 1859, covering a rectangle of ground, some eighty yards by twelve, with fish. (For a long time it was supposed that none had landed outside this extremely limited area, but one recent researcher has shown that a few came down in the surrounding hills.)" [73]

None of these theories explain my one brush with a fafrotskie. If the Celestial Sargasso Sea is an innate part of the way things are, then surely the creatures would not have been dried and desiccated when we found them - they would have been fresh and possibly even still alive. The children had been playing in the garden all afternoon and were adamant that they had not been there earlier.

The same would seem to be the case if they had been transported there by virtue of a mysterious waterspout. Firstly, there had been no rain for days, and secondly, even if there had been an isolated shower which had managed to evade the detection of both us and the metereological Office, and even if this reticent rainstorm had contained a number of fish, then why were both the fish and the grass around them as dry as a bone?

The last theory that anyone has come up with is that the fish could have been dropped into my friend's garden by a passing seabird. My only answer to that is that if one is forced to hypothesize a mysterious flying piscivorous predator that lived exclusively on dried and desiccated fish, then we would be faced with a putative phenomenon far more bizarre than the one that we are actually examining.

Like so much in this book fafrotskies in general, fish falls in particular and my experience with the three pipe fish specifically are just part of the way things are, and are presently completely inexplicable. I included this little anecdote in this book purely to underline (as if any such underlining were needed) that Exmouth, and in particular Littleham, has the potential to be an extremely strange place.

But these two were not the only anomalous falls in the Exe Estuary area at that time.

Sometime during the first week of March 1983, a few months before I had my encounter with the unidentified flying pipefish, and several months after the couple from Exmouth had their unfortunate encounter with a block of falling ice, Mrs Rita Gibson, of Topsham, on the other side of the Exe Estuary from Exeter, found a "scattering" of strange pink beans in her back garden. *"They could not have been thrown,"* she says, *"because our house is surrounded by three walls around a courtyard."* But if they fell, where did they come from? The nearest Mrs Gibson could come to identifying the beans, which were larger than rice grains and smaller than orange pips see photo - is that they looked a bit like iris seeds; but iris seeds are orange, not pink. Another oddity is that the seeds/beans are quite out of season. Mrs Gibson adds*: "They do not look like last year's because they are fresh, not dried out."* [74]

The *Exmouth Journal* for the 23rd of July 1998 reported a strange episode:

"Mystery still surrounds the arrival of three Royal Marine beret badges on housewife Jane Stevenson's patio. Mrs Stevenson walked out to the garden of her home in Cranford Close, Exmouth on a recent morning

and suddenly saw a sparkling badge on the patio glinting in the early morning sunshine.

She picked it up and within feet on a lower level of the patio were another two of the badges. She is mystified as to where they came from and how they managed to find their way into her enclosed garden.

Magpies, she thought.......

But, could a bird fly four and a half miles, as the crow flies, from the Commando Training Centre at Lympstone, with one of the Stay-Bright badges?

No, says local naturalist Trevor Bartlett. He said, "It is feasible for a magpie to take an object and fly a considerable distance with it. But, I cannot see one flying four and a half miles, three times, and dumping the badges in the same spot".

Could the badges have been stolen in a burglary and dropped by a raider trying to break into Mrs Stevenson's home?

No, says Sgt Ian Frazer-Rowe. He said "I have checked all recent burglary and car thefts and no items like these badges have been reported stolen".

Could they have been dumped by Royal Marines as a prank?

"No," says Lt Cdr Edwards at the base. He said "They are ordinary ranks beret badges. They are something that any marine would cherish and value and not something that they would even contemplate throwing away. We have no idea how they ended up in this lady's garden. All we can think is that it may have been the work of a magpie"." [75] [76] [77]

However, we have to go back a century and a half from the main body of events described in this book to find a mystery from both Topsham and Exmouth that was so weird that it has entered general parlance as `The Great Devon Mystery`.

On the night of February 7, 1855, there was an unusually heavy snowall right across Devon. When the people awoke the next morning they found that the fresh snow had been broken by what appeared to be footprints, of a very mysterious sort.

According to *The Western Luminary & Family Newspaper for Devon,*

Cornwall, Somerset & Dorset of 13th February 1855

"DAWLISH. MYSTERIOUS. - Since the recent snow storms, some animal has left marks on the snow that have driven a great many inhabitants from their propriety, and caused an uproar of commotion among the inhabitants in general. The markings, to say the least about them, are very singular; the foot print, if foot print it be, is about 3½ inches long by 2½ inches wide, exactly, in shape, like a donkey's hoof: the length of the stride is about a foot apart, very regular, and is evidently done by some two-footed animal. What renders the matter more difficult of solution is, that gardens with walls 12 feet high have been trodden over without any damage having been done to shrubs and walks. The animal must evidently have jumped over the walls. It has also left marks all over the churchyard and between the graves. Many parties have traced the prints for miles, but as yet, without any solution to the mystery. Several of the very superstitious draw long faces, and say it must be the marks of Old Nick: others conjecture that it must be some monkey which has escaped a travelling menagerie, with something on its feet; but all wish the enigma unravelled." [78]

At one place, the tracks marched right to the edge of the Exe River near where it meets the sea. The river there is two miles wide and was not frozen, yet the trail continued on the opposite shore just as if the creature had swum or walked across the water. The line of prints was found to zig-zag its way from the town of Topsham southward to the town of Totnes, a distance of approximately ninety-seven miles along the south Devon coast. The prints didn't make an unbroken line; sometimes they followed an irregular course and at others they disappeared for a distance of several miles.

The strange tracks seemed to be anywhere and everywhere. Practically every town in village in the area, as well as isolated farms, were marked by the horseshoe-shaped tracks. They were found in town squares and lonely beaches; cemeteries and public roads; woodlands and even on tops of houses.

The snow had stopped falling in Devonshire at about midnight. The tracks had been made between that hour and about 6:00AM, when people arose and first began to notice them. Yet not a single person reported seeing or hearing anything unusual during the night, and certainly no one reported seeing whatever it was that made the tracks.

When people first saw the prints, they had a good deal of fun speculating what they might be, but as the day wore on and the extent of the trail of strange prints became known, the fun went out of the speculation. The rumor spread that the prints were not horseshoe-shaped at all, but were the prints of a cloven hoof! It was said that the Devil had been abroad that night in Devonshire.

The following night people in the district locked themselves indoors, for fear of meeting the Prince of Darkness walking about that night. But the next morning there were no fresh footprints. Nor were there any the next morning, or the next, and gradually the hysteria died down.

What made the "Devil's Footprints"? A local clergyman suggested that they really had been made by the Devil and that they were a warning against the swearing, drunkenness, and general poor morals of the district. But another clergyman said that this was a "gross and incredible superstition." He had heard that a couple of kangaroos had escaped from a nearby zoo, owned by a gentleman called Mr Fish whom we shall meet again in a later chapter and that, unlike any of the local wildlife, they might be capable of jumping over walls.

It must be said, however that the prints in no way resemble those of a kangaroo.

Sir Richard Owen, one of the most distinguished biologists of the day, had a more reasonable explanation. he suggested that the prints had been made by a group of badgers that had been driven out of hibernation by hunger and were scurrying about the countryside in search of food. The badger's characteristic print, he said, had been distorted by melting and refreezing of the snow.

Other animals, such as otters, geese, great bustards, and of course ponies, were put forth as possible sources of the prints. Someone even suggested a swarm of frogs, but none of these explanations gained even general acceptance. It has to be said that although many hundreds of thousands of words have been written on the subject of the Great Devon Mystery, to this day no one really knows whether the strange prints were made by an animal, or if they have some other origin. Perhaps they were made by something that fell from the sky, or by a change in weather. The phenomenon of "Devil's Footprints" however, has been observed in a few other places and is generally connected , at least in the popular mind, with the appearance of some sort of devil or monster. [79]

It is interesting, we think that three different sets of phenomena have seemingly travelled the same route. The medieval dragon, the 19th Century Devil`s footprints and the contemporary UFOs. Whether these three phenomena are actually one and the same, or whether, as seems more likely, they are all manifestations of a single greater whole, or whether indeed there is no connection between them at all, is a moot point. However, there can be no doubt that the matter does provide food for thought.

Copplestone Cross: where Mrs Carbonell saw the black dog

The Haldon pet cemetery

◀ *Filming at Otter Cove*

▼ *Nigel Wright at Otter Cove*

◄ *The lane at Aylesbeare where Genette Tate disappeared*

Clyst St. Mary –the home of the `weird warbling whatsit`

 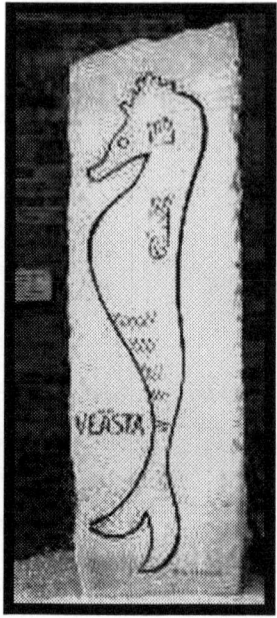

▲ In August 1995, a strange creature described as a gigantic sea horse, was allegedly seen by Martin Ball at Chesil Cove, Portland, Dorset.

▲ The stone engraving outside the Ferrybridge Inn, Portland, depicting Veasta, the Chesil Beach Monster.

▲ An artist's impression of the Chesil Beach Monster

MARK NORTH/CFZ © 1995

The Jurassic Coastline of Lyme Bay

Jon and Nigel a little worse for wear at the 1999 LAPIS Conference - on tour to promote the first edition of this book.

The mutilated whale - Exmouth 1997

Dame Alexandra David-Neel

Wilhelm Reich

Woodbury Common

Woodbury Castle - where Jon and Nigel saw the UFO

PART THREE: WHAT?

"From many a mud wall cabin eyes were watching through the night, many a manly heart was beating, for the blessed morning light, murmurs ran along the valley, like the banshee's lonely croon, and a thousand pikes were flashing at the rising of the moon"

***Trad arr* Shane McGowan**

VIII

A UFO book would not be a UFO book without some allegations being made of a conspiracy or cover up. Many authors writing within this genre have made the most extraordinary claims for the fruit of their `researches`. Depending on whom you believe, a malevolent race of aliens contacted certain officials high up in the hierarchy of Nazi Germany in about 1937. They were, or so the accounts by people of the ilk of the self styled "Commander X" [1] attracted by some of the bizarre occult rites performed by Himmler and his henchmen. In return for unspecified favours these aliens worked together with the Nazis only to rather unfortunately crashed one of their flying saucers in a desert near Roswell in New Mexico two years after the war [2] which the Nazis lost despite the aid of their extra-terrestrial colleagues. Of course, everyone knows that the surviving members of the Nazi High Command were secretly flown in flying saucers to a base far beneath the Antarctic Ice Cap where Admiral Byrd's 1947 expedition only just failed to expose them. [3] [4]

An alien rescued from the Roswell crash lived on until 1953 on a diet of strawberry ice-cream [5] until, on finally dying of sheer boredom, he was hacked up in what must have been the first space age splatter movie which was conveniently lost until a bloke with an Italian name [6] who was in search of lost footage featuring Elvis Presley (who of course ain't dead but living on Zeta Reticuli with JFK) discovered it and made a mint of money flogging a dead horse (or should that be dead alien?) to a gullible public until the bubble burst soon after the fiftieth anniversary of the crash and everyone went off to play computer games instead. (Except for Elvis, JFK and the tribe of Nazis living beneath the South Pole).

Of course, some of what I have said above is true, but most of it is undeniably rubbish that I cobbled together after a cursory read of a pile of third rate paperbacks. It is amazing how much rubbish people will believe, but it is also important, I think to note how easy it is for even the best intentioned writer to put two and two together only to make 666.

For example, *something* most certainly *did* crash in the New Mexico desert during the summer of 1947. In the same year Admiral Byrd *did* lead an expedition to Antarctica. The Nazi High Command *were* fascinated by occult symbolism [7] and what is crudely (and usually inaccurately) known as black magic. Ray Santilli *did* release the so-called `Alien Autopsy` video to the general public. Italians *are* known for manufacturing excellent ice-cream and there`s a guy works down the chip shop swears he`s Elvis. [8] QED You have a great conspiracy.

In this book, however, we have curbed the temptation to make figurative literary mountains out of equally figurative fortean molehills and when, as in this chapter, we *have* come across what looks suspiciously like a Government cover-up we have done our best to treat the matter as calmly and rationally as a fat, manic-depressive fortean and a skinny Jew are able to do. [9]

The first piece in this particular jigsaw comes from an item in the *Round and About with Dennis H. Pratt* column in the *Exmouth Journal* of December the 9th 1950. We make no apologies for quoting what may seem at first to be excessive amounts of verbiage, but we feel that it is important to see these events in as wide a cultural context as is possible.

Mr Pratt`s column reads:

"If there were, as the song says, `two little men in the flying saucer`, we saw [it] *at Exmouth last Saturday afternoon, then it must be admitted that, again as the song says, `they quickly flew away`. We saw it from Raleigh Park, and there was really nothing so bad in the match between the reserves of Withycombe and Crediton to cause the `two little men` to be in such a hurry to get away. The `flying saucer` was seen by some of the Saturday afternoon gardeners on the Hamilton-Cranford allotments. Things are certainly pretty bad up there, thanks to the weather, but even such a mess need not have caused those `two little men` to scoot across the sky at such a furious rate. They could, at least, have had a look at the Brussels Sprouts that were not all that bad. Down on the Maer the town reserves took a toss in the Geary Cup competition, but the `two little men` were apparently not the least bit interested. They whizzed away towards Exeter - as we thought - as if Old Scratch was after them.*

If they were taking pictures at that speed then all we can say is that our moving pictures are standing still.

It seems that the 'two little men' had a look at the football matches in Somerset just about the same time, a little before four o'clock. Please let me make it clear that we didn't actually see the 'two little men' they just came out of the song.

Oh, but we did see the flying saucer and we have never before seen such a thing. It flipped us across the sky just as other folk said these things do flip across the sky and looked like a small watery moon, and left some sort of trail.

Of course, we have never before seen a meteorite in daylight, but that is what we really and truly believe we saw on Saturday. We shall have to see something a lot more convincing to make us believe in flying saucers!" [10] [11]

The flippancy with which this piece was written teaches us two things. Firstly, although I would love to claim that Mr Pratt was engaged in a complex campaign of disinformation by the failing Labour Government led by Clem Attlee in a vain attempt to stave off the onslaught of the Conservative party under Winston Churchill , in order to cover up the British Government's collaboration with a sinister alien race, that would be nonsense. At least I THINK that it would be nonsense. Anyway, I'm not going to make any such claims as I think the real reason is far more important. It is simply that the modern age of UFOs was still in its infancy, and they were still seen as amusing 'silly season' novelties. Only three years before Kenneth Arnold, a pilot in his thirties had ushered in the 'age of the UFO' with a sighting, described here by John Spencer:

"It was on 24 June 1947 that Kenneth Arnold sighted the nine objects in formation which were to lead to the modern UFO era. He was a lone pilot in a Callair aircraft informally engaged on a search for a crashed C-46 marine transport plane, which he did not find. During the flight near Mount Rainier in the Cascade Mountains of Washington State, USA, he witnessed objects in flight formation; he estimated their speed to be between 1,300 and 1,700 miles per hour, which would have been faster than any plane of the day could fly. He estimated the length of their formation to be some five miles, at around twenty-three miles' distance from him. He believed the individual size of the objects was approximately two-thirds that of a DC-4 (one of which happened to be sharing the sky with him and gave him some point of reference).

The sighting was of short duration, at far distance, not corroborated by radar or other sightings, and in fact adds very little to our knowledge of the UFO phenomenon. The significance of the sighting has always been the media attention it attracted and the enormous public interest which started at that time and has never seriously abated." [12]

Two things are usually forgotten about this sighting, however. Firstly, Arnold was not responsible for coining the appelation `flying saucer`. That dubious honour must go to a Texas rancher who in 1878 described the object that landed on his farm as a `large saucer`. [13]

Secondly, and by far the most importantly - Kenneth Arnold never claimed that what he had witmnessed were extra-terrestrial craft. He remained convinced that what he had seen were experimental military aircraft of some description and perhaps they were! The idea that these were `space craft` piloted by `two little men` (let's face it, if I can't beat Mr Pratt, I might as well join him), came much later in socio-cultural terms at least and at the time of the 1950 Exmouth sighting of what (if the description is to be believed) most certainly wasn't a meteor was still very much a cultural joke.

The level of flippancy with which Mr Pratt treats the subject can be seen in the next paragraph when he compares the `flying saucer` to a hat worn by actress Judy Holiday. He then goes on to say:

"Well, well, next thing we'll be hearing that diving teapots have been seen by submarine crews". [14]

Of course, they may not have been teapots (it would be left to David Allen to invent that particular brand of *rara avis* two and a bit decades later), [15] but Unidentified Submarine Objects were to be seen, observed, and even photographed in a number of locations across the world over the next half century. As we have seen, they even turned up near Exmouth in 1997. Perhaps the `two little men` had returned to wreak their revenge upon Mr Pratt for lampooning them in execrable prose, and on not being able to find him they vented their spleen upon the most sentient being that tyhey could find - a hapless pilot whale? [16]

However, back in 1950 the extent of Mr Pratt's witticisms were not over yet. He then proceeded to discuss the subject in a cod Devonshire dialect that would, these days at least, make any true blue Devonian cringe.

"The Riddle Solved...

Still, we need worry no more about the stories of these strange things in the sky, for the riddle has been solved by Zam Brown who emerges from Rogue's Roost, apparently after prolonged consultation of astrological

charts and other paraphanalia, with the solution.

'I remembers years an years ago, must ave been about 1891 er zumwhere near to it that I seed for mezelf plenty o 'flying saucers' an t'was down Chapel Street tu that I saw em. Thaair was me an 'Ginger' Chandler, (gone now, dear old chap) an Tom Pinecombe. All of us boys together gwain tu Dicky Grove's school auver the Parade, whair Woolworth's is now.

This appened on a market day, when they used to bring cattle in frim the farms an auction 'em orf auver to the cattle market whair the church hall is standing now.

Us wuz comming out o school and gwaine ome tu dinner an was stude outzide Mr Prittlejohn's ous down to th' corner o The Parade where 'tis knawn now as Knowlings' Corner.........." [17]

The punch line to this excrutiating piece of prose was that the bullocks got free and one of them ended up into Bennet's china shop causing some saucers to 'fly'. Very amusing!

Devonshire dialect happens to be something that I know a little about. My father is the author of a renowned dictionary of which, in many ways, is a separate and individual language. [18] What Mr Pratt wrote is neither funny nor good Devon dialect but it is, in its own way highly significant.

As we approach the new Millenium and beyond Devonshire is easily accesible from the rest of the country by means of the M4 and M5, and also by the A303 which is, as I write this in the autumn of 1998, a dual carriageway for most of its length. But it was not always like this. When I first came to Devonshire as a boy of nine in 1969 the journey to Devonshire from London was a long and arduous one which could only be accomplished by a tortuous cross country trek involving a number of small market towns with impenetrable one-way systems. The westcountry was relatively isolated from the rest of the UK and prided itself upon this isolation. Nearly two decades previously the social gulf between a Londoner and an Exmouthian would have been an almost insurmountable one and the gulf between their two mindsets even greater.

However, people like Mr Pratt, whilst priding themselves upon their Devonshire roots, took a great pride in the fact that they were up-to-date and relatively cosmopolitan. In my opinion, at least, this is why his lampooning of the 'two little men' in the 'flying saucer' in cod-Devonian is so important.

It was only three quarters of a century ago, well within living memory that, as the great Devon folklorist the Rev. Sabine Baring-Gould wrote

In 1879, a farmer on the west side of Dartmoor, whose name I know, and also the name of his farm, having had sickness among his cattle, sacrificed a sheep and burned it on the moor above his farm, as an offering to the pygsies. The cattle at once began to recover, and did well after, nor were there any fresh cases of sickness among them. He spoke of the matter as being by no means anything to be ashamed of or that was likely to cause surprise. I do not, however, wish to give his name [19]

and the same year a newspaper report read:

"Counteracting Witchcraft by Pin Sticking.-~ Mr Chown, cooper, of the parish of Honiton Clyst, owns some houses; and a tenant of one of them having left, certain repairs were found necessary to prepare for the next. In carrying out the work the chimney had to be explored, and in the course of the operation there was found secreted a pig's heart stuck all over with thorn-prickles. This is said to be the third curiosity of the kind found here. It is supposed to have been done by direction of some "White~witch," as a method of taking revenge on the witch to whose incantations the party considered some mischief due, in the belief that the heart of the ill-wisher would be pierced in like manner until it became as pulseless as that of the pig." [20]

I believe that Mr Pratt would have had a sneaking suspicion that a belief in the `two little men` in a `flying saucer` would have been too close to his father's generation's belief in witchcraft and `pygsies` and therefore to give any credence in a public arena to a story such as this would have been tantamount to declaring himself to be an ignorant country bumpkin. However, he was still immensely proud of his Devonshire heritage and mildly resentful of the fact that the increasing urbanisation of the region had resulted in changes like "Dicky Grove's School" being replaced by a branch of F.W.Woolworth.

It is important, I believe, to try and understand the mindset of a social commentator like Dennis Pratt, for it is through his eyes, and through the eyes of his contemporaries that we must see the few, but intensely valuable UFO reports that we have from the early 1950s. The canon of ufological literature is full of the socio-political impact that the advent of the age of the flying saucer had upon the populace of the United States, but one has to realise that the populace of a small market town like Exmouth was both literally and figuratively half a world away from that of their transatlantic cousins. Where the United States had Frank Sinatra, the jitterbug and anti-communist witch-hunts, Great Britain still had an Empire, ration books and Dennis Pratt.

We must now move on a year. The British had done what they always do best and revelled in nostalgia by re-electing wartime leader Winston Churchill as Prime Minister and trying to recapture the spirit of 19th Century gunboat diplomacy by seizing the Suez Canal in the name of democracy. Neither option worked. But we weren't to know that at the time. The next piece in the jigsaw that, despite our better judgement, may indeed lead us to the conclusion that the British Government was activelly involved in a minor-league UFO related cover-up half a century ago is also from the *Exmouth Journal* and is dated October 13th 1951.

"Another Flying saucer?

A small number of people on Exmouth's Sea front on Sunday evening at about 8.30 witnessed a curious phenomenon. What appeared at first to be a brilliant blue sky rocket travelled in a straight and horizontal course towards the North West and vanished in mid-air after a few seconds.

The head was a cone of brilliant light blue and there was a comparatively short tail of golden light. The speed was much slower than that of the usual meteorite and there was nothing in the nature of a flash.

The progress of the light was steady and the height did not appear to be great. The suggestion has been made that the apparition was a guided missile used in practise". [21]

A week later the front page carried the headline *"Flying Saucer was Guided Missile!"* and ran the following story:

"Reported exclusively in the Exmouth Journal *last week, the `Flying Saucer` seen from Exmouth Sea Front on the night of October 7th proves to have been, as we suggested, a guided missile. It was in fact, the biggest and fastest guided missile yet built by scientists in Britain and it was on the secret list until late on Monday night. Two powerful motors drive the thirty foot rocket upwards at a speed of 2,000 miles per hour. The missile is then guided along a radar beam to the target.*

A huge jet of flame is then thrown out by the motor to launch the rocket and then boost it to high speed and when this fuel is spent the booster drops off.

What was seen from Exmouth was undoubtedly the sight of the streamlined front half travelling under its own power". (22)

The story was complicated by another report the following year which, apparently at least, provides some vindication for this interpretation of events.

"We saw Secret Weapon ten months ago.

A number of Exmouth people are possibly amongst the first `civilians` to have seen Britain's answer to the Atom Bomber, a self guided rocket in actual flight. Ten months ago the Journal *exclusively reported on the sight at night from Exmouth Sea Front of a strange missile travelling at great speed with a jet of flame coming out of its tail.*

Last Saturday Mr Duncan-Sandys, Supply Minister, reveals of a fantastic new weapon, a guided rocket for use in defence against Atom Bomb air attack.

Mr Sandys who saw trials at an experimental establishment at Aberporth...." (23

This was presumably at the range now controlled by Defence Evaluation and Research Agency (DERA) Aberporth, with target drones flying from DERA Llanbedr which has been conducting research since the mid 1950s,... (24)

"......South Wales, and afterwards that because of military security he could not state precisely the actual performances, but the guided rocket can travel at well over two thousand miles per hour and reach heights greater than a bomber is likely to reach for years". (25)

Nigel checked with an ex BAe engineer and military historian [26] who confirmed his suspicions that the figures given, ostensibly by Duncan Sandys [27] were hyperbole to say the least. A thorough Internet search implied that the missile referred to by Dennis H. Pratt was probably an early version of the `Blue Sky` or `Fireflash` missile [28] which, although an impressibve weapon for the time could not approach the figures claimed for it in Pratt's column.

Missiles with that degree of performance were not tested for several years and then only at the Woomera Testing Range in Australia. [28] So what happened?

There is no evidence whatsoever that the British Government claimed that the Exmouth sightings were of their guided missile,. And all the evidence that we have points towards the guilty party as being Mr Pratt. It seems that he put two and two together and dreamed up a solution that would fit in with his self-styled role as arbiter of truth and honesty in the New Elizabethan age. He also did his patriotic `bit` to foil the menace of the Russian Bear by announcing an extraordinary weapon that didn`t really exist. In short he made the whole thing up.

No Government cover-up! Sorry Commander X Fans.

There are, however, a couple of points to do with the affair which are of interest to the fortean. I placed a request on the Internet for information on British Government missile research during the 1950s and quickly received the following reply.

Yes. The British government made the missiles here in Cumbria and sent them to Woomera Aus. for testing. A photograph was taken by a fireman in Cumbria of his daughter, near the missile factory. when the photo was developed, a mysterious figure was seen behind the girl. The photo became known as 'The Cumbrian Space Man', and was investigated by Jenny Randles.

Oddly enough, it transpires that at the same time the photo was taken in Cumbria, UK, a missile test in Woomera, Australia had to be aborted after two figures were seen on security camera near the launch pad. The figures were described as wearing suits and helments...the same garb as in the Cumbrian photos! Jenny found reference to the Woomera incident last year in the public records office and it mentioned film footage was in existence of that very moment the countdown stopped. The fellow who took the photo was visited by two apparently 'MIBs' who warned him to stay out of the way.

Hope this helps

Jerry Anderson [29]

Before we leave the subject it is, perhaps, apposite to quote from Nick Redfern`s 1997 book *A Covert Agenda* (Simon and Schuster)

"This period is notable for one other reason: it saw the publication of the Air Ministry's 'Secret Intelligence Summary' which sought to provide appropriately down-to-earth answers to the UFO mystery. Although I have

yet to ascertain exactly when the summary was written, it can have been no earlier than July 1, 1954, and no later than March 13, 1955.

I base this belief on the following: the four-page summary references a well-known and much-reported UFO sighting which took place over Canada on June 30, 1954.20 Hence, the paper could not have been written prior to the beginning of July of that year. In addition, a copy of the summary was forwarded to Duncan Sandys MP on March 14, 1955, so it had to have been written at some point before that date." [30]

So, even though it can be shown that Dennis H. Pratt was talking palpable nonsense Duncan Sandys, who in March 1955 was Minister of Housing and Local Government *was* taking an interest in `Flying Saucers`. It is hard to see the relevance of this subject to his particular Government post, so maybe there is a mystery to be solved after all...

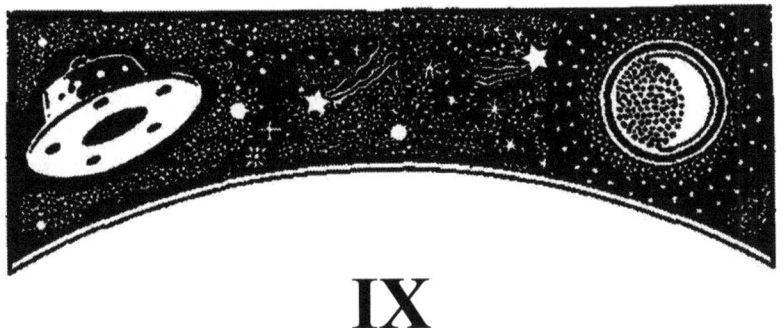

IX

The phenomena now known as UFOs have been reported for many years over Exmouth. We discovered the earliest account in our records almost by accident. At the time that Nigel discovered it, the paranormal press was full of the 50th Anniversary of the Roswell UFO crash. There had been several major TV series on the subject and quite a number of books had been sent for review at ESP HQ. Nigel, being the inquisitive little fellow that he is was interested to contrast the social mindset of the American public at the time of the Roswell Crash with that of their Exmothian counterparts.

Therefore in a spirit of inquisitive good humour he spent a morning looking at the 1947-9 newspapers in Exmouth Public Library. In one 1949 paper he found a column entitled "40 years ago" which read:

"Exmouth was thrown into a state of amused excitement on Thursday by an allusion to the `flitting` about in the firmament of an airship with the accompanyimng fears of foreign invasion and its attendant horrors. Whatever was the `mysterious` affair which was noticed by two girls as long ago as last Friday night, it was only on wednesday that it was `licked into airship shape` and remembering the elusive - may it be suggested the illusive (sic) - quality of the craft, it became quite natural to speculate as to its mission or presence. That it was only seen by two young girls - Miss Violet Woodcock, and Miss Cissie Webber - and had evaded the vigilance of the coastguard men, gave the story the same mysterious complexion that those from various parts of the country bore. Indeed, its ubiquitous quality surrounded it with quite an air of wonder.

However, the story of two young ladies, who did not themselves proclaim that they had seen an airship is very simple, and can be explained in two ways. At the time - between nine thirty and ten p.m they were returning home by way of Alexandra Terrace, after a walk on the Esplanade. They noticed a light flash over the ground, and looking upward in the direction of the sea, they saw anopther flash or two.

They appeared to be frightened a little, and went home, where they incidentally alluded to the matter. They had no idea themselves of airships at the time, nor had they imagined since that they had seen lights flashed from an airship, imaginary or real. What they saw is suggested to be what is popularly called `shooting stars` or possibly searchlights from vessels at sea. Very little notice was taken of the matter generally, as from the first it was regarded as an idle rumour." [1]

The 1909 papers were full of the spate of UFO sightings that had taken place across the country. Although there were no other accounts from Devonshire, we have included the full stories that Nigel found because this is an episode in British UFOlogy that has not been satisfactorily dealt with elsewhere.

(All these accounts are, by the way, from the *Exmouth Journal* of 21.5.1909)

The first story reads:

"Early on wedensday morning an airship was seen in the neighbourhood of Cardiff by a number of persons.

The facts of the occurrence are stated in the following official statement, which has been made to the Cardiff Stock Company, by Mr Robert Westlake, Signalman at the King`s Junction of the Queen Alexandra Dock. "At 1.15 this morning (May 19th), while attending my duty signalling trains at the King`s Junction, of Queen Alexandra Dock, I was startled by a weird object flying in the air. In appearance, it represented a boat or cigar shape and was making a whizzing noise. It was lit up by two lights which could be plainly seen. It was travelling at a great rate, and elevated at a distance of half a mile, making for the eastward."

There were many men working at the time loading the S.S Arndale and the airship was seen by most of them. Five workmen, as well as the third mate of the Arndale all testified to the facts recorded above. The airship came from the direction of Newport, took a curve over the docks and passed over the channel towards Weston being clearly in view for a minute or two. It could, it is stated, have been longer, but that the lights on board were suddenly extinguished. "Had the Dowlais Works blast been on", observed one of the eye-witnesses, "we should have had the airship clearly discovered, but we saw enough to put at rest all doubt about it.

The night was clear though there was no moon, and the airship could be distinctly seen and the whizzing of its motors heard by all".

Several of the night workmen who have been interviewed corroborate the story of Westlake. It may be recalled that on Saturday the employees of Messrs Smith`s Star Mill, newport (M.O.N), reported that they saw an airship in the district during the night." [3]

The same newspaper carried another story which corroborates the above account nicely. It was accompanied by the headline *Strange Story from Norway* and reads:

"A correspondent forwards to the Daily Mail *a copy of the* Norwegian Journal *containing accounts of the appearance of a mysterious airship over the North Sea. The journal - The Shipping Gazette of Norway - publishes a report made by Captain Egenes of the Norwegian steamer St. Olav. He states that on the night of May the 14th, when the St Olav was in the eastern part of the North Sea an airship sailing at low altitude approached his vessel and directed a searchlight upon the decks. After making a close examination of the St Olav, the airship moved off and scrutinised another steamer in the same way.*

The Norwegian journal suggests that the airship is carried by day in one of the German warships manouvering in the North Sea" [4]

In order to understand the significance of these reports we have to take a brief look at the political situation in Europe at the time. In Britain, the elderly King Edward VII, who had spent so many years waiting for his mother to die so that he could finally achieve his birthright and become ruler of the greatest Empire that the world had ever known, was in poor health. Europe was in turmoil, the old order was changing fast, and a number of events had brought the entire continent to the brink of war. The annexation of Bosnia and Herzegovina by Austria-Hungary in October, 1908, led to a controversy between the Dual Monarchy and Turkey. It also led to international complications which for several weeks early in 1909 threatened to end in a general European war. This was the Bosnian crisis.

From the beginning of the occupation Austria-Hungary counted upon ultimately obtaining permanent possession. Serbia, however, continued to hope that the provinces, or at least such a portion of them as would give access to the Adriatic, would some day come to her. The crisis in 1908-1909 sprang from the fact that Serbia believed that she must prevent the consummation of annexation by Austria-Hungary or give up permanently her long-cherished hopes.

Soon after the proclamation of annexation Serbia called a part of the reserves to the colours and lodged a vigorous protest with the powers, demanding either a return to the status quo ante or compensations calculated to assure the independence and material progress of Serbia. Serbian newspapers demanded a strip of territory extending across Novi-Bazar and Bosnia-Herzegovina to the Adriatic. The Government of the Dual Monarchy refused to receive the Serbian protest. It denied that Serbia had any right to raise a question as to the annexation. [5] [6]

For a time the attitude of the powers was uncertain. With the exception of Germany, whose attitude at first was extremely reserved, all of the powers objected to the action of Austria-Hungary, but apparently more to the form than to the fact of annexation. As the controversy developed Germany came quickly and decidedly to the support of its Austro-Hungarian ally. In Russia public opinion expressed itself strongly in support of Serbia. The Russian Government, which at first had shown a disposition to do no more than record a formal protest against the infraction of the Treaty of Berlin, responded by supporting the demand first made by Turkey for an international conference to consider the matter. The British and Italian Governments then supported this demand with considerable vigour, while France sought to play a conciliatory role.

Germany was also flexing its political and military muscles. In 1908, Kaiser Wilhelm II gave an extraordinary interview to *The Daily Telegraph* which sent ripples across the entire continent. The interview is, even ninety years later, both horrific and compelling:

"You English," he said, "are mad, mad, mad as March hares. What has come over you that you are so completely given over to suspicions quite unworthy of a great nation? What more can I do than I have done? I declared with all the emphasis at my command, in my speech at Guildhall, that my heart is set upon peace, and that it is one of my dearest wishes to live on the best of terms with England. Have I ever been false to my word ? Falsehood and prevarication are alien to my nature. My actions ought to speak for themselves, but you listen not to them, but to those who misinterpret and distort them. That is a personal insult which I feel and resent. To be forever misjudged, to have my repeated offers of friendship weighed and scrutinized with jealous, mistrustful eyes, taxes my patience severely. I have said time after time that I am a friend of England, and your press --, at least, a considerable section of it -- bids the people of England refuse my proffered hand and insinuates that the other holds a dagger. How can I convince a nation against its will ?

"I repeat," continued His Majesty, "that I am a friend of England, but you make things difficult for me. My task is not of the easiest. The prevailing sentiment among large sections of the middle and lower classes of my own people is not friendly to England. I am, therefore so to speak, in a minority in my own land, but it is a minority of the best elements as it is in England with respect to Germany. That is another reason why I resent your refusal to accept my pledged word that I am the friend of England. I strive without ceasing to improve relations, and you retort that I am your archenemy. You make it hard for me. Why is it?" . . .

His Majesty then reverted to the subject uppermost in his mind -- his proved friendship for England. "I have referred," he said, "to the speeches in which I have done all that a sovereign can do to proclaim my good-will. But, as actions speak louder than words, let me also refer to my acts. It is commonly believed in England that throughout the South African War Germany was hostile to her. German opinion undoubtedly was hostile -- bitterly hostile. But what of official Germany? Let my critics ask themselves what brought to a sudden stop, and, indeed, to absolute collapse, the European tour of the Boer delegates, who were striving to obtain European intervention? They were feted in Holland, France gave them a rapturous welcome. They wished to come to Berlin, where the German people would have crowned them with flowers. But when they asked me to receive them -- I refused. The agitation immediately died away, and the delegation returned empty-handed. Was that, I ask, the action of a secret enemy ?

"Again, when the struggle was at its height, the German government was invited by the governments of France and Russia to join with them in calling upon England to put an end to the war. The moment had come, they said, not only to save the Boer Republics, but also to humiliate England to the dust. What was my reply? I said that so far from Germany joining in any concerted European action to put pressure upon England and bring about her downfall, Germany would always keep aloof from politics that could bring her into complications with a sea power like England. Posterity will one day read the exact terms of the telegram -- now in the archives of Windsor Castle in which I informed the sovereign of England of the answer I had returned to the Powers which then sought to compass her fall. Englishmen who now insult me by doubting my word should know what were my actions in the hour of their adversity.

"Nor was that all. Just at the time of your Black Week, in the December of 1899, when disasters followed one another in rapid succession, I received a letter from Queen Victoria, my revered grandmother, written in *sorrow and affliction, and bearing manifest traces of the anxieties which were preying upon her mind and health. I at once returned a sympathetic reply. Nay, I did more. I bade one of my officers procure for me as exact an account as he could obtain of the number of combatants in South Africa on both sides and of the actual position of the opposing forces. With the figures before me, I worked out what I considered the best plan of campaign under the circumstances, and submitted it to my General Staff for their criticism. Then, I dispatched it to England, and that document, likewise, is among the state papers at Windsor Castle, awaiting the severely impartial verdict of history. And, as a matter of curious coincidence, let me add that the plan which I formulated ran very much on the same lines as that which was actually adopted by Lord Roberts, and carried by him into successful operation. Was that, I repeat, an act of one who wished England ill ? Let Englishmen be just and say!*

"But, you will say, what of the German navy? Surely, that is a menace to England ! Against whom but England are my squadrons being prepared? If England is not in the minds of those Germans who are bent on creating a powerful fleet, why is Germany asked to consent to such new and heavy burdens of taxation? My answer is clear. Germany is a young and growing empire. She has a worldwide commerce which is rapidly expanding, and to which the legitimate ambition of patriotic Germans refuses to assign any bounds. Germany must have a powerful fleet to protect that commerce and her manifold interests in even the most distant seas. She expects those interests to go on growing, and she must be able to champion them manfully in any quarter of the globe. Her horizons stretch far away." . . . [7]

Is it any wonder therefore that faced with a continental political situation which looked as if a horrific and bloody war was imminent that the news stories in the edition of *The Exmouth Journal* that contained the sightings of mystery airships give such coherent hints of a military build-up?

Taken at random:

"The King and his Army- The King went to Aldershot on Tuesday and witnessed field operations by the troops. His Majesty, accompanied by General Sir John French, left Waterloo by a special train at a quarter past ten. After lunching at Government House, whither all the General Officers of the Command are invited, the King made an exhaustive tour of the garrison, during which he opened the new Cavalry Club at the Cavalry Barracks.(....) The King repeatedly expressed pleasure at what he saw. After watching the Irish Fusiliers at Bayonet practise and the Lancers swimming with their Horses, His Majesty visited the wireles

telegraph and the Connaught Military Hospital. The King then motored to the coal plateau to see the new dirigible............" [8]

Against a background such as this, is it any wonder that mysterious objects seen in the skies over Britain were immediately interpreted as being secret weapons owned by the German Empire? However, with the advantage of hindsight we can see that whatever these objects were, it is highly unlikely that they had anything to do with Kaiser Wilhelm or his empire. For one thing - similar spates of UFO activity were being reported from the other side of the Atlantic Ocean.

The *Willimantic (CT) Chronicle* 1 Jan 1910 reported a sighting of a "Mysterious Airship". This is only one of several dozen reports in our files, and we have chosen it almost at random because it has a number of similarities to the news stories from the United Kingdom which we quoted earlier in this chapter.

"Where does it come from? What is it? Who does it belong to? These are the questions which have come to the mind of newspaper readers all over New England and in New York during the last fortnight. From a score or more localities reports have come of a wonderful mechanism, which has been seen skimming along, high in the air, above out cities. It has invariable come in the night time, when big searchlights of tremendous power have gleamed from out of the darkness like the eyes of some monster living creature of the imagination. It is quite impossible to believe we are all suffering from a common hallucination.

If the wonderful flying apparatus is the product of the brain of Wallace Tillinghast of Worcester, as the public tends to believe, then that gentlemen has good reason to be secretive about it. Apparently, as compared with this creation, the flying machines of the Wright brothers, who have been generally recognized as being the leaders of the world in aeronautics up to the present moment, seem very crude. Mr. Tillinghast, presuming him to be the owner and inventor, undoubtedly has in mind a thorough perfection of this airship before giving the public more than an inkling about it. He may realize that this or almost any government would pay a fabulous sum for airships as successful as this one is, provided their details have been kept in strict secrecy. On the other hand, it is scarcely to be believed that such a phenomenal invention could be successfully and continually kept secret.

The Springfield Republican *suggests a gigantic hoax in this connection. "The idea suggests itself," it says, "that the* Worcester Telegram *is trying to emulate the* New York Sun *by bringing out a sort of semicentennial* edition of Edgar Allan Poe's celebrated balloon hoax. In that story, it will be remembered, Poe pictured a "dirigible balloon's voyage across the Atlantic ocean with a party of seven or eight men." But the stories of how this strange craft of the air had been seen have come from so many different localities that it is well-nigh impossible to be believe there could be any hoax back of it. Indeed, as the Republican *says, undoubtedly referring to the recent Cook affair:* "it will be observed that hoaxes are not popular just now." [9]

(For a longer exploration of the Mystery Airship sightings of 1909, we must refer the reader to a paper by Joseph Treanor in Steve Moore`s Fortean Studies *Volume One (1994) which contains far more information than we can include in this volume).*

The explanation was unlikely to be either the mysterious Wallace Tillinghast or the Kiaser because similar objects were being seen over what is now Uzbekistan. The *Japan Weekly Mail* of 19th June 1909 contained the following news item:

"A number of observers were struck by the apparition in Tashkent of a mysterious aeroplane, which traversed a considerable area of the Province, as attested by eyewitnesses. No explanation is forthcoming of this manifestation, but newspapers from widely separated districts report the occurrence. A suggestion has been made that the aeroplane is from British India, which it is said, experiments have been in progress for some time in secret". [10]

These accounts destroy the widely held belief that modern UFO reports started with Kenneth Arnold in 1947. There are some that are even earlier, and some which even invoke a primitive version of the Extra Terrestrial Hypothesis as this letter from the *Sacramento Bee",*
a local Californian newspaper during the 'Airship' flap of 1896-1897 shows. It is dated November 24, 1896 and reads:

"The Lord Commissioner of Mars has evidently sent one of his electric craft on an exploring expedition to the younger and larger worlds. The airships are constructed of the lightest and strongest fabrics and the machinery is of the most perfect electrical work. Aluminum and glass hardened by the same chemical process that forms our diamonds contribute the chief material of their most perfect airships.

When in use these vessels at a distance have the appearance of a ball of fire being operated wholly by the electric current generated on such vessels. The speed of our Martian ships is very great and can be regulated to the rapidity of 1,000 miles per second. In fact, with the Martian inventions, space is almost annihilated. These aerial craft can so adapt their courses that when they desire to rest they can anchor within certain degrees of latitude and wait for the revolution of the Earth, for instance, to bring any particular locality desired nearer them without the necessity of any aerial navigation.

- W.A." [11]

However we must return to Exmouth in 1909. In the same newspaper which has already provided us with mystery airship sightings in two countries comes another story of potentially great fortean significance:

"Invasion Scares - Queer story from Humberside

A strange story was told to the Yorkshire Post *Grimsby correspondent by workmen from Killingholm near Immingham new dock works on Tuesday night. They declared that they were seated at noon on the roadside at Killingholm, when a large motor car drove up and two men alighted who walked to the bank on which the workmen were seated and asked if any airships had been recently seen near. The workmen replied "No" wherupon the motorists asked the distance between Killingholme and Spurn, and whether any mines were laid in the Humber between the two places. The workmen referred their two interrogators to a coastguard, saying he would be able to answer them. "It does not matter" replied the motorists, and after enquiring the way to the nearest refreshment house, they jumped into their car and drove quickly away".* [11]

This is wonderfully reminiscent of the Men In Black (MIB) accounts which have bedevilled modern ufology. Beginning in the late 1950s, reports surfaced of strange men arriving, unannounced, sometimes alone, sometimes in twos or in threes, at the homes of particular UFO witnesses usually before they had reported their sightings to anyone. Often seeming to know more than a stranger should know about the witnesses, MIB caution against reporting their sightings or close encounters. MIB typically walk with a strange limp, speak in mechanical monotones or annoying sing-songs, wear black suits and black shoes, often arrive driving black cars, and convey an overall eerie 'otherworldly' aura. [12] [13]

John Spencer described the phenomena in depth in *The UFO Encyclopedia*:

"The "Men in Black" were a curious phenomenon of early years of UFO stories in North America; typically they went around in twos and threes,

were well dressed -- always in dark suits -- and looked not unlike FBI agents. There is a suggestion that they were in fact government agents suppressing stories of UFOs, and one of the more specific claims was that they were agents of the Atomic Energy Commission who were suppressing stories of an accidental leakage of radioactive material at Maury Island.

Of more interest is the theory that the "Men in Black" were themselves alien and suppressing witnesses' stories in order to carry on conducting their own clandestine activities. There are claims that they wore bizarre make-up, with the men often wearing lipstick as if somehow not quite appreciating the difference between the sexes on Earth. Typically they would drive old cars that were in pristine condition, suggesting somehow that they had been "created" for a specific purpose.

Although they have not completely gone away, the "Men in Black" are now much more rarely reported, possibly coinciding with an era of much greater openness world-wide about the subject of UFOs." [14]

We tend to think of the MIB more in terms of a socio-cultural phenomenon than an actuality and this 1909 report would tend to confirm that. It is tempting to theorise that a century before when Bonaparte was rampaging across Europe, that two mysterious figures were seen to alight from a phaeton and enquire about coastal defences, and that this scenario is a necessary part of the innate huiman paranoia rather than anything more sinister.

However, as with so much else in this book, it is an answer that we are unlikely ever to have.

The history of fortean investigation is full of tiny, and otherwise silly co-incidences which have despite all odds, turned into something far more significant. One day Nigel was having a cup of coffee in Exmouth when he was approached by a man who until a few months before had lived next door to him. He gave him a little booklet entitled *Flying Saucers over the West* by A.B.Bearne. It had been privately published in 1968 and Nigel`s ex-neighbour had bought it for him as a present for the princeley sum of 10p in a local charity shop. [15]

This random and seemingly unimportant act of kindness was to prove a major breakthrough in the search for historical sightings of UFOs in the area.

Bearne`s are a well respected Devon firm of Auctioneers and for a scion of this noble family to have leant his name to something gives the subject of west-of-England UFO research a level of gravitas (in Devonshire socio-cultural terms at least) that it would not have been able to have otherwise.

Bearne's interest in the subject started with his own sighting (taken here verbatim from the booklet):

"On Monday, 30 October 1950, my wife and I had gone to play at our Badminton club at about 7 p.m. (and, readers please note, this club had no liquor licence! -and I had drunk nothing stronger than a cup of tea that evening, thus I cannot be accused on that score of "seeing things"!) Towards the end of the evening we were joined by our daughter and when play finished at about 10.30 p.m. we returned home by car.

I dropped my wife and daughter at our front gate then drove around to the rear of our property in Southfield Avenue, Paignton, opened up the outer double-doors, and the garage doors and drove my car into the garage, switched off the car lights and closed the garage doors. There being no artificial light in or around the garage at that time, my eyes had time to get adjusted to the darker conditions whilst I had closed the two pairs of doors and I could then easily discern my surroundings as I walked slowly down the rear garden path, which runs almost due north and south. There were no bright lights visible anywhere near me, and a street lamp which was outside the front of my house at that time, was quite obscured from my view.

Walking in a southerly direction down towards the kitchen door, at the side of my house, I became aware of a light high over my head, westward of the direction in which I was slowly walking; looking upwards I was mystified to observe a funnel-shaped stream of flames, chiefly white, descending, pointed-end first, in an absolutely silent and very peculiar manner-peculiar inasmuch that the point of the flames seemed to be "creeping" or "fingering" downwards .(This I will refer to more fully later in this account).

I stared most intently at this unusual and unaccountable sight, trying to think what it could possibly be, and very mystified indeed. I at first wondered whether it could be a burning part of a plane which had caught fire and burst asunder at some high altitude, but this solution did not satisfy me because it was not falling straight down but coming at an unvarying angle and at a steady and apparently not very fast speed, and there was something peculiar about the forward point of the flames which at first I could not understand.

After having been in my view for possibly about half a minute, the flames-or flaming object or objects ~ disappeared from my sight below the top of the roof of my house. Therefore, still very puzzled, I continued walking forward down towards the kitchen door at the side of my house, gazing straight ahead between my house and the next in the direction where I expected this strange object to again appear on its downward path. In a very short while it again came into view, but now more strange still I observed not a long stream of flames, but a roughly spherical "ball of fire," and instead of continuing in its former path downwards it was now travelling horizontally straight away in front of me in a southerly direction over Paignton towards Churston Ferrers and Higher Brixham, and at no very great height, possibly not more than 500 feet-but this was difficult for me to judge correctly, although a trained aircraft observer could probably have given an accurate estimate of the height.

I was now more than ever at a loss to account for this very strange sight, and having, as I have previously stated, so far seen only flames, no thought whatever of "flying saucers" had as yet entered my mind. This was probably because I had read that "flying saucers" were supposed to be large luminous discs, or globes, and I cannot recall up to that time having read of flames issuing from, or surrounding, these objects.

Now comes the climax! From standing there on my garden path, by the side of my house, perfectly calmly but very puzzled, and watching very intently, I observed this animated bunch of flames, by now apparently some miles away, suddenly take an upward course and to my amazement I then saw appear ahead of the flames the forward portion of a huge disc, from which the flames appeared to recede as it climbed upwards. In a flash I thought "flying saucers", and, greatly excited, I banged on the kitchen door of my house and shouted loudly for my wife to come out, but by the time she had come to the door and unlocked it and hurried out it was too late, as this object had disappeared miles away in the night sky; in any case, coming from a lighted kitchen out into darkness, it is unlikely that her eyes could have discerned the object described even had she come out a few seconds earlier. Actually it could have been two discs (as stated in later reports by other witnesses) because in front of the disc mentioned by me appeared to be the faint outline of a second disc just ahead of the other; whether this was possibly only a reflection on a cloud I cannot say, but as far as I remember there were few, if any, clouds in this area at that time." [17]

In the light of such a reasoned and sensible account it seems appropriate to treat his other records with a certain amount of respect. There are dozens in the the booklet, but only a few which have direct relevance to the area where the other sightings in this book took place half a century later.

This is the first:
"In the Herald Express, *2 November 1954, was the following report of a sighting on the previous day: Two Torquay men yesterday saw about 15 mysterious balls of fire in the sky, one of the men claimed today. Mr. J. Branson, of 50 Bampfylde Road, Torquay, stated that yesterday afternoon at about 3.45 he was near the coast at Babbacombe. With him was Mr. Cox, who is in charge of the tip. Suddenly, said Mr. Branson, he looked out to sea and in the direction of Weymouth, several miles away and at quite a considerable height, he saw a cluster of flying objects. "They were an orange yellow colour like balls of fire," he said, "and as I watched I saw them go into a straight line and counted about IS of them. They were moving quite slowly then, but they went into a cluster again and climbed very rapidly into the clouds and out of sight." Mr. Branson said that Mr. Cox also saw the objects quite clearly. "I never believed stories about flying saucers and such things before," said Mr. Branson, "but seeing is believing."*

In the same newspaper on the following day, was this account:

More witnesses came forward today, to confirm reports, published in yesterday's Herald Express, *that objects like fireballs had been seen from Torquay over the sea. Mr. S. J. Hines, of Stover Golf Club, Newton Abbot, said he was on the Esplanade, Exmouth, on Friday afternoon when his son drew his attention to a number of round objects floating in the sky above the sea in the Weymouth direction. He added "They looked like balls of fire, just as they have been described in your newspaper."*

Mrs. G. H. Bean, of 4 Eugene Road, Preston, Paignton, told the Herald Express *that her mother and brother were both on Babbacombe beach at the same time on Monday as was mentioned in the first report. On returning home they had described what they had seen, and it was exactly as observed by the first two witnesses. Mrs. Bean said: "They remarked that no one would ever believe their story as they, too, had always doubted the many reports of strange objects seen in the sky recently."*

Mr. J. J. Sutton, of 14 Redburn Close, Paignton, states that while watching from his bedroom window he saw the "fireballs" break one by one from the clouds and move slowly in a line over Thatcher Rock and then disappear towards Babbacombe." [18]

The *Exmouth Journal* has a number of historical reports. A strange object

was seen in the night sky in October 1957.

"In an interview with the "Journal" Mr. Bulling said: "I was coming out of my house about ten minutes past five on Tuesday morning and I looked across a clear blue sky to the west. I saw a light travelling at great speed. It was like a star but larger and at first I thought it was a jet plane but it was travelling too fast for a jet. It It was was moving east towards the moon. As it approached the moon it changed colour to orange and then I lost sight. of it. I saw it for about 30 seconds".

Mr. Bulling, who does odd jobs at the Holly Tree Inn, Withycombe, was on his way to work. [20]

P.C. H. L. Sandercock, of Exmouth walked out of Exmouth police station shortly after five a.m the same morning and *"saw the object, like a large star. racing towards the moon. I lost sight of it after about a minute"* he said to a reporter at the time. [21]

Ten years later on 28th April 1967 (UFO Encyclopedia) eight coast guardsmen, including Brian Jenkins, reported sighting, through binoculars, a cone-shaped UFO which they described a 'shining brilliantly'. Their description indicates that they believed it was made of metal. There appeared to be some sort of hatch on the underside. [22]

In 1978 as the police investigation into the Gennete Tate mystery was at its height there was another spate of UFO activity in the area. The *Exmouth and East Devon Journal* for October 28th 1978 reads:

"Five young Lympstone girls talked excitedly this week about the UFO they claim to have seen hovering over Candy's Field on Monday night at about 7.00 and their statements were backed up by twelve year olf Julie Hawkins, who said she saw the object from her bedroom, which overlooks the top of Meeting Lane.

The five, Sharon Tooley (13), Clare Johnson (14), Angela Eyres (14), Tracey Bright (13) and Glynis Uphill (13) were sitting on top of a Wendy Hut in the field when they saw the object stop. "I was walking up the field with Tracey when we first saw it" said Glynis. "At first we thought it was a shooting star, but we could see a cigar shape. It was silvery coloured, with lights.

When we got to the hut, we watched it for a while until it stopped over a tree. It was silent. We were scared, and we went into the hut and put a tyre against the door as a barricade. But we could see it through the cracks in the wall. It moved overhead and seemed to be starting to land. Then it went forward and sort of vanished".

Paula Marker (14) who did not see the object said that she reached the hut shortly afterwards and said that she found the girls scared and screaming, one of them was crying". [23]

There was a spate of UFO sightings almost a decade later in the summer of 1987. The first report of a particularly problematical object described as a `Flying Fairground` was reported in the *Exmouth Herald* in August.

"A mystery object, described as "looking like a flying fairground," was spotted high in the night sky over Exmouth on Tuesday. Mr. Gordon Baker spotted it travelling slowly in the sky. He had gone out into his garden in Blackmore Court, off Dinan Way, armed with a telescope in the hope of catching a glimpse of the planet Jupiter, which should have been visible in the clear sky. Instead, he said, he saw this object, which he sketched as it tracked over the town from the north-east to the south-west.

After training a pair of binoculars on the two cross-shaped objects travelling close together, Mr. Baker called his wife Gloria and asked a neighbour, Miss Heather Palmer, to look at the brightly-lit object. While watching it, the three saw an aircraft pass underneath much faster than the mystery object was travelling. Mr. Baker said: "I was out looking for Jupiter when I saw these two cross. shaped objects lit up like a fairground. It was definitely not an aircraft. There was no sound whatsoever. I called my wife and my neighbour, Miss Palmer.

I helieve the object was travelling at about 35,000 feet. Then I heard the noise of a jet aircraft. I saw it pass under the lit objects and I even checked with Exeter Airport to see if the pilot had reported seeing it. They said they had not received any reports. However, a man in air traffic control said he had had a couple of objects on his radar, but did not know what they were. We watched it for about 15 minutes until it disappeared on the horizon.

I don't know what it was but it certainly had hundreds of lights on it."

Miss Palmer said: "Mr. Baker knocked on my door and said 'have a look at this.' I went out on to the pavement and I could see these two lit-up crosses straight away with my naked eye.

"He gave me a pair of binoculars to look at it, but I could see better with

my own eyes. As I went out of the house, I looked at my watch and the time was eight minutes past ten. There was no noise at all. It was just moving slowly across the sky. Living here, you often see aircraft at night and they have flashing lights. These lights were all constant and white. I just don't know what it was." [24]

This report spawned a number of other reports of what appear to be the same object that were published in the same newspaper a week later:

"Last week's U.F.O. sighting over Exmouth has been confirmed by three more people. But the Ministry of Defence is not interested. A spokesman said this week: "If U.F.O.'s were hovering over one of our R. A.F. bases, we would look into it. Otherwise the sightings are of no interest to us. In most of these reports. there is a logical explanation."

He did not offer one for the object - described as "looking like a flying fairground - seen over Exmouth on August 4th by at least six people, including Mr. Tony Millington, a former R.A.F. technician. Mr. Millington and his wife Claire. who run Shear's Place, a Lympstone restaurant, were leaving the Globe public house in the village when they saw brilliant lights towards Starcross. Mr. Millington, who served in the R.A.F. for 15 years, said: "It certainly was not an aircraft. When we got to the Green, we looked over the water towards Starcross and we saw these two large lights which were a sort of orange colour.

"It is very difficult to say how high they were, but there was no noise at all. That is what seemed so odd to me. As we watched, the two objects seemed to get close together and I thought it was very, very odd. We watched the objects for about 15 minutes before they disappeared over the horizon towards Haldon Hill. The lights were uniform in brilliance.

They were also seen by Mrs. Elizabeth Tunmer from her mother-in-law's home in Granary Lane, Budleigh Salterton. Mrs. Tunmer sketched the object before returning to her home in Sussex Her mother-in-law, Mrs. Elizabeth Tunmer, said: "My daughter-in-law saw it quite clearly and watched it for several minutes.

"To her, it appeared to be a lit-up object like an aircraft on its side. There was no noise but the lights on it were so strong and it was moving very slowly. She watched it until it was hidden from view by trees at the bottom of our garden. We just don't know what it was."

Another witness was Mrs Pat Sampson of Withycombe Village Road,

Exmouth, who thought at first the U.F.O. was a Hercules plane refuelling from a tanker. But the curious thing was that there was no noise. There were a lot of separate lights and one of the aircraft sent out an orange flare - which we have never seen before," she said. "Also, the Hercules is smaller than the tanker, but these two aircraft were the same size.

The first report of the object came last week from Mr. Gordon Baker, of Blackmore Court, off Dinan Way, Exmouth, whose sketch of it was published in the Herald. He described it as two cross shapes flying together and said it had so many coloured lights that it reminded him of a fairground in the sky." [25]

A further note, the following week, effectively solves this particular mystery:

"102, Bradenham Beeches,
Walters Ash,
High Wycombe, Bucks.

SIR - Recently, I received a copy of Exmouth Herald *of August 7th. via my father who lives in Dawlish, in which you reported the appearance of a mysterious object in the night sky over Exmouth. From Mr. Gordon Baker's graphic description, of his sighting on August 4th. I deduced that he had most likely observed a number of aircraft engaged in air-to-air refuelling.*

For this particular manoeuvre, the aircraft fly in close formation and at night the undersides of the tanker are illuminated with white floodlights to help the receiving aircraft to acquire visual contact. Enquiries at our main RAF tanker base revealed that a pair of VC1O tankers conducted a refuelling exercise over South West England on the night in question. Furthermore, one of the pilots was able to confirm that the aircraft flew over Exmouth in formation towards the South West at a height of 25,000 feet shortly after 10 p.m. He also recalled that both aircraft had the floodlights switched on.

Air-to-air refuelling is carried out at a lower speed and engine power setting compared with airliners flying at similar heights. It is understandable, therefore, that the sound of the VC1Os was inaudible to observers on the ground.

The flight path of the tankers would not have been known to the authorities at Exeter Airport because aircraft flying high over Devon and Cornwall are controlled directly from the London Air Traffic Control Centre.

I hope my explanation solves the mystery of the "flying fairground" to the satisfaction of Mr. Baker and your other readers who shared his unusual experience.
MICHAEL WESTWOOD
Squadron Leader" [26]

I must admit that I agree with Nigel when he says that it is a little odd that a former RAF technician was unable to identify such a common manoeuvre. It is also hard to reconcile the drawing by the original witness, Mr Baker, with the account given by Squadron Leader Westwood. However, it seems unlikely that a more bizarre explanation will be forthcoming. However, it should be noted that whilst the furore about the `Flying Fairground` was at its height, Mr Baker, together with friends of his, witnessed several other objects which, if his sightings are to be believed, bear no resemblance whatsoever, either to aircraft of RAF Transport command or to a `Flying fairground.

"Thirteen mystery objects, all shaped like an inverted cup on a saucer, were seen above Exmouth at the weekend. The sightings were made and double-checked by a newly-formed net-work of U.F.O. watchers based in and near the town. When one member of the group sees an object, he or she calls another keen amateur astronomer to check the sighting after giving the subject's description and course.

Mr. Gordon Baker of Blackmore Court, Exmouth, formed the network of sky watchers after people contacted him two weeks ago saying. like him, they had seen a mysterious "flying fairground" object over the town. Mr. Baker checks the sky for two hours every evening through a powerful telescope. On Friday night he spotted three saucer~like objects, another three on Saturday and seven on Sunday evening. He described each as being lit brightly when travelling at speed, but dim when they slowed down.

He said: "These are a new lot of objects. They are not aircraft or comets, which can be easily recognised by their tails. "They are shaped very much like a saucer with an inverted cup on them. When they go slow, their lights dim and then they change direction, before going off again at a terrific speed. "As soon as I saw them I telephoned Mr. Bill O'Shaughnessey at Woodbury. He saw them and gave me a running commentary over the telephone. His wife was outside with a friend and kept relaying the information to him while I was on the phone.

"Now we have a way of checking the direction in which these objects are

travelling. I am making a record of the times and dates of all the sightings and who has seen them. Mrs. Caroline O' Shaughnessey, of New Way, Woodbury Salterton, said: "I saw three objects travelling together and then split up and go different ways in the area of the Plough in the sky. They were certainly not something made on earth. They were too high and too bright."

Mr. Baker, who has spotted numerous unidentified objects from his home, a high point in Exmouth. is now planning to learn how to capture them on film." [27]

A few months later Mr Baker saw another object in the sky::

"Alien beings from outer space have apparently returned to take another look at Exmouth. Years after the last published reports of U.F.O.s being sighted over the town, a flying saucer is claimed to have been spotted on Saturday evening. Mr. Gordon Baker, of 17, Blackmore Court, off Dinan Way, drew a rough sketch of the flying object which, he said, was moving at a speed which he thought was around ten times the speed of a jet plane.

He told the Herald*: "I thought that people would say I had gone strange in the head, so I called my wife and neighbours who came out and saw it as well. "The U.F.O. had blue and white lights running around its rim. It was like neon signs flashing in a row of windows all around the edge."*

Mr. Baker, an amateur astronomer, owns four powerful telescopes, one of them capable of magnifying sixty-fold, which he used at the time.

He said: "The sky was completely clear of cloud at 8.30 on Saturday evening and there was almost a full moon when I went outside. "I heard a sound in the sky, looked up and saw the lights of a Tristar airliner with three vapour trails behind it. "Through my telescope, I could see the plane's fuselage, although you wouldn't have been able to do so with the naked eye. "Suddenly I saw a large circular object three times as big as an airliner towards the east. Blue and white lights were flashing around the edge of it. "It was moving west. Then it stopped and hovered above the town for about three minutes. It headed north at great speed, stopped five miles away and hovered again.

"That was when I called my wife and neighbours, thinking I might need witnesses who would say it really did happen. "They didn't have to look through the telescope because they could see the circling blue and white lights quite clearly. "After that, the U.F.O. headed away to the west and

hovered over the Exe Estuary before continuing to the west and vanishing." [28]

The self consciously 'humorous' tone of this report shows how little the newspaper had progressed since the days of Dennis H.Pratt! However the fact that Mr Baker was responsible for so many sightings may be significant. The available evidence suggests that some people are more susceptible to witnessing a series of sometimes disparate phenomena than others. For example, a family in Cornwall have encountered so many strange things over the years that, in one magazine article I dubbed them 'the strangest family in the land'. [30] [31]

St. Neot is a small village on the southern edges of Bodmin Moor in Cornwall. In recent years we have become interested in the area mainly because of the big cat sightings on the moor but also because of the activities of several witches in surrounding villages. During a recent investigation into Cornish Alien Big Cat sightings we contacted Kevin and Sue Wright. They told us such a bizarrely fascinating story that we were forced to investigate further. It must be stressed that we are still at a relatively early stage of our investigation but this is a summary of our case notes so far.

Kevin and Sue have been married for over twenty years. They used to live in a haunted house in Yorkshire where they experienced several bizarre and frightening poltergeist incidents. They moved to Cornwall about five years ago. They have three children, Julian, Ed and Heloise.

They have all experienced different paranormal phenomena in the area and on discussing their experiences with their friends and neighbours it appears that many people in the area have also experienced 'weird' phenomena.

We have conducted extensive interviews with various members of the family, and the information presented here is only a relatively small part of what is available to us including sketch maps, drawings and the plaster cast of a mysterious cat print. They have also furnished us with the names and telephone numbers of a number of other witnesses, many of whom have agreed to talk to our investigating team.

In this document we shall cover the main events in the story in brief with the aim of providing a concise overview of what is, by anybody's standards a most peculiar story.

THE HORNED GOD
In the autumn of 1994 when Julian was 16, the family were walking home from the pub at about 9pm. It was late dusk and there was still some visibility. None of the family are known epileptics, none had drunk more than half a pint of beer and none of them had taken recreational psychoactive drugs.

Julian was walking in front of the party and saw a figure that he thought was his father. He spoke to the figure and Kevin answered him from behind. The figure turned around and Kevin could see that the figure was about six feet tall and had the antlers of a stag apparently sprouting from the top of his head. He compared them to the antlers of a Red Deer rather than those of a Roe Deer.

Similar figures have been seen in the area both known and unbeknownst to the family. There is an ancient wall in the lane containing what appears to be a shrine to Cernunnos, the Celtic Horned God.

There are, however certain aspects to the story which suggest the Romano-British deity Sylvanus, the God of the Oak Trees and the springs. Manifestations of Sylvanus in the west country have been noted by Rodney Legg and others (1988).

It is possibly significant that an oak tree nearby grew four feet in 12 months.

THE PHANTOM PLAYGROUND
Kevin has good night vision. In view of some of the recent events Sue doesn't go out at night. On several occasions Kevin and others have experienced rustling of beech trees in what appears to be an ex-furniture plantation and faint sounds like a children's playground, from the aforementioned oak tree eastwards. Kevin said it definitely wasn't the sound of the stream.

ECTOPLASMIC EARTHLIGHTS
This next series of events is particularly interesting because it ties in well with one of our other ongoing investigations. The synchronicity of dates and numerology may also be significant.

On or about the week of the 15th April 1996 Kevin was putting a lake into a field on his property. He built a bank and by about 2am they had

dug a channel to divert their stream into it.

Julian thought he saw flickering lights in the treetops (1OO ft mature beeches), visible only by starlight. Kevin suggested that they were will-o'the wisps. This is, however, a phenomenon of incandescent methane or marsh gas, and physically can not occur one hundred feet from the ground.

These tiny points of light formed into a group all flickering at once. It started to move around, following the line of the hedgerow and circled the group. They coalesced into white lights. The dog didn't appear to be worried, just interested. Humans went off, feeling apprehensive. A similar phenomenon was reported in the Torridge estuary during 1936 and at various times in Cornwall over the past twenty years.

Sue experienced a similar phenomenon a few months later and less than a week before this document was prepared Ed also experienced swirling ectoplasmic lights in one of the paddocks.

THE ALIEN BIG CATS

Their first sighting was in November 1993. Kevin and Sue were driving from Launceston through Tremaddock, down a hill. In the headlights of their car they saw a black cat which jumped out of the hedge, landed in the road, and ran away. They described an animal approximately 3' high and 4' long (excluding the long tail). It had strong legs.

We separated the two and Kevin and Sue drew independent pics. Sue said it was sleek and black with an arched back. She described it as a "proud" cat. Kevin said that it had pointed ears, but they were not tufted. They both described it as having a blunt face (ie not pointed).

The animal had a long solid tail; Sue described it as being clubbed-ended (ie not pointed). Unfortunately neither of them could describe the feet of the animal although its legs were gracile.

On another occasion their lurcher chased the same, or a similar animal up a tree. They managed to obtain a plaster cast of the footprint. We showed both witnesses pictures of various cat species as described by Hvass (1966), Guggisberg (1975) and Green (1984).

Both Kevin and Sue compared 'their' cat with the leopard in Green's book. David noted that it didn't have the distended underbelly of leopard in Guggisberg's book. He said that although in many ways it was similar to the lynx in Green's book, it lacked its face whiskers.

Kevin remarked on the similarity of the morphological characteristics of 'their' cat with the Oncilla in Green's book; and was struck by the resemblance to Shuker's mounted Jungle Cat.

Sue thought that 'their' cat was most similar to a slightly more gracile version of the puma in Guggisberg's book. David then looked at that picture and agreed.

Neither Sue or Kevin had any knowledge of scratching posts or scent markings in the area.

The second time that they encountered the animal was on or about the 20th February 95. It was about noon and Kevin saw it from the landing window of their house. It walked along the hedge in an adjoining field and at first he thought it was one of the two family cats until it reached a telegraph pole and in comparison Kevin could see that it was really rather large. While Sue watched from the window, Kevin, armed with a long pole, went outside and pursued it but it loped into some scrub, aware of being followed.

Kevin and Sue have provided us with a number of telephone numbers of other witnesses in the area and we presently have eight or nine reliable sightings, together with accounts of attacks on livestock and other substantative supporting evidence.

OTHER APPARITIONS.

An interesting incident happened to Heloise and a student friend of hers who stayed with them for the summer of 1996. During a full moon (August) they set off to the village and were scared by seeing a figure of a woman in the trees.

Julian said he saw a figure of a person which, as he went along, merged into the horse that usually occupies the field. (This spot is where Kevin leaves "offerings" to the earth spirits). Another family friend has also seen the figure of a woman in the trees and a local farmer has reported seeing a ghostly couple in a local field when he was ploughing.

Kevin has speculated on the connection between these apparitions and Cornish faerie apparitions. It is a matter of record that such phenomena are not at all uncommon in the region and I have many such incidences on my files.

THE WOLF PACK

The last wolf in Cornwall was supposedly killed in the eighteenth century although it is a matter of speculation as to exactly when and where the last British wolf met its untimely end. Recently, however, Kevin's daughter Heloise said she saw a pack of wolves running up the lane; blinked; and they had disappeared. All she could see then were leaves blowing in the wind.

I interviewed Heloise separately and was impressed by her plausibility as a witness.

It seems apparent that there are two forces at work here. The family are, by their own admission susceptible to paranormal phenomena, and it seems extraordinarily synchronitic that they have come to live in an area which appears according to many authorities to be a 'window area' for parapsychological phenomena. However as Tony 'Doc' Shiels was once fond of telling me:

"There's no such thing as a coincidence, you GOBSHITE..." [33]

and there has been nothing so far in our careers as fortean investigators which would lead us to believe otherwise.

With one exception, the rest of the sightings in our records are of amorphous balls of light. The earliest of these is from 1987 when the *Exmouth Journal*. Printed a picture of a glowing light surrounded by clouds and flying over the Exe Estuary. Apart from the 1983 picture taken by Eric Morris which, although it could be a plasma ball is more likely to be the result of a drop of water on the lens than anything else, this is the only photograph of an Exmouth area UFO and is actually quite impressive:

"Exmouth amateur photographer Jim Brady, is wondering if he inadvertantly sighted the UFO/Unidentified Flying Object while taking a sunset shot over the Exe Estuary. For, after collectimng his newly developed slides from the chemist, when Jim came to project the slide on the wall of his flat at Rivermead Court, there it was in all it's glory - a shining white object in the western sky above Haldon Hills. "It's all a bit of a mystery how it got there. I've tried to rule out all the possibilities and I'm still baffled".

It was about 4.30 p.m on a winter's evening when Jim took the shot, so he ruled out the Evening Star. "There was no high flying aircraft around at the time and if the mark had been a spot of emulsion from the printer's it would have shown up more positively on the transparency", said Jim.

"I suppose it could have been a Met Office balloon", he said, "but if it was it was a big one and why wasn't it there about fifteen seconds later when I took a second shot of the same sunset? It had just vanished". [34]
Three years later in 1990 there was another sighting:

"Three trainee teachers who spotted a mystery light over Exmouth at the weekend have asked if anyone can explain exactly what it was they saw. The three students at Rolle College reported the UFO sighting to Exmouth police but checks with the coastguard and other authorities have failed to come up with an answer. Coincidentally, police all over the Westcountry received numerous calls at the weekend after what is thought to have been a meteor was reported to have have "scorched" across the night sky before coming down with a "bang" in Bridgwater Bay.

The Exmouth students say the strange 'moon-sized' orange ball of light they saw was moving East to West and falling towards Lyme Bay Off Exmouth - the wrong direction for the Bridgwater reports. First year B.E.D students Lee Jones, 19, from Weston Super Mare, and Mark Marsden, 20, from Sussex, were watching a video with fellow third y year American exchange student Stephanie Glover, in a ground floor flat at Kingsthorpe Hall of Residence, Rolle Road, at 9.45 pm on Sunday evening.

They said their attention was attracted to the strange light in the dark night sky through the seaward-facing window of the flat.

"We saw this light like an orange hall moving very slowly across the sky from our left to right. We saw it go down very, very slowly and then go out of sight below the trees on our horizon," said Mr Marsden.

"It was like nothing we had ever seen before. We went down to the beach to see if something had come down in the sea but we could see nothing and two people we spoke to who were walking their dogs along the seafront said they had seen absolutely nothing," he added. The three have been the subject of some attention from fellow students since reporting the sighting and would now like to know if anyone else saw anything or can explain what the mystery light was." [35]

We tried to contact Mr Brady, but according to residents at Rivermead Court, he had moved several years before and no-one knew where he lived anymore.

A year later, the *Exmouth Journal* printed a letter containing another sighting of an amorphous ball of light:

"I visited Exmouth for three days last April and on the second night (April 3rd I think), in my hotel on the Beacon I couldn`t sleep, and stood at the window - it was around 3.40 a.m and a still moonlit night - when suddenly an orange coloured "ball" rolled from one side of the bay (on the right) and disappeared at the other side. It was not so high as the stars (at least I don`t think so) and was quite large. I could see the surface of it was not smooth but sort of rouhghed up. It was not shooting along but rolling over and over as a billiard ball does on a table. I intended to write to you directly I got home but kept putting it off.

I would be most interested to hear if anyone else has reported seeing it. It was a sort of "lit up" orange colour - not just orange if you know what I mean.

I can tell you I did not sleep after that! And, people in the train going home were all interested to hear about it. My friend who lives in Exmouth reminded me to write to you.

*Barbara M.Bellinger,
28 Privet House,
Cumberland St
Portsmouth Harbour"* [36]

Nick Pope is one of the more contentious characters in British UFOlogy. For some years he was the Civil Servant in charge of Dept. AS2a of the Ministry of Defence where he was in charge of collating civilian UFO reports. In an interview with Michael Lindemann he talked about another wave of westcountry UFO activity:

"I think the moment where I really felt, "Okay, this is it, I'm not playing any more," was a wave of sightings that occurred on the 30th and 31st of March, 1993. We had several hundred reports that came our way. Many of the witnesses were police. A lot of police in the southwest of the country, in Devon and Cornwall, saw something. Now, as with all of these big waves of sightings, quite a lot of the reports were fairly mundane, lights in the sky. But even so, it was quite late at night -- most of these reports were between, say, 1:00 and 1:30 in the morning -- and because there were police officers on night patrol, you're dealing with more than average recognition training, and people used to being out and about, and used to seeing lights and other things in the sky. Repeatedly, I heard the phrase, 'This was like nothing I'd ever seen before in my life.' People

were genuinely quite spooked by this.

What was generally reported was two lights, flying in a perfect formation, with a third, much fainter light -- our old friend the flying triangle, really. The lights were described as being in a triangle formation. It's difficult to say, of course. It's quite possible they could have been three separate things flying in formation, but the impression from talking to witnesses was that this was a triangular craft with lights mounted on the underside, at the edges. The most interesting reports, of course, were the ones which occurred at close distance. There was a family in Staffordshire who apparently saw this thing so low -- and they described it as either triangular or diamond shaped -- that they leapt into their car and tried to chase it. They didn't succeed, although at one point they thought it was so low that it had actually come down in a field. It wasn't there when they got to it. They described a low, humming sound, a very low-frequency sound. They said you didn't just hear this sound, you felt it, like standing in front of a bass speaker.

The really intriguing thing was that this object, whatever it was, then proceeded to fly over two military bases. It was seen by the guard patrol at RAF Cosford, about three or four people, [who] made an instant report of this, obviously because it had flown over their base. They checked radar. There was nothing on the screens, nothing at all, and there was nothing scheduled to fly. No military or civil aircraft should have been airborne in that area at all. They phoned the nearby base at RAF Shawbury, about 12 miles away from Cosford. The meteorological officer there took the call. He was a man with about eight years experience of looking into the night sky and then doing the weather report for the next day. So he knew his way around objects and phenomena. Now, to his absolute amazement, he saw a light in the distance, coming closer and closer.

That light eventually resolved itself into a solid structured craft that he saw again flying directly over the base, but at much closer proximity than the guard patrol at Cosford had seen it. He estimated that the height of the object was no more than 200 feet. Its size, he said, was midway between a C-130 Hercules transport aircraft and a Boeing 747. He heard the low hum, too. He had not spoken to any other witnesses, except the Cosford people, who I don't think had reported the sound. He reported this low-frequency hum. Perhaps most disturbingly of all, he reported this thing throwing a beam of light down at the nearby countryside and fields just beyond the perimeter fence at the base. And this light was tracking backwards and forwards, he said to me, "as if it was looking for something." The beam of light then retracted, and the craft moved off. It was traveling very slowly, I should say, probably no more than 20 or 30 mph. Then it gained a little bit of height, and then it just shot off to the horizon in little more than a second. Needless to say, that was a description I had come across many times in other UFO reports, the virtual hover to the high-Mach accelerations in an instant.

I launched a full investigation. I made all the usual checks, trying to track down aircraft movement, satellite activity, airships, weather balloons, meteorites, etc., etc. I drew a blank -- with one exception -- and then put a report up the chain of command. The exception was a ballistic missile early warning sensor at RAF Fylingdales, in North Yorkshire. It is estimated that at some stage in the night there had been a rocket reentry of, I think, Cosmos 2238, which might have caused a very brief firework display in the high atmosphere. It's just possible that some of the vague lights-in-the-sky sightings might have been explained in that way, although Fylingdales didn't seem very sure on whether [the satellite reentry] was actually going to be visible from the UK at all." [37] [38]

The next year, another letter referring to a ball of light appeared in the *Exmouth Journal*:

"My husband and I were visiting Exmouth for a family wedding. On Sunday evening, March 22nd, we were driving towards Topsham at about 8 p.m with some friends, when, on the left, I saw a bright light in the sky. It was light a glowing flourescent ball, not red but bright pink. It was not moving. It then appeared on the right side and much higher. After a few more seconds it just vanished.

I have received two articles from your newspaper, one suggesting a distress flare - but I have never seen one move sideways across the sky - or a rabbit hunter's torch beam - I don't think so - cat lights, certainly not.

Ever thought about UFOs?

Mrs S.E.Smith
Guildford
Surrey". [39]

The main focus of UFO activity over East Devon, however does appear to take place in roughly a ten year cycle. Although there are few reports from the sixties there were highly publicised outbreaks of activity in 1997, 1987 and 1977/8 when the sightings were so common and so regular that it became quite a regular night out for students from the local colleges.

Nigel remembers seeing them on a number of occasions. In September 1977, together with a varying number of his friends, he drove up to Woodbury castle where the car park overlooks the Exe Estuary. They would take a picnic tea, which being students consisted mostly of beer, and they would sit and watch in awe as nearly every night glowing balls of orange light - sometimes as many as four in an evening - would gently float inland from the Estuary, following the river towards Exeter in a rolling motion. They would get nearly as far upriver as the city and then disappear into a pinprick of light. [40]

One final occurrence that we have put in this chapter, mostly by default, because it doesn't really fit anywhere else is taken from Delderfield's *Exmouth Milestones*:

"Living in the 20th Century, when we accept as nothing unusual the fact that an airplane crosses the Atlantic by means of radio control, it is not easdy to appreciate what must have been the amazement of Exmothians in 1845, when at daybreak one morning a man strangely clad was observed to leave the beach near the sea wall by a series of motions similar to those of a bird attempting to fly. It was indeed a singular attempt, and we read that this unknown pioneer did in fact fly, crossing the water and landing safely on the Warren. The flight took him ten minutes. This is recorded in Woolmer's Gazette, *the Exeter newspaper of the time"*. [41]

The distance from Exmouth sea-wall to Dawlish Warren is no more than three hundred yards and if, indeed this mystery aviator were travelling by hitherto unsuspected mechanical means he was doing it extremely slowly. Is this just a local legend with no basis in reality? Was this really an `unknown pioneer` of manned flight? Was it, perhaps the first and only sighting of a hitherto unknown Exmothian analogue of the Point Pleasant Mothman or the Owlman of Mawnan? In the words of one well known character from a much loved television Science Fiction series, we have insufficient data to proceed further with our enquiries.

X

I am a naturalist as well as a fortean, and I think that is important to note that certain parts of the Lyme Bay area have a peculiar ecosystem all of their own. For example Lulworth Cove in Dorset is one of the favoured sites for a particularly peculiar re-occurent mutation within certain species of British butterfly. The semi-legendary British Entomologist L.Hugh Newman noted on a number of occasions how, on collecting expeditions to the area a mutation known as halved gynandromorphism was particularly prevalent in the area. [1]

This is a mutation which...

"shows indications of both sexes apparent in one specimen. In the past these specimens were described as hermaphrodites but this term is incorrect. The most striking examples occur in the Blues where the blackish-brown female may be streaked with the blue of the male, or in more extreme cases may be completely halved, male on one side and female on the other. These are referred to as bilateral gynandromorphs; the antennae, thorax and abdomen can be affected in the same way. Some striking examples are illustrated in the Adonis and Chalk-hill Blues, and the Scotch Argus. Intersex specimens have a similar appearance but are genuinely of one sex; this occurs most often in the Silver-studded Blue where a female may have a dusting of the blue scales of the male or even areas of blue on the wings." [2]

The coastal areas of Lyme Bay also provide ine of the few known habitats for Britain`s rarest snake:

The smooth snake (length up to 70 cms) lives on heathlands in Dorset, Hampshire and Surrey where it can lay its eggs in sandy soils. These snakes have round pupils to their eyes, greyish background colour with usually two rows of darker brown or black markings along the back.

Smooth snakes feed on other reptiles, mostly slow worms and lizards, but small mammals such as pygmy shrews and young birds are also taken.

However, something which is relatively little known is that the area, until the end of the 19th Century at least, was that it was also the haunt for a bizarre animal known as the scarlet viper. Although these days it is commonly agreed that it was nothing but an unusual colour morph of the common viper, for many years it was thought that this animal was distinct enough to be granted full specific status.

There is also question about some of the lizards reported from the Lyme Bay area. There is no doubt that whilst extremely rare, the rarest known species of British lizard lives in the area.

The sand lizard prefers to lay eggs into shallow hollows dug in sandy soil. Like the smooth snake, it is found mainly in southern Britain, but also on the dunes of the Merseyside coast. These lizards, which can grow to 20 cms, have a grey-beige background with dark brown blotches. Sand lizards have the ability to take food in large quantities when it is freely available and will eat most types of insects, worms, slugs, and can eat their own young too, if necessary. [4]

However, there is some evidence to suggest that another species of lizard; *Lacerta viridis* - the European Green Lizard - a species not officially known from the British Isles may also live in the coastal areas adjacent to Lyme Bay. [5]

I have shown elsewhere that these are probably escapees from animals brought into England inadvertently in baskets of fruit and flowers shipped from the Channel Islands (where they live) to Weymouth, from whence they have colonised part of the surrounding area. It has also been claimed that any mysterious animals reported during the 19th Century from East Devon were likely to be escapees from the collection of a mysterious Exmouth naturalist called Mr Fish. [6] He was blamed for the escaped wallabies which some people claimed caused the so-called Devil's Footprints, and he was also blamed for releasing these emerald green lizards into the verdant countryside of this portion of the westcountry. The irony is, that, apart from these two references, we have one last group of reptilian inhabitants of the area which, though not extant in the true sense of the world, are, we believe, important from a socio-cultural viewpoint.

The undoubted heroine of all naturalists in Southern England is Mary Anning who was born in Lyme Regis, on May 21, 1799 and died on March 9, 1847. She lived through a life of privation and hardship to become what one source called *"the greatest fossilist the world ever knew."*

Her biography reads:

"Anning is credited with finding the first specimen of Ichthyosaurus acknowledged by the Geological Society in London. She also discovered the first nearly complete example of the Plesiosaurus; the first British Pterodactylus macronyx, a fossil flying reptile; the Squaloraja fossil fish, a transitional link between sharks and rays; and finally the Plesiosaurus macrocephalus.

Her history is incomplete and contradictory. Some accounts of her life have been fictionalized, and her childhood discoveries have been mythologized. She was a curiosity in her own time, bringing tourism to her home town of Lyme Regis. Only her personal qualities and her long experience brought her any recognition at all, since she was a woman of a lower social class and from a provincial area at a time when upper-class London men, gentlemanly scholars, received the bulk of the credit for geological discoveries.

Anning learned to collect fossils from her father, Richard, a cabinet maker by trade and a fossil collector by avocation. But he died at 44 in 1810, leaving his family destitute. They relied on charity to survive.

Fossil collecting was a dangerous business in the seaside town. Anning walked and waded under unstable cliffs at low tide, looking for specimens dislodged from the rocks. During her teenage years, the family built both a reputation and a business as fossil hunters. In 1817 they met Lieutenant-Colonel Thomas Birch, a well-to-do fossil collector who became a supporter of the family. He attributed major discoveries in the area to them, and he arranged to sell his personal collection of fossils for the family's benefit. Most of Anning's fossils were sold to institutions and private collectors, but museums tended to credit only people who donated the fossils to the institution. Therefore, it has been difficult for historians to trace many fossils that Mary Anning located; the best known are a small Ichthyosaurus discovered in 1821 and the first Plesiosaurus, unearthed in 1823.

Mary had some recognition for her intellectual mastery of the anatomy of her subjects, from Lady Harriet Silvester, who visited Anning in 1824 and recorded in her diary:

the extraordinary thing in this young woman is that she had made herself so thoroughly acquainted with the science that the moment she finds any bones she knows to what tribe they belong. . . . by reading and application she has arrived to that greater degree of knowledge as to be in the habit of writing and talking with professors and other clever men on the subject, and they all acknowledge that she understands more of the science than anyone else in this kingdom.

Visitors to Lyme increased as Anning won the respect of contemporary scientists. In the last decade of her life she received an annuity from the British Association for the Advancement of Science (1838). The Geological Society of London collected a stipend for her and she was named the first Honorary Member of the new Dorset County Museum, one year before her death from breast cancer. Her obituary was published in the Quarterly Journal of the Geological Society--*an organization that would not admit women until 1904.* " [7]

Her legacy to the world is that her discoveries defined the modern science of palaentology and forever linked the southern coast of East Devon and West Dorset with the study of dinosaurs and she re-awakened the subject of dragons within the collective psyche of a country that had long forgotten them. I would love to be able to say that her discoveries prompted a string of dragon sightings, but they didn`t. Her legacy is important however in terms of the other subjects discussed in this book because it did change the perception that he contempories held of the world around them.

This change may well have had extreme repercussions.

Now for what is perhaps the strangest animal mystery in the history of the United Kingdom.

In 1982, a Tasmanian wildlife officer, Hans Naarding, was surveying birds in a remote part of North-West Tasmania. At two o`clock one morning he woke from a fitful sleep in his vehicle. As always on such occasions, he switched on his spotlight in order to scan the surrounding area for any passing, nocturnal wildlife. There, caught in the beam, is a fully grown Thylacine. For three spellbound minutes Naarding has a clear view of an animal declared `probably extinct`, in 1936! This exciting encounter is by no means unique and is only one of a growing number of sightings being made in Tasmania, and, more controversially, on mainland Australia and even in New Guinea.

The following description, along with much of this section is extrapolated from an article by Alan Pringle in *Animals & Men* no 2. The Thylacine, Tasmanian Wolf or Tasmanian Tiger *(Thylacinus cynocephalus)* is the largest known marsupial carnivore to have survived into historic and modern times. Superficially dog like enough to explain the popular name, its most striking characteristic is the series of 15-20 dark brown, vertical stripes ranging down its back to the long, inflexible tail. Hence the name `Tiger`.

Thylacines measure up to 160 cm in length, including a 50 cm. They are unique amongst marsupials in that the male has a rudimentary pouch, and they are also famous for their enormous gape, the largest of any mammal. They are known from fossil records to have existed on mainland Australia over 3000 years ago and in Tasmania until the arrival of European settlers in the early 1800`s. Although their natural prey is small mammals they soon developed a taste for sheep and were persecuted by farmers, and systematically exterminated until the last wild one was shot in 1930. A captive specimen lived on at the now defunct Beaumaris Zoo in Hobart until September 7th 1936. About ninety Thylacines were held by Zoos between 1850 and 1936, but as far as we know they never bred.

Since 1936 there have been many expeditions to various parts of Tasmania in an attempt to determine whether or not the species has survived. No hard evidence has been obtained although many tracks were found and hair and faecal samples collected.

Sightings have been steadily increasing, however, over the years, and many believe that the animal is not extinct. Because of the island`s vast tracts of rugged mountains, temperate rain forests and steep river valleys very few people are ever IN the position to see one. The anglers, hikers and bushmen who do are usually, however the sort of experienced people who know what they are seeing. More often though, thylacines are fleetingly glimpsed in the headlights of vehicles traversing the island`s lonely roads. Ironically it will probably be as a result of a road kill rather than as a result or organised research that the first post 1936 specimen will be obtained.

In 1990 to two fishermen were driving home through the Cradle Mountains in the north of the island saw what appeared to be a Thylacine in their headlights. In the same year an adult with cub was seen not far from the same spot. One of the most recent sightings, in July 1993, involving an alleged Thylacine crossing a road witnessed by two motorists. This sighting, however, occurred in Western Australia, where the species is supposed to have died out thirty centuries ago! Recent colour photographs taken in Western Australia are of doubtful authenticity and scientists are divided on the motives of the photographer.

In New Guinea, like mainland Australia, the Thylacine is known only from fossil evidence, but recently one researcher has received reports of Thylacine like animals known to the highland people of the Indonesian province of Irian-Jaya where some of the upland country is similar to parts of Tasmania, but much less explored, and would provide ideal conditions for Thylacines. The people there seem to know the animal well and claim that they are NOT confusing it with wild or feral dogs.

With over a thousand sightings of this enigmatic animal SINCE its official demise in 1936, it may not be long until irrefutable proof in the form of a road kill or a good, clear, film is obtained. A dead animal would, no doubt satisfy the scientific community, but, with a species obviously as rare as this, they need to be left alive, as the population, although recovering, is still very valuable indeed. Besides, the animal still has official protection in Tasmania because of a law passed in 1936 - ironically the same year that the last known Thylacine died! [8] [9] [10]

At 3.30 AM on the 7th April 1974 Joan Gilbert saw a strange creature at Branksome in Dorset. Her description was uncanny:

"It had stripes, a long thin tail, and seemed to be all grey, though it might have had some yellow on it. It was thin and definitely not a fox".

She later identified the animal as a Thylacine from a picture in an illustrated book! [11]

We live in what Ted Holiday, (a researcher we have already met due to his groundbreaking research linking UFOs and lake monster sightings, and also with reference to his musings on the problems encountered when trying to photograph fortean subjects) called a Goblin Universe.

In a manuscript eventually published after his death in 1979 he wrote:

"We inhabit a strange cosmos where nothing is absolute, final or conclusive. Truth is an actor who dons one mask after another, and then vanishes through a secret door in the stage scenery when we reach out to grab him. All he leaves behind is a sardonic chuckle which we record, take away, analyse and debate. But we never see his face.

Human beings have thought crookedly since history began. Such thinking afflicts us because we relate cause to effect falsely or inaccurately. We imagine that a man, a rainbow or a piece of quartz is a thing; but these are not things-they are really ideas manifesting in space and time. Moreover, they are immensely complex ideas, far surpassing any scientific description we care to advance. Each idea is related to all other ideas in an infinite progression of subtle links which leave the mind spellbound with awe at the sheer majesty of creation.

If we were not petty and provincial in our dealing with phenomena, we would go insane. A professional biologist in Chicago publishes satirical mock-scientific papers on a private press for circulation to his friends. These are his relief from the serious technical papers he also publishes throughout the world through normal scientific channels. Some scientists gleefully play ingenious hoaxes on their colleagues. Such activities are essential to preserve mental stability in a cosmos which slopes away rapidly into the Goblin Universe.

The Goblin Universe is the place in the play where the actor switches one mask for another. Suddenly you have the weird sensation of falling through the floor. The lights change colour. The clocks all go wrong. And the villain who died in Act 1 is alive and well again in Act 3. Now is the time to smile and order ice-cream, to murmur a dirty joke to your partner and wonder what won the 2.30. otherwise you will end up being escorted firmly from the theatre by hospital attendants towards a padded ambulance." [12]

It took a long time for me, at least, to come to terms with the fact that in essentials Holiday was correct. We can no longer afford to look at the mysteries of the cosmos in terms of three Euclidean dimensions, Newton's laws of physics, Darwin's theory of evolution and Mendel's Laws of inheritance. The omniverse is a far more subtle and extraordinary place than that. This is something that children's authors have known for many years, and which the rest of humankind has yet to wake up to.

One of the pieces of writing that best encapsulates the holistic view of a fortean universe comes from someone who would, I am sure, have been horrified that her work was included in a book such as this one. She was a children's author called Frances Jenkins Olcott's who wrote this forward to her 1929 book, *Wonder Tales from Fairy Isles:*

"The British Isles are preeminently above all other isles, the home of the Fairies. England, Wales, Scotland, with Man, Ireland, and the islands in the British seas are said, in Fairy Cult, to be inhabited by multitudes of soul-less little people that go invisible.

Airy faerie beings of fantasy are they, appearing, vanishing, and disappearing, in lovely, quaint, or grotesque forms. They are the People of Peace, Good Folk, Little People, Gentry, Kind Neighbors, Fair Family.

They are, also, Leprechauns, Cluricauns, Brownies, Pucks, Hobgoblins, and other "Fairies and Elves! shadows of night," filmy and tiny, or of puckish shape, or expanding to human size. Of various colors are they, "Fairies black, gray, green, and white." And of a moonlit eve they dance and sway to ravishing elfin music in Fairy Rings; they frolic and gambol on green heights, or float in misty wreaths along hillsides. They hold goblin markets in the meadows. From harebells they quaff nectar of dew, dine off spreading mushroom-tops, feast on elfin food, cradle their babes in flowers, turn burgs, raths, or forts--the fairy mounds--into elfin palaces gleaming with treasures. They guard Fairy Gold. They steal pretty maids and brave youths, kidnap human infants and leave changeling brats instead. They pixy-lead the traveller, tease the foolish, hound the wicked, reward the kind, and spin and churn and reap and thresh for the good farm-folk all for a bannock and a bowl of cream.

Capricious and captious are the Fairies, generous and grateful, whimsical, mischievous, and tricksy as elfin fancy leads. And such fine wee things they are with their protective coloration of spring green and the hues of flowers, or starting up from earth arrayed in pointed red cap and green jacket. There are sociable Fairies, hosts of them, following King Oberon and Mab his Queen. There are odd little fellows who love solitude and tap fairy brogues, sitting lonely under quiet hedges.

Innocent imaginings are these, joys of the nursery, fair flowers from the garden of fancy, magic seed of poesy, bewitching alike the Morning Star of Song and the Swan of Avon --Fancy's Child--and charming the stern moods of the titan Milton.

And the Fairies are rhythmic creatures. They may not be approached through prose alone. The pulse of fairy-life beats in swaying rhythmic verse. So in this book will be found tales of Elves and witchery strung like precious fairy jewels on a gossamer thread of pale moonbeam, alternating with tiny beads of clan song, madrigal, and charm. And this wonder necklace, this chain of fairy gems flashing with morning dew, may it delight our children by its freshness.

The nursery tales they know so well, like "Jack the Giant Killer" and "Jack and the Bean Stalk," they must look for in the Fairy Books of Mr. Lang, Mr. Rhys, Mr. Jacobs, and other folk-lorists who have collected and edited for children. And fairy doings from all the world over they will find in my own Book of Elves and Fairies. But when they pass through the magic portals of this Wonder Tales from Fairy Isles, may they wander delightedly in new elfin realms. Even the snatches of fairy song and verse, we hope will be new to them. In order to preserve the illusion of Fairy Land, the authors of the verses and rhymes are given only in the table of contents.

The irrational side of folk-lore with its death raps, death lights, banshees, howling ghosts, bloody beasts, and other gruesome wights, is not here. Such lore is of deep interest to the student of folk-custom and belief, but is not for our children.

The British Fairies are scientific data to the antiquarian who is busy drawing their history from mounds, dusty archives, and the lips of old folk who remember what their grandparents taught them. For the origin of the Fairy Cult of the United Kingdom is bound up with the history of early Britain.

The several theories advanced for the origin of British Fairies are discussed elsewhere by learned folk-lorists. One theory, widely accepted, is that they are survivals of the Druid Cult.

In my Foreword to Wonder Tales from Baltic Wizards, I have tried to show how such favorites as "Aladdin and the Wonderful Lamp" and other folk-tales of magicians and enchanters, have had their genesis in the soul enslaving Cult of Shamanism.

And it would seem that the witcheries of the Fairy Folk are but the miasmas from expiring heathen superstition. Under the spell of folk-fancy, these noxious exhalations have been transmuted into a Fairy Cult, one side of which is mirky and sinister. But the poetic childlike side is as beautiful as the pure white waterlily that arises from the breast of the stagnant pool.

It is claimed by many folklorists, that the Celtic gods and goddesses came under the transforming influence of Christianity. These heathen deities were worshipped and placated in ways largely evil, even with human sacrifice. The inhabitants of Britain, newly converted, were taught by their missionaries that followers of Christ Our Lord should abstain from worshipping these false gods. The partly Christianized people, loath to let their house hold gods go and still half believing in their eerie power to harm or help, in time dwarfed or etherealized them by the action of folk imagination. They believed them to be soulless diminutive people. And even today, largely in country districts, specially in Man and Ireland, there are people who speak fearfully or affectionately of the Fairies, though they dare not call them that fearing to offend, but say Good People or other placating names.

As the stories in this book show, the fairy lore of the racial divisions of the United Kingdom has distinctive characteristics. Ireland is a treasure house of Celtic fairy survivals, folk tales homely and humorous, fairy charms, beliefs and legends; and ancient literary Celtic romances and poems colorful and heroic with the deeds of the semi-mythological Daanan race that came to be thought fairy. In Wales, the Cambrian Tylwyth Teg, the Fairies, are not so omnipresent, but they sport and play; while at times appear the Fays, or Fairy Ladies as in the Mabinogion. In quiet secluded spots in Man, the Good People frisk and gambol in blue and green and red; they hunt, steal, tease, and reward; while that sad outcast Fairy, the Phynnodderree, serves the good housewife.

Giants cumber the land of Britain, but Cornwall has a special brand of Giants possibly borrowed from the Danish invaders; and Cornwall swarms with hosts of tiny Spriggans, Knockers in the tin mines, and tricksy Piskies. Over the border in Devonshire dwell multitudes of the little Pixies, for Devonshire is as rich in fairy lore as in cream. And saucy Pixy Folk hold their elfin fairs in Somerset.

The Anglo-Saxons "believed in the existence of a certain race of little devils, that were neither absolutely spirits nor men, called Duergar or Dwarfs," we read, so Dwarfs lend their quota of wonders to our book. In Scotland the Witches toil and boil, bubble and trouble; while Brownie helps the housewife and teases the dairymaids." [13][14]

As we have seen in the preceeding chapters of this book, the apparently disparate and heterogenous phenomena described here are all, apparently inter-related in some subtle (or possibly not so-subtle) way.

Fortean researchers have long been aware of a phenomenon called window areas. The term was first coined by John Keel who postulated that phenomena such as mysterious animals whose existence could not be explained within conventional zoological terms of reference, UFOs and even ghosts and other apparitions were in fact inhabitants of another dimension who/which were only visible in this one by means of some mysterious trans dimensional portal or window. He postulated that these `windows` only occured in specific places, and his term `window areas` has become part of the accepted parlance of the fortean researcher. [15][16]

As will become evident in the final chapters of this book, I do not believe that one has to postulate a series of different `dimensions` in order to explain such phenomena. However, the term window area is a good one and we shall continue to use it.

American researcher John Horrigan has dscribed visiting one such area in an un-named area of Colorado in the United States:

"Visited "The Mysterious Valley" and interviewd its brilliant and eloquent author Chris O'Brien. Met his lovely girlfriend Isadora. Chris may very well be the foremost authority on the mysterious as he claims that the valley is "the most paranormal place on earth". Odd lights, "Cheap Fireworks", flying triangles, battleship-sized cigar-shaped craft, aliens, prairie dragons, men-in-black, ghosts, bigfoot, black helicopters, cattle mutilation and the devil himself are making appearances in this sacred valley to Native Americans. The San Luis Valley got onto the supernatural map nationally in 1967, when a mare known as "Lady" was found mysteriously mutilated. O'Brien is a gifted musician and composer, but when he speaks one is immediately tantalized and mesmerized. He's that good.

Although I only saw one aircraft in the three days that I spent in the valley, the military uses the Sangre de Cristo mountains (part of the Rockies) and the area east near La Veta frequently. They call it the M.O.A. Military Operations Area. The military has conveniently chosen this active U.F.O. region as an area to conduct low-level flying maneuvers, complete with C-130s and a wide variety of sophisticated helicopters. Thrown in a few of the 10,000 flares dropped by aircraft in the M.O.A. annually, and you'll have either the UFO sightings explained or simply a diversionary tactic employed by the military. A lot of cattle have fallen victim to odd mutilations. O'Brien calls them "U.A.D.'s - unusual animal deaths." Chris thinks that over 600 head have had laser-like incisions inflicted upon them; had their alimentary canal (esophagus to the anus) cored out; had eyes or organs plucked out or in one case had their brain and spinal chord removed! Some are the results of predatorial action. Could some be snacks for the aliens? No footprints are found. Sometimes no sign of blood. An electromagnetic charge emits from some of the bovine carcasses. UFOs, odd flashes and precede the event. "Black" helicopters appear following the incident. Crestone is a real hip place. I crossed the Rio Grande more times than I did my old man as an adolescent. Route 17 is a straight 50-mile drag. The sweeping vistas are magnificent. And Chris O'Brien rocks!" [17][18]

During my career as a fortean researcher I have visited several others. There is a specific slice of southern Cornwall which is undoubtedly a `window area` and I have described the gamut of high strangeness that has occurred there in *The Owlman and Others* (1997,8). [18] The island of Puerto Rico is another, as are parts of Mexico (see *Only Fools and Goatsuckers [1999]*), [19] there seems little doubt that several areas in South

East Devon, including Littleham, Woodbury Common and parts of Lyme Bay itself are another one.

What common factors (apart from having more than their fair share of quasi-fortean occurences) are there between these different areas? In order to find out, we should take another look at the range of phenomena described in the first three parts of this book, and try to decide which of them have any direct link to each other and which are figurative red herrings.

PART FOUR: WHY?

"All along that singing River, a black mass of men was seen, and above their shining weapons, hung their own beloved green, death to every foe and traitor whistle loud the marching tune and hoorah my boys for freedom, 'tis the rising of the moon"

Trad arr. Shane McGowan

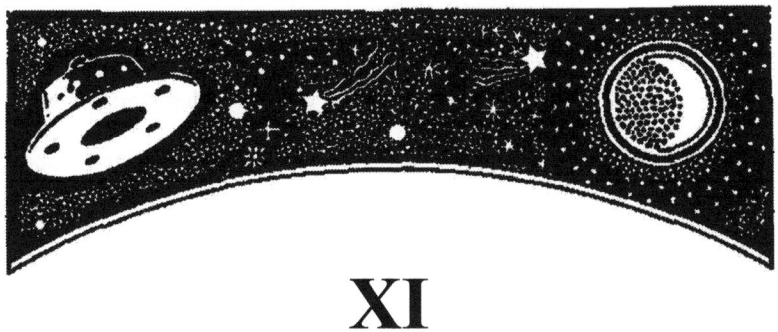

XI

We are faced with a large amount of apparently heterogenous data and it is now time to take a pace back and try to make sense of it all.

The first thing that is apparent is that the events in south-east Devon during the summer and early autumn of 1997 cannot be seen in a vacuum. As we have shown, such spates of apparently disparate phenomena are well known within the canon of fortean literature. Over the years I have been involved in investigating several of them, most notably the events of the long, hot summer of 1976 in southern Cornwall. [1]

Although, if you read any of the books on general mystery animals such as *Alien Animals* by Janet and Colin Bord, [2] or indeed any of the contemporary copies of *Fortean Times* [3] the claim that Cornwall had been particularly weird at the time is often made, it is not until you visit the Cornish Studies Library in the back streets of Redruth, sit yourself down at one of their microfiche machines, and physically examine twelve months or more`s issues of the *Falmouth Packet*, the *West Briton* and the *Western Morning News* that you can see quite how strange the time actually was. For a period between the late autumn of 1975 and the early spring of 1977 it seems that Southern Cornwall was seized by a period of collective madness. Much of this is chronicled in some depth in my book *The Owlman and Others* [4][5] but even there I think that I failed to give a true picture of quite how strange the area had become.

There were dramatic extremes in the weather - droughts and floods - heatwaves and frozen wastes. The local animal life went (figuratively and literally) crazy; one unfortunate woman was imprisoned in her house by hordes of attacking birds which literally beat themselves to death against the walls of her house, which was dripping red with their blood.

Another woman was similarly imprisoned by a mob of feral cats, dog attacks trebled, swimmers were attacked by dolphins (who also saved other swimmers from drowning), and there were reports that cattle belonging to local farmers had developed the power of teleportation. [6]

Most interesting to the fortean, however, were the burgeoning numbers of UFO sightings and the reports of three entirely different sets of mystery animal in the region; Morgawr (the Cornish Sea Serpent), the Cornish mystery big cats and the Owlman of Mawnan.

Whereas this is far from being the only `flap` of apparently disparate quasi-fortean phenomena united purely by geographical location and time on record it does have the advantage of being (apart from the events in this book) the one that I have investigated most thoroughly, and so, for statistical purposes, therefore, it would seem a useful exercise to compare the two.

The first, and most obvious correlation is the weather, which was uniformly good, during the summer of 1976 in Cornwall, and during the summer of 1997 in Exmouth. It should also be noted that, according to the records, the summer of 1978 which saw a UFO flap, Genette Tate's abduction and a number of other events described at various points during the first ten chapters of this book, was also an unusually good one as was the summer of 1917 (when Emily Bamsey disappeared) and even the summer of 1909, which saw the spate of worldwide mystery airship sightings. [7]

I noted in *The Owlman and Others* [8] how Mawnan Smith, and in particular the areas adjacent to Mawnan old Church were surrounded by a particular sinister reputation. According to Delderfield, Exmouth was once similarly tainted:

"In those early days, and indeed well into the eighteenth century, Exmouth had a distinctly unsavoury reputation, so much so in fact that, when Lady Glenorchy, widow and heiress of Viscount Glenorchy, had her Chaplain preach in the town in 1776, the good lady felt that Exmouth was so much in need of reform that she suggested to a Mr. Holmes of Exeter that she would like to have a house licensed for the spreading of the Gospel in Exmouth. That worthy gentleman expressed the opinion that Exmouth was so wicked a place that it would be in vain to attempt anything there. Lady Glenorchy went on with her plans, however, and in 1777 opened a chapel. The good results were not immediately noticeable, for ten years later tribute is paid in some old records to the indefatigable exertions of a Samuel Eyre "to improve the morals of the in-

habitants, then most notoriously depraved."

As late as 1850 a petition was passed to the General Health Board, and the inspector's report subsequently issued included had never seen human habitations more utterly devoid of the precautions necessary for the preservation of health and cleanliness ~ more crowded, dark, close, filthy and loathsome than those in the part called South Town .

These conditions applied to all small towns at this date and to some much later. The result of this inquiry was that a Local Board of Health was set up in the town. The boundaries of the district affected were the Withycombe Brook, Marpool Road, Long Lane and Lime Kiln Lane (now known as Watery Lane)." [9]

There are several accounts in the records of the brutal and primitive behavious of people in the vicinity, and Delderfield notes one particularly unpleasant episode, which took place under the aegis of the Church of England:

"*It was a Sunday morning in Summer. From the small town-ship the population, behaving as if on holiday bent, streamed along the main road out of the town. Gesticulating, laughing and talking excitedly, they made their way to the Parish Church. Hundreds gathered at the church gate, and the path to the church itself was lined by excited crowds as if awaiting a spectacular procession. Just before the service was about to start, a quiver of excitement ran through the throng, followed by a silence worthy of the graves on which the people stood.*

A strange procession drew near the waiting crowd. Carrying a white wand, a middle-aged woman, dressed in a white sheet, approached. Her grey hair hung unkempt about her shoulders; her face was bathed in tears.

On either side of her a churchwarden, also carrying a white wand, attended the poor wretch, and as the group neared the Church the three principals halted while the woman removed her shoes. Then with a sob she proceeded, walking with the agony that the sharp flints bring to feet seldom bared. On arrival at the Church door she was halted, and there remained in the public gaze during the church service, at the conclusion of which the sentence of excommunication was read out to her.

This, one of the. last cases of open penance in this country, took place at Littleham Church in 1805. The woman, Susan Chamberlin, who lived in a cottage on the Littleham Road, had been sentenced to this rigorous act of discipline by the Spiritual Court and in such a way was her "flagrant act of wickedness" purged. What this act was, history does not record, but in the Churchwarden's Accounts for 1806 the following entry appears :-

" Paid ye expenses for S. Chamberlin's penance, £3 5s. 8d." [10]

There are other links as well. Both areas are predominantly rural, with agriculture, fishing and tourism being the major economic forces. Both areas are adjacent to the sea and both areas have large numbers of ancient archaeological sites in the vicinity. Both areas have an interesting range of wildlife living there, and as we shall see in Chapter XIII there are other links as well.

For the moment, however, it is important to examine one of the most important links, because, apart from the animal mutilations and the UFO reports, both areas have reports of zooform phenomena - in Mawnan Smith, the eponymous Owlman and in Exmouth/Littleham/Woodbury we have various four footed furry fiends; the strange beasts of Hullham Road and the animal that was "all lit up". [11]

We must now take a look at Zooform Phenomena and attempt to reach some conclusions about the nature of this particularly elusive beast. There are three main types of mystery animal. The first are simple. They are `cryptids` - species of animal whose existence is unrecognised by mainstream science. The second grouping are quasi- or pseudo-cryptids. The animals in this group are a little more problematical as they are members of a species which is KNOWN to exist in a place where it is not SUPPOSED to be. This can either be because it is presumed to be extinct in that specific area or, more commonly, because they are exotic species that have escaped or been introduced

The third, final, and in some ways the most contentious of the three groupings of apparently unknown creatures are the ones that may well not be creatures at all!

At the risk of severely angering the folk in the Yeti, and Bigfoot camps and indeed some of my friends and colleagues who have spent so much of their lives sitting on the shores of Loch Ness waiting for something to happen, this is the category into which most of the most well known members of the iconography of Cryptozoology fit in.

This is not the time nor the place to enter into a long discussion about the veracity or otherwise of the most `media friendly` cryptids, The Yeti,

Bigfoot and the Loch Ness monster, but even the most hardcore nessiephile or traditional cryptozoologist would admit that the volumes that have been written about these phenomena includes a fair amount of evidence that suggests that some if not all of their manifestations may not necessarily be of physical origin.

One of the most important books to have been written on the subject of Fortean Zoology in the forty years since Heuvelmans first published in English, is *Alien Animals* by the well known husband and wife team of Janet and Colin Bord. [12]

In their book they outline five types of what they call "Animals that aren't" but what in a paper published by the now defunct Society for Cryptozoology and Anomalies of Nature (SCAN), I first described as `Zooform Phenomena`: apparitions which take the form of animals-usually living but which are not living things-at least in the way that we understand the term [13]

In my original paper I added a sixth category (mystery kangaroos), to the original five propounded by the Bord's and the list of Zooform Phenomena/Alien Animals/Animals that aren't now reads:

MYSTERY CATS
MYSTERY DOGS
LAKE MONSTERS AND SEA SERPENTS
MAN BEASTS (BHM)
WINGED THINGS
MYSTERY KANGAROOS

The very strange thing about each of these categories is that in nearly every case zooform phenomena of a particular case live alongside actual flesh and blood cryptids of similar form and sometimes the definitions get muddied to such an extent that it is difficult to tell where one ends and the next begins.

This is a phenomenon which is well known, but which, until now has baffled all researchers who have dabbled in this particular arcane area of forteana. [14] [15]

The examples given in this book are just a few of the many zooform phenomena on record. They are often linked with a specific geographical location such as a church (Owlman), a mountain (Am Fear Liath Mor), or a road.(The `cats` of Higher Hullham Road). One particularly interesting incident was recounted by Graham McEwan in his book *Mystery Ani-*

mals of Britain and Ireland (1986):

"On the night 0f the 21st January 1879, a man was driving his cart home from Woodcote in Shropshire to Ranton in Staffordshire. At 10.00 p.m., as he was crossing a bridge on the Birmingham and Liverpool Junction Canal (now part of the Shropshire Union Canal), about a mile from the village of Woodseaves, a horrible black creature with enormous shining eyes jumped out of the trees by the roadside and landed on the horse's back. The man tried to push it off, but his whip just went through the creature and in his fright he dropped it. The horse broke into a gallop, the creature clinging to its back. Eventually though, the phantom vanished and the exhausted horse and its terrified owner made their way home, stopping to rest at an inn in Woodseaves where the man described his ordeal. He was so shocked that he spent the next few days in bed. His whip was found next day at the spot where he had dropped it.

The story has an interesting postscript. A few days later, after a garbled version of the story had been circulating, the witness's employer, Mr B., was visited by a policeman who was investigating a report that he, Mr B., had been attacked and robbed on the Big Bridge on the night of the 21 January. Mr B. described the true incident to the constable who responded, in a disappointed manner: Oh, is that all, sir? Oh, I know what that was. That was the Man-Monkey, sir, as does come again at that bridge ever since the man was drowned in the cut [canal].

Mr B. described his employee's frightening encounter to the folklorist Georgina F. Jackson just a week after it happened." (16) (17)

Ape and Monkey Ghosts such as `The Man Monkey of Staffordshire`, and more appositely the ghost ape of Marwood in Devon and `Martyn`s Ape` of Athelhampton in Dorset, which although they are explicable within the terms of purely regional folklore as `animal ghosts`, exhibit in my opinion, characteristics analogous to those exhibited by the smaller BHM phenomena of parts of the United States.

Unlike the phenomena in America, however these British phenomena each have a convenient little folk story to explain their presence in the occult infrastructure of the region. The Ghost Ape of Marwood was, when alive a pet of a local landowner who one day grabbed the landowner`s young son and climbed a tree with him, refusing to come down, whereas the well known spectre of "Martyn`s Ape" is supposed to have its origins in the unfortunate pet of an earlier female scion of the Martyn family who was either accidentally walled up alive during building work, or entombed (also alive) when the daughter either committed suicide in a locked, secret room or was walled up by an unforgiving parent, (depending on which account you read). [17] [18]

It is my supposition that rather than the apparitions being a result of these, rather far fetched stories, the stories were rather invented by local people to explain the sightings of monkey shaped apparitions, or small BHM as we should really refer to them, that had been seen in the vicinity since times immemorial.

We noted earlier in this chapter that Exmouth and Mawnan Smith both have gained extremely bad reputations. This is something which can be noted in a number of locations where Zooform Phenomena are prevalent.

* In *The Owlman and Others* I described how the zooform entity known as the Jersey Devil had arisen to haunt a place whose reputation was already so evil that the original inhabitants had named it *popuessing* (place of the dragon), but this is a scenario that one can note again and again. [19] [20]

* In *The Mothman Prophecies* (1973), John Keel notes that the mothman appeared at a disused ammunition dump, and was also a precursor to the disaster at Point Pleasant bridge. [21] [22]

* The Nahanni River valley in Canada is known as Headless Valley. Early in the 20th century the Nahanni became a land of mystery and legend. Tales of gold deposits lured prospectors, and when the headless bodies of some of these adventurers were discovered, legends of fierce natives and mythical mountain men grew. In recent years, however, there has been little trapping and prospecting, which may still be partially in response to the old legends. It is a well known site for Bigfoot reports. [23] [24]

* Doone Valley in North Devon is not only a place with a grim reputation and an unpleasant history but it is the reputed haunt of a local werewolf. [25] [26] [27] [28]

But these are not isolated examples. Loch Ness, for example, has a fearsome reputation for a number of reasons.

Heading northeast along the loch side road towards Inverfarigaig past the Foyers Hotel - a place with a fine view over Loch Ness - you come to the hamlet of Boleskin. Here a little above the road is Boleskin House which, for fourteen years, was the home of Aleister Crowley, the self styled 'Great Beast.' [29]

The following chronology of his life was extrapolated from *Crowley: Just the Facts* by 'Nuamicus'

* He was born in Leamington Spa, Warwickshire, on October 12, 1875
* Christened Edward Alexander Crowley
* Raised as a preacher's son among the Plymouth Brethren, a fundamentalist Christian sect
* Young Aleister deeply devastated when his father, Edward Crowley, dies, 1887
* Attended the Trinity College high school in Cambridge, graduating in 1895
* First mystical experience, 1896
* Met George Cecil Jones and Gerald Kelly for the first time; initiated into the Hermetic Order of the Golden Dawn; privately published several important poems, 1898
* Undertook the Abramelin Operation at the recently acquired Boleskine House, located on the South-East side of Loch Ness in Scotland; met Allan Bennet and McGregor Mathers, 1899
* Initiated in Paris by McGregor Mathers; spiritual pilgrimage in Mexican deserts; became 33rd° Mason; travelled into the Far East, 1900
* Returned from the East; established his own publishing house called the "Society for the Propagation of Religious Truth"; married Gerald Kelly's sister, Rose, 1903
* Honeymooned Paris, Naples, Cairo, and India, 1904
* Took first Astrum Argentinum [A∴A∴] oath, March 21, 1904
* Revelation of Liber Al Vel Legis received in Cairo, Egypt, April 1904
* Published numerous poems and books, 1904-1907
* Traveled through Spain and Morocco, 1908
* Met Leila Waddell, 1910
* Travelled to the Sahara, 1911
* Travelled to Moscow; Initiated into the O.T.O. by Theodore Reuss, Frater Merlin X°, 1913
* Moved to the United States, 1914
* Attains grade of the Magus - Prophet of the New Aeon, 1915
* Magical Retirement in New Hampshire, 1916
* Became the Editor of 'The International', 1917
* Numerous publications, 1908 - 1920
* Established the Abbey of Thelema in Cefalu, Sicily, 1920
* Attains the Supreme Grade of Ipsissumus, 1921
* Became Outer Head of the O.T.O., remaining so until his death, 1922
* Crowley banished from Sicily by Mussolini, 1923
* Israel Regardie becomes Crowley's secretary, 1928
* Crowley banished from France; married Maria de Miramar, 1929

* Israel Regardie leaves Crowley, 1932
* Crowley declares bankruptcy, 1935
* Died: Hastings, England; cremated in Brighton; passages from *Liber Al Vel Legis* were recited at his burial, December 1947 [30]

Crowley was many things including a mountaineer, but he will always be remembered as the writer of books and poetry about satanic rites, the occult and devil worship. He lived in Boleskin house during the early part of this century and during his time there managed to feed all sorts of myths and rumours about devilish goings on beside the loch. Local tradesmen, it is said, would never approach the house but left their deliveries at the gate.

Boleskin House was said to have an 'air of evil' about it. It has had several owners since Crowley including Jimmy Page of the rock band Led Zeppelin. His daughter died tragically some years later and Page sold the house. Another owner tragically shot himself for no apparent reason. All this adds to the myth and perhaps it is just as well that Boleskin House is not open to visitors. [31]

My one and only (to date) visit to Loch Ness was in the spring of 1991 during a three day break from a tour by *Steve Harley and Cockney Rebel,* a band for whom I worked at the time. [32][33]

We drove right around the Loch, keeping our eyes firmly on the cold black water below us, convinced that we would see the elusive monster. As we drove past the gates of Boleskine House I felt a chill run down my spine. I realised that we were within figurative spitting distance of one of the most notorious sites (from the point of view of both a fortean and a Led Zeppelin fan) in the British Isles. I made the others stop the car and I got out to investigate. There were obviously people around, so I didn't dare to investigate too closely but I gazed in awe at the stone eagles on the pillars of the gate and looked longingly at the driveway, but I decided that as Jimmy Page was a notoriously reclusive bloke with a reputation for giving unwanted visitors short shrift, that I had better not investigate further. [34]

I got back in the car and we drove off. This report from *Highland News,* however, encapsulates the strange vibe that the place still has for so many people:

"A chilling warning has been given over restoration work planned for Boleskine House at Foyers, the former home of magician Aleister Crowley, the self-styled "Beast 666." On the 50th anniversary of the death of

Crowley the "word of the wise" has come from Malcolm Dent, former buddy of millionaire pop star Jimmy Page and custodian of the house for Page for 20 years. He is urging Dingwall architect Sandy Gracie, who's to restore the North Wing of the 18th century mansion, to get cracking when he starts and be sure he finishes what he has begun - or face the unexpected.

Malcolm, a 6ft 3in very streetwise Londoner when he arrived in the sleepy Loch Ness-side hamlet where locals avoided Crowley's old home, said his experiences changed him from being a total sceptic.

"I have witnessed what can happen," he said. "My former wife and I got our eyes - and ears - opened over the time we spent at Boleskine. Most of the oddities occurred during upheavals in the house. I am not talking about wallpapering, but structural alterations. Any time there was anything major in hand, it was almost as though the house didn't like it. If we didn't get on with the job and get it finished, something would let us know about it. We would be wakened up during the night with heavy doors banging all over the place and carpets and rugs being rolled up. It was as though it was a reminder to get on quickly and get the job over. Once the work was finished, the house settled down."

Another upheaval was when Malcolm, who is now making hand-crafted furniture in Embo, was getting ready to leave Boleskine about six years ago, and again "something" made itself known. "There had been an upheaval getting the house ready for viewing," he said, " and I had started moving some of my possessions. I was outside at the time when, without warning, and in what I can only describe as a great booming voice came 'What are you doing?' When I got back inside the house, I was as white as a sheet. That little experience really scared me!"

Another more visual experience was when Malcolm friends were discussing the occult, a few drams having been taken.

"We were discussing the house, Crowley and what had happened in it and had all started off with contrary views," he said. "As the evening wore on , we eventually found ourselves in agreement and there was a moment's silence. At that point, something happened that, looking back, was like a very emphatic exclamation mark! A small porcelain figure of the Devil rose off the mantelpiece to the ceiling, then smashed into smithereens in the fireplace."

The most horrific experience of all was something Malcolm heard. but was too terrified to open the door to.

"I was awakened in the wee sma' hours," he said, "and just knew something was wrong. I was petrified. Something outside the bedroom door was snorting, snuffling and banging. It sounded like a huge beast. I had this clear picture in my mind of what it looked like, but there was no way I was going to open the door. I had a knife on the bedside table and I opened the blade and just sat there. The blade was so small it wouldn't have done any good, but I was so frightened that I had to have something to hang on to. The noise went on for some time, but even when it stopped, I still could not move. I sat on the bed for hours and, even when daylight came, it took lot's of courage to open that door. Whatever was there, I have no doubt, was pure evil."

Malcolm said he was glad that the old house above Loch Ness had been taken on and was now being treated as a home.

"I have quite a few drawings of what Boleskine House looked like back in the twenties," he said. "If Sandy, the architect, or anybody else wants any help, I will be only too glad to give it."

But architect Sandy Gracie, of MacGregor's Court, Dingwall, who has been working on the house for 20 years on and off, says he is not worried.

"The North wing was destroyed by fire and we are rebuilding what was there so that the house will be as it was," he said. "We are building up one room and doing reroofing work. The latest work will go ahead as soon as we get listed building planning consent. I have been working on the house on and off since Jimmy Page had it 20 years ago.

I'm afraid I can't say I have personally seen or heard anything strange over the years I have been involved with the house. The latest owners, the MacGillivrays, are basically taking on the work Jimmy Page started. Of course, with the 50th anniversary of Crowley's death coming up, you never know. Anyway, I'm not bothered. I'm not afraid." [35]

Lake Monsters and Black magicians are not the only strange things to have been reported at Loch Ness. As alluded to briefly in *The Owlman and Others* (1997,8) there have also been reports of a strange winged humanoid called the boobrie, as well as the ubiquitous UFO reports. [36]

We found this undated story from the *Inverness Courier* on the UFO Scotland web site:

"There's something strange flying about in the night sky over Inverness.

An Inverness father and his 10-year old daughter became the second local family in a fortnight to see an unidentified flying object over the area. And it seems that air traffic controllers at Inverness Airport have also had some sort of close encounter, but they are not saying very much about it.

A spokesman yesterday would only confirm that a report had been filed with the MoD, about a possible UFO sighting earlier this week [week of Feb 5]. On Wednesday [Feb 7] journalist Paul Breen and his daughter Susan believe they spotted what could have been a mystery object at 9pm when travelling home to Westhill. Mr. Breen added: "I haven't a clue what it was. At first I thought it might have been a balloon, but it was far too luminous".

The sighting by Mr. Breen and his daughter comes days after the Courier *reported that a Black Isle family had spotted a UFO and tried to capture the craft on video. Pauline Mackay of Drumsmittal said the object seen by her, her husband and two sons in the sky near Inverness had three lights and stayed in one place.*

"We could see circular lights on the outside. It seemed to pulsate." [37]

Trying to discover links between the various areas where anomalous phenomena of the same types have occurred was not as easy as one would have hoped. Indeed, it has proved to be almost impossible.

We have discovered a number of areas in which there does appear to be correlation, but there is nothing that gives us more than a vague overview of the situation that we are attempting to unwravel. Perhaps we are approaching this problem from the wrong angle. We have spent this investigation so far amassing data until, perhaps we have too much of it.

The time has now come to get rid of some of it, interesting though it is. We have to separate the wheat from the chaff in a vain attempt to actually make sense of it all.

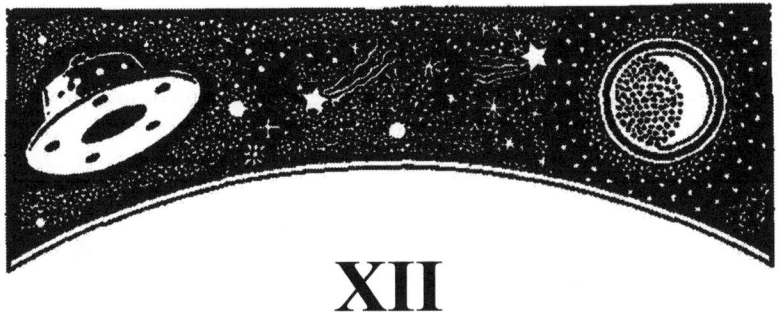

XII

Now you have read everything that we have been able to uncover about the series of weird and anomalous events which took place in the vicinity of Woodbury Castle, Littleham and indeed in several other locations across South Devon. Some of them are directly relevant to each other and some are not. It is now time to sift through the available evidence and to attempt to make some kind of sense of it all.

Let us we disregard the UFOs for the moment - there is no doubt that in the broadest sense they existed. They were objects, they were flying and we were unable to identify them. In many ways they are the easiest of the mysteries listed in this book to solve.

It does seem as if there are some bizarre links between many of the incidents listed in this book, but which ones? In order to find out which of these incidents are related we must first decide which of the plethora of apparently inexplicable accounts contained in this book we should discard.

* Gennette Tate

Despite the efforts of all and sundry to provide a paranormal explanation for the abduction of this unfortunate girl it seems almost certain that her disappearance can be explained in a horrifyingly prosaic manner. It seems certain that she was abducted, (almost certainly for sexual purposes), and then murdered. A Westcountry TV documentary aired in the summer of 1998 named the most likely suspects

* Her father. John Tate was convicted of sexual offences against Genette`s half-sister whilst the furore surrounding her disappearance was still at its height. He has never denied his paedophile tendencies, but he claims that since intensive psychotherapy he is no longer a risk to chil-

dren. Genette's half-sister claimed during the documentary that Genette had almost certainly been a witness to her father's sexual activities with her. It was implied that this could have been a compelling motive for John Tate to murder Gennete. Unfortunately for those conspiracy theorists who like to believe that the simplest solution is the most likely, John Tate has an unimpeachable alibi for the time that Genette disappeared. [1]

* Robert Black. This British convicted child killer serving 10 life sentences for the murders of three other girls was offered immunity from prosecution for Genette's murder if he was able to provide information leading to the discovery of her remains. Black was linked to the area where Genette disappeared by tracking his petrol station receipts.. However, he has always denied that he had anything to do with the case and it seems unlikely that any further evidence can be obtained to link him with Genette's disappearance. [2]

* Ian Bealey. In the summer of 1998 the Devon and Cornwall Constabulary took the unprecedented step of publically naming Bealey as a prime suspect in the case. After his 1981 conviction for the murder of student Virginia Maunder, Bealey's friends told police that he had told them details of the police hunt for Genette before they had become public knowledge. There are a number of pieces of evidence linking Bealey to Ayelsbeare on the day that Genette vanished and it is generally believed that Bealey, now serving a life sentence in Dartmoor Prison is guilty of Genette'a abduction and murder. [3][4][5]

There is one final irony about the case, however. As the *Exeter Express and Echo* reported on the 21st June 1998:

"..if Bealey wasn't involved and Black was, it does throw up an astounding coincidence -n that afternoon on the airport road two men later proven to be murderers passed within yards of each other" [6]

There seems no doubt that one can explain the tragic events of August 1978 without having to resort to fanciful speculation about UFO reports, alien abductions or the predations of a passing leopard. However, as we have seen, there are a number of quasi-fortean links to the case, especially the apparent synchronicity with the disappearance of Emily Bamsey so many years before. Although all these factors point vaguely towards the disturbing *genius loci* of the Woodbury Common area, the available facts indicate that Genette's disappearance is atrributable to a 'monster' of a very human kind.

* The Flying Fairground

Unfortunately we must also discard this gloriously bizarre series of sightings from 1987. Having read Squadron Leader Westwood's interpretation of events, there is little doubt that he is correct. The description given by all the witnesses is highly reminiscnet of the inflight refueling operation carried out by *"a pair of VC10 tankers"* engaged in *"a refuelling exercise over South West England"*. As Squadron Leader Westwood has managed to confirm that *"one of the pilots was able to confirm that the aircraft flew over Exmouth in formation towards the South West at a height of 25,000 feet shortly after 10 p.m."* with *"the floodlights switched on"* and that *"air-to-air refuelling is carried out at a lower speed and engine power setting compared with airliners flying at similar heights."* [7]

This essentially disposes of the subject of "The Flying fairground" to our satisfaction.

The Vickers Super VC10 was the last of the first generation of jet airliners, prior to the arrival of wide bodied and jumbo jets. It entered service in 1964 and could carry 170 passengers at a speed of 600 miles per hour. It had a range of approximately 5000 miles. [8]

The RAF's VC10 tanker force operates four variants of the aircraft: the C1Ks are military transport aircraft, carrying 120 passengers or freight, and can be adapted for tanking with the addition of wing-mounted refuelling pods; the K2s are ex-civil VC10s and the K3s and K4s are ex-civil Super VC10s although the K4s lack the additional fuselage fuel tanks of the K3s. The K2s, 3s and 4s all have wing refuelling points for fighters and a centerline refuelling capability to provide additional support for large aircraft. [9]

Interesting, but no mystery there.

* The mermaid of Topsham and the Veasta of Portland.

These reports are too vague and ill-defined to be brought into the equation. Despite the many hundreds of man-hours that we spent researching the subject we have to admit that we neither know what the `creatures` are/were nor how they got there, and therefore we are unable to quantify the synergistic effect they may have had upon the other phenomena in this book.

However our researches in this area DID show us a number of things.

When I was in Puerto Rico at the beginning of 1998 I spent a considerable time investigating the local folklore, which, influenced by television programmes such as *The X-Files* made some extraordinary claims about the covert activities of the American Government, claiming that they were directly (or at the least indirectly) responsible for various outbreaks of vampirism, UFO activity, the appearance of strange creatures and spates of animal mutilation and `alien` abduction, as well as for the anomalous disappearance of an American College Professor who vanished for several days whilst walking through the rain forest at El Yunque, and the supposed murder of a "soldier" found clutching what appeared to be a jar containing an alien embyo. Of course, we found no link between these anomalies and the U.S Government, although we did manage to discover some of the reasons why the shadowy figures of Capitol Hill are portrayed so badly in Puerto Rican socio-cultural affairs. [13]

The results of our investigations can be found in *Only Fools and Goatsuckers*. It is interesting, however, to note that in the case of the strange "beast" from Benbecula in the Outer Hebrides, many of the same cultural cliches were invoked. The young woman who allegedly discovered the "carcass" felt constrained to comment that: *"It was beside some land owned by the Ministry of Defence and there were big notices all over the place saying that if people found anything on the beach they were not to touch it......"* Later in the same interview she unconsciously mirrored the peasant farmers of Puerto Rico by suggesting that the `monster` was a result of a mutation triggered by nuclear pollution. [14]

However, even the most cursory investigation into the social and economic infrastructure of Benbecula would suggest that whilst her conclusions are almost certainly erroneous (doubly so when one considers that practically every `expert` who has investigated the affair has suggested that the `creature` is nothing more exciting than a crudely sculpted `sandcastle` manufactured as a joke), the same social and economic constraints which I noted in Puerto Rico have apparently taken place in the Outer Hebrides. [15]

Helen McSkimming claimed in 1994 that: *"This is now the busiest part of the island since the army base arrived in 1958. There was resistance to their arrival initially although the island now seems to be of mixed opinion with the argument put forward that the army has added much to the island economy. It was the RAF who were responsible for the building of the airfield at Oitir Mhor in the very north of the island. The airfield does provide a valuable link for the island with regular flights to Stornoway on the Isle of Lewis."* [16]

Just as in Puerto Rico, the advent of new technology, which perforce HAS to belong to the military has had irreversible conequences for the area.

There is just possibly a parallel link with this scenario in the Lyme Bay area. According to local legend there is a tunnel between Otter Cove and Littleham Church. This was apparently built by smugglers in the 19th Century. [17] [18] We have not been able to substantiate this, but what we have found is clear evidence linking Littleham Church with the local `Gentlemen`. [19] [20] According to Delderfield, a well known local smuggler of dubious reputation lived in a cottage next to the Plough Inn (demolished in 1930), in Littleham Village. These cottages backed onto the graveyard. When under suspicion he was known to throw the kegs of illicit liquor up to an accomplice in the churchyard behind the cottage to be hidden. This gave rise to a local saying *"They would let Lady Nelson tend them `till the coast was clear"*. Lady Nelson`s tomb was right behind the cottage. [21] [22]

The main link that this story has with the events in Benbecula, Puerto Rico and other locations mentioned in this book is the alleged use to which these tunnels (if they actually existed) were later put by the Ministry of Defence. There is a MOD Rifle Range at Otter Cove, but when Nigel lived there at the end of the 1970s, the MOD carried out a vast programme of construction work in the area, building a system of underground tunnels, (which may well have incorporated the putative 19th Century ones discussed above), ostensibly in order to transfer the rifle range underground. Although the tunneling work was completed, presumably succesfully, the rifle range on the top of the cliffs is still in use, and many local residents wonder what (if anything) the vast underground tunnels are used for. [23]

We would not want anyone to think that by recounting this anecdote we are taking unwarranted steps into *X-Files* territory. Enough of that is done in British UFOlogy as it is by the likes of Matthew Williams. We are including this account purely as en example of how military activity, both here and elsewhere can effect the atmosphere of a locality through rumour and popular belief. [24] [25]

Even an island as tiny as Benbecula is a rich source of folklore, all of which mirrors other events in other places described in this book. Two examples at random taken from the collection of Helen McSkimming:

* *The place in the Gaelic is called Baile nan Cailleach, the town of the Nuns (or Hags). A number of years ago a stone vault was uncovered on*

the east side of the village which contained a number of bones. A great many rumours went about as to what the bones were from including the idea that they were the bones of children that the nuns had given birth to. Whatever they were, the vault was quickly closed up again and left in peace. [26]

We have already seen how the spectre of organised religion has prompted widespread folk beliefs in quasi-religious apparitions and stories like this one and like several of the ghost stories we have collected from Littleham. When we discussed Zooform Phenomena we discovered that extraordinary events can be given mundane interpretations and *vice versa*. This is merely another example of that syndrome in action.

* The ClanRanald estates once stretched over Moidart and Arisaig on the mainland and included the islands of South Uist and Benbecula here in the outer Isles. In 1938, Ronald George MacDonald, eighteenth Chief of ClanRanald, sold both Benbecula and South Uist to John Gordon of Cluny and so began the removal of the people from the Isles. This signalled the end of the traditional relationship between the Clan Chief and the people of the Clan. Prior to that time the Clan Chiefs not only had the support of the people. but also the support of the Sidhe of the land. Numerous folktales recall the Clans gaining help from the Sidhe in times of trouble. Apparently different factions gave their support to different Clans and they would also give warning to the household, like at Borve Castle, if the Chief was going to return home unexpectedly or if some tragedy had come about. The Sluagh, or Hosts of the Sidhe were also known to visit Borve Castle whilst on their travels although their visitations were not so welcomed. Other tales also recall the people's connection and respect for the Sidhe as the tale of the Smithy shows. This particular Smithy would never open his forge on a Friday for it was reckoned the Sidhe were abroad on this day and he had no wish to offend them with his use of Iron. [27]

As will be seen in the concluding chapters of this book, there have long been hypothesised links between the 'wee folk' and UFO activities. Yesterday's fairy folk or *sidhe* (in this instance) are today's aliens. Truly there is nothing new under the sun.

The most important thing that we have learned from this particular part of our investigation, however, is that wheareas the true nature of the merfolk of Lyme Bay may well remain obscure, there is an undoubted connection between sightings of strange creatures in the seas and woods, and strange lights out amongst the stars.

* The 1952 "conspiracy".

As we have shown this was in fact no such thing, and unfortunately we had, for a short time at least, allowed ourselves to be drawn into the mish-mash of lies, half truths and wishful thinking that we so abhored in the previous section when it concerned the `beast` of Benbecula or the Puerto Rican chupacabra. However, our lengthy investigation into the journalistic ethics of Dennis H.Pratt proved one thing and that is that even as seasoned investigators and hard nosed sceptics we are just as likely to be fooled by an episode of *The X Files* as is anybody else.

* Black magic on Woodbury common.

Although as we showed in the text, there is no evidence whatsoever to suggest that anything even approaching a genuine Satanic Ceremony was being practised on Woodbury Common in 1982 when an unnamed teenage witness reported seeing shadowy figures in robes cavorting through the woods, recent evidence has cast doubt on it even having been a harmless wiccan ceremony. A few months after the report appeared in the *Exmouth Journal* a very similar story appeared penned by David Bazell:

"Was another black mass ritual held on Woodbury Common this week? Two youths claim that they had seen a hooded figure with a knife - on the road to Yettington on Monday night and there is evidence they were so frightened by what they saw that they drove off terror stricken.

The youths may have been good actors with only the demon drink driving them on but it is by no means the first report of such figures being seen at certain times of the year. A young man saw what he is convinces was some sort of mass in progress, and these two cases happened only about half a year apart.

Farmer, Colin Bolt was flagged down on on his way to Kerslake Farm at yettington on 9.20 p.m on Wednesday. Two youths beside a Ford Cortina rushed to Mr Boult`s side and after saying what they had seen pleaded `you must help us`. Mr Bolt told me "They spoke of seeing one man with a knife in a roble looking like the Klu Klux Klan. They certainly seemed very distressed. One of them was clutching onto my car 0- they were very frightened - or extremely good actors".
Bolt promised to `phone the police and did so, making a 999 call when he got home.

Another youth from Colaton Raleigh repeated with some nervousness his previous experience. He was walking home in the early hours of the morning when, not far from Borden Barn on the road leading down to Yettington, when he saw through a clearing a group of people in Robes and Hoods standing around a central light in a small valley. A chanting and rattling sound could be heard.

He ran home frightened. And despite accompanying police the next day in a fruitless search for any evidence that a mass had taken place, he remains convinced to this day that what he saw was real.

A Police spokesman said that although more credence to the youth's story if they had themselves reported the matter to the Police he admitted there might be one of a number of reasons why they would not want anyone to know of their presence at the spot at the time. Someone interested in the subject told me that on one occasion she had seen a bull or bullock's skull attached to the trunk of a tree in the same area, and that on another occasion also in the vicinity green and blue nylon fur strands were hanging from bushes." [28]

Just in case one was wondering about the occult significance of green and blue nylon fur strands, the final sentance is one to strike you completely dumbstruck.

"It has been established that no Royal Marine training activities were taking place at the relevant times." [29]

Even the most rabidly anti-militaristic conspiracy theorist would be hard pushed to suggest a scenario whereby the forces of the Royal marines are inducted into the service of the Goat of Mendes in arcane midnight ceremonies. It just don't work that way.

So what did happen?

The newspaper report claims that the unnamed youth *"remains convinced to this day that what he saw was real"* and as we can prove conclusively this is because it WAS. However what he was seeing wasn't what he THOUGHT he was seeing.

I now have to be very careful whilst recounting this next smidgeon of det ective work, because I am not too sure that no crime was committed that night, and I have promised my sources that I wouldn't reveal any details that could attach them to the events of that night in 1982.

Nigel and I were appearing at the Exeter Univewrsity's Science Fiction Convention *Microcon* soon after my return from Puerto Rico and Mexico

in the February of 1998.

And as part of a general discussion about the weird goings on on and about Woodbury Common we described the alleged `black masses` but added that there was absolutely no evidence that a mass was taking place.

We were just about to continue with our theory that what was actually being carried out at that time was a harmless and relatively restrained wiccan ceremony when a voice piped up from the back of the lecture hall:

"Too Damn Right there was no black mass taking place! It was us!"

and everybody in the audience laughed uproariously. When the laughter had died down he explained himself further. Apparently back in 1982 he had been a student at the University and had been a member of the Science Fiction Society. He was also involved with another group of students who were keen amateur film-makers.

One night, for no particular reason apart from the fact that it had seemed a good idea at the time, he and his *compadres* had been on Woodbury Common making a short film in which they re-enacted certain scenes from a Dr Who serial called *The Stones Of Blood*. [30] [31] [32]

The addition of an unwary but totally innocent spectator merely made the film more exciting and even more highly amusing than it would have been otherwise.

Unfortunately another mystery is solved.

He was not able to shed light on the second incident and so it is just possible that Wiccan ceremonies are performed in the midst of Woodbury Common after all, although the lack of any proper identification for the two youths makes one suspect that it was another student prank that managed, much to the hilarity of everyone involved (exccept for Mr Bolt, Mtr Bazell and the Police) to make the local `papers.

Sad but true!

* The 1957 `UFO` wasn`t any such thing!

The date and the description given gave it away. In October 1957 the Soviet Union stunned the world by launching Sputnik 1, the world's first artificial satellite. Although Sputnik 1 was only about two feet in diameter, weighed only 184 pounds, and could only send radio beeps towards the United States as it flew overhead around every ninety minutes, Sputnik 1 had a profound effect on the world.

Shook up by the persistent beep-beep-beep reminder of Russian skill in space, the U.S. government began a crash program to improve America's standing in science, technology, and engineering. Within a year after Sputnik, both NASA and ARPA (the Advanced Research Projects Agency) had been created. The National Defense Education Act provided loans to students and funding for educational programs, especially ones in math, science, and foreign languages, and in faraway Devonshire some elderly men were scanning the skies when they thought that they had seen a UFO..[33]

* The Oliver`s Castle Crop Circle Video.

Even the case of the Oliver`s castle crop circle video, with which we began this book, and this search, is not as clear cut as it seemed when we first viewed it back in October 1996.

According to Freddy Silva and Colin Andrews:

"Peter Sorenson, who is himself a computer graphic design specialist, says he immediately saw the Oliver's Castle video as a computer generated image. Several graphic design specialists say that yes, this video could have been generated by computer, with two qualifications. It would take time and money. Because the video was being shown by the evening of the same day the formation arrived, the timing suggested a real event. However, if the video being shown in the pub the first night was not the same version being shown six days later, which I have every reason to believe is true, the time constraint is considerably altered. Additionally, crop circle researcher and computer specialist Paul Vigay saw the version of the video currently released and went home to create his own computer generated rendition. From a photograph of a circle, he recreated the same general sequence in six hours." [35]

I have seen Paul Vigay`s video animation and I have to state that I was not at all impressed. Yes, he did manage to overlay an image of balls of light flying over the field in which the crop circle appeared but the end result was similar to the old video game `pong` and looked nothing like the video that we were shown so long ago. [36]

However, it should be said that Freddie Silva claims that the video which was eventually publicised was NOT the one that he was originally shown in the pub on the lunchtime of August 11th 1996 and if this is correct then it does place the provenance of the video in considerable doubt. It also should be noyted that various researchers including Colin Andrews and George Wingfield have implied that far from there being no financial motive for the hoaxing of the film, it was in fact `made to order` with finance from one of several major television networks. However, despite the increasingly complex miasma of truths, half-truths and downright lies which have surrounded the matter from the beginning I have to agree with Dan Drasin who said:

"It would be presumptuous and unscientific to declare that this video absolutely could not have been hoaxed." [37]

...And there, until further evidence one way or the other surfaces we must leave the matter. However, with regret, we should also exclude it from our deliberations until its provenance is no longer in question.

* Devil`s footprints

Although the problem has never been solved beyond all possible doubt, these days it is generally accepted that whatever it was that caused the anomalous lines of footprints along the snowy pastures of South Devon in the middle of the 19th Century, it was NOT Satan. In fact, it was probably not anything supernatural at all.

Like so many others of the phenomena discussed in this book the Great Devon Mystery is almost certainly the synergistic result of a great deal of different mysteries which well meaning local people and journalists with an eye to the big chance blew up out of all proportion.

After scrutiny of the original source materials it is certain that:

* Despite the claims made again and again in books about what is broadly lumped together as "The Paranormal", that the footptints did NOT all appear on the one night. They appeared over a period of about four days, giving limitless scope for copycats and hoaxers.
* The footprints were NOT all the same size and shape, implying that they were made by a variety of different meansd.
* Some of the footprints were certainly hoaxed by means of a hot donkey shoe and a stick.
* There is evidence that some were hoaxed as a protest against the new Vicar of Woodbury who had committed the unforgiveable crime of allowing "Good King Wenceslas" to be sung in church over the previous Christmas.

...And they only conclusion that one can bring is that the whole matter is so highly confused that it needs far more research before we can even hope to find how much (if any) of the material that is left is apposite to the case in hand. [38]

* Unusual flesh and blood animals in the Lyme Bay Region

We included the accounts of unusual animals from the region in Chapter X, not because we believed for a moment that they had any direct relevance to the main body of events discussed in this book, but because this provides a glowing example of the enormous range of data that has to be sifted through when one is investigating an affair of this nature. The peculiar beasts of the region, are, however, an indication of quite how different this area is from the rest of the British Isles.

In geological terms, the region is quite young. Around 210 million years ago, fully marine conditions prevailed leading to Blue Lias, Black Ven Marls and Belemnite Marls being slowly deposited on the sea floor over a period of about 12 million years. Throughout the Mesozoic era, Dorset (and the U.K.!), was positioned approximately 35degN of the equator. A flourishing marine life in the shallow warm seas provided a continual supply of dead organisms to the sea bed, where many became fossilised. These sediments hardened with age and burial before being uplifted and tilted eastwards by earth movements and subsequent erosion.

Around 131 million years ago, the area was again under water and the Cretaceous seas resubmerged the earlier deposited sediments. The deposition of the Upper Greensand and then (around 97 million years ago), chalk. Because of the easterly dip of the earlier Jurassic rocks, the Cretaceous sediments now deposited on the sea bed lie on progressively older Jurassic and then Triassic rocks as you move westwards. The boundary between the Cretaceous strata and the underlying Jurassic and Triassic rocks represents a huge gap in time.

In the last few thousand years the advancement of the English Channel has exposed the local geology in a series of fine cliff sections. This coastal erosion is aided by the massive landslips that can occur at any time. These are caused by groundwater flowing along the unconformity surface, and have revealed large portions of Dorset's primordial past. [39] [40]

We believe that the real importance of the palaeogeological and zoogeographical uniqueness of the area is, as Martin Ball described it:

"Portland's Jurassic landscape lives in a cycle of submergence and emergence revealing its pre-historic existence. This isle traces the evolution of life ~ quarried stone denudes petrified ammonites and trilobites locked in the fossils of the moment." [41]

Petrified reminders of an exotic and frightening past have been so much a part of Dorset life over the last two centuries that we feel that in some way it must have effected the essential atmosphere of the area in more ways than one. Perhaps this is why strange creatures are still seen in the seas and flying dragons still haunt the skies?

However, as far as the flesh and blood inhabitants of the area are concerned we must consider the matter again.

Whereas, we feel sure that the occurrence of colour variations of the common adder, or even the existence of a species of lizard hitherto unsuspected from British shores has nothing at all to do with the main gamut of quasifortean occurrences in the Lyme Bay region there may actually be some connection between quasi-fortean and the occurrence of halved gynandromorph butterflies.

Gynandromorphism is a particularly rare syndrome within comparative entomology, and the discovery of a population which exhibits a larger than average proportion of gynandromorphic individuals is a case for some comment. Andrei Soureakav of the Department of Entomology, at California Academy of Sciences wrote the following report in 1994:

"An unusual population of the lycaenid butterfly, Meleageria daphnis (Lepidoptera: Lycaenidae), is found in the Kislovodsk area (43.80N lat., 42.70E long.) of southern Russia; 60% of the observed females in the adult population have been partial gynandromorphs or sexual mosaics during the period of 1988 to 1993. This site is within 30 km of the center of the refining area where uranium was processed for the first Soviet atomic bombs, and is also within the southeastern boundary (extent as of 2 May 1986) of the cloud of radiation released from the Chernobyl disaster on 26 April 1986. The situation may reflect a high level of radiation-induced somatic mutations or a genetic alteration in the Y-chromosome carried by most of the females in the population." [42]

We should note that Kislovodsk and the surrounding region of Stavropol Krai was not only one of the key agricultural regions of the USSR, but is also famous for its mineral waters and vacation resorts, the best of which

were reserved for high party officials, and was therefore a region of both miliraty and political importance. [43]

However, it is also the location for one of the best known UFO reports from the former Soviet Union. The source document for this information is no less a document than The Statement on Unidentified Flying Objects" submitted to the U.S Senate Committee on Science and Astronautics on July 29, 1968, by James E. McDonald, Senior Physicist, Institute of Atmospheric Physics, and professor, Department of Meteorology, The University of Arizona, Tucson, Arizona. [44]

"5. Case 24. Kislovodsk, Caucasus, August 8, 1967.

Zigel, who is affiliated with the Moscow Aviation Institute, reports in the same article (Ref. 38), a sighting at 8:40 p.m., 8/8/67, made by astronomer Anatoli Sazanov and colleagues working at the Mountain Astrophysical Station of the USSR Academy of Sciences, near Kislovodsk. Sazanov and ten other staff members watched an " asymmetric crescent, with its convex side turned in the direction of its movement" moving eastward across the northern sky at an angular elevation of about 20 degrees. Just ahead of it, and moving at the same angular speed was a point of light comparable to a star of the first magnitude. The crescent-like object was reddish-yellow, had an angular breadth of about two-thirds that of the moon, and left vapor-like trails aft of the ends of the crescent horns. As it receded, it diminished in size and thus "instantly disappeared".

If we may accept as reliable the principal features of the sighting, how might we account for it? The "faintly luminous ribbons" trailing from the horns suggest a high-flying jet, of course; but the asymmetry and the reddish-yellow coloration fail to fit that notion. Also, it was an object of rather large angular size, about 20 minutes of arc, so that an aircraft of wingspan, say, 150 feet would have been only about five miles away whence engine-noise would have been audible under the quiet conditions of a mountain observatory. More significant, if it had been an aircraft at a slant range of five miles, and at 20 degrees elevation, its altitude would have been only about 9000 ft above the observatory. For the latitude and date, the sun was about ten degrees below the western horizon, so direct sun-illumination on an aircraft at 9000 ft above observatory level would be out of the question.

Hence the luminosity goes unexplained. Clearly, satellites and meteors can be ruled out. The astronomers' observation cannot be readily explained in any conventional terms. Zigel remarks that the object was also seen in the town of Kislovodsk, and that another reddish crescent was observed in the same area on the evening of July 17, 1967."

During the summer of 1997 I did a fair amount of research on some documents 'liberated' from the official KGB records of UFO reports. The most interesting thing about them was that they show that the same types of phenomena that have been reported in the western world for half a century were also noted (though less well publicised) in the USSR, but probably the most poignant document I received was from a senior Soviet Civil Servant:

"Dear Pavel Romanovitch,

The State Security Committee has never been engaged in systematic gathering and analysis of information on anomalous phenomena (the so-called Unidentified Flying Objects). At the same time the SSC of the USSR has been receiving statements from a number of persons and agencies on cases of observations of the above phenomena. We forward you copies of such statements. At an earlier date the same material was sent to the Central Machine Building Research Institute, the town of Kalingrad.

N.A.Shem: Deputy Chairman of the Committee" [45]

In an article for *Sightings* I commented on this letter:

"One big question remains, and this is the question that has been puzzling, intriguing and frightening UFOlogists for half a century now. Is the apparent disinterest in UFOs by 'the establishment' in the USA, the UK and in the former USSR, because they simply do not believe in such things, or is it because they already know what they are?" [46] [47]

However, with the benefit of hindsight I think that responses like this, are what one would expect from Civil Servants worldwide - the mindset that if it is not actually jumping at your throat it is far better to let sleeping dogs lie.

However, the 1967 UFO report is not the only report of an anomalous quasi-fortean event from the Kilovodsk region of the Causacus, for this is where, for centuries now there have been reports of anomalous man-beasts lurking undiscovered in the wild and rocky mountains.

Jeanne-Marie Koffman explored this area extensively, and during her travels met Talib Kumyshev, 67, a Kahardian, who was a highly respected elder man of the rillage of Kamennomos. His testimony is highly revealing:

...It was probably in 1930, or 1931, or 1932, in June or at the end of May, when our cattle left for the alpine pastures of Elbrus. I was chief of the group. We had left to inspect the herds with the veterinarian.

Well, rain had surprised one of my shepherds, Shaghir Zagureyev, very high up on the slopes, and he had gone to take refuge under a rocky overhang. As he approached it, he saw there were three almastys sitting under it. Shaghir was a little frightened, but as the rain was by then falling much harder, he decided to stay there anyway, though at a distance from them. They looked at one another. Then, the rain stopped and Shaghir came down to the farm. He did not say anything to anyone.

Very early in the morning, I was awakened by cries, a tremendous noise, and I saw that the shepherds were running to assemble their herds and were taking the cattle down the valley. "Why are they leaving?" I asked. "There are almastys under the rock, up there." . . .At that moment Shaghir declared: "It's true, there are three almastys sitting up there, I saw them yesterday evening." I was then really angry... I said to Shaghir: "You're an idiot. You were frightened by a bush."

"No," said Shaghir, "I saw them.".

"Well, why didn't you tell anyone?"

"Because the old people have warned: when you see an almasty for the first time, if you tell anyone about it you'll get a bad headache. Well, for me, it was the first time that I have seen one."

I continued not to believe all this. They said to me: "OK, go ahead, go see for yourself."

We were about 10 to 15 people making a half-circle around that rock. We stayed there until dinnertime. Some went away, and others came up. Three almastys were seated under the overhang, two of medium size, and the other bigger. The one which was the biggest was in the middle. They were sitting on rocks, facing us, hunched over, with their heads down. From time to time they raised their heads slightly, and looked at us from under their brows.

Their heads were very ugly, not nice at all. Their faces resembled human faces, but the nose is shorter and flattened. The eyes are slanted and red-

dish. The cheeks are very prominent, like those of a Mongol or a Korean, but more so. The lips are thin. The lower jaw is receding, as though cut on a bias.

The hair is long, like that of a woman, and tangled. The entire body is covered with shaggy hair, resembling that of the buffalo. In some places this is long (torso, chest) and in other places it is shorter (arms, legs).

The big one had the chest of a man. The others had the breasts of a woman, but extremely long and covered with hair. The hair was very dirty. The stink was so strong that we could not stand it. The odour was like that of wild flax, when it grows thickly. Once, the one seated on the right mumbled something. I did not see their hands clearly, as they were held between their legs. The legs are rather short and bowed. The foot is like that of a man, but more spread out. All were wearing, wrapped around their waists, an old piece of a shepherd's cape. A young shepherd proposed to throw a lasso around one of them and bring it into the village. But all the others cried out that it is forbidden, that they must not be harmed, and that they must not be disturbed. I watched them from a distance of three or four metres, and I even approached to within about one metre. Did I touch them? I should say not! If you touch them, as Allah is my witness, you could no longer eat with your hands afterward, they are so dirty, stinking and repulsive. I remained 1.5 - 2 hours. When I left, other shepherds were arriving. I have heard my father recount that they suckle on cows." [48]

Even a cursory look at the folklore of the region provides a number of leads which would no doubt be of great interest to any researcher who wishes to follow up the work that we have chronicled in this present volume.

Another connection which would be worth investigation is that of background radioactivity. As we have seen Andrei Soureakav postulated a connection between the abnormally high rate of gynandromorphism and the level of background radiation following on from the nuclear weapons testing that had taken place in the region. We would only add that although Lyme Bay has been used for bacterial warfare experiments, it has never (we are sure) been used for testing nuclear weapons, but that outcrops of several mildly radioactive minerals have been reported from the area. This is something that needs to be investigated in further depth.

Obviously there is a connection beyond that of mutated butterflies and it is one that could well be of paramount importance to those who would understand the manifold mysteries of a quasi-fortean multiverse. Regretfully, however, we have had to leave this avenue of enquiry to those who come after us, as we attempt to sift through the rest of the material that we have gathered.

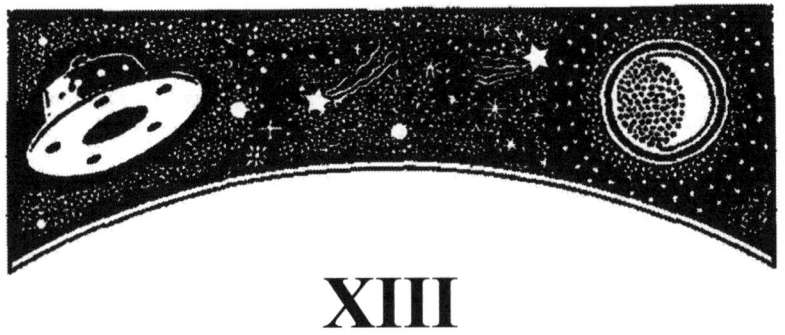

XIII

Littleham is one of the oldest parts of Exmouth.

According to *The Winchester Chronicle* (1001).

"And thence (i.e from Hampshire) they (the Danes) went westward until they came to the Defnas (men of Devon), and there to meet them came Pallig, with the ships that he was able to collect; for he had revolted from King Aetheldred in spite of all the treaties he had made, and notwithstanding that the king had well endowed him with landed estates and gold and silver (.........) And thence they went to Exanmouth (mouth of the Exe), so that they disposed themselves in one course upwards until they came to Pinhoe......." [1]

From Florence of Worcester's translation of the word Exanmutha, (*ostium fluminis Eaxse*) it is clear that he considered it as meaning merely the mouth of the river, and not a town of any kind. However as J. B.Davidson suggested (1898) the available evidence suggests that there was some sort of settlement there even at this time. As the Danish ships were left moored in the inner bay of Exanmutha whilst the harrying of Devonshire, and most particularly the Battle of Pinhoe, was going on, it is at least probable that a few dwellings stood on the shore of the bay, but there can be no doubt that the village, if any, formed a very subordinate member of the manor of Littleham, in which it stood. [2]

According to Davidson:

"Littleham is the name of a manor and parish, which is bounded by Withicomb [sic] on the north, Budleigh on the east and the river and seacoast on the west and south, and extends for about two miles, more or less, inland. Mainly it consists of one valley, watered by a little stream called The Brook flowing from north-east to south-west. Of this manor

we happen to posess some information from the Anglo-Saxon deed above mentioned & In the cartulary of Sherborne Abbey, now in the Phillipps Library at Thirlestane House, Cheltenham, at folio 27, is entered an instrument of the year 1042, whereby half a mansa of land at Littleham is granted by King Eadweard [Edward the Confessor] to a thegn of his named Ordgar..." [3]

What is obvious is that for many years it was Littleham that was the centre of the social and economic infrastructure of the area and that its place was only usurped by Exmouth several hundred years later. Davidson wrote in a particularly turgid style, but it seems apparent from his paper that Littleham was of much more socio-economic importance than it is now well into the nineteenth century:

"Littleham Church was, as we have seen, confirmed to the church of Sherborne in 1146; and on the 17th of March, 1234, it was, by Bishop William Brewer, with the assent of tithe lords of the manor, the abbot and convent of Sherborne, granted to the canons of the church of Exeter, reserving 100 shillings yearly for the maintenance of a resident vicar. In the Valor Ecclesiasticus the vicarage is valued at £15 12s. 6d. a year. In the valuation of 1831 it is entered at £191, including the annexed curatcy of Exmouth.

In 1842 the rectorial tithes were commiuted for £383, and the vicarial tithes for £112. The patronage of the living still belongs to the Dean and Chapter of Exeter.

Dr. Oliver states that Littleham Church formerly had three altars, one, no doubt, in the chancel, and a second in the ancient chantry on the south side of the chancel. Hence the double dedication to St. Andrew and St. Margaret. A third altar stood, it is presumed, in the north, commonly called Drake's aisle, which cannot, says Dr. Oliver, be earlier than the reign of Henry VII.

On the 25th of June, 1329, Bishop Grandisson licensed the performance of divine service in a chapel within the place called Pratteshide ; i.e. Exmouth. This chapel was dedicated to the Holy Trinity. It stood on the Beacon Hill, and probably served as a sea-mark. On the 1st June, 1412, Bishop Stafford licensed the inhabitants of Exmouth to assist at divine service in the Chapel of St. Trinity, "there situate," until the following 24th of June, provided that no prejudice thence accrued to the mother church; and to secure this the inhabitants were required to attend the Church of Littleham on Sundays and festivals." [4]

Exmouth therefore didn't even have a church of its own until two hundred years after Littleham, and three hundred years after Edward the Confessor (1002-1066) had granted the deeds of the Manor of Littleham. As recently as 1830 Exmouth was still very much a `poor relation` of Littleham and the situation may have continued even more recently than that. Now, however it is merely a suburb (and not a particularly preposessing one) of Exmouth.

Domesday Book also mentions Littleham:

"Horton Church holds LITTLEHAM. Before 1066 it paid tax for half a hide, land for eight ploughs.

Meadow, 6 acres; underwood, ¾ acres; pasture 6 furlongs in length and width. 1 cob 8 cattle; 139 sheep. Value 40s".

[Terra Aecclae De Hortone. Eccla Hortvnens ten Liteham. T.R.E. geldb p. Dim hida. Tra.e.viii.car. In dnio.e una v trae.7 xv.uitti 7 xx. Bord cu. Viii.car. Ibi.vi.ac.pti.7. v.ac filuae minutae. Paftura vi. Qz in lg 7 lat . Valet. XL. Folid] [5]

We have already seen how the eighteenth century craze for sea bathing irrevocably changed the economic infrastructure of coastal regions. A book called *Exmouth Milestones* by Eric Delderfield, the brother of the famous novelist R.F.Delderfied (author of *To serve them all my days* - a book set at the minor public school of which I am one of the less distinguished scions) [6] included the following passage which implies that the events that we have already seen at Weymouth and Brighton took place even more markedly at Exmouth:

"THE first beginnings of the growth of Exmouth when regarded as a watering place, can be said to have commenced about 1720 when a Lord Chief Justice spoke so glowingly of " . . . . its natural beauties and excellence of climate," that people of quality began to come to the town and make it into a fashionable resort, but, of course, the difficulties of travel even for those days made the progress of necessity slow.

So it remained until the close of the eighteenth century, when the natural amenities of the site and the wonderful prospects began to be realised. In 1792, the first six of the dignified terrace of Georgian houses, the Beacon, were erected. The Rolle Estate began in earnest then to develop the town.

At this time the population of Exmouth was 1909, 570 of which were re-

turned as being employed in trade. There were 406 houses. As a point of interest, East Budleigh then had 1014 inhabitants and 203 houses. Sir John Colleton, Bart., can be said to have been one of Exmouth's first publicity agents. He was for many years in South Carolina and on his return to this country settled in Exmouth." [7]

It was this that heralded the eventual decline of Littleham as the centre of the local economy, and I believe, were a major causative factor in the events discussed in the main body of this book.

A similar scenario can be presented vis a vis the other epicentre of episodic high strangeness that is discussed in this book - Woodbury Castle. According to Aileen Fox's *Prehistoric Hillforts in Devon* Woodbury castle is:

"A conspicuous hill-top fort, on the crest (175m) of a ridge of the Bunter Pebble Beds on Woodbury Common, two kilometres east of Woodbury village. The B3180 runs through the fort, passing through the two entrances.

The main enclosure of 2 hectares is defended by a massive steep rampart and deep ditch, supplemented on the north and east sides by a substantial counter-scarp bank. On the west side the defences are doubled and the end of the second rampart is expanded to create a fighting platform beside the northern entrance. The main rampart turns inwards to flank the southern entrance, now under the road. Other gaps are modern.

60m to the north there is another smaller rampart and ditch across the ridge, extending to Soldiers' Well, a spring on the western side, which probably served as the water supply for the hillfort. On the southern and western sides there are intermittent earthworks that are earlier than the main hillfort.

Limited excavation of a narrow strip alongside the road in 1971 by Henrietta Quinnell showed that a palisaded enclosure pre-dated the defences. The inner rampart was found to have a turf revetment at the back and was topped by a timber breastwork; subsequently it was heightened and the breastwork renewed. At the northern entrance, the rampart ends were revetted with timber and later strengthened with stone, whilst in the interior there were post-holes indicating rectangular timber buildings, possibly granaries. Finds were very few but the pottery suggested that the defences were completed before 300 BC." [7]

In close proximity to the castle are a number of burial mounds, scattered

around the common. It is believed that, nearly two thousand years after it was first built, the Castle was used again between 1798 and 1803, because of the threat of invasion during the Napoleonic wars. [8][9]

For many years, therefore, Woodbury, like Littleham was far more important as a social, cultural and spiritual centre of activity than it is now, and this is, we believe, extremely important, for this is the greatest thing that the places which appear to be the epicentres of an unusual degree of quasi-paranormal activity have in common.

* Littleham. The spiritual, social and economic centre of the area, only usurped by Exmouth after the rise in popularity of sea-side holidays made Exmouth reasonably popular as a resort at the end of the eighteenth century. Exmouth was also relatively isolated until the advent of the railway in 1861, and until at least 1830 it was the superior parish in Ecclesiastical terms.

* Woodbury. One of the first locations on the east side of the river Exe. It was the most important settlement in the area until the Middle Ages, but even as recently as the Napoleonic Wars it played an important role within the socio-economic and military-industrial infrastructure of the area. Now, however, it is deserted.

Compare these two locations with the other epicentres of broadly paranormal activity described in my last two books:

* Puerto Rico. Once the last refuge of the Carib Indians, it was the political centre of the region for many years because of its integral place within the Spanish Empire in the Western Hemisphere. Now it is a shadow of its former self - politically it is neither independent nor an integral part of the United States. Now it is only visited by western journalists in search of the chupacabra and emissaries from the mainland of the United States intent on discarding their industrial waste. [10]

* Mexico. Once the centre of Montezuma`s mighty empire, even after the Spanish invaded it was a powerful and large nation. Now, having lost Colorado, Texas and New Mexico to the United States it is a country on the verge of penury whose ex-President absconded to Dublin with most of the contents of the National Treasury and his beautiful (if dumb) mistress. The Aztec Empire is now a haven for Child Prostitution and Drug Money. [11]

* Falmouth Bay. Once a thriving sea-port, recession after recession has meant that it is now visited mostly by tourists and the once proud seafar-

ing industries are very much on the wane. Falmouth is no longer a mighty sea port and the whole area is rapidly diminishing in importance. (12)

* Mawnan Smith. A great blow was stuck to its spiritual heart - Mawnan Old Church, when it was reconsecrated (see *The Owlman and Others*). Further damage was done to the area with the wave of redundancies in the rural industries over the past thirty years which have meant that once thriving agricultural communities are reduced to a shadow of their former selves. (13)

At last we have a link between the areas which demonstrate an unusual level of fortean phenomena. It may not be the definitive link, it may not be the only one, but it is, for the moment at least, all that we have, and it provides us with an extremely useful like of investigation.

XIV

We would like to begin our penultimate chapter by stressing that we have always kept an open mind in our research, and also that whilst we believe that we are presenting an answer in these pages we do not presume to suggest that we are presenting THE answer.

We started this book with Unidentified Flying Objects and this is where we shall finish.

It is certain that the `things` that have been classified as UFOs are many and diverse. It is equally certaion that the objects described in this book are equally as multifarious. The irony is, that whereas we are attempting to present a theory which can effectively explain how so many apparently disparate types of paranormal phenomena can be reported from the same place at the same time, we are having to, perforce, admit that we can`t even group all the UFO sightings together under one convenient catch-all heading.

That is because the only things that UFOs have in common is that:

1. They are Unidentified
2. They are Flying
3. They are Objects

and even these three descriptions are by no means always accurate.

Sometimes UFOs are on the ground, which means they are not FLYING. Sometimes it appears that they are not tangible or even three dimensional, so they can`t be described as OBJECTS
It has been alleged on many occasions that many people within the higher echelons of various world governments know perfectly well what

they are, so *per se* they cannot be UNIDENTIFIED
We would like to state categorically that:

* We believe that at any time various Governments have secret military hardware that is at least fifteen years in advance of anything seen at Farnborough Air Show, and that a proportion of UFOs reported are in fact sightings of these craft. [1]
* We believe that many UFOs are misidentified reports of conventional aircraft, weather balloons, birds, lenticular clouds, stunt kites and practically everything else that you can think of.
* We are even prepared to admit the possibility that a TINY proportion of UFOs might even be alien spacecraft, and that on the odd occasion a visitor from another planet MIGHT actually land on the Green Hills of Earth [2] in order to do his own inimitable thing.

So, if we are prepared to accept that such a range of hypotheses may indeed be true, is there anything that we are NOT prepared to believe.

The answer is 'not much'. As forteans we have come to accept that the world is an infinitely strange, beautiful and wonderful place where all sorts of wonderful things happen and there are only two hypotheses that we are not prepared to accept.

* Aliens from Zeta Reticuli are not conniving with various earth governments to take over the planet. [3]
* "Flying saucers" are not driven by malaevolent aliens who land in our fields to damage our crops whilst letting out their pet chupacabra to mutilate our cattle. [4]

Apart from that anything goes!

So what have we got apart from a heterogenous collection of "things" that are mostly seen in the "sky" and which some "people" are unable to decide what they are?

The answer is: Not Much. Although the list of explanations given above is a comprehensive one and provides an explanation for a wide range of the UFO activity covered in this book, there are three things that it can't explain.

* What are the glowing balls of light seen above crop circles, in the sky and coming out of the sea?
* Although we accept that a large proportion of the objects reported currently can be categorised as terrestrial hardware or known or unknown

origin, this does not explain the historical sightings of objects that appeared to be machinery in the skies of the world when manned flight was in its infancy.

* How come (if we reject the theories put forwards by `Commander X` and his kind) so many of the UFO reports happen at the same time and in the same place as a dazzling and disturbing array of other quasi-fortean phenomena?

The irony is that we are nearer to reaching at least a partial understanding of the phenomenon if we approach it from a phenomenological viewpoint.and that far from digressing up a varying number of blind alleys during our search for the truth. The time has come to approach the matter holistically and from an avenue that we have never tried before.

Born on October 24, 1868 in France, Alexandra David-Neel was the first woman to be granted the title of Lama in Tibet (Lama is a title equivalent to the sanskrit guru; in Tibet the title is reserved for the high-ranking priests). During all her life of a hundred years she travelled extensively through Asia, especially in the Himalayas (at a time when Tibet was not in the blood-stained hands of China) where she followed an incredible spiritual path. In 1932 she wrote a remarkable book about her travels. Called *With Magicians and Mystics in Tibet* and later reissued as *Magic and Mystery in Tibet* it contains a passage which, I firmly beliefve, holds the key to understanding not only the link between all the apparently heterogenous phenomena contained in this book, but, indeed, their very nature: [5]

"Once the tulpa is endowed with enough vitality to be capable of playing the part of a real being, it tends to free itself from its maker's control. This, say Tibetan occultists, happens nearly mechanically, just as the child, when his body is completed and able to live apart, leaves its mother's womb. Sometimes the phantom becomes a rebellious son and one hears of uncanny struggles that have taken place between magicians and their creatures, the former being severely hurt or even killed by the latter.

Tibetan magicians also relate cases in which the tulpa is sent to fulfil a mission, but does not come back and pursues its peregrinations as a half-conscious, dangerously mischievous puppet. The same thing, it is said, may happen when the maker of the tulpa dies before having dissolved it. Yet, as a rule, the phantom either disappears suddenly at the death of the magician or gradually vanishes like a body that perishes for want of food. On the other hand, some tulpas are expressly intended to survive their creator and are specially formed for that purpose. These may be considered as veritable tulkusl and, in fact, the demarcation between tulpas and tulkus is far from being clearly drawn. The existence of both is grounded on the same theories.

Must we credit these strange accounts of rebellious "materializations," phantoms which have become real beings, or must we reject them all as mere fantastic tales and wild products of imagination?—Perhaps the latter course is the wisest. I affirm nothing. I only relate what I have heard from people whom, in other circumstances, I had found trustworthy, but they may have deluded themselves in all sincerity.

I could hardly deny the possibility of visualizing and animating a tulpa. Besides having had few opportunities of seeing thought-forms, my habitual incredulity led me to make experiments for myself, and my efforts were attended with some success. In order to avoid being influenced by the forms of the lamaist deities, which I saw daily around me in paintings and images, I chose for my experiment a most insignificant character: a monk, short and fat, of an innocent and jolly type.

I shut myself in tsarns and proceeded to perform the prescribed concentration of thought and other rites. After a few months the phantom monk was formed. His form grew gradually fixed and life-like looking. He became a kind of guest, living in my apartment. I then broke my seclusion and started for a tour, with my servants and tents.

The monk included himself in the party. Though I lived in the open riding on horseback for miles each day, the illusion persisted. I saw the fat trapa, now and then it was not necessary for me to think of him to make him appear. The phantom performed various actions of the kind that are natural to travellers and that I had not commanded. For instance, he walked stopped, looked around him. The illusion was mostly visual, but sometimes I felt as if a robe was lightly rubbing against me and once a hand seemed to touch my shoulder.

The features which I had imagined, when building my phantom, gradually underwent a change. The fat, chubby-checked fellow grew leaner, his face assumed a vaguely mocking, sly, malignant look. He became more troublesome and bold. In brief, he escaped my control.

Once, a herdsman who brought me a present of butter saw the tulpa in my tent and took it for a live lama.

I ought to have let the phenomenon follow its course, but the presence of that unwanted companion began to prove trying to my nerves; it turned

into a " daynightmare." Moreover, I was beginning to plan my journey to Lhasa and needed a quiet brain devoid of other preoccupations, so I decided to dissolve the phantom. I succeeded, but only after six months of hard struggle. My mind-creature was tenacious of life." [6]

Richard Freeman is not just my house-mate and fellow toiler in the Cryptozoological vineyard but he is a Goth with the predilection for high strangeness which often accompanies a taste for doomy music and stupid haircuts. During the summer of 1997, whilst the rest of our core-investigation team was hard at work investigating the UFOs over East Devon he conducted some experiments to create a tulpa-like thought form of his own. However, Richard being Richard, he decided that *his* tulpa experiments wouldn`t involve anything as simple as a fat and jolly monk, but would instead be of something altogether more terrifying - a giant spider!

At a party he and his friends constructed an altar to "Athlac-Nacha" the grotesque spider-god invented by horror writer Clark Ashton-Smith in the 1930s. The fact that this hideous deity never existed outside the author`s imagination didn`t seem to worry them as they decorated the altar with strange and arcane artefacts, and erected a huge cloth spiders web in the middle of which they placed a mechanical toy spider.

Then, being students, they all got drunk. Over the next few days they meditated in front of the altar and visualised the image of a huge, glowing spider. After a few weeks it began to appear as if something was beginning to happen. One day Richard entered the cellar where they built the altar. Silhouetted against the darkness of the cellar wall was the image of a huge spider. It was white on black "like a photographic negative", and as he moved his gaze to other walls of the room, and even the ceiling the image remained with him as if it were etched into his retina. A friend of his who visits the cellar, but who hadn't been aware of Richard's arachnid-raising activities also experienced strange sensations, but within a few weeks the whole affair got REALLY weird.

During the latter part of the summer and the early autumn there was a plague of outsized spiders across Leeds and Wakefield and a number of specimens were taken to the Environmental Health Offices by concerned citizens who were worried that they might be poisonous foreign immigrants. Their display of Arachno-xenophobia was unjustified as it turned out that they were all UK species which had grown to an enormous size because of the warm weather. The fact that there were so many of them, however, suggests that something more esoteric than a mere Indian Summer was afoot. [7] [8]

Then in the autumn, a hapless employee of a well known firm of fruit importers, working at a warehouse in Wakefield, was attacked by a giant spider (a bona fide exotic specimen this time) as he was unpacking a case of bananas. He was rushed to hospital where (reportedly) he was told that there was no anti-venom available and that the only way of finding out whether the animal that had bitten him was poisonous or not was by seeing if he was still alive eight hours later. As he survived, presumably the animal's bite was relatively innocuous. The poor chap, bent on vengeance tried unsuccessfully to sue his employers for damages.

His solicitor came out with the classic comment that if a man was unable to carry out his employment duties without being at risk of attack from dangerous foreign invertebrates then there was something rotten in the state of Denmark (or words to that affect).

At this point Richard (who is - believe it or not - an even bigger self publicist than I am) stepped back into the limelight claiming not only to have been responsible for the tulpa in the cellar but also for the plague of Yorkshire spiders and the incident in the fruit warehouse. Whether he was or not goodness only knows but it was a great story and I volunteered my services to tout it around the various representatives of Her Majesty's Press. They loved it and it would certainly have made the daily newspapers (complete with dramatic pictures of Richard and a Goth chick in long black robes waving ritual swords around beneath the huge mechanical spider toy), if a completely pointless story involving one of *The Spice Girls* and a soap star hadn't appeared miraculously across the tabloids consigning my memorable headline of "GOTH APOLOGISES FOR SPIDER PLAGUE" to newspaper heaven.

That proves that the world really is weird! [9]

According to Graham, McEwan:

"Another case where a thought form was allegedly created occurred in Russia in 1912, when a group of noblemen, known as the Brotherhood of the Rising Sun, was led in an experiment by a guru of Chinese or Tibetan origin. The guru prudently suggested that they should concentrate on a humorous and harmless creature, such as Puss in Boots, in the uniform of a musketeer. After about half an hour of intense concentration the form began to appear. At first it was just a light cloud but gradually the form of a red-haired cat began to appear. Its dress remained unclear, though, and the guru intervened: 'Obviously you cannot imagine the musketeer's uniform,' he said, 'your thoughts are various. Now, think only of a red-haired cat in common Russian boots.'

Within a few moments the features of the cat stabilised and on its hind feet was a pair of Russian boots. The egrigor was motionless and looked like a poorly developed photograph.

The guru ordered the assembly to cease thinking about the egrigor, and slowly the form disappeared. This incident was described by Nicholas Mamontoff, a son of one of the witnesses, in Fate magazine in 1960." [10]

We now have to hypothesise the first of a number of questions. What happens to a thought form once it has become a quasi-independent entity? In all texts we have cited (with the notable exception of Richard Freeman's) the thought form, like Frankenstein's monster was always destroyed by the vengeful villagers (or in this case by its creator) before it could do any harm.

According to Alexandra David-Neel:

"Once the tulpa is endowed with enough vitality to be capable of playing the part of a real being, it tends to free itself from its maker's control. This, say Tibetan occultists, happens nearly mechanically, just as the child, when his body is completed and able to live apart, leaves its mother's womb. Sometimes the phantom becomes a rebellious son and one hears of uncanny struggles that have taken place between magicians and their creatures, the former being severely hurt or even killed by the latter.

Tibetan magicians also relate cases in which the tulpa is sent to fulfil a mission, but does not come back and pursues its peregrinations as a half-conscious, dangerously mischievous puppet. The same thing, it is said, may happen when the maker of the tulpa dies before having dissolved it. Yet, as a rule, the phantom either disappears suddenly at the death of the magician or gradually vanishes like a body that perishes for want of food. On the other hand, some tulpas are expressly intended to survive their creator and are specially formed for that purpose. These may be considered as veritable tulkusl and, in fact, the demarcation between tulpas and tulkus is far from being clearly drawn. The existence of both is grounded on the same theories.

Must we credit these strange accounts of rebellious "materializations," phantoms which have become real beings, or must we reject them all as mere fantastic?" [11]

The second question that we have to ask is more complex. In all the examples we have cited the thought form was created intentionally as an act of will. Is it possible that a thought form could be created spontaeneously, or in a more likely scenario accidentally over a number of years.

The answer appears to be yes.

Dion Fortune (real name 'Violet Mary Firth') was born on December 6, 1890 and died on January 8, 1946 and is argued by many to have been one of the leading occultist's of her time. Although she was born in Bryn-y-Bia near Llandudno, she never described herself as Welsh, but prefered to adopt the mantle of being a Yorkshire woman (her father was a Yorkshire man). The family motto was 'Deo, non Fortuna' which translated means 'By God, not by Chance', and from this, she obtained her magic name (Dion Fortune).

Very little is known of her early life except that she is reputed to have had visions of 'Atlantis' when she was four and later in her life she believed that she had once been a temple priestess there (presumably in a previous incarnation). During puberty she is said to have developed mediumistic abilities. In 1906 she joined the Theosophical movement when her family moved to London, but did not find their ideas inspiring. When she was twenty Dion worked under a woman who had travelled to India and studied occult techniques which Dion claimed she used against her in the form of 'Psychic Attacks'. Dion fought off these attacks suffering a nervous breakdown in the process. By the age of twenty-three she was a lay psychoanalyst having studied psychology, but felt that neither Carl G. Jung or Sigmund Freud really understood the complexity and ability of the mind. During the end of World War I she met and worked with the Irish occultist and freemason Theodore Moriarty which led to her write her well known book *Psychic Self Defence* (AD1930) which is seen as her magical autobiography.

Fortune was initiated an outer order of the Hermetic Order of the Golden Dawn known as the London Temple of the Alpha and Omega Lodge of the Stella Matutina in 1919, but she formed her own order known as the 'Fraternity of the Inner Light' which was based upon esoteric Christianity. It was also originally part of the hermetic Order of the Golden Dawn but it became independent after Moina Mathers (one of the founders of the Golden Dawn) asked Dion to leave.

During the winter of 1923/24 Dion then spent time in Glastonbury which became a place she would retreat to regularly involving her own thoughts in the Celtic Otherworld (See Otherworld) she claimed lay beneath the 'Tor'. During this time she claimed to have been in spiritual contact with the Greek philosopher Socrates, the nineteenth-century Chancellor of

England Lord Erksine, and later the great Arthurian magus himself 'Merlin'. She wrote many of her experiences down in the book 'Glastonbury : Avalon of the Heart'.

Fortune married Thomas Penry Evans in 1927 and he was nicknamed Merlin/Merl by many of Fortune's followers. They divorced in 1939. Fortune also formed a pilgrim centre known as the 'Chalice Orchard Club' whilst in Glastonbury, along with a temple dedicated to the 'Mysteries of Isis' in West London known as the 'Belfry'. During her life, and since, she has received a large following. Many of her books are still read by occultists/neo-Pagans. Just after the World War II she was struck down with leukaemia and died at the age of 54. [12]

According to Graham McEwan she:

"described in her book Psychic Self Defence *how she unintentionally created a werewolf. She was lying in bed, half asleep and brooding resentfully against someone who had injured her. The thought of vengeance entered her mind and she suddenly thought of Fenris, the huge, malevolent wolf of Norse mythology. 'Immediately,' she later wrote, 'I felt a curious drawing out sensation from my solar plexus, and there materialised beside me on the bed a large wolf.' As she moved, the beast growled at her, but she summoned all her courage and pushed it off the bed. The animal vanished through the wall of the room, but next morning another occupant of the house told of dreaming about wolves, and of waking in the night to see the glowing eyes of an animal in the darkness."* (12)

Other examples of incedences where a tulpa was apparently created spontaeneously come from the work of Polish medium Teofil Modrzejewski (1873-1943), who worked under the pseudonym of Franek Kluski.

"As a contemplative child, Kluski had experiences of OBEs (Out of Body Experiences), and seeing deceased relatives and animals. Relevant in view of what he would do in the future, Kluski recorded how other children, when with him, would also see those who had died. However, it was not until 1918, after a seance with Jean Guzik, that Kluski's mediumistic potential was recognized and the spectacular seances began. The number of those attending ran into the hundreds and included a variety of people, e.g. professors, soldiers, professional magicians and parapsychologists; these undoubtedly witnessed what must have been some of the most evidential demonstrations of life continuing after death. Those attending 'were not the "usual crowd", but were totally random and very numerous', and 'the testimony left by many of these people is...an encounter with a magical world, that could not possibly be achieved using pa-

thetic little tricks and sleight-of-hand'.

During the period of Kluski's mediumship, the seances were conducted at different locations, and a lighted environment was sometimes present by means of a red lamp and a luminous plaque. There were over eight hundred occurrences of visitants, with sitters recognizing some of these as people who had died: 'They would start out as a kind of haze, and gradually take shape and become more visible, with greater detail, such as wrinkles and facial hair'...Great numbers of them appeared virtually simultaneously, and often there would be an impression of other presences'. Prof. F. W. Pawlowski noted how the apparitions appeared at some distance from Kluski, and while some walked around normally, others would fly above the sitters' heads. Those who could speak did so in his/her own language, and it appeared that they could read the sitters' minds as they responded to what a sitter was thinking before anything was said. Some chose to communicate by raps, but the voices of those who did speak were reported to have been 'perfectly clear and normally loud, but sound like a loud whisper'.

Kluski is also important to Spiritualist belief as he dealt a death-blow to Christian anthropocentrism (that, illogically, teaches only human beings survive death), as his seances enjoyed the presence of animals returning. Sylvia Barbanell cited Pawlowski's testimony that sitters experienced the materialization of various types of animals; he recorded an instance of a dog materializing and jumping upon the laps of the sitters, and in a seance with a red lamp, a hawk-like bird flew around, with its wings beating against the walls: this occasion was photographed. Validating a further feature of Spiritualist belief, i.e. that bonds of affection are not broken by death, when certain persons materialized in the Kluski seances, they would be accompanied by an animal that left as soon as their human companion departed. The significant feature, as Mrs Barbanell observed, is that the Kluski seances demonstrated that all, rather than some, animals survive death.

One materialization brought an animal that resembled a lion that would lick the sitters: this 'would stalk around, lashing its tail against the furniture and leaving behind it a strong acrid smell'. Another visitor, referred to as the Pithecanthropus, was clearly intent on making his presence known to the sitters: an ape-type being, it moved the furniture and behaved 'rather roughly with regard to the sitters, trying to lick their hands or faces'; often the seance had to be prematurely ended when it became over-enthusiastic. Pawlowski related how it grabbed one woman's hand to rub this against its face, and 'this frightened her considerably and caused her to shriek'. Those who came to the seances from 'the other side' would comply with requests to move furniture; despite being in darkness, they would do this without any obvious difficulty; one such instance was the moving of a heavy bronze statue. Kluski's seances may have been many things, but they were hardly uneventful.

Relevant due to the present popularity of the idea that communicators are really only fragmented personalities ('psychons' or 'mindkins'), Dr Gustave Geley, who participated in Kluski's seances at the Paris Institut Metapsychique International, and in Warsaw, reported how 'All these phantoms give the impression of being alive, and as normal as living people'. Pawlowski reiterates this view, adding that 'They made a round of the sitters, smiling an acknowledgement of the familiar sitters and looking curiously at the sitters they had not seen before'.

In addition to the materializations, there was the appearance of lights swiftly moving around the room, apports and noises. Admittedly, Kluski was hardly a typical medium: he was not only a proficient materialization medium but adept at producing automatic writing, and deriving no financial benefit from this. He was also seen in different locations away from where he was physically situated, and was accompanied by lights and followed by noises and odours; apparitions would appear in the daylight when he was not even conducting a seance. Pawlowski mentioned how 'the apparitions' persisted in interrupting Kluski's sleep by walking around his room and going as far as illuminating themselves for his benefit. Pawlowski also referred to a report that he had 'no reason to distrust', that Kluski was not only transported to the seance room by the apparit-ions, but also transported from the locked room and found asleep in a another location. Furthermore, tests demonstrated there was a dramatic reduction of temperature in the seance room with Kluski present, and compass needles would move about violently when he was nearby." [14]

This hypothesis is confirmed by Alexandra David-Neel who says:

"In a general way, Tibetans distinguish two categories of psychic phenomena.

1. The phenomena which are unconsciously produced either by one or by several individuals.

In that case, the author—or authors—of the phenomenon acting unconsciously, it is obvious that he does not aim at a fixed result.

2. The phenomena produced consciously, with a view of bringing about a prescribed result. These are generally—but not always—the work of a single person.

That "person" may be a man or may belong to any one of the six classes of sentient beings which lamaists acknowledge as existing in our world. Whosoever be its author, the phenomenon is produced by the same process, in accordance with some natural laws: there is no Oracle." [15]

The third and most important question that we have to ask is in many ways the most cerebral of them all. In all the examples that we have cited, the tulpa has taken the specific form decided by its creator. In other words it has been created "in his/her own image". If a thought form can, indeed, arise by an unconscious act of will, and if, as we shall see hypothesised in the next chapter, it is created by a group of people who not only do not realise that they are engaged in the act of creation, but are doing it over a long period of time - probably many lifetimes - what form would it take?

Here, we should perhaps question the very nature of what are popularly known as `ghosts`. Although they are popularly believed to be the spirits of the dead, left to wander the earth in limbo, we believe that the available evidence leads us to reason that they are nothing of the sort.

This is not the time nor the place to discuss the true nature of such phenomena in any length, but we would like to note two aspects of ghosts and other paranormal occurrences which are often grievously misinterpreted.

These are the apparitions which appear to drug users and the mentally ill, which are usually dismissed as being schizophrenic/chemically-induced delusions, but which we believe are in actuality are sometimes at least no such thing.

I am not psychic and I have had very few experiences in my life which I can count as true encounters with a ghost. However, what few I have had were all in and about the hospitals for the Mentally Handicapped where I worked for so many years. I spent some months on night duty alone at a semi-disused Victorian asylum in East Devon. [16] During my hours alone on the ward I often heard the sounds of footsteps and the unmistakeable noises of people moving around from a locked ward on the floor above me which had been empty for several years. My ex-wife reported similar occurences at Redhills Hospital in Exeter and I have collected a number of similar stories from old hospitals around the country. [17]

Nigel's mother was a patient in the RD&E Hospital in Southernhay, Exeter (now decommissioned and the headquarters of the Exeter Health Care Trust). She was suffering from quinsy during WW2. At midnight every night she would have to close her eyes because the locked door would open of its own volition and she would feel cold 'breath' upon her face. She could hear the 'breathing' as well, and the room would have an apparent severe drop in temperature. The one night when she managed to summon up the courage to open her eyes there was no-one there.

She told this story to the medical staff who were convinced that she was suffering from febrile hallucinations, but apparently she was so insistent that one night a doctor and two nurses sat in the room with her and at midnight they saw the locked door open and the shadowy figure of someone wearing what appeared to be old-fashioned nursing uniform come over to Nigel's mother's bed, and bend over her. [18]

An almost identical account comes from an anonymous source in Australia:

"Being in a private room of a well known hospital I woke up in the middle of the night for no apparent reason. The door to my room was a sliding one with a large glass window pane that allowed you to see any one approaching my door and out into the hallway. The door was slightly ajar. I was looking towards the door when to my surprise and shock an arm came through the gap, slid across the wall towards the light switch located just inside the doorway and turned the overhead light on. I expected a nurse to come in to give me medicine but no one appeared, I then buzzed for a nurse when no one came. The nurse appeared at the window in the door and came in. I angrily asked who turned on the light and why? She said that she had been just down from my door for the past 10/15minutes and had seen no one there. She also said that there were no patients out of their beds and no other nurses or staff in the hallway, just her. We both thought it was really, really strange. After everything had settled down I thought about the whole thing and suddenly realised a few things, when the arm came in I could hear no one in the hallway, it was dead quiet and I could see no one in the window of my door!!!" [19]

Medical and Surgical hospitals are also full of 'ghosts'. This story, taken at random, is a typical account:

"My wife is an RN at our local hospital. She works on the Medical Floor (Medical covers all people who don't require surgery but are sick enough to stay in the hospital). Most of her patients are elderly and many pass away there.

There are two rooms on her floor that are "haunted". In one, the equipment will turn itself on. They will be alerted to this because the call button is also activated. One night this happened while she was alone on the floor. The call button for the room went off but there wasn't a patient in it.

When she walked into the room, the TV, the lights, and other equipment standard for a hospital room were on. She thought that another nurse had been assigned and that a patient had been admitted. After several hours and no patient or nurse, she turned off the stuff and went back to her station.

About ten minutes later, the call button sounded again. She went into the room and found it just the way she had before. This room was close to her work station and noone could have entered it without her seeing them.

She turned the equipment in the room off again and that was the end of that night. When the next shift came on, she asked the head nurse about the room. The Charge nurse told her that the room had always been weird and that the electronic equipment didn't work correctly when in there. There had been several deaths in the room but none that were traumatic or anything. Unlike some of the other rooms.

Another room that is "haunted" is called the Rose Room by the nurses because every once in a while they will hear someone in the room calling out the name 'Rose'. Patients who are heavily drugged or close to death have reported having been visited by a very pleasant elderly man dressed in a suit and tie. They have conversations, etc. but usually don't remember when he arrived or when he left.

A final story that doesn't end in a haunting but is interesting:

A young man was dying and had developed a serious condition where he was bleeding internally but had used up his clotting factor.

My wife was working that night, but did not have him as a patient. When she walked by his room, she heard what sounded like water being poured onto the floor. She went into the room and saw that he was vomiting blood consistenly, and this was flowing onto the floor.

Immediately she called the doctors and nurses and tried to help the poor guy. He continued to vomit black blood all over. I'm not sure about the *exact nature of the events, but at some point just before he died, he became conscious. He seemed to know he was going to die and was very afraid, but there was nothing the doctors could do. He went into convulsions while vomiting and blood covered everyone.*

As he died, the hospital bed started to freak out. It began to move up and down and into all the different positions without anyone touching the controls. Finally, when the poor guy died, the bed stopped moving. They tried to opperate the controls but they wouldn't respond. They were never able to fix the bed so that it worked again.

Although there was a creepy feeling in the room when the guy died, there hasn't been any problems with it since then.

Just thought I'd contribute a fun couple of stories for the folklore files." [20]

I used to live at Staplake House, in Starcross. It was the nurses home adjunct to the Royal Western Counties hospital at Starcross and it was the `home` of a large number of ghosts. Although I never saw anything, various girls living in the building did, and it was commonly believed that these apparitions dated back to the days when Staplake was actually an annexe of the RWC Hospital. [21] [22]

The accepted paradigm is that these ghosts are the spirits of dead patients/staff who for reasons of their own still haunt the coridoors of the location where they once upon a time lived and/or died. But what if the explanation is far more obvious and less "woolly" than that?

The other group of people whose paranormal occurences are often misjudged are long term drug takers. This account is taken from an interview I conducted with a one time New Age Traveller called Trish Lovelock, who, whilst not a drug user herself, was at the time sharing an old school bus with her boyfriend who:

"......had a series of encounters with what he described as a `little grey alien`, very similar to those depicted on the front cover of Whitley Streiber's book `Communion`.

One night he was driving along the road together with my daughter Jenny who was about eight years old at the time. She remembers seeing a ball of white and yellow light `about the size of a football` suspended in the road in front of them. With no time to stop they drove straight through the light which appeared to enter the car and go straight *through it. She remembers how the light felt strangely warm although she can remember suffering no ill effects from her experience. My recollections of Mark`s account at the time, howeve, are somewhat different. I remember him telling me how, terrified, he reversed away from the light and drove away as fast as he could, and that another car on the same road did exactly the same thing and both cars reversed down the road as fast as they could.*

My boyfriend started to suffer from unusual tiredness and used to go to bed extremely early. Each morning when he awoke he had strange triangular red `burns` on his arms, and I think once, on his neck. Although they appeared to be burns these regular isosceles triangles did not blister and seemed not to cause him any pain. He was convinced that these marks were somehow linked to the alien entity that he nicknamed `George`. He even claimed that `George` had sat in the car with him one night and attempted to communicate with him. A Druid friend of mine, known to the cognoscenti as `Badger` was driving my car one night when she had a momentary sighting of what appeared to be a very similar entity in the rear view mirror. This activity seemed to be inextricably linked to the location where we were camped because when we left Stibb Cross we seemed to leave `George` behind us.

Jenny also saw what she described as little figures running off into the undergrowth on a number of occasions, although now, she has half convinced herself that they were rabbits or birds going about their natural business. Other weird things happened at the same time. On a number of occasions we saw strange flickering lights in the night outside our bus. On one night a car which was parked outside rolled downhill into a convenient bush but although the ground was wet there were no tyre marks. A few days later a similar incident happened but this time the events were even more inexplicable as the car seemed to roll uphill into a muddy ditch from whence it had to be pulled out by a tractor!

Another day we found a burnt out car in the middle of the moor. The strangest thing about it was that there were no scorch marks on the ground around the vehicle and it seemed as if it had somehow been transported to the place where we found it.

My boyfriend became obsessed with the imagery of the archetypal Grey after his encounters with `George`, and for months afterwards he made tiny alien heads out of modelling clay. Long after we left Stibb Cross, the psychic reverberations of that sinister spot haunted our whole family, and even now the memories leave us all with a chill down the back of our necks. ".... [23] [24]

I make no apologies for the fact that much of this book has been about mental illness - specifically my mental illness. In many ways this book is the chronicle of my own struggle with sanity and I make no apologies for that either. However, I have been undergoing succesful treatment for my disorder for well over two years now, and I am well on my way towards being cured, insofar as I ever will be. Much of my treatment, and the greater part of my psychotherapy has been targeted towards my dysfunctional perception of what is fondly known as reality. As I came out of the protective shell in which I had languished for so many years I began to see things in a new light and I began to realise that in fact despite what I had always thought, I had never been insane at all, but that like so many people with what is diagnosed as a mental disorder, I had not been able to handle my emotions, and that this inability had clouded both my behaviour and my perception of the universe around me.

Vaguely, over a period of months I began to realise, that those people, like me, who were unable to control their emotions and who therefore wasted a lot of emotional energy were often (but by no means always) those who found themselves at the centre of unusual bouts of quasi-fortean activity. I realised that this piece of information was important, but I didn't know what to do with it.

As the months progressed and slowly turned into years my perception of the whole nature of outbreaks of quasi-fortean occurences began to change and I realised that, slowly, as my life got better, so did my understanding of the nature of the phenomena that I had spent so many years studying.

Russsell Hoban wrote:

"Wherever they have shamans, they are always the unstable, the epileptics, the weird ones of the group, people prone to terrors and depression like I am".. [25]

I have always agreed with his statement. Now I was very close to understanding it.

The history of human involvement with hallucinogenic drugs probably goes back many thousands of years since DMT usage is associated with South American shamanism. The "Spanish friar Ramon Paul, who accompanied Columbus on his second voyage to the New World, was the first to record native use of ... *'kohhobba' to communicate with the spirit world"*. Plant tryptamines are used by Amazonian shamans in the form of ayahuasca, a dark Liquid formed by boiling sections of a vine from the

Banisteriopsis genus, usually *B. caapi*. This vine contains harmala alkaloids, in particular, harmine and harmaline, which are sufficient in themselves to induce visions. Usually another plant is added to the brew "to make the visions more intense" (according to the native shamans). Ayahuasca is frequently consumed at night by a group of people, although there are large variations in its mode of usage among the Indian tribes of the Amazon. In Brazil there is an interesting religious organization known as Santo daime, whose members use ayahuasca within a Catholic/Christian context . [26]

Writing in *The Use of Psychoactive Plants Among the Hupda-Maku* Pedro Fernandes Leite da Luz describesthe use of other hallucinogens amongst Peruvian Tribes:

"Patu
Erythroxylum coca var. ipadu is known by the Hupda as "Patu" and is used daily. There are three distinct types: Ipadu de Peixe, Ipadu de Pau, and Ipadu Abiú. These are valued according to flavour, Abiú being the strongest. Close to all Hupda villages in the region you encounter small fields with enough mature Patu plants for the Hupda's traditional use of the species. Starting at 4:30 pm the sound of the "pilão" (wooden mortar and pestle) can be heard in almost all of the households. The recently collected Patu leaves, dried in a manioc toasting pan, are beaten and the resulting powder is mixed with ashes of dried Embaúba (Cecropria sp.) leaves. The final product is then sifted through cloth to be taken orally in doses of a teaspoonful, or more, at a time in the "roda dos homens" (the circle of men). The events of the day are discussed. Taking Patu has an important role in the socialisation of the Hupda men, acting as a stimulant while they relate to each other the trails used in hunting, discuss problems affecting the group, or organise a party. These conversations last from 5:00pm to 10:00 pm. When the Patu prepared for the day is finished, the Hupda begin preparing for sleep, which they will all be doing by midnight. In spite of testimonies by the Hupda of persecution by the Brazilian Federal Police because of their use of Patu, they do not want to give it up because they recognise the medicinal and stimulant virtues of the plant.

Patu is also important in the preparations for the ingestion of "Carpi" (Banisteriopsis Caapi), because it allows the shaman to acquire the mental state and the physical purification necessary for the Carpi ceremony. Patu is chewed in great quantities while fasting for several days before the ceremony. The Hupda frequently associate the two plants, Carpi and Patu, considering both to be "professors" which emerged together when the world was created. Xenhet Another related plant, used simultaneously with Carpi is "Xenhet", a red powder made from trees of the genus Virola. The Hupda utilize two species: Virola theiodora and Virola calophylla, and consider this plant to be Carpi's relative. Xenhet is at the same time a tree, a powder made from the tree, and an "enchanted being." This being, the "Xenhet", is considered to be a man about eight centimetres tall who, when the shaman inhales the powder for the first time, starts living in the shaman's ear. Here he teaches the shaman about the visions and knowledge which come from "Carpi" consumption. The Xenhet is seen as the son of everyone who has sniffed him but his help and teachings can be invoked even without inhaling the powder; all you have to do is call him affectionately and he will answer. Extremely valued by the Hupda, the use of Xenhet is fundamental for those who want to be a shaman. Only with Xenhet's help can someone be successful in understanding Carpi's effects and become a healer. The powder must be acquired from an experienced shaman who will teach the apprentice about its use and preparation. The apprentice then becomes indebted to the shaman for favours and gifts which he must honour under penalty of death. Indeed, the shaman who has not been satisfactorily paid for his Xenhet can blow in the direction of the apprentice and cause him to die within three days.

The tree is well known and common in the region occupied by the Hupda and the preparation of the powder is simple and known by all Hupda men. The bark of the Virola is cut 50cm from the ground, a piece 40cm wide and 1.2 metres long is then stripped from the trunk. The exuded resin is put in cold water where it solidifies, later being dried, pulverized, and mixed with tobacco snuff to be inhaled. Even given the high esteem and the enthusiastic terms with which the Hupda refer to Xenhet, and in spite of the recognized strength of its effects, Xenhet is thought of as an auxiliary entity to Carpi.

Carpi
For the Hupda, Carpi existed at the time of creation, in the "Parmuridúi" when humanity emerged. Carpi formed the bones of the first man, the ancestor of all Hupda. In this way Carpi can be seen as a distinctive legacy of the Hupda. They say that by having the Carpi body they share the knowledge that it has, thus justifying their alleged superiority in knowledge of the world in relation to other peoples. Indeed, in Hupda culture, Carpi is the principal vehicle for attaining wisdom. Identified in another myth with the veins of the "sloth man", the "owner of caxiri" (a fermented drink made from manioc), Carpi metaphorically represents the strength and the vital sustenance which enables the user to learn and grow.

In taking Carpi the Hupda first see "how the world moves," as they say, which means the reason for the creation of the world, how it was done, and the laws which govern its workings. Carpi reveals the "movement" of all things, the reasons they exist, and the role they play in the great cosmic drama. Under the effects of Carpi everything acquires life. Even a rock or a piece of firewood reveals its true identity. Everything appears as if it were human and that is the hidden aspect of being which is revealed to whoever drinks Carpi. To obtain knowledge, to be intelligent and have good vision and discernment, it is necessary to take Carpi and to learn from it the true form and meaning of all things. In spite of being the same plant, Banisteriopsis caapi, the Hupda distinguish seven different types of Carpi in accord with the maturity of the plant, the part used and the general appearance of the vine, e.g. if it is smooth, if it has knots, if it is twisted, etc. Each type has its own specific use. For instance, there is one which is drunk to learn, another to give knowledge, another is a stimulant to be taken before work or war, one is used to relate and listen to the tribal myths, and finally, those which are used for dancing at parties and for healing.

To ingest Carpi with the goal of having good visions, one must observe certain procedures. For some days beforehand one cannot eat anything roasted, salted, warm, or prepared by a menstruating woman. It is necessary to clean the body repeatedly by taking an emetic drink, as well as by maintaining sexual abstinence. According to the use for which the vine is being prepared, the plant additives are changed, but generally the preparation is similar. The vine is scraped and the bark, the only part utilised, is put in a pan of water to cook while the other desired plants are added. As soon as the liquid boils the pan is removed from the fire and left to sit in the sun. The Hupda believe that the sun has an active role in the "birth" of the Carpi, by boiling and cooking it. Both the preparation and the ingestion of Carpi take place far from the eyes of women and children, otherwise the drinker may get sick. The vine is cultivated and harvested by the shaman, or by a dancer, who must always be the oldest of his sibling group. The oldest brother brings the vine, tied in a bundle, and drops it at the entrance to the "maloca" (communal hut) and sings and dances around the vine before its preparation.

In the Dabacouri celebration (ritual exchange between siblings and/or village), the drink is ingested by the dancers so that they will "lose their shame", chanting and dancing to meet the expectations of the village. The songs, in these cases, have as their objective the fertility and growth of animals and fruits. When the effects of Carpi start to be felt, the Hupda encourage each other by saying: "It's started, we must be strong, we must be men," and eventually they discuss the visions they are having. In these situations, the Carpi is used not as an end in itself but as a tool, *a necessary aid to the harmony of the song and the dance.*

"Huamp Carpi", on the other hand, is used by the shaman to heal and is drunk for its capacity to show sickness and its causes. Under the effects of "Huamp Carpi" the shaman sees illness in the form of a venomous substance foreign to the patient, and also sees who has sent the illness. The shaman sucks the back of the left hand of the patient, taking away his/her evil, meaning the cause of the illness, an invisible poison which the shaman then spits away. The illness, however, can't be left there alone where it could contaminate someone else passing by. So the Shaman then takes the illness in his hand, as if it were solid, and puts it in a magical invisible bag. To drink Carpi is also thought of as a preventative medicine, turning the blood of the drinker bitter, thus making him immune to any external aggression. During the healing ceremonies, a specific song is sung which lists different flowers from which water comes to extinguish the fire which represents illness. [27]

Some users of psychedelic drugs have reported that they have experienced what appears to be contact with non-human entities whilst `tripping`. When it was attempted to recreate these experiences under laboratory conditions, some astounding results were achieved.

A few accounts at random:

* <u>Subject S (no previous experience with DMT; written communication)</u>:

My first attempts with DMT have left me with some serious thoughts... I did less than 10 mg on my second attempt and had a very weird experience. Not only did I have what I can only call a "close encounter," I was left with two thoughts. First, they were waiting for me, and they were not "friendly."... ion the] third attempt lit] seemed like they could not wait for me to experiment. In this event, I did not have actual contact, but rather "felt" them wanting to get into my consciousness. The actual experience was far more frightening than any major "trip" previously experienced.... I was profoundly affected.

* <u>Subject O (description of first DMT experience; written communication)</u>:

Remember to breathe. Recline and get into position, subsumed by the momentum; before me I see an irridescent membrane, taut and gently pulsating, something stretching and pushing towards me, on the other side, straining to emerge. fissure rends, tears and inside I glimpse the existence of something/place consisting of a dense whirling body of brilliantly multicolored primordial life/thought stuff, seeping and beckoning... I breathe and return into the plexus, center of my being, to witness myself as an outline-constructed 2-0 diagramatic shell of many coherent light-points, revolving quadrated vortices, large central to smaller and then tiny outer, phosphorescent green and I... enter into utter emptiness, space matrix....

[I]mpression of basic colors, unmuted blue, yellow and red, shimmering into being depth imperceptible yet defined within the space, endlessly recurring back from/into the corner when, slowly, from around the edges they peer towards me, watching eyes bright and watching in small faces, then small hands to pull themselves, slowly, from behind and into view; they are small white-blond imp-kids, very old in bright, mostly red, fogs and caps; candy-store, shiny, teasing and inquisitive, very solemn and somewhat pleased (ah, here you are!) watching me as I meet only their eyes bright and dark without any words (look!) or any idea remembered they only want to convey (look!) through their eyes that I must know that THIS is what they/we are doing...

* <u>Subject O (second DMT experience; written communication)</u>:

...I found myself once again in the company of the "elves," as the focus of their attention and ministrations, but they appeared much less colorful and altogether preoccupied with the task at hand, i.e., pouring a golden, viscous liquid through a network of long, intertwining, transparent conduits which led into the middle of my abdomen...

* <u>Subject G (very experienced with DMT; Gracie [44], #5)</u>:

We each had taken 150 mg of pure MDA.... About hour 4, I decided to try smoking some DMT.... This time I saw the "elves" as multi-dimensional creatures formed by strands of visible language; they were more creaturely than I had ever seen them before.... The elves were dancing in and out of the multidimensional visible language matrix, "waving" their "arms" and "limbs/hands/fingers?" and "smiling" or "laughing," although I saw no faces as such. The elves were "telling" me (or I was understanding them to say) that I had seen them before, in early childhood. Memories were flooding back of seeing the elves: they looked just like they do now: evershifting, folding, multidimensional, multicolored (what colors!), always laughing weaving/waving, showing me things, showing me the visible language they are created/creatures of, teaching me to speak and read.

* Subject V (very experienced with DMT; verbal communication):

I was in a large space and saw what seemed to be thousands of the entities. They were rapidly passing something to and fro among themselves, and were looking intently at me, as if to say "See what we are doing" ... I noticed what seemed to be an opening into a large space, like looking through a cave opening to a starry sky. As I approached this I saw that resting in the opening was a large creature, with many arms, somewhat like an octopus, and all over the arms were eyes, mostly closed, as if the creature were asleep or slumbering. As I approached it the eyes opened, and it/they became aware of me. It did not seem especially well-disposed towards me, as if it did not wish to be bothered by a mere human, and I had the impression ! wasn't going to get past it, so I did not try. [28]

For at least thirty years, the use of psychedelic drugs has been widespread within western cultures. We have tended to use them recreationally. I tried both LSD and Psilocybin when I was in my early twenties, but I have to admit that I didn't particularly enjoy the experience and I certainly didn't gain any great insights into the workings of my inner psyche from my chemical experiences.

Whilst I, Graham and most of our contemporaries just swallowed a handful of `magic mushrooms` and listened to a Led Zeppelin album some users of hallucinatory drugs do claim to have had some extraordinary experiences and even experienced great spiritual revelations whilst using such chemicals. Many of these people have been heavily influenced by writers such as Terence McKenna [29] and Carlos Castaneda, [30] who introduced the concept of the use of pscychoatice chemicals for spiritual, rather than purely recreational purposes. However, I believe that although the spiritual awakenings that they wrote about may well have been genuine ones, they did an awful lot of harm to the people who read their books and used them as an excuse to experience life through drugs rather than through `real` experiences. If my experiences with psychoactive chemicals are anything to go by, it is terribly easy, whilst using them. to see whatever you want to see. [31]

When I was doing drugs I thought I was near the truth; when I was mad I thought I was the most important man in the world.

I was still using recreational drugs when I started to investigate paranor-

mal and fortean phenomena and I believed that my drug use was in some subliminal way helping me to understand the nature of the phenomena that I was investigating. As will be seen in the final chapter, if my theory to explain the true nature of some of the phenomena described in this book is indeed correct, then I was correct by my assumption. However, I was terribly wrong in so far as my explanation for this truism went.

The strange thing is that I was far from being the only one. For thirty years now successive generations of starry eyed hippies have thought that, by taking enormous quantities of chemicals and lying in empty fields, gazing up at the stars, they were being `pretty damn cosmic`. The ultimate irony is that they were right, and that the successive generations of "straights" condemned them for it. The successive generations of `starry eyed hippies` were however, far from being in control of what was happening.

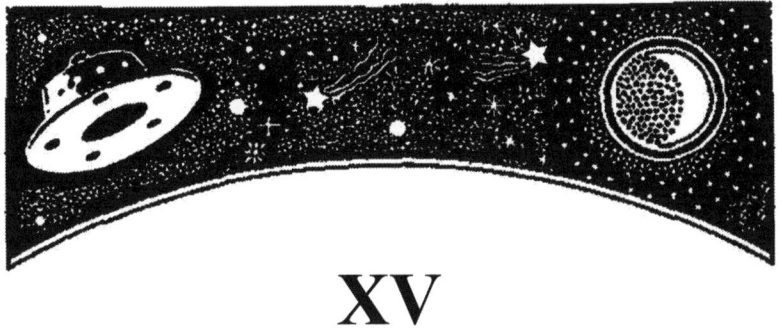

XV

But where is all this leading us? To be more accurate, because this is the last chapter of the book, where has all this led us? What started as a simple account of some UFO sightings in the west of England which happened to coincide with the break-up of my marriage has now become something else entirely. The truth is, as Oscar Wilde once said, rarely pure and never simple [1], but it has been staring us in the face all the time.

It has taken me something in the region of a decade to get this far along the path of my quest for the truth, and although I am quite pleased with my progress I am the first to admit that I have a long way to go before I can finally say - when the UFO Buffs tell me smugly that **"The Truth is Out There"** - *"Yeah, I know, and furthermore here it is"* [2]

I believe that we have now formulated the beginnings of a theory which can explain the nature of not all, but a large proportion of anomalous phenomena, and especially those which cluster in so-called "window areas". However, to do so, we must first examine the work of some unjustly ignored scientists.

Firstly, Wilhelm Reich. He was a Freudian analyst born in Austria in 1897 and spent much of his life trying to prove the energetic reality of the "Libido" which Sigmund Freud had coined. Reich worked on his own version of biophysics for many years, but by 1933 he had to leave Germany as Hitler's Nazi regime and the threat to his own well-being increased. Eventually after moving to Oslo he moved to the United States in 1939. Using what was, for his time at least, a high quality microscope, Reich observed that under high magnification he could see that what appeared to be luminous blue/green globules which were released by decaying food. He described these as some form of biological ether. He likened these globules to *Bions* which were named and researched by H.

Charlton Bastian, a contemporary of Louis Pasteur. Reich claimed that the particles he could see in the microscope were actually an unidentified energy or radiation form which in turn caused conjunctivitis and skin tanning. Reich named this energy 'Orgone'. (3)

An uncredited article on the Mystical www reads:

"In 1948 Reich founded the 'Orgone Institute' at Rangeley, Maine, USA. It was here that the experiments with orgone energy and electromagnetism were carried out and discussed in the 1951 publication, 'The Oranur Experiment' (first report 1947-1951). As experiments were being carried out, it is reputed that menacing clouds formed above the institute, lab workers and visitors became sick and it was said that the general area felt oppressive, with an impending sense of doom. Even trees and shrubs were reported to have blackened and died. It was then that Reich maintained that he had started to produce what he called 'DOR'. (Deadly Orgone Radiation). 'OR' (Orgone Radiation) was believed by Reich to be a life giving process, DOR was the reverse which is why people fell ill and plants died." (4)

Reich was not the only researcher to hypothesise a measurable `life energy`. Franz Anton Mesmer (1734 - 1815) had similiar ideas. He theorised a connection between Newtons theory of "universal gravitation" and the power of the human mind and body. Newton had commented the body contained an invisible fluid that responded to planetary gravitation and Mesmer believed that a body's well-being depended upon whether the body's "animal gravitation" was in harmonic alignment with the planets and chose the term "animal magnetism" for life energy.

Baron von Reichenbach (d. 1869) also hyothesised an electro-magnetic life energy "Odic Force." He conducted thousands of tests with more than hundred sensitive people and he developed a comprehensive theory concerning this energy, much of which was contained in a book called *Researches on Magnetism, Electricity, Heat, Light, Crystallisation and Chemical Attraction, in their Relations to the Vital Force.* which was translated into English by Prof William Gregory and first published by Taylor, Walton and Maberly, London, 1850 (5)

This concept of a measurable `life energy` is nothing new. These three scientists were, however the first to attempt to codify it. This `life energy` (call it what you will) is of course what priests and magicians have been using for centuries. The savants of every culture have developed effective and complex mechanisms to create and project this energy. Various cultures have used everything from human and animal sacrifice, chanting, emotional build up in congregations or magical groups, walking in circles, sex magical practices, and other rituals. In the Bible, for instance, you will find no less than 23 passages that tell how to sacrifice animals. In most instances the shaman or priest used energy that was available and accumulated it up for release in a religious-magical operation.

However, as we have seen from the experiments described by Alexandra David-Neel, it does seem that it is possible to create a *tulpa* that can achieve some degree of independent existence.

Geoffrey Ashe, writing in *The Ancient Wisdom* confirms Alexandra David-Neel's claims:

"If the concentration of thought and will is powerful enough - perhaps a joint effort by many people - a human tulpa [thought form] can be more than a phantasm . It can come into being by normal birth, as a stable physical form with personality. It is then called a tulku or 'phantom body'. A tulku child is not, or need not be, distinguishable from others by inspection alone. But he embodies a god or a demon or another person deceased, or an intention or hope; whatever it was that inspired the thoughts which formed him. Repetition of this process through a series of lives produces a chain of tulku personas who are fundamentally the same, though they may develop quiet differently.

This accounts for the mystic succession of Dalai Lamas. One of Madame David-Neel's informants told her that the Mongols would 'construct' the returning Messianic Gesar by their own thoughts, their own yearning for him. He would be reborn as 'the tulku of all of us whom the foreigners wish to make their slaves." [6]

Writing in *The Tibetan Book of the Great Liberation* -W. Y. Evans-Wentz, claims that this act of creation need not be done on a conscious level:

"...'mediums' in the Occident can, while entranced, automatically and unconsciously create materializations which are much less palpable than the consciously produced Tul-pas [thought-forms], by exuding 'ectoplasm' from their own bodies. Similarly, as is suggested by instances of phantasms of the living reported by psychic research, a thought-form may be made to emanate from one human mind and be hallucinatorily perceived by another, although possessed of little or no palpableness" [7]

We now have to ask whether it is possible for a thought form to be inadvertantly created in a spontaeneous act as a by-product of magickal and religious ritual activity? Or, possibly, whether a tulpa-like being can be created as a necessary byproduct of social religious and/or magickal behaviour. If one person, albeit a medium, can do as Evans-Wentz has claimed, maybe we should hypothesise the synergistic effect (on an etheric level at least) of generations of people who worship and perform rituals in the same place.

Despite our refutation in Chapter XIII of claims that Woodbury Common has been used in recent years for satanic rituals, it is clear that over the years it, and indeed the other epicentre of high strangeness in Littleham, has been used for two, if not three, groups of religious practises:

1. The Druid religion of the Celts
2. Christianity

and possibly

3. Contemporary Wiccan and Neo-Pagan worship

Despite the many thousands of words written on the subject we actually know very little about druids, or their religious beliefs, but what we do know implies very strongly that their religion was extremely ritualistic in nature. As Peter Beresford Ellis has noted:

"Many Celtic gods were worshipped in triune or triple form. The concept of a three personality god seems to have its roots in IndoEuropean expression. In Hindu belief the Trimurti consisted of Brahma, the Creator, Vishnu, the Preserver, and Shiva the Destroyer. Pythagoras saw three as the perfect number of the philosophers -the beginning, middle and end - and used it as a symbol of deity. Indeed, the ancient Greeks saw the world ruled by three gods -Zeus (heaven), Poseidon (sea) and Pluto/ Hades (underworld). Three permeates Greek myth: the Fates are three, the Furies three, the Graces three, the Harpies three, the Pythia or Sibyl (the Delphic oracle) sits on a three-legged stool, the Sibylline books are three times three, the Muses are three times three and so on.

As in the Greek world, so among the Celts, who saw homo sapiens as body, soul and spirit; the world they inhabited as earth, sea and air; the divisions of nature as animal, vegetable and mineral; the cardinal colours as red, yellow and blue and so forth. Three was the number of all things. Most of their gods were three personalities in one. Combinations of the figure three occur often in Celtic tales such as nine (three times three) and thirty-three.

Ireland itself is represented in the female triune goddess - Eire, Banba and Fótla. There were three Celtic craft gods - Goibhniu, Luchta and Creidhne. The goddess of fertility, of smiths and of healing and poetry, even the Dagda himself, were worshipped in triune form. The most famous war goddess was the Morrigan, sometimes Morn'gu', 'great queen', and she also appears interchangeable as Macha, Badb and Nemain. She embodies all that is perverse and horrible among the supernatural powers.

Mother symbols were also worshipped in triple form; in Gaul the title matres or matronae was used, because the dedications on the monuments survive only in Latin. Mother Earth was the symbol of fertility and figures with children, baskets of fruit and horns of plenty are found all over the Celtic world. From Vertault in Burgundy comes a triple mother goddess sculpture with a baby held by one while the other holds a towel.

Christianity later adopted this triune godship (Father, Son and Holy Ghost) - not from Judaic culture, to which it is alien, but from the Greek interpretation aided by the concepts of early Christian Fathers. The Gaulish Celt, Hilary, bishop of Poitiers, (c.AD 31 Sc.367) is regarded as one of the first native Celts to become an outstanding philosophical force in the Christian movement. And his great work was De Trinitate, *defining the concept of the Holy Trinity, which is now so integral to Christian belief. Diogenes Laertius observed that the Druids taught in the form of Triads. This is confirmed by the literary traditions of both Ireland and Wales."* [8]

In many ways, therefore, although it may well be heresy to say it, the practise of religion, if not the main tenet of the spiritual beliefs expressed was largely the same for the best part of two thousand years. The spiritual beliefs of the celts and those of the usurping Christian newcomers were not that far apart.

We have also seen that the beliefs of contemporary Wicca are also much the same at least in principle, and although the practitioners of each religion would be aghast at the suggestion at in many essentials at least, their religious practises were much the same.

* All three religions are based on prayer and ritual
* All three religions deal with a triune deity
* All three religions have a ritual roughly analogous to the rite of Holy Communion

Unlike Wicca and the religion of the Druids, Christianity, however, is not, except in the most abstract and metaphysical way, a religion whose devotees or priests consciously attempt to create thought-forms. However, as we have shown, the `life-force` (by whatever name you like to call it) is a necessary, nay a logical by product of ritual and religious activity, and as David-Neel and Evans-Wentz have both shown, under certain circumstances this life-force can achieve an independent (or quasi-independent) existence, even after rituals lasting days, hours, or weeks. Imagine, if you will, a life-force created without form as an unconscious by product of the prayers and rituals of worshippers over many centuries.

How many times have you gone into a church or some other building and said *"this place has a good feeling about it"*?

Imagine if you will that the creation of a life force, is a necessary side effect of worship, and that if such rituals are, as was certainly the case in all the areas that we have discussed, carried out over a period of many centuries, then an extremely powerful tulpa-like entity is a logical result. Indeed, if Evans-Wentz is to be believed there can be little doubt about it.

However, there is are great differences between a tulpa created as a conscious act of will by a skilled magician and our hypothesised Odillic Life-Force entity created as a necassary but unconscious by-product of years of ritual and worship.

* The *tulpa* is created with a specific goal in mind or to carry out a specific task. Our hypothesised Odillic Life-Force entity has no such goal. Although we can have no more than the most minimal understanding of the natural history of a life-form (if indeed it can be described as such) which is completely unlike any other that we have ever studied, it would be reasonable, I suspect, to suggest that such an entity would not stray far from the place where it was created.

* The *tulpa* is created with a specific form. Alexandra David-Neel created a jolly and fat monk. [9] Dion Fortune created a fearsome wolf. [10][11] However, if our hypothesised Odillic Life-Force entity has been created in the way that we suggest, then it would be unlikely to have a specific form. It would just exist.

We have also seen from Reich`s experiments that both Orgone energy and `Deadly Orgone Radiation` can be produced through much the same means. If thought forms are the result of a conscious attempt to manipulate this energy then we must assume that a life-force created in the way I have hypothesised behaves in much the same way.

We should then re-examine David-Neel's statement that:

"The features which I had imagined, when building my phantom, gradually underwent a change. The fat, chubby-checked fellow grew leaner, his face assumed a vaguely mocking, sly, malignant look. He became more troublesome and bold. In brief, he escaped my control" [12]

and remember Trish Lovelock's account of 'George' - an originally benign and even friendly entity that eventually started to leave strange burns on her boyfriend's skin. [13]

How many times have you gone into a disused church or a ruin and said *"this place feels evil"*?

This dichotomy between positive and negative thought forms is not a new concept. The mystic Nicholas Roerich wrote the following passage in 1929:

"Upon completion of a shrine (suburgan or stepa) dedicated to Shambhala:

"A sunny, unclouded morning - the blue sky is brilliant. Over our camp flies a huge, dark vulture. Our Mongols and we watch it. Suddenly one of the Buriat lamas points into the blue sky. 'What is that? A white balloon? An aeroplane?' - We notice something shiny, flying very high from the north-east to the south. We bring three powerful field glasses from the tents and watch the huge spheroid body shining against the sun, clearly visible against the blue sky and moving very fast. afterwards we see that it sharply changes its direction from south to south-west and disappears behind the snow-peaked Humboldt Chain."

According to a lama - "Ah- you are guarded by Shambhala. The huge black vulture is your enemy, who is eager to destroy your work, but the protecting force from Shambhala follows you in this Radiant form of Matter. This force is always near to you but you cannot always perceive it. Sometimes only, it is manifested for strengthening and directing you." [14]

Carl Jung also suggested a psychological explanation for some UFO reports:.

"The whole collective psychological problem that has been opened up by the Saucer epidemic stands in compensatory antithesis to our scientific picture of the world...[the scientific picture] consists, as you know, very

largely of statistical or average truths. These exclude all rare borderline cases, which scientists fight shy of anyway because they cannot understand them. The consequence is a view of the world composed entirely of normal cases. Like the "normal" man, they are essentially fictions, and particularly in psychology fictions can lead to disastrous errors. Since it can be said with a little exaggeration that reality consists mainly of exceptions to the rule, which the intellect then reduces to the norm, instead of a brightly colored picture of the real world we have a bleak, shallow rationalism that offers stones instead of bread to the emotional and spiritual hungers of the world. The logical result is an insatiable hunger for anything extraordinary. If we add to this the great defeat of human reason, daily demonstrated in the newspapers and rendered even more menacing by the incalculable dangers of the hydrogen bomb, the picture that unfolds before us is one of universal spiritual distress, comparable to the...chaos that followed A.D. 1000 or the upheavals at the turn of the fifteenth century. It is therefore not surprising if, as the old chroniclers report, all sorts of signs and wonders appear in the sky, or if miraculous intervention, where human efforts have failed, is expected from heaven." [15]

Although, as already noted, to study the natural history of an entity whose nature we do not even pretend to understand, and whose existence is hypothetical is an almost impossible task. However it is this that we now have to do.

As David-Neel, Evans-Weltz and other sources quoted in this book have implied a *tulpa* needs constant nurturing in order to grow. This implies that its source of energy; its food (if you like), is emotion. If one takes this line of thought and extrapolates it together with what we already know (or guess) about our hypthosised Odillic life-force entity it makes perfect sense.

We are not the only people to have hypothesised a life-force, indeed an independent entity whose nature is not defined by the strictures of a carbon-based DNA led structure. We have already discussed the `sky beasts` hypothesised by Trevor Constable et al, but these are not the only hypothetical entities of this type that have been proposed.

Writing in a complex analysis of the great Scottish BHM phenomenon known as *Am Fear Liath Mor* [The Big Grey Man of Ben McDui], Dr Karl P.N.Shuker presented an overview of research into other hypothesised lifeforms which, it has been suggested, live in parts of the e.m spectrum invisible to mankind.

"Conversely, a hypothesis which may be of notable significance to An Fear Liath Mor is the compelling suggestion that phantoms could be energy forms occupying the immediate boundaries of electromagnetic radiation, i.e the Infra Red (IR) and Ultra Violet (UV) regions. For there is incontravertible evidence that certain ghost like images unseen to photographers have been captured on film sensitive to these wavelengths, as affirmed by researcher of psychical phenomena, Andrew Green relative to IR and George Kanigowski of the Nottingham based Strange Phenomena Research and Notation Group (S.P.R.I.N.G) relative to UV. (`The Unknown` February 1987).

According to Andrew Green, for example, NASA have testified that they have obtained locality photographs that reveal ghostly heat (IR) images of people and vehicles which left the locality many hours before it was photographed. Heat (IR) images may explain many `photographed phantoms` - especially those in contemporary attire.

Could the phantom of the UV wavelengths be the genuine article - real ghosts? According to frequent documentation in literature appertaining to paranormal phenomena, investigations of notable psychics have often revealed that their eyes` colour sensitive perception is displaced to the right of that of everyone else. That is to say, the eyes of psychics appear less sensitive than those of other people to the red zone of the visible spectrum but overly sensitive to the violet extreme and seemingly even beyond that, into the UV (astral) zone (normally invisible to human eyes). If this is indeed true, and psychical phantoms (whatever they may be) reflect UV light, this would account not only for their visibility to psychics and invisibility to everyone else, but also for many examples of mysterious photographs which clearly depict forms unseen by the photographer but which are evidently something more than mere heat images.

Could the Big Grey Man be an electromagnetic phantom - an entity beyond the vision of most humans (hence the rarity of sightings compared with the frequent reports of footsteps), but whose presence is still sensed?

What might be revealed one day, I wonder, by a climber on Ben MacDui who points a camera containing UV sensitive film in the direction of crunching footsteps being produced by an apparently invisible agent?" [16]

I started this chapter by promising an explanation for certain types of UFO activity, especially that which is reported in conjunction with a wide range of other fortean phenomena. I believe that they are conscious manifestations of an inherently formless entity created from Odillic life-energy as a perfectly natural result of one of the most basic of human activities - prayer.

If, as we have hypothesised, such a "creature" (and although I don't like using the word "creature" I can't think of a more apposite term), is nurtured by the emotions disippated during prayer and religious ritual, then it is logical to suppose that it could also feed from excessive outpourings of emotion from other sources. Having been both a drug user and having suffered for many years from a debilitating mental illness I can testify to the immense outpourings of wasted emotion that each condition can produce.

I do not know whether the food needed by these "creatures" is chemical (the endorphines or pheremones produced by people and animals *in extremis,* in agony, in ecstasy or in prayer) but I believe that these "creatures" will, like any other living thing, do whatever is in their power to provide themselves with sustenance.

I believe that the perception of these creatures is inherently linked with the part of the psyche awakened during the psychedelic experience and that in many ways the two scenarios can be linked. I would suggest that these "creatures" can produce situations whereby a human or an animal can produce the emotion (or chemical by-products of same) that is necessary for its well-being. This would explain how so many fortean phenomena are strangely religious in nature. It would explain visions of the Blessed Virgin Mary and the great Icons of other religions which on occasion appear to unwary believers in a semi-corporeal form.

It would also explain, how in places where religious activity has continued for so many years the level of quasi-fortean phenomena is so much higher.

Why do such phenomena appear in cycles - in Lyme Bay, Woodbury and Littleham, cycles of about ten years?

Maybe that is when the "creature" gets hungry.

If, as we have also hypothesised, these "creatures" somehow inhabit a part of the electro-magnetic spectrum that is invisible to human beings then it is perhaps apposite to notice that several geophysical events that can also have grave repercussions within parts of the e.m spectrum also happen on ten year cycles. Sunspots and the 'wobbles' of the earth on its axis being only two of these. However, we are nearly at the end of this book, and I do not wish to do more than indicate further lines of investigation that I presently have done no more than glance at for a fleeting instant.

The further one extrapolated the natural history of our hypothesised Odillic Energy life-form, the more options become obvious to us.

If, as Alexandra David-Neel has stated, a benign *tulpa* becomes vicious and generally unpleasant when it escaped the control of its creator then surely the same can be said for our hyptohesised Odillic-energy life-form. Thus, a benevolent entity originally formed by years of prayer and rituasl, and fed by the same, is now, to a certain extent at least, out of control The `life-form` that originally fed on prayer now feeds on fright, creating situations, either by conscious manipulation of its environment or, more likely by manipulating the nuances of the perception of the human being it is feeding off.

In an earlier chapter I condemned Di Francis for her revolting suggestion that Genette Tate was killed and eaten by a rogue leopard. [17] I do not want to fall into the same sensationalist trap, but it seems highly likely that if my hypothesis is broadly true, whether or not the Woodbury `life-form` actually caused her abduction and probable rape and murder, it would have fed hungrily on the lust of the abductor and the terror of his victim.

This leads us neatly onto another subject that we have briefly touched on already in this book, but which is of great interest to contemporary UFOlogists. That of alien abduction.

Kevin McClure has derided much of the sensationalist nonsense printed about the subject in recent years:

"If I'm right, and there never has been a single, physical, enforced act of abduction of a human being by an alien, non-human being, the belief in abductions has left some very confused people out there." [18]

I tend, as always, to agree with him in principle if not in fact. I believe that in order to understand the realities of the `abduction` experience we should, perhaps examine the testimony of an abductee in some detail. It so happens, that during the summer of 1997, (coincidentally, on the same day that Graham and I met the two witnesses to the Exmoputh Harbour red lights from the 13th August), I met and interviewed the lady who is quite probably the most famous abductee of all time.

Several years ago, American researcher and author Bud Hopkins wrote a book called *Intruders* which became an international bestseller and is still one of the best known books ever written on the subject of Alien Abductions. During an interview with Hilary Evans who is probably the best known British researcher in the field, we discussed Hopkins' book. He said:

"I have a lot of respect for Bud Hopkins. He is a very conscientious, and I think an honest person, and I treat his books with a great deal of respect. If you look at his second abduction book, the girl involved who was called Kathie Davis claimed to have been abducted by the extra terrestrials who saw her as a suitable mother for their children. She was a young lady in her twenties who as a teenager had not been exactly promiscuous, but had experienced a relaxed and easy going sexual life. On top of that she had undergone almost every illness that was going - she was not a well girl. At about the age of twenty she found herself pregnant and she persuaded her young man to marry her. It turned out that she was not pregnant because "the foetus had been removed by aliens" but she eventually had two babies, after which he said that enough was enough and left her."[19]

A few weeks later I was at the BUFORA conference in Sheffield where I met a young lady called Debbie Jordan who had just published a book called *Abducted* (co-written with her sister Kathy Mitchell). I found her to be a charming and completely genuine person who, like so many other people that I have met during my career as paranormal researcher and journalist, came across as a perfectly ordinary person whose life had been completely disrupted by a series of extraordinary events.

It wasn't until about a week later when she sent me a signed copy of her book from the States that I discovered that Debbie Jordan and Kathie Davis were one and the same person! I found it impossible to reconcile the charming and attractive lady I met in Sheffield with the neurotic, promiscuous adolescent described to me by Hilary Evans. Having read her book, (which is excellent by the way even though, so far it is not available in this country), I was still unable to make any connection between these two, apparently disparate, characters!

"I have had strange things happen to me all my life. I don't like to use that word, although that is what I am. I don't think of myself as an abductee. I am just an ordinary person who had some kind of extraordinary experience, and I don't know what it was. It's a long story, it really is. I

can cut it down into a nutshell, and say that I was staying with my parents and we saw some strange lights up in the sky, and in the pumphouse in the back of the house. Eventually I found my way out there to investigate. I thought it was burglars actually, but I realised that it was kind of weird.

When I got out there I didn't see anything and I ended up out by the side garage looking around, and as I came back in I was hit in the chest by some kind of light. I thought that I had been hit in the chest by lightning, and I thought I was dead. Whilst the effects wore off, and though it felt like it lasted forever, it couldn't have been for more than a couple of seconds, but whilst the effect wore off I couldn't move and I could hardly see anything.. All I could see ddidn't make any sense because I didn't understand it and I didn't know what it was. I still don't know what it was for sure.

All I can do is tell you what I saw, because it still doesn't make any sense to me. It was small and egg shaped and it wasn't more than twelve feet tall. There were six 'people' moving around and about in the back of the house. They looked like kids. I couldn't see a whole lot of detail because I was still blinded by the light.

That's about all I remember, although there is an hour missing out of my life that I still don't remember to this very day and probably never will.

After the brightness wore off I could feel somebody pulling down on the back of my shoulder and it felt like something was stuck in my arm, like a burning needle that went all the way up to my head. I couldn't scream or yell or do anything to fight it. I heard someone behind me saying that it was unfortunate that I had to feel the pain, and a few moments later I had gone from the doorway of this garage out to the back patio, and that's when I saw the egg shaped thing and those people, but I don't remember how I got there. I don't remember wailing or even being toted." [20]

(While she was telling this story to me, and to my colleague Dave Simons, Debbie was obviously becoming quite distressed at reliving what was, I am certain, the most traumatic event of her life. I have met several 'professional abductees' who travel around the lecture circuit, recounting their story and getting paid for it, but the sheer distress that Debbie was undergoing whilst reliving her experience, convinced both of us that she had written her book and was now telling her story for the umpteenth time in order to undergo some kind of personal catharsis, rather than for any less noble commercial motives)

"I can't remember anything else after that except for someone saying "It's Over!" and my only thought was for my children who were in the house with my Mom at the time. I got scared for them, and this voice said to me that "your children are alright" and suddenly I could move again. It was like I had metal shoes on and someone had suddenly turned off the magnet. I turned around and walked to the back of the house and with every step I took the memory of what had just happened was fading away and I was just thinking about my children and I had an overwhelming desire to get wet or to have a swim.

It started at about eight o'clock and by the time me and my girlfriend went off for a swim it was ten or so. Be the time we had done with swimming, my Dad had pulled into the driveway. He'd been working second shift and didn't get back 'till five past eleven or so. There is a lot of stuff missing. There are many things that I just can't remember.

As we were walking across the yard to the pool, my girlfriend's daughter went 'Yow!'. We thought she had stepped on a bee or something. She was jumping up and down in pain. Then she said that her foot got numb and then her leg was numb up to her knee. By the time we got to the pool the numbness had worn off, but all three of us were feeling sick - nauseated. My eyes started hurting real bad and I couldn't see. Everything had a white halo around it like from swimming-pool chlorine, but I hadn't put my head under the water and I couldn't figure it out!

We gave up on the swimming idea. They went home and I went to bed. When I got up the next morning, my eyes were swollen completely shut. I was taken to the hospital, immediately to the Emergency Room. They sent me across the street to the opthalmologist who swore up and down that I had been welding without a mask. But I don't weld.

I was given pills and drops, medicines and all that crap, and they told me that I had the worst case of conjunctivitis that they had ever seen. They couldn't believe that I hadn't been bothered by it the day before because it would have had to have built up to have become that bad. From that point on my eyes were never the same. I became very far sighted (I wear bifocals now though I don't have them on) and my night vision is poor." [21]

I asked her what happened next and her reply startled me.

"Well two days after that night we were all out in the back yard for the first time since the incident. All the family had come over for the fourth of July holiday and when I got out there there was this mark in the yard. It *was like an eight foot in diameter circle with a nine foot swathe coming off it. It was two feet wide all the way down.*

That mark stayed in the yard for five years, Snow melted off of it, animals wouldn't walk on it. Soil samples showed that it was sixty percent depleted of calcium and low in what they call biological life. They were unable to reproduce it - it was rock hard and repelled water down to fourteen inches below the surface.

Eventually they managed to reproduce it by baking it in an oven for eight hours at 850°. Then I got all sick. My hair started falling out. My finger nails got all wavy and peeled off like paper. My dog (who was out there that night with me) ended up having to be put to sleep because all her hair fell out as well as her teeth. Her gums started to bleed and her eyes whited over..." [22]

I think that I should point out here that Debbie's eyes were obviously damaged and that the skin around the eyes had the tight, artificial look that one usually associates with heavy sunburn..

"I developed life threatening allergies and had two anaphalactic shock episodes (most people won't even survive one)... That was terrifying. I developed an irregular heart beat that I am still taking beta blockers for, and it turned out that the condition which caused my arrhythmia is kind of common in some radiation exposures. All this time I was getting all my sicknesses I was not connecting them in any way with what had happened to me that night..." [23]

I wondered what had made Debbie aware of what had happened to her. What brought these events to the front of her consciousness again?

"It was when I saw the mark in the yard. I had trouble sleeping. I couldn't sleep at first I was in pain. I also had a lot of anxiety, and I was also having a lot of anxiety. I would spend long periods during the night sitting up watching my kids and waiting for something, but I didn't know what. I would sleep during the day when I could, when I knew that someone else was awake. That went on for months, if not years afterwards.

But it was when I saw the mark in the yard. Its never changed. It showed up. It didn't grow that way. My Mom said ,"Oh yeah, that's where the UFO landed". This was the first that I had ever heard of that.

She then laughed like she was making a joke, and I suddenly started looking at that mark in the yard and it was like someone had pulled their

finger out of the dyke and it suddenly came flooding back!

My Mom remembers calling me and telling me to come back, but for a while she couldn't remember why. Finally one day she was standing in the kitchen doing the dishes and looking at that mark in the yard when she turns round to me and says: "Oh My God. I suddenly remember why I called you that night!" I asked "why", and she said "I was standing here clearing up the mess after you'd all finished dinner when I saw a basketball shaped ball of white light around the area outside the window. I looked around to see if it could be the reflection from a headlight of a car in the driveway and then I realised that there was no way in hell, there could be any headlight coming from anywhere back in the woods like this. As I stared at it I saw it fade and fade until it was gone. As soon as it disappeared she got a strong thought in her head that she had to call me and get me home..." [24]

I am convinced, that whatever actually happened to Debbie, she is 100% certain that what she told me, what she told Bud Hopkings and that what she wrote in her book was the absolute truth. Although I have no real idea what happened to her, it is interesting to note the dreadful illnesses that she suffered, apparently as a result of this incident. This is highly reminiscent of the effects of `Negative Orgone Radiation` as noted by Reich. Also reminiscent of Reich is the appearance of sunburning around her face and eyes. This is something that I can testify to having seen it myself.

The basketball shaped balls of light are reminiscent of the balls of glowing (orgone>) energy filmed in farmer's fields in conjunction with crop formations.

The most interesting things about the experience, however, are firstly that there is (unsurprisingly) no evidence whatsoever that her experience has anything at all to do with extra-terrestrials, and secondly that it is somewhat reminiscent of episodes which have been reported for centuries from the westcountry.

Here, taken almost at random is an account of an event that happened a century or so before Debbie's "Abduction", but which is surprisingly similar. The following story was submitted to the *Folklore Report of the Devonshire* Association in 1892:

"Pixies in North Devon ~ The following appeared in the **Western Daily Mercury** of 6th June, 1890:

A few days ago a party of men were ripping bark in a wood about four miles from Torrington. In the evening, when it was time to pick up the tools, one of the men had occasion to separate himself from the party to fetch an iron which he had been using in another part of the wood. He avers that on stooping to pick up the tool a strange feeling came over him, and while totally unable to raise himself lie heard peals of discordant laughter all around. It flashed across his mind that he was being pixie-led, and though he has many times heard stories of people being in a similar state, his presence of mind forsook him, and he was unable to turn big coat inside out-a sure talisman against the spells of pixies. This was about half-past five in the afternoon. At seven o'clock his wife became uneasy at his non-appearance, and started off to look for him. Happening to meet one of the rippers, she enquired whether he had seen her husband. "Yes," replied the man, "he left work when we did." This added to her troubles, and when ten o'clock came, and still no husband, she was greatly alarmed. When she arrived near the place where the men had been working, she met her husband dripping wet. "Where have you been?" said she "I have been pixy-led," he replied, and told his story. It appears from his account the pixies held him under their spell for nearly five hours, and at the end of the time he was able to crawl away on his bands and knees, scarce knowing where lie was creeping, tumbling head over heels into a stream. Directly he rose, he knew where lie was, and made the best of his way home. "You girt fule, why didden 'ee turn your pockets inside out?" was all the comfort he received from his better-half; "Then you would have been able to come away tu wance." The man firmly believes in pixies, and what strengthens his belief is the fact that a tailor named Short was "pixy-lead" in the same wood some years before, and remained under their spell until morning. It may be said the man was drunk, but it can be proved on the best authority that no intoxicating liquor was drunk that day by any of the party." [25]

Although there is always the danger whilst involved in research into these sorts of subjects that one is sometimes tempted to interpret the available evidence according to whatever theory you are trying to prove at the time, it does seem to all four of us that this story is extremely reminiscent of many contemporary accounts of Alien Abduction.

Unfortunately, whilst there is no doubt in my mind at least that experiences like those of Debbie Jordan, and the unnamed woodcutter from North Devon, were very real to her at least, there is, like Kevin McClure has said, absolutely no evidence that they have anything to do with visitors from another planet. Indeed, there is every reason to suppose the exact opposite.

I disagree with Kevin in as far as I believe that these events are most definitely worthy of investigation, although I agree with him wholeheartedly that much of what is written about the subject is not only misleading, but distasteful in the extreme.

This excerpt from an article by Don Worley, was taken from the pages of *Flying Saucer Review,* a well respected magazine within UFO circles that really should be ashamed of itself for printing such heinous rubbish. Worley was speculating about the numbers of people who had actually *been* abducted:

"Estimates run from hundreds of thousands to possibly millions. Important in the estimates is the fact that there is an unknown percentage of our citizens who do not suspect that it has happened to them! I have by accident discovered some of these folk myself and it has convinced me that there is a great unknown total in this classification.

Another element in the equation is the fact that once you have been "chosen", or "selected" --- usually in babyhood --- there is no escape. At least not until they are finished with you, or you get up into your 50s maybe. This shocking ability of theirs to find an abductee again, no matter where, is most un-nerving. In my "Kim" case (Illinois) the lady had been "picked up" or "taken" in two West Coast States. Then she moved to Illinois, where she hoped that she had at last escaped. But no --- she had not --- and they also "selected" her little daughter.

This child always referred to the Aliens as "That nice Mister" or, maybe, "them bad little Misters." "Kim" herself had never discussed the subject of "Aliens" anywhere in the presence or vicinity of the child, but one day she chanced to leave a copy of Whitley Strieber's book Communion where the child was able to catch sight of it, and was able to see the face on the dust-cover. The child at once seized the book and hugged it, and said "Mister! It's Mister! Momma, he loves me!"

This lawless kidnapping of an innocent little girl makes me mad, and it is sad to see the helplessness of the parents."

Throughout this book we have noted the preconceptions that many people have made about matters apertaining to quasi-fortean occurences. It is time to re-examine them in the light shed by our hypothesised Odillic Life-Force entity.

* Many people have noted the correlation between the rise in interest in UFOs and other branches of fortean phenomena and the drop in the numbers of practitioners of organised conventional religions. They have usually explained this as "sheep-like" people needing "something to believe in" and choosing to believe in aliens rather than God. If my hypothesis is true then the correlation is still there but the rise in interest about such phenomena (and as a result the rise in reports) is actually a result of undoubted the fall in the numbers of devotees of organised religion rather than its cause.

Here it should be noted that whilst more traditional forms of devotion are attracting fewer and fewer followers, there is a rise in the importance of fundamentalist religious beliefs that place a heavy emphasis on what could unkindly be described as the more hysterical outpourings of religious devotion than was commonplace in the more traditional forms of worship such as the ones that I practise. This is not just notable in Christianity but can be seen in every other major religion as well.

* The tendancy for what can be broadly labelled paranormal phenomena to be witnessed by drug users, the physically and the mentally ill has been noted elsewhere in this book. Generally these phenomena are disregarded by serious researchers who claim, with some justification, that they are nothing more than psychotic delusions or chemically induced hallucinations. What if they are wrong?

As a one time user of psychoactive chemicals and also as someone who has suffered from a Bipolar psychiatric condition for many years I have already testified in this book to the enormous outpourings of emotion that both scenarios can produce. If we are to believe my (admittedly tenuous and fledgeling) hypothesis, then what better "food source" can there be for our hypothesised Odillic-energy life-form?

* We have already noted how there is a significantly greater level of broadly paranormal phenomena in places which have suffered a drastic loss of socio-culturasl significance. If one follows my theory to its ultimate end, this makes perfect sense. If our hypothesised `life-form` has been created by years of prayer and ritual in a place of importance, once it ceases to be of importance, and thus the level of religious devotion is greatly lessened, then it stands to reason that the `life-form` would look elsewhere for sustenance, and as we have already seen, its main souce of sustenance is the end result of the manifestation of broadly paranormal phenomena.

This would also explain why so many ghosts, UFOs, corn circles, and outbreaks of animal mutilation occur in the vicinity of places like Stonehengre, Avebury and other sites of great historic importance like Hampton Court Palace and the Tower of London. When the hapless visitor to The Tower sees the ghost of Anne Boleyn with her head beneath her arm, he is, like the unwary recipient of a `bad acid trip` only seeing what the darkest side of his or her psyche is expecting to see. As I found out during the darkest days of my illness, there are no bounds to the horrors that one's psyche can conjure up and I am now convinced that when this occurs, somewhere an Odillic energy life-form is feasting well.

* We have seen how at times of great political and socio cultural instability paranormal phenomena are prevalent. I discuss this, with regards to events in Puerto Rico and Mexico at far greater length in *Only Fools and Goatsuckers.* [1999]. [27] In this present volume we have seen this scenario repeated in the affair of the 1909 Mystery Airship reports which were concurrent with a period of great political instability across Europe. In the light of my new theory this makes perfect sense.

* Also in *Only Fools and Goatsuckers* [1999] [28] I have noted the correlation between the ancient Aztec blood sacrifices and the contemporary accounts of the *chupacabra* from modern Mexico. Now they begin to make sense.

* This theory could also be used to explain vampires, incubi and succubi.

The precise method by which PHYSICAL phenomena such as animal/human mutilation and even crop circles are produced remains unknown. I would suggest that one of three scenarios is correct. Either the `life-form` can carry out these acts directly which seems unlikely, or it can produce a temporary physical form, perhapss analogous to the ectoplasm reported by early spiritualists, with which to perform them, or, more prosaically, as we have already hypothesised with regards to the abduction and disappearance of Genette Tate, that it can influence people to do its will.

Doug and Dave could never explain exactly WHY they started to make crop circles.

* Something else which begins to make sense is the universal legends of mischievous gods and spirits, most notably the Norse deity Loki:

Loki is one of the major deities in the Norse pantheon. He is a son of the giant Farbauti ("cruel striker") and the giantess Laufey. He is considered one of Aesir, but is actually their enemy. He is connected with fire and magic, and can assume many different shapes (horse, falcon, fly). Loki is handsome and has a friendly appearance, but an evil nature. He is crafty and malicious, but is also heroical: in that aspect he can be compared with the trickster from North American myths. The ambivalent god grows progressively more evil, and is directly responsible for the death of Balder, the god of light.

Loki's mistress is the giantess Angrboda, and with her he is the father of three monsters. His wife is Sigyn, who stayed loyal to him, even when the gods punished him for the death of Balder. He was chained to three large boulders; one under his shoulders, one under his loins and one under his knees. A poisonous snake was placed above his head. The dripping venom that lands on him is caught by Sigyn in a bowl. But every now and then, when the bowl is filled to the brim, she has to leave him to empty it. Then the poison that falls on Loki's face makes him twist in pain, causing earthquakes.

On the day of Ragnarok, Loki's chains will break and he will lead the giants into battle against the gods. Loki is often called the Sly One, the Trickster, the Shape Changer, and the Sky Traveller." [29]

Perhaps our hypothesised Odillic life-force entity should really be given the title of a 'Lokiform'. However, I have enough respect for the powers of elder gods not to wittingly provoke them by means of parody.

* In both *The Owlman and Others* [1997,8] and *Only Fools and Goatsuckers* [1999], I have noted the malign power of psychic backlash. In *Only Fools and Goatsuckers* I write:

"One thing that I do know about monster hunting, however, is that those who practice it are susceptible to what "Doc" has called "Psychic Backlash". This is a series of inexplicable and horrific outbreaks of bad luck that can overtake the hapless seeker asfter monstrous truth on his way to his goal. I never believed in it until, during the months that I was working on "The Owlman and Others" two of my pet cats died suddenly, two computyers blew up (as did two cars) and my wife left me." [30]

It is tempting to hypothesise that this very real effect is the result, either of Reich's N.O.R or, even more sinisterly, of a conscious effort by a malign entity composed of Odillic Energy attempting to stop the hapless seeker after truth from reaching his goal.

The one thing I have never been diagnosed with is clinical paranoia.

* Also explainable by the effects of Rechian N.O.R is the feeling of doom which Keeling-Basford and others have noted at various locations on Woodbury Common and which may well have been responsible for

the extremely high numbers of suicides in one specific location there.

It should be noted, as well, I think, that this same sense of 'dread' is also described in some accounts of mystery animal sightings, which again provides a useful link between the two types of apparently disparate phenomena. Two good examples can be found in Graham McEwan's *Mystery Animals of Britain and Ireland* (1986):

"Over the years, there have been several encounters with an unpleasant creature at the village school of Goodhurst in Kent. One witness was the writer, Joan Forman, who worked there during the mid- 1950s. She was spending the first few days of the summer holiday at the school, most of the staff already having left, and was sleeping alone in the oldest part of the building. At about 3.30 a.m., on her second night there, she awoke suddenly out of a deep sleep. Something was crouching on the floor to the left of her bed:

It was about two feet in length, I suppose, the size of a large cat or a small corgi. It resembled neither of these. It had a pair of huge nocturnal eyes like those of a lemur, and these were the clearest features of the apparition. I noticed them particularly because they were unwaveringly fixed on me. I think it was the most revolting gaze I have ever had to endure, for what emanated from the thing was an atmosphere of extreme malevolence and obscenity. With all its exudation of evil it was at the same time mocking. It stared at me for what seemed half an hour (although I suspect it was only a few minutes in chronological time) and I stared back, playing rabbit to its snake. I could not move to switch on the light, and in any case the creature itself seemed to emit some kind of glow in which I could see the shape of its face and head and the huge eyes, and a dim suggestion of the rest of its body.

Eventually, the room, which had been bitterly cold, grew warmer with the early dawn, and the thing began to fade away, and in a few minutes had disappeared altogether. Joan Forman's successor at the school had a similar experience, though in a different bedroom" [31]

Another, and possibly even more bizarre encounter comes from the same book, where McEwan describes what he calls "The Monster from Over The Hill":

"In 'The Powers of Evil' Richard Cavendish described a bizarre case which involved a person whom he calls Mrs Smith. One evening, about the year 1940, she was chatting to her husband and her neighbours when she said, quite out of the blue, 'It will come over the hill when it

comes.' She later had no recollection of saying this, and doubted it even when the others assured her that she had spoken these words. Shortly after though, she became increasingly nervous of being out of the house after dark. About three months later, she woke up in the middle of the night, trembling and shivering. Waking her husband she told him that the thing from over the hill was nearly upon them. Almost at once they heard one of the outside doors opening and the heavy tread of something which sounded wet coming up the stairs. The Smiths clung together, terrified, as a hideous creature came into their bedroom. It was naked, bloated and had a blotched skin of yellow, green and purple with a head that came nearly to a point on top and ear lobes reaching almost to its shoulders. It had a massive bull neck and what appeared to be webbed feet. It crossed to the window, giving the impression of wading rather than walking, and disappeared. Mrs Smith, who said that she and her husband had both seen the thing clearly, later commented:

'It was horrible and the absolute essence of ...... I have never experienced anything so dreadful before or since and I hope I never shall, God willing. I still experience the same horror when I talk about it or write as I am doing now. I have never been able to discover why I saw it and I have never been able to find out what it was.'" [32]

It seems that everywhere we look we are presented with more vindication for this exciting new theory. Even Trevor James Constable's theory of sky-beasts, which has been heartily scoffed at by zoologists and UFOlogists alike can be seen as supporting evidence. It has been suggested that such hypothetical sky beasts could not only be the explanation for UFOs, but also for Crop Circles. Andrew Collins's book *'The Circlemakers'* (1992), was the first to suggest such a theme. Resurrecting the work of Wilhelm Reich, the discoverer of the somewhat speculative force of 'orgone energy', he suggested that these 'critters' were actually comprised of 'orgone energy', and that the highly complex patterns which have been appearing in corn fields across the world were, in fact, the perfectly normal result of an encounter between such an animal and the earth. [33] [34]

It is tempting to hypothesise that these 'balls of light' (BoL) reported so often by witnesses to UFO and crop circle activity, and perhaps even filmed by John Wheyleigh (Wabe?) at Oliver's Castle in 1996 are the only 'true' face of our hypothesised 'creatures' of Odillic energy.

Writing in the *Exmouth Journal* of the 25th June 1998, Geoff Naish reported the arrival of the first crop circle to have been reported from the 'Woodbury Triangle':

"UFO experts were yesterday investigating the origin of mystery `crop circles` that had appeared in a field of winter barley near Yettington. The circles of flattened barley, which are about 25m in diameter, were discovered early yesterday morning by Bicton College Farm Manager Don Causley. He spotted them in a field owned by the college along side the narrow road leadimng from Brick Cross, Otterton to Yettington village. "They are clearly visible from the road. There is a huge circle of flattened corn and then a circle of standing corn and another circle of flattened corn around the outside," said Mr Causley.

Nigel Wright, the Journal's *Strange Phenomena Research Expert, when told of the appearance said that he was keeping an open mind on the cause of the circles but would he examining them as soon as possible. He add "It is very interesting as this coincides with a period of intense UFO activity over - Woodbury Common over the past two weeks."*

Mr Cauley was not keeping such an open mind on the likely cause of the circles pointing out that the field is very close to the college and that the agricultural students had finished their exams and are currently waiting for the official prize presentations ceremony on Friday. He added: "It seems obvious to me that this I sa student prank. I certainly haven`t seen any little green men around yet and, as my son pointed out, the circles have appeared on a sloping field facing the road - why didn't the Martians land on the flat bit above it?" [35]

The Editor of the Exmouth newspaper telephoned Nigel for the comment that was included in the above newspaper. He telephoned us and Graham and I made our way out to Yettington where we met Nigel and Sue (accompanied by small child) in a narrow country lane.

There, in a field on the left hand side of the road was an impressive looking crop circle. We gingerly tramped across the barley, doing our best to do as little damage as possible, as we approached the formation. Although I had seen crop circles before in Dorset during the summers of 1994 and 1995 I had never investigated one closely. I have to admit that it was a bit of a disappointment.

Seen from close up it was rather crude and gave all the indications that it was man made. We wandered aound doing the things that we had come to do and then made our way back to Exeter.

A week after the original report appeared Nigel Wright tried to effectively put the matter to bed with his own comments on the affair written in his own inimitable style, in which he gave a highly flattering account of our technical prowess:

"As some of our Journal *readers may have read in last week's edition we had, at first sight an alien invasion in a field at Yettington! Overnight, a circle twenty-five metres across had appeared. When first told of this I must admit that I was pretty excited! Unlike some other parts of this country, East Devon has not been graced with the really quite pretty sight of the huge and complicated crop circles seen over the last few years. Suddenly it seemed that our luck had changed. I, and the investigation team from the Exeter Strange Phenomena Reseach Group arrived on site, complete with all the necessary equipment to conduct a full scientific analysis on our strange visitor!*

We started out across the field towards the circle. The first thing that we notivced was a number of tracks leading from the edge of the field towards the circle itself. These tracks could, of course have been made by rabbits, or indeed the farmer himself after discovering it. So, to try and establish what caused these tracks, we got one team member to walk across the field, whilst we filmed the resulting marks in the crop. This established that these tracks were indeed man-made. This was not looking good.

Having made our way to the circle we first took samples of the crop from areas both inside the ring and outside it. These have been sent away for DNA analysis. We next looked at the pattern of the crop stalks lying on the ground inside the main inner circle. On other circles regarded as genuine, this pattern is nearly always plaited in some way. Unfortunately on this example it was merely bent low on the stem. We also went to the centre of the circle and took a reading from a compass. The reason for doing this is that for some unknown reason, in other circles, compasses react in a strange way. They either spin around continuously or alter from the true reading by a considerable margin. This I am sorry to report didn`t happen here.

By this time, I`m sorry to say, that we were all nearly 100% certain that this circle, nice as it was to see it, was a man-made fake. We concluded our investigation by fully recording the circle both on video and still film. I will of course let you know the results of the DNA testing as soon as we have the results back. But in the meantime my message to the person or persons who took the time to make this circle is that it was pretty to look at, but I am sorry to say that researchers like us are rather more scientific minded today! So any fake has to be rather better than this one to fool us. PLEASE, don`t try again. For one thing, it's really not fair on the farmers who toil long and hard to grow the crops in the first place.

My, and the society's thanks go to Mr Causley of Bicton College Farm for allowing us to enter his field and take the samples. I'm sorry Mr Causley that I can't say that it's real". (36)

A week later, he was back and to a certain extent at least, eating humble pie, because new evidence suggested that the crop circle may have been genuine after all:

"If Only I had Listened to my Dear old Ma!

Well, dear readers, no sooner had I written my last article than my telephone rang. A lady from East Budleigh 'phoned me to report a bright orange light hovering over the fields between East Budleigh and Bicton College. It seems that this light remained still in the sky for a full fifteen minutes or so until the lady returned to her bed. This happened at approximately 1.30 a.m on the morning of the 23rd of last month. This all goes to prove that I should have learned the lesson my dear old Mum tried to teach me when, at the age of seven or so, she said to me 'The wise old Owl sat in the Oak, the more he saw the less he spoke!'. Evidently I am no wise old owl!

The really interesting thing about this sighting is that it happened over the field where a crop circle appeared. You know the one I mean dear readers - the one that I declared was a fake. Who knows? Perhaps I was wrong about that as well. It is often the case that crop circles appear in conjunction with bright lights in the sky so it is not inconceivable that these two incidents are related in some way. I will let you know on that one!" (37)

On the first Monday in June 1998, Nigel and various members of the ESP group were on Woodbury Castle. I was in Leeds visiting Richard Freeman (who had not at that time come to live in Exeter), and Graham was at home with a bad bout of sciatica so I must leave it to Nigel to describe what happened:

All was quiet until 10.44 p.m when as myself, and two other members of the group watched, a strange triangular type of craft came into view from the direction of Torquay. The most noticeable thing about it was the total lack of sound as it passed over the castle and headed towards Ottery St Mary. It displayed three constant white lights, one on each apex of the triangle with a rotating white light in the middle of the underside of the craft.

It did NOT, however display any recognised navigation lights usually used on aircraft namely red and green on each side......" [38]

Whether this was a piece of conventional hardware or whether it was something less substantial it is incontravertable that it flew directly over the field where the crop circle was to appear a few days later.

In view of the suggestion that the BoL phenomena is the only true manifestation of our hypothesised Odillic energy life-forms we should, I think, examine some eyewitness accounts of this phenomenon from other locations away from South East Devonshire.

The first comes from *Balls of Light Over Liverpool* by Andrew Lunn (British UFO Research Assoc. and ISUR)

"What Maureen saw was three orange balls of light. As she watched they started to move and another two appeared either out of or from behind the two base lights, as they travelled towards the mouth of the river. Here they reformed into what seemed a diagonal line from where Maureen was standing. Another witness MS, was walking on the other side of the estuary and reported seeing three orange balls of light in a triangle formation. Throughout detailed discussion, many reasons were thrown into the hat, not least the idea that maybe they were geese, made to look orange, due to the light reflecting off the estuary. Maureen dismisses this out of hand, but the idea is not preposterous, considering the position of the two witnesses from the estuary.

Both witnesses reported having an 'aura' effect after seeing these balls of light, only when they started to move. The majority of ball of light cases include observations of a luminous 10-20cm diameter oval, round or spherical form (often yellow, orange, red, blue or silver). However there have also been cases where balls of light have looked anything but like a ball. What one has to ask here, is that are balls of light capable of producing any effect, such as some form of aura? In other reports of balls of light there have been cases of car stalling and radio disturbances, but they are also meant to emit some biological effect. This can range from anything like 'pins and needles' to supposed instances of dermal 'tanning' and 'klieg conjunctivitis'. Also balls of light, due to their very nature, should occur in the same spots, explaining the use of the term 'Hot Spot'.

Maureen tried to explain here 'aura' effect. Did you get 'pins and needles'? I asked. Maureen explained that it was bordering on some form of tranquillity, but would not directly define it as this. It is perhaps more accurate to state that Maureen was physically affected by these balls of light, but in a way that is very hard to put into words. It is fair to suggest that the actual effect of the aura was to transfix Maureen, displacing the thoughts in the mind for a momentary minute. It is during this time, that an effect in the body will take place, perhaps due to the energies being given of by these balls of light." [39]

The second from researcher Jeffery Jones:

"I also experienced balls of light in a house. This happened in Denver, Colorado, USA. It happened to me in 1972. I was at a friends house, fairly old for this city. There were 3 of us in the house at the time. A young lady got up and went to the restroom, which was at the top of a horseshoe shaped hallway, which continued around into the kitchen, which continued into the dining room. I was sitting at the mouth of the kitchen and dining room with one leg propped over the other. The girl turned off the light to the bathroom. At that moment two balls of light the size of a raquetball with about 8 inch tails came from the direction of the bathroom down through the kitchen and flew directly over my legs on past the other fellow and made a sweeping turn into the living room and continued behind a wall blocking my vision and out I assume through the front door. I asked my friend if he saw them and he nodded yes. He did tell me that his parents had at one time been A Priest and Nun. Left the church married and when they died were cremated stored in jars and buried under rose bushes in the front yard. I do not know if that was coincidence or not. I did not feel threatened but, when I left I walked swiftly across the front lawn to my car. A few years later, a young lady that I knew lived in the house with those people and said many strange things happened there. It is possible that the two people were prior owners and not his parents. It has been too long ago for me to remember. It was one of the oldest areas settled in Denver, and at one time had been a log cabin." [40]

BoL phenomena is often confused with a little known metereological phenomenon called Ball Lightning. Ball lightning is thought to be made up of Plasma - the state of matter beyond Gas. (Stars are made up of Plasma). The process by which it can be produced terrestrially is open to some speculation as, according to "orthodox" science, it is very difficult - if not impossible - to reproduce in a laboratory. It seems clear, if one accepts its existence, that it is strongly associated with electrical storms - common in many reports. Some people seem to think its appearance may also be associated with high voltage power lines. Or even high power tv transmitters. It is often seen in clouds, or dropping down from them. It seems it is commonly spherical in shape, but can be discoid or ellipsoid. It can penetrate solid walls and if it is indeed made up of gas plasma, it will be electrically charged and will therefore be influenced by magnetic fields and possibly metal objects. [41]

It would be facile to suggest that ball lightning is in fact a manifestation of our hypothesised life-forms, but perhaps the laws of physics which define this well known but ill understood phenomenon can be used to explain more about the nature of our hypothesised `life-form`. However, I am a fortean with no pretensions to being a scientist. In actuality this book is a work of philosophy based on personal experience rather than a scientific treatise and it should be treated as such. It is up to the scientists to try and prove or disprove my theory. Unfortunately, knowing the mindset of many conventional inhabitants of the sacred groves of Academe, they will probably just ignore it.

That is, I believe, their loss, not mine.

EPILOGUE

A month after I saw the strange blue light on Woodbury Common, the long awaited letter arrived offering me a trial period of six month's psychotherapy. On the appointed day, it was raining as Graham drove me up the long, driveway towards the forbidding grey-stone facade of Wonford House Psychiatric Hospital.

To say I was nervous would be a complete understatement. My G.P had already warned me that psychotherapy was likely to be harrowing in the extreme, and even worse that my behaviour and state of mind was likely to deteriorate dramatically before it started to get better as a direct result of what was, if it was to be done properly, a gruelling and testing process. [1]

I got out of the car, hugged Graham and Toby the dog and strode as bravely as I could towards the door to the reception area. I would love to be able to say that there was a huge triangular craft hovering above the roof of the old Victorian Asylum, but if there was, I was too scared to notice.

I took a final drag on my cigarette, and flicked the remnants to the ground where I stubbed it out with my foot. I took a deep breath and walked through the door. It was time to get on with the rest of my life.........

REFERENCES

[A small number of references from the original edition which no longer apply are still to be found in the endnotes, lest their deletion cause numerical confusion - *publisher*]

PART ONE

INTRODUCTION

1. Southwest Witness Support Group
2. D.Smyth pers. comm.
3. M.Crook pers. comm
4. ESP Records
5. I had been diagnosed with a Bi-Polar condition for several years but no-one, especially me, had ever done anything about it.
6. I make no apologies for dwelling on the subject of my mental illness in this book. It is important, not only from my own point of view, but, as will be revealed in part four it has great relevance to the main strands of the text.

I

1. We made seven albums, the last of which was "The Case" (STP CD 1995) A new CD may be released before the end of the century but don't hold yer breath
2. Although, as will be seen, much of the events surrounding the Oliver's Castle video are open to a certain amount of interpretation, this account

is essentially the one given us originally by Pete Glastonbury in October 1996.
3. Shiels, T. *"Monstrum - A Wizard's Tale"* (Fortean Tomes, 1989)
4. A pub at Alton Barnes in Wiltshire much frequented by `Croppies`
5. This statement was told to us by Peter Glastonbury, presumably in good faith. However several researchers, including Lee Winterson have cast doubt on this claim suggesting:

"After this daring escapade, a request was made with John Lomas for John Wabe to come clean and admit his involvement. Afterwards, John Wabe has been in phone contact, stating he WAS involved in the production of this video but could not comment further due to an exclusive contract with a broadcast production, DISCOVERY CHANNEL, USA. He did make it clear that he would like this all to "Just go away". He is not hiding the fact that it IS a HOAX.

In our opinion he has been paid well to perform this duty, and he almost go away with it. The British side of this hoaxed production team has raised questions as to the exclusive use of the Oliver's Castle footage. They were to air this program on August 11th or 12th. However, due to a phone conversation just after Lee's Barge Inn announcement, we found out that the DISCOVERY CHANNEL USA have moved ahead of schedule to air their program titled ?? "Oliver's Castle Fraud Explained" on Monday night, July 28th, 1997. Look in your listings and stay tuned for the next chapter of disinformation! As an aside, the woman heading the Discovery Channel production team named "Jane" has talked to us by phone, but is reluctant to give the real production name, or WHO is really behind it. Are they on the run because we are into their game?"

6. "The Exe Files" October 1996
7. Although we weren`t present at the Westcountry TV screening were were present at the Exeter University screening and can confirm that Philip Head was extremely impressed with the video.
8. Tony "Doc" Shiels cited in Downes., J. *The Owlman and Others* (1997,8)
9. This was a quote given us by Peter Glastonbury and we cannot find which Roy Harper album it came from even though we have most of the CDs in our collection.
10. www. Agrolawn.com/Fairy.htm
11. I first got this from *Rewards and Fairies* by Rudyard Kipling (1910)
12. www.nmufo.simplenet.com/index.html. (*The Earliest Crop Circle?* by Bob Kingsley)
13. It would be amusing, I suppose to put this as A.S.Huntingford *nee* Downes pers.comm

14. Internet Report
15. www.shogun.demon.co.uk/dorset/maidenca.htm
16. www.cseti.org/freports/dd2.htm
17. Internet Report
18. An annual event run until 1997 by veteran zoologist Clinton Keeling
19. See *The Owlman and Others*
20. It is not the purpose of this book to criticise the *modus operandi* of the Exeter City Community Psychiatric Services However it has to be said that their treatment of me as an emergency case left something to be desired. I was told repeatedly that I needed long term treatment, but no one was prepared to do anything in the short term and it took three months before I was able to secure a place at the local drop-in centre. However it must be said that once I started at the *Victory Centre* they were marvellous.
21. www.cseti.com/crashes/crash123.htm
22. Author and Civil Servant
23. He had just published *Open Skies Closed Minds*
24. House of Lords records on the Internet
25. The Buzzcocks *"Have you ever fallen in Love"* (UA, 1978)
26. One of the few 1977 punk bands whose music still stands up two decades later.
27. Richard Freeman started to write for *Animals & Men* in 1996
28. The CFZ is a non profit making organisation founded by Jon Downes in 1992.

II

1. South West Witness Support Group (Brigitte Grant)
2. Whenever possible we interviewed the witnesses in person. On this occasion Yvonne contacted us after one of the stories that was run about our activities in the *Exeter Express and Echo* and we got back to her immediately interviewing her at length.
3. See *The Owlman and Others* Ch 6
4. Published by Rapide Publishing
5. A large number of these `witnesses` were small boys of about 10-11 who were obviously intent on having as much fun at our expense as possible by making up as wild stories as they could.
6. Unfortunately we have not been able to identify him
7. Some witnesses have asked to remain anonymous although we have their true identities on file. This is not one of those.
8. See *Only Fools and Goatsuckers*
9. Why Greys are supposed to come from Zeta Reticuli is a complicated story and one that is explained to a certain extent in John Spencer`s *UFO*

Encyclopaedia.
10. The ins and outs of my divorce hearings are not relevant to this book but my state of mental health at the time of the events described most certainly is.
11. Jan Scarff pers.comm. I know the identity of this witness but have been asked to keep it secret. It is on our files.
12. An unemployed man in his late 40s. Again the identity of the witness is on file.
13. Warren, L and Robbins P., *Left at East Gate* (Michael O'Mara, London 1997)
14. Tina Askew
15. As documented in *Sightings Magazine* October 1997
16. Trish Lovelock pers.comm
17. Jan Scarff pers.com.
18. I have a copy of the video in my possession
19. *Roswell* starring Kyle Machlachan
20. Why anyone *ever* believed that load of horse shit I have no idea!
21. As I will show in the concluding chapters of this present book, I believe the truth to be somewhat different!
22. The original report appeared in the *Western Morning News*
23. *The Exmouth Journal* (14.8.1997)
24. ibid
25. We have this witnesses name and telephone number on file. He first contacted the *Exeter Express and Echo* who passed him on to us.
26. Ian Wright pers.comm
27. An anonymous telephone call to the ESP office
28. These were the first witnesses to contact us and did so as a result of one of our radio shows for BBC Radio Devon. We have their name and telephone number on file although we have honoured their requests for anonymity.
29. Of *Fortean Times*
30. Dash, M., *Borderlands.* (W.Heinemann, London, 1997)
31. See *Travellers Tales* by Jon Downes and Trish Lovelock, *Alien Encounters* August 1997
32. No names no packdrill. To provide a reference here would spill the beans so tough!
33. Jan Scarff pers comm. Barry Payne was an acquaintaince of Jan's who was quite happy to co-operate with us and didn't mind his identity being made known.
34. Another anonymous telephone call.
35. David Nelson contacted us after the first *Exeter Express and Echo* story
36. We have the lady's details on file. She contacted first Nigel and then us through the first of the articles in the *Exmouth Journal*. By this time

we had appointed Nigel as Exmouth `rep` for the ESP group, and he was beinning to field telephone calls for us!
37. Jan Scarff pers.comm
38. The story appeared in a number of local papers but they got it from us first c/o our friends at the Devon News Agency.
39. Trish Lovelock et.al. pers.comm
40. We were in the peculiar situation here whereby although the original witness didn`t want to be identified, her sister and co-witness didn`t mind. We decided to err on the part of caution and not identify either of them although we have all their details on file.
41. Janet left the BBC at the end of July 1998
42. Tina Askew
43. Since 1977
44. I lived in Hong Kong between 1961-1971
45. The female (which retains the larval form) of a *Lampyris noctiluca* predatory beetle which exhibits bioluminescence.
46. *Gyrinus natator*
47. The "Truth is Out There" brigade are known for their paranoia
48. The Exeter based commercial radio station.
49. Jan Scarff and Nigel Wright pers.comms.
50. I have a sneaking suspicion that this is because of their innate uselessness and inefficiency rather than because of any weird conspiracy!
51. Jenny Wright pers.comm.
52. And the Channel Islands.
53. An anonymous telephone call whilst me, Nigel, Graham and Jan were trying to collate the information
54. The whole of this account comes from Nigel and his wife Sue who rang me up repeatedly from various locations across the town.
55. Nigel Wright pers.comm
56. Witness letter to Nigel W. On file
57. Nigel Wright pers.comm
58. ibid
59. Holiday, Ted, *The Dragon and the Disc* (Sidgewick and Jackson, London 1973)
60. ibid
61. ibid
62. Author of *Ring of Bright Water* and *The Rocks Remain* etc
63. Holiday, Ted, 1973 op cit
64. Both published by Domra Publications
65. She telephoned me after hearing our radio show. We have her details on file.
66. Many references including McEwan, G. *Mystery Animals of Britain and Ireland* (Robert Hale, London, 1985) and various references in the Transactions of the Devonshire Association

67. http://dialspace.dial.pipex.com/town/plaza/aan26/shkworld.htm
68. McEwan op.cit.
69. Nigel Wright pers.comm
70. *Alien Encounters* October 1997
71. I do not know why he opted to remain silent. His name was actually featured in early reports but he asked us to remove it after the end of August.
72. This was for a story for *The Times* due to be published on 1st September. However, Princess Diana was killed the day before it was due to come out and so the story never appeared.
73. This story is quoted on dozens of web sites, none of which are ours!
74. Sunday People 10.8.97
75. K.McClure *Abduction Watch* 2
76. K.McClure *Abduction Watch* 3
77. ibid
78. K.McClure *Abduction Watch* 4
79. K.McClure *Abduction watch* 5
80. Uncredited
81. They are all on file either with me or with Nigel

III

1. *Exmouth Journal* September 15th 1997
2. *Exmouth Journal* September 21 1998
3. ibid
4. ibid
5. This has been the subject of a number of articles in *UFO Magazine*
6. [URL: www.fas.org/sgp/library/ciaufo.html]
7. *Daily Mail* newspaper: Tuesday 17th March 1998
8. *Animals & Men* 15
9. For the record it was *Stretch/We had it all* [BGO CD]
10. Jan has never really been given the credit that he deserves for his part in the events of the summer of 1997 and this is the place to set the record straight.
11. The guest was Terry Hooper of the Exotic Animals Register
12. Terry Hooper pers.comm
13. As will be seen, the old Lady wished to remain anonymous for fear of undoubted ridicule.
14. See my forthcoming book *The Mystery Animals of Hong Kong*
15. HERKLOTS G.A.K *Hong Kong Birds* (SCMP, Hong Kong, 1968)
16. One of the most notable examples is a large male black browed albatross that has been haunting the Shetland Isles for nearly three decades
17. It didn`t help that this report took place at the time of my obsession

(fuelled by Doc Shiels) with the movie and book of *Moby Dick*. See *Uri Geller's Encounters* October 1997 and *Animals & Men* issue 17.
18. And keen member of the ESP Group
19. The Cat and Fiddle, Clyst St Mary. The landlord's account was later substantiated and confirmed by interviews with bar staff past and present who reported sounds of footsteps and breaking glasses, as well as barrells being rolled around the cellar in a scenario wonderfully reminiscnet of the moving coffins of Barbados described by my old pal Lionel Fanthorpe.
20. Tawny Owl (*Strix aluco*) The Tawny Owl can be found in woodland, parks and even large gardens. It likes to sit on its perch until it spots its prey then pounces. It diet is varied and it will even eat fish and small birds when times are hard. Its cry is very musical and can be heard most often in autumn and winter.
21. Jan Scarff pers. comm
22. ibid
23. BBC Radio 4 *Today* 27/28 September 1997
24. Directed by Harry Salzman

IV

1. Sick Tim (pseud) pers.comm
2. Personal Observation (snigger) and this is NOT a reference to foot fetishism
3. Ironically when I went back to find this story again for the reference I couldn't find it.
4. Report by NW 1.10.97
5. Nigel Wright pers.comm
6. Report by NW September 1998
7. Referring to Dorchester UFO Conference April 9th 1998
8. ibid
9. See Chapter Three
10. Nigel Wright pers comm
11 David Bolton from the Royal Albert Memorial Museum in Exeter confirmed that although no autopsy had been carried out no cause of death had been found.
12 The *Exmouth Herald* for September 25th 1987
13 Sandy Bay Holiday Park
14 [URL: www.nsrl.ttu.edu/tmot/ziphcavi.htm]
15 COFFEY, D.J. *An Encyclopaedia of Sea Mammals* (Hart Davis/ McGibbon, London, 1977)
16 The *Exmouth Herald* October 2nd 1987
17 I don't know who first coined this appellation but I *think* it was

French cryptozoologist Michel Raynal
18. HEUVELMANS B *In the wake of the Sea Serpents* (Hart-Davis, London, 1968 1st English ed.)
19. Chris Basford pers.comm.
20. As cited in *Sightings,* Dec 1997
21. See Chapter III
22. (Dossier Editor pscpdocs@aol.com)
23. He was drunk
24. J.T and M Downes (my Mum and Dad) pers.comm
25. *Exmouth Journal* October 16th 1997
26. Nigel Wright pers.comm
27. *Exmouth Journal* October 16th 1997
28. Nigel Wright pers.comm
29. *Exmouth Journal* October 16th 1997
30. [URL: ufobc.org/underwat.htm]
31. [URL: www.ufo.no/english/articles/iur2.html]
32. [URL: ufobc.org/underwat.htm]
33. *ibid.*
34. I would, indeed question whether ANYONE has
35. Cumberland Clark (Words) Mark Strong (Music)
36. Thanks to Dr Karl Shuker
37. COSTELLO P. *In Search of Lake Monsters* (Garnston, London, 1974)
38. SHUKER, K.P.N *The Unexplained* (Carleton, London, 1996)
39. From the sheet music in the collection of Dr Shuker
40. Costello op.cit.
41. *Exmouth Journal.* October 16th 1987
42. [URL: www.andrewjd.demon.co.uk/rn/rm.html]
43. *Exmouth Journal.* October 16th 1997
44. Tinnitus is the name for ringing in the ears or head noises, and they are very common. Nearly 36 million Americans suffer from this discomfort. Tinnitus may come and go or you may be aware of a continuous sound. It can vary from pitch from a low roar to a high squeal or whine, and you may hear it in one or both ears. When the ringing is constant it can be annoying and distracting . More than 7 million people are afflicted so severely that they cannot lead normal lives. [URL: www.nyee.edu/otolaryn/Tinnfaq.htm]
45. *Exmouth Journal.* October 30th 1997
46. N Wright pers comm
47. *Exmouth Journal.* October 30th 1997
48. See above
49. 44. *Exmouth Journal.* October 30th 1997
50. Nigel Wright pers.comm
51. Roy Richardson pers. comm

52. http://www.pufori.org/brasil/campeng.htm
53. TDH Press Release July 1997
54. c/o Dave `daev` Walsh pers.comm c/o fortean list.
55. *http://www.cornwall-online.co.uk/falfish/mackerel.htm*
56. *ibid.*
57. URL: www.indian-river.fl.us/playing/fishing/s...r/mackking.html]
58. Various sources, mostly [URL: www.state.ma.us/dep/files/mercury/hgch2.htm]
59. [URL: www.reast.demon.co.uk/pw953.htm]
60. ibid
61. Roy Richardson pers.com
62. [URL: www.aufon.com/issue2.htm]
63. [URL: ufoinfo.com/roundup/v03/rnd03_07.shtml]
64. [URL: www.nacomm.org/news/1998/qtr1/9712na4.htm]
65. [URL: www.ufoinfo.com/news/]
66. Kolosimo, P *Timeless Earth* (Sphere, London, 1974)
67. The Lithuanian page about Mercury (parada in Sanskrit) in the Tantric Alchemy. URL: www.vartiklis.elnet.lt/mitai/indai/alchemy.ht
68. ibid
69. *Daily Post (London)* 23.1.1738
70. Dance. P *Animal Fakes and Frauds* (Sampson-Lowe, Maidenhead, 1975)
71. Fitzsimmons R. *Barnum in London*
72. Dance op cit
73. Fitzsimmons op cit
74. ibid
75. ibid
76. Shuker K.P.N *"The Lost Ark - New and Rediscovered animals of the 20th Century"*:
(Harper Collins, London 1993)
77. ibid
78. Napioer, J cited in Shuker op. cit.
79. Various Internet Soucres and Loren Coleman pers. comm
80. Shuker op cit
81. Richard Freeman pers.comm
82. As recently as 1990 Bernard heuvelmans was still defending his experience
83. Various Internet Sources
84. NORDENSKJOLD A.E. *Voyage of the Vega* (MacMillan and Co, 1886)
85. Cited in MACKAL. R.P. *Searching for Hidden Animals* (Cadogan Books, NYC, 1980)
86. Rudyuard Kipling Home Page.
87. Kipling, R. *Puck of Pook`s Hill* (1902, London, Macmillan)

88. Downes J. *The Owlman and Others* (CFZ 1997, Domra 1998)
89. In publication
90. Kipling, R. *The Jungle Book* (1894, London, Macmillan)
91. Mackal op.cit
92. ibid
93. ibid
94. M Ball, *Veasta* (Dorset Life undated)
95 ibid
96. Holinshed R et al. *Chronicles of England, Scotland, and Ireland* (1577).
97. URL: www.encyclopedia.com/articles/05970.html
98. Holinshed et al op cit
99. Ball. M op cit
100. URL: www.alltheway.com/html/ergot.html
101. URL: www.elite.net/~ergot/ergot.html
102. Graham Inglis pers comm
103. M Ball op cit
104. Downes J op cit
105. HITCHING, F. *The World Atlas of Mysteries* (Pan, London, 1978)
106. ibid
107. Various Internet Sources
108. Various Internet Sources
109. Various Internet Sources
110. Hitching op cit
111. Various Internet Sources
112. Various Internet Sources
113. Various Internet Sources
114. Downes J op cit
115. This skull is now in my personal collection
116. I have to protect my sources.
117. Herklots, G.A.K. *The Hong Kong Countryside* (SCMP, HK, 1951)
118. A&M #6/Uri Geller's Encounters Nov. 1997
119. SA (Johannesburg) Sun Times 13.9.98 via Loren Coleman
120. Shuker Dr K.P.N. *The Unexplained* (Carleton, London, 1995)
121. A&M 12
122. URL: www.parascope.com/articles/1196/monster.htm
123. Tom Anderson pers comm
124. Hitching op cit
125. ibid
126. Shiels, Tony 'Doc' *Monstrum - A Wizard's tale* (Fortean Tomes, London, 1989)
127. McEwan G *Mystery Animals of Britain and Ireland* (Robert Hale, London, 1985)
128. Gerry Connelly pers comm

129. URL: crs.uvm.edu/profiles/brighton/history.htm
130. ibid
131. Downes J op cit
132. ibid
133. Ball M op cit
134. Benchley, P *Jaws* (Pan, Pb Ed 1974)
135. Ball op cit
136. ibid
137. ibid
138. Holiday, Ted, *The Dragon and the Disc* (Sidgewick and Jackson, London 1973)
139. Bord J & C *Alien Animals* (Granada, Manchester, 1980)
140. Coleman, Loren *Mysterious America* (Faber and Faber, NYC, 1983)
141. Bord J & C op cit
142. Richard Freeman pers comm
143. Coleman L op cit
144. ibid
145. R Freeman pers comm
146. Coleman L op cit

PART TWO

V

1. Keeling-Basford C. pers comm
2. ibid
3. *Exmouth Herald* Friday 5th November 1982
4. Unfortunately we were unable to contact Mr Morris to confirm this story
5. *Exmouth Herald* March 1st 1991
6. *Exmouth Herald* May 28th 1982
7. Encarta OnLine
8. LaVey Anton *The Satanic Rituals, by Anton LaVey* (London, Avon Books, 1972)
9. Note the Charlie Manson connection and see Alan Moore`s quote from the front of this book.
10. Rosemary's Baby. Directed by Roman Polanski. Starring Mia Farrow, John Cassavetes, Ruth Gordon, Sidney Blackmer, Ralph Bellamy, Charles Grodin.

"By turns comic, grotesque, and genuinely terrifying, this 1968 tale of a really difficult pregnancy proves the old adage that it pays to be paranoid - sometimes they really are out to get you.

John Cassavetes and Mia Farrow play Guy and Rosemary Woodhouse, a newly married couple who move into a gloomy old Central Park West apartment building. (One of the great effects of cinematographer William Fraker, who also worked on great films like One Flew Over the Cuckoo's Nest and Close Encounters of the Third Kind, is to make the dark apartment grow increasingly light and airy as the heroine's suspicions deepen.) They live next door to Roman and Minnie Castavet, played by Sidney Blackmer and Ruth Gordon (of Harold and Maude), an eccentric old couple who turn out to be witches. Soon Guy, a struggling actor, lands a lead role in a successful Broadway play - for which he had previously been turned down - when the actor chosen in his place mysteriously goes blind. To celebrate, he suggests to Rosemary that they have a baby. And then the fun begins.

One of the reasons this film works so well is its setting, emphasized by the leisurely pan across Manhattan with which it opens. It's hard to believe that a successful coven of witches could be operating in such an urban environment. And the witches are played by veterans like Gordon, Blackmer, Elisha Cook Jr., and Patsy Kelly, which seems more ludicrous than frightening. Also, the story is told entirely from Rosemary's point of view, and the possibility that her fears are induced by the hormonal changes that accompany her pregnancy always hovers in the background.

Rosemary's Baby marks the final high of an interesting career in horror movies for producer William Castle. Most of his previous efforts were low-budget thrillers like House on Haunted Hill and The Tingler, which succeeded more because of Castle's promotional stunts than for any inherent qualities of the films themselves. Watch for Castle playing a man at a phone booth in this movie."

URL: the-tech.mit.edu/V116/N41/rosemary.41a.html

11. The Eagles "Hotel California"
12. [URL: 207.238.20.223/magic.htm]
13. Unlike the much publicised quote by *Black Sabbath* guitarist Tony Iomni who is quoted as saying that the nearest thing that the band ever got to Black Magic was eating the chocolates....
14. This came to my attention in a book called *Job* by Robert A Heinlein
15 Cruden's Concordance to The Bible could not verify this account
16 Many thanks to my father for his huge amount of fruitless research

here
17 [URL: 207.238.20.223/magic.htm]
18 There is no evidenmce that she actually existed
19 From *The Meaning of Witchcraft*, which was published in 1959.
20. [URL: 207.238.20.223/magic.htm]
21 ibid
22 Richard Freeman pers comm
23 [URL: 207.238.20.223/magic.htm]
24 W. Petrovic pers comm
25 *Exmouth Herald* Fri Nov 27th 1987
26 N Wright Pers comm
27 N Wright Pers Comm
28 Various Newspaper reports and Westcountry TV Documentary July 1998
29 ibid
30 Phil Johnston pers comm (originally published in *Uri Geller's Encounters* May 1997)
31 ibid
32 As Forteans we are sparing with our credulity but are open to a wide variety of conceptualisations
33 Francis D *The Beast of Exmoor* (David and Charles, Newton Abbot, 1993)
34 Big Bang #4 (Primal Dribbling Dreambook) 1987
35 In *Unsolved* (Orbis Publications)
36 *Exeter Express & Echo* 12.08.1978
37 cited in *Exmouth and East Devon Journal* 12.9.1978
38 N Wright pers comm

VI

1. *Transactions of the Devonshire Association* Folklore Report for 1899
2. E.R.Deldefield *Exmouth Milestones* (Raleigh Press, Exmouth 1948)
3 N Wright pers comm
4. Delderfield op cit
5. A term first used by Colin Wilson
6. Brown T *Devon Ghosts* (Jarrold, Norwich, 1980)
7. Underwood, P *Westcountry Ghosts* (Bossiney, Boscastle, 1978)
8. N Wright pers comm based on interviews with witnesses
9 ibid
10 Sue Wright pers comm
11. URL: www.rpi.net.au/~ghostgum/castle/ghosttrain.html]
12. Roy Richardson pers comm via Nigel Wright
13 N Wright pers comm

14 Roy Richardson perscomm
15 URL: sol.zynet.co.uk/imprint/Tucson/5.htm
16 Downes J op cit
17. [URL: www.livingspirit.com/ghost6.htm]
18. URL: www.roma1.infn.it/rog/group/frasca/parafaq.html]
19. N Wright pers comm
20. [URL: www.altnews.com.au/nexus/Polter.html]
21. ibid
22. Nigel Wright pers.comm
23. Exmouth Milestones E.R.Deldefield (Raleigh Press, Exmouth 1948)
24. ibid

VII

1 His name and address are on file
2 Downes J *Mystery Animals of the Westcountry* (Domra,Corby, 1999)
3 ibid
4 ibid
5 M Crook pers comm
6 His name and address are on file
7 M Crook pers comm
8 ibid
9 I have never encountered anything quite like this before. This is unprecedented in my experience, and I felt quite awestruck at being able to examine bona fide physical evidence for animal attacks..
10 M Crook pers comm
11 ibid
12 ibid
13 *Exmouth Herald* February 4th 1983
14 *Exmouth Herald* March 4th 1983
15 *Exmouth Journal* Oct 20 1997
16 *Exeter Express and Echo* Nov 20th 1997
17 Downes J op cit (1999)
18 ibid (Quoting PC Eddie Bell)
19. [URL: library.advanced.org/11234/puma.html]
20. [URL: library.advanced.org/11234/leopard_any.html]
21. [URL: library.advanced.org/11234/lynx.html
22. [URL: www.oit.itd.umich.edu/bio/doc.cgi/Chorda...Felis_chaus.ftl]
23. Loren Coleman op cit
24. ibid
25. Bord J&C op cit
26. Goblin Universe #7
27. Parsons K *The Chicksands Enigma* (published in *The Truthseeker`s*

Review)
28. http://deville.demon.co.uk/glosabc.html
29 Constable, T.J. *Sky Creatures - The Cosmic Pulse of Life* (Kangaroo Books, New York, 1978)
30 ibid
31 ibid
32. W Petrovic pers comm
33 URL: astrologix.de/artikel/bessler2.htm
34 Fort, C *Lo* (Kendall, New York, 1931)
35 URL: www.borderlands.com/archives/1949-5-5.htm
36. [URL: www.ufobbs.com/txt3/2428.ufo]
37. ibid
38. Karl Shuker pers comm (and URL: www.gafintl-adamski.com)
39. Downes J 1998 op cit
40. Arthur Conan Doyle, b. 1859, Edinburgh, Scotland; d. 1930, Crowborough, Sussex, England. (Conan was originally his middle name, but in later years he began using "Conan Doyle" as his surname.) Doyle came from an aristocratic and intellectual Irish family; he was mainly brought up in Jesuit boarding schools, and entered the University of Edinburgh in 1881, receiving a medical degree in 1885. One of his professors, Dr. Joseph Bell, was to serve as a model for Sherlock Holmes.

He began writing while still in school in order to earn money, and sold his first story ("The Mystery of the Sasassa Valley") to Chambers' Journal in 1879. Later that year his father fell ill and entered a convalescent home, and Arthur became the head of the family, assuming its financial burdens.To earn money, he spent some months as ship's doctor on two vessels, and eventually opened a medical practice in Southsea, Portsmouth. Like Dr. Watson's, his practice was "never very absorbing", at least at first, and he began writing novels in his spare time. His third try was "A Study in Scarlet", the first Sherlock Holmes story, published in 1887 as the annual Christmas novel of Mrs. Beeton's magazine. "The Sign of the Four" followed in 1890, under encouragement from the American publisher Lippincott; and with further novels and stories his literary reputation grew to the extent that he closed his medical practice. The first Sherlock Holmes short story was published in The Strand magazine in 1891 ("A Scandal in Bohemia") and two dozen more followed shortly; when Doyle grew tired of Holmes in 1894 and killed him off (in "The Final Problem"), public outcry was so great that Doyle was forced to explain away Holmes' death and continue his career. In the final Holmes story (published in 1917 as part of His Last Bow), he has come out of retirement to aid His Majesty in the war effort.

By the turn of the century, Doyle had determined to concentrate on "serious" novels, and created several other characters, such as Brigadier Etienne Gerard and the boxer Rodney Stone; but none of his other novels have remained at all well-known.

Doyle was married to Louise Hawkins in 1885, and had two children with her; she was seriously ill 8 years later and died in 1900. Doyle married again to Jean Leckie in 1907, and fathered three more children. Following his first wife's death, and eager to witness the Boer War, Doyle sailed for South Africa as doctor and unofficial diplomat, and eventually wrote a definitive account of the war, The Great Boer War. In the period leading up to the First World War, he became a sort of unofficial statesman and advocate, famously championing the cause of several men unfairly convicted in criminal trials, and campaigning for lifesaving equipment and body armour for the Navy. He had always been interested in spiritualism, and when his son died in the war, he devoted the rest of his life to its pursuit, becoming almost a fanatic. He toured Europe and America in search of converts, and wrote a few books on the subject, making arrangements to contact his wife after his death.

Sherlock Holmes, Doyle's enduring creation and the most famous of fictional detectives, was the world's first consulting detective, operating from his rooms at 221B Baker Street in London, which he shared with his friend and biographer, Dr. John Watson. A steady procession of the distressed, the set-upon, and the criminal make their way through the door of the parlour to enlist Holmes's help; the supporting characters (Mrs. Hudson, the housekeeper; Lestrade, an inept Scotland Yard inspector; Hopkins and Gregson, policemen of greater ability; and the Baker Street Irregulars, a pack of street urchins who Holmes employs to ferret out information) have entered with Holmes into literary immortality. In the early stories, when he has no cases under investigation, Holmes-- who cannot face mental inactivity-- uses cocaine for stimulation, but Watson has exhorted him out of this habit by the end of the series. Holmes possesses amazing deductive powers, a giant intellect, and a formidable athleticism; he has an encyclopedic knowledge of any area touching his criminal interests (but hardly any knowledge of, for example, astronomy or politics). He seems to have no need of ordinary human friendship or romance, and Watson occasionally compares him to a machine, so arrogantly cold and detached could he be toward his clients. (In "A Scandal in Bohemia", in which he first meets the only woman who ever impressed him-- Irene Adler-- Holmes explains that emotions and romantic passions would get in the way of his logical, deductive mind). Watson eventually marries and moves out of Holmes's rooms, but drops by for visits now and then and continues to chronicle a few of Holmes's more interesting cases. In 1891 Holmes was said to have perished at the

Reichenbach Falls in Switzerland at the hands of his arch-enemy, the crime boss Professor Moriarty, but reappeared in London three years later, having taken the opportunity to fake his disappearance in order to fool his enemies in the underworld. Before the war, he retired to the South Downs to keep bees, but returned for a final adventure on behalf of the government during the War.

41. Published in 1928 (I believe)
42. Karl Shuker pers comm
43. A popular London publication of the late 19th-early 20th Centuries. Also published fiction by Oscar Wilde amongst others
44. Conan-Doyle A *The Horror of the Heights* as cited by Shuker Dr K.P.N in the 1996 CFZ Yearbook
45. ibid
46. Shuker Dr K.P.N in the 1996 CFZ Yearbook
47. ibid
48. D Spoor pers comm
49. M Pearson pers comm
50. Shuker Dr K.P.N in the 1996 CFZ Yearbook
51. ibid
52. cited in ibid
53. Dickinson P *The Flight of Dragons* (Paper Tiger, London, 1998 re-print)
54. Freeman, R in A&M 15
55. R Freeman pers comm
56. Whitlock R cited by R Freeman
57. R Freeman op cit
58. Muirhead R in in the 1996 CFZ Yearbook
59. Exeter *Express & Echo* 20 June 1983;
60. *Transport 2000, Devon Group Newsletter* Summer 1984.
61. A long defunct ITV Soap Opera remarkable only for its terrible production values and worse acting
62 S Johnson pers comm
63 Sticklebacks and pipefish : Gasterosteiformes
A commonly caught group in both fresh and sea water. There are 3 species of stickleback, 1 snipefish and 8 pipefish and sea horses in N. Europe.

The British species are:

Greater Pipefish, *Syngnathus acus*. Very common, widespread.
Lesser Pipefish, *Syngnathus rostellatus*. Very common, widespread.
Deep-snouted Pipefish, *Syngnathus typhle*. Local, frequent.
Straight-nosed Pipefish, *Nerophis ophidion*. Local, uncommon on the

shore.
Worm Pipefish, *Nerophis lumbriciformis*. Very common in the south and west only. Unknown from the east coast.
Snake Pipefish, *Enterulus aequoreus*. Uncommon, west coast only, frequent in some areas.

64 I do not know which species these were
65 Complete Works of Charles Fort (Dover, 1974)
66 Dash.M *Borderlands* (Heinemann, 1997, London)
67 ibid
68 Complete Works of Charles Fort (Dover, 1974)
69. Dash M ibid
70. Exeter *Express & Echo* 12 March 1983.
71 *Exmouth Journal* 23.7.98
71 ibid
72 ibid
73 ibid
74 Cited by Mike Dash in *Fortean Studies Vol One*
75 CFZ Archives

PART THREE

VIII

1 In my opinion a complete Charlatan. See my reviews and comments in *Sightings* Magazine Summer/Autumn/Winter 1997
2 Yeah right!!!!!!!!
3 hahahahahahahaha
4 For God`s sake........
5 Various sources including issue 1 *The X Factor*
6 Ray Santilli
7 D Suster, *Hitler Black Magician* (Gazelle, 1998, UK dist)
8 Song by Kirsty McColl
9 No prizes for guessing which is who
10 Pratt D.H in *Exmouth Journal* Dec 9th 1950
11 Intrigued by Pratt`s repeated use of the `Two little men in a Flying Saucer` motif. I posted a request for information on the Interet. A few days later Andrew Dennis replied:

Jon Asked:

>Does anyone know about a popular song from about 1950 either called or about: "Two Little men in a Flying Saucer"
>
>I would be grateful for a sample of the lyrics and also details of who sang/wrote it?
>
>Thanx
>
>Jon

Can't help with author/original artist/date details, but the song (actually "Five Little Men In A Flying Saucer") is still current on, for example, the BBC's utterly psychedelic "Fun Songs Factory" which is a
massive hit with the under-fives. (This is one of those shows that you have to be either a toddler, insane or full to the gunwales with Class A recreationals to appreciate).

It's a counting-down song, like ten green bottles or the speckled frog song, and it goes like this:

Five little men in a flying saucer,
Flew round the world one day,
They looked left and right and didn't like the sight,
So one man flew away,

Whooooooosh! (You've sort of got to do the actions at this point. Well, I have if I don't want to get hit with Pos'm Pat's van, anyway)

Four little men in a flying saucer.... etc., all the way down to the last verse, which is:

One little man in a flying saucer,
Flew round the world one day,
He looked left and right and liked the sight,
So that man decided to stay.

The tune is now, thank you Jon, rattling around in my head and will give me no peace until I kill someone. I hope you're proud of yourself.

I have a fanciful idea that the tune is actually an older one, played to a slightly different rhythm, but for the life of me I can't place it. I think I've got a video of Ozzie Octave (Don't ask. You thought Big Bird was scary? Brrrr.) performing the thing, and I'll take a look in the credits to see if there's any hint as to where it came from.

Down by the Station,
early in the morning,
See the little puffing-billies,
standing in a row...

(a genuine forteana list no-prize for anyone who can remember the rest of this one. That or the lyrics to the dinosaur version.)

Andrew Dennis

12 Evans H and Stacey D *UFO 1947-1997* (John Brown Pubs., London, 1997)
13 Spencer J *The Encyclopaedia of UFOlogy* (Headline, London, 1997)
14 Pratt op cit
15 *Radio Gnome Invisible* (Virgin Records 1973)
   Angel's Egg (Virgin Records 1974)
   You (Virgin Records 1975)
Three albums by *Gong* which chronicled the story of the Pothead Pixies from the planet Gong who travelled around the universe in a flying teapot. Since leaving Gong Daevid Allen explored the mythos on some of his solo albums and has now (surprise surprise) reformed *Gong*.
16 see part one
17 Downes J.T *The Dictionary of Devonshire Dialect* (1988)
18 Downes J (1988) op cit
19 Transactions of the Devonshire Association 1879
20 Dennis H Pratt in *Exmouth Journal* 13 October 1951
21 *Exmouth Journal* 21 October 1951
22 *Exmouth Journal* 2 Aug 1952
23 URL: www.dra.hmg.gb/html/products/testeval/airsect/asccaabp.ht
24 S Johnson pers comm
25 N Wright pers comm
26 ....and would not have been operational until about 1956
27 various Internet Sources
28 S Johnson pers comm
29 Gerry Anderson pers comm
30 Redfern N *A Covert Agenda* (Simon and Schuster. London, 1997)

IX

1 *Exmouth Journal* May 21st 1949 (40 Years Ago)
2 *Exmouth Journal* May 21st 1909
3 ibid

4   http://mirrors.org.sg/ww1/index.htm
5   Various Internet Sources
6   http://mirrors.org.sg/ww1/tldts.htm
7   *Exmouth Journal* May 21st 1909
8   *Willimantic Chronicle* 1.1.10
9   *Japan Weekly Mail* 19.6.09
10 *Sacramento Bee* 24.11.1896
11 *Exmouth Journal* May 21st 1909
12 John Spencer op cit
13 Keel J *The Mothman Prophecies* (NEL, London, 1973)
14 Spencer op cit
15 Nigel Wright op cit
16 Bearne N *Flying Saucers over the West* (PP 1958)
17 ibid
18 ibid
19 ibid
20 W Petrovic pers comm
21 *Exmouth Journal* Oct 28th 1978
22 *Exmouth Herald* August 7th 1987
23 *Exmouth Herald* August 14th 1987
24 *Exmouth Herald* September 11th 1987
25 *Exmouth Herald* August 21st 1987
26 *Exmouth Herald* April 17th 1987
27 I stole this headline from one in The Sun about `Doc` Shiles from 1978
28 Goblin Universe #4
29 Jan Williams wrote to me after reading the first draft of this book suggesting that the `horned God` was actually St Neot himself. I asked for references and she wrote back:

Hi Jon, I've surfaced again. I can't find the specific ref to St Neot being patron saint of beasts of the chase I was thinking of at the moment, but here are some other bits which give the general idea (all fully referenced - see I can do it if I really try!) Anthony D Hippesley Coxe: Haunted Britain:Hutchinson and Co. 1973 *St Neots: Upstream is St Neots Well. It will be found in a meadow down a lane to the right of a garage. St Neot is said to have been (i) a dwarf; (ii) brother of Alfred the Great; (iii) a monk from Glastonbury; and (iv) all three. He was particularly kind to animals, particularly those which were the quarry of the hunt. This curative well is most effective on the first three mornings in May.* John and Caitlin Matthews: An Encyclopaedia of Myth and Legend; British and Irish Mythology: Diamond Books, London 1995 *St Neot (d 877). Trained as a monk at Glastonbury, he became a hermit near Bodmin Moor at Neotstoke. He is said to have appeared to King*

Alfred the Great on the eve of the Battle of Ethandun. When Neot's oxen were stolen, he yoked stags to plough his fields. Guy Williams: A guide to the magical places of England, Wales and Scotland: Constable, London, 1987. *St Neot is said to have been a dwarf, and was famed for his miraculous achievements with animals, birds and fishes. One of the saint's most remarkable feats, in which he restored two dead fish to life, is recalled in a stained glass window in the church.* New Shell Guide to England: Ed. John Hadfield: Michael Joseph: 1981. *St Neots .... Just up a lane beside the garage in the village centre is St Neot's Holy Well; its waters were once believed to strengthen delicate children.* So there you go. One very confused saint, but with definite connections to the well, and to stags. Makes you realise how boring life was in the ninth century, though, doesn't it? Two dead fish, and he gets a whole stained glass window. Hope all is well with you lot. All the best, Jan

30 Downes J 1998 op cit
31 *Exmouth Herald* February 28th 1987
32 N Wright collection (Undated)
33 N Wright collection (Undated)
34 N Wright collection (Undated)
35 Interview with M Lindemannn on Internet [URL: www.cninews.com/Search/CNI.0645.html]
36 N Wright collection (Undated)
37 N Wright pers comm
38 Delderfield op cit

X

1 Newman L.H *Living With Butterflies* (1967)
2 Russwurn A *Aberrations of British Butterflies* (1978,London, Classey)
3 Burton J., *National Trust Book of British Animals* (Cape, London, 1984)
4 ibid
5 A&M2
6 CFZ Collection (Trans Dev Assoc)
7 Various Internet Sources
8 Pringle, A. *The Thylacine - the liveliest mystery animal around* (A&M#2)
9 ibid
10 ibid
11 Bord, J & C *Alien Animals* (Granada,London, 1980)
12 Holiday., F.W and Wilson C *The Goblin Universe* (Llewelyn, NYC,

1986)
13 Alcott F.J *Wonder Tales from thre Faerie Isles* (1929)
14 ibid
15 McEwan G op cit
16 ibid
17 Downes J (1998) op cit
18 Downes J *Only Fools and Goatsuckers* (Domra, Corby, 1999)

PART FOUR

XI

1 Downes J (1998) op cit
2 Bord J&C (1980) op cit
3 Seiveking P (Ed) *Diary of a Mad Planet (FT 16-25)* (Fortean Tomes, 1990)
4 Downes J (1998) op cit
5 ibid
6 ibid
7 *Exmouth Journal* May 21st 1909
8 Downes J (1998) op cit
9 Delderfield op cit
10 ibid
11 See Part One
12 Bord J&C (1980) op cit
13 SCAN News #3
14 McEwan op cit
15 Bord J&C (1980) op cit
16 McEwan op cit
17 ibid
18 Coxhead J *Devon Folklore* (pp 1955)
19 Green A *Our Haunted Kingdom* (Pan, London, 1974)
20 Downes J (1998) op cit
21 Coleman L op cit
22 Keel J *The Mothman Prophecies* (NEL, London, 1974)
23. ibid
24 Richard Freeman pers.comm
25 [URL: www.treasure.com/j3895.htm]
26 Beer T *The Beast of Exmoor* (Countryside, Barnstaple, 1976)
27 McEwan op cit
28 CFZ archives

29 We have the witnesses name on file but are respecting his request for anonymity
30 URL: members.xoom.com/horuskings/aleister.html
31 Unreferenced Internet Source
32 *My Only Vice is the Fantastic Prices I charge for being Eaten Alive* #8
33 ibid
34 Graham Inglis pers comm and various other sources including a book called `Hammer of the Gods` that no-one can remember who wrote...
35 Unreferenced Internet Article
36 Inverness Courier via UFO Scotland Web Site

XII

1 Westcountry TV documentary Summer 1998
2 Petrovic W pers comm
3 Nick Beer (E&E) pers comm and docs
4 ibid
5 ibid
6 ibid
7 *Exmouth Herald* September 11th 1987
8. [URL: www.dra.hmg.gb/html/news/design98/imgsup.htm]
9. [URL: www.raf.mod.uk/front_line/vc10.html]
10 see above
11 Downes J (1999) op cit
12 http://www.dalriada.co.uk/Archives/benbec.htm
13 Downes J (1999) op cit)
14 http://www.dalriada.co.uk/Archives/benbec.htm
15 Delderfield op cit.
16 Nigel Wright pers comm
17 Delderfield op cit.
18 The term comes from a poem by Rudyard Kipling.
19 Delderfield op cit.
20 Nigel Wright pers comm
21 ibid
22 Matthew Williams is best known for his unauthorised explorations of such military installations as Rudlow Manor
23 cited in http://www.dalriada.co.uk/Archives/benbec.htm
24 http://www.dalriada.co.uk/Archives/benbec.htm
25 Undated story from *Exmouth Journal*. We have a photocopy but have not been able to find the original.
26 ibid
27 The first weekend of March 1998

28 *The Stones of Blood* was the 100th Doctor Who adventure and the third story in the 1978 Key to Time season. David Fisher's original storyline entitled "The Nine Maidens" was commissioned by producer Graham Williams in early 1978. Williams hoped to repeat the success of the previous season's gothic horror tale, Image of the Fendahl. After very few rewrites, the more Hammer-esque sounding "The Stones of Blood", went into production in June, beginning with location filming at the Rollright Stones in Oxfordshire. The story's small but strong cast included Susan Engel in the dual role of Vivien Fay/Cessair, Nicholas McArdle as Leonard De Vries, and in her last acting role Beatrix Lehmann as Professor Rumford...

Arriving on Earth, the Doctor and Romana trace the third segment of the Key to Time to a stone circle, "The Nine Travellers" of Boscombe Moor. There they meet archaeologist Professor Rumford and her friend Vivien Fay. Following a visit to the local Druidic priest, De Vries, the Doctor is almost sacrificed by his local pagan cult, who worship the Celtic goddess; the Cailleach. De Vries is killed by one of the stones from the circle. Several stones are discovered to be blood plasma dependent Ogri, carbon based lifeforms from the Tau Ceti system. The Cailleach is revealed to be Vivien Fay, in reality the alien criminal - Cessair of Diplos, who brought the Ogri to Earth 4,000 years previously. Cessair sends Romana to a hyperspace vessel above the circle. The Doctor follows and inadvertently releases the Megara justice machines, who as a result threaten him with execution. The Doctor tricks the Megara into probing Vivien's mind and they discover her true identity. They sentence her to imprisonment as a stone megalith for theft of the Seal of Diplos (the third segment of the Key to Time), which the Doctor secures at the last moment. (http://www.jeremy.co.uk/cve/story2.html)
29 No names no packdrill
30 *Emouth Journal* Sat 19 Oct 1957
31 URL: crop-circles.sip.fi/OC1.html
32 This is of course assuming that Paul Vigay has not made a superior version since the one we were shown in November 1996
33 URL: crop-circles.sip.fi/OC1.html
34 The best overview of this phenomenon was presented by Dr Mike Dash in *Fortean Studies Volume 1* (John Brown Publishing, London, 1995)
35 URL: www.ucmp.berkeley.edu/history/anning.html
36 URL: geoclio.st.usm.edu/anning99.html
37 URL: www.ucl.ac.uk/geolsci/edu/ugrads/fieldtr.../day1_text.html
38. [URL: www.calacademy.org/research/entomology/staff/gynand.htm]
39. [URL: www.ukans.edu/kansas/cienciala/342/ch8.html]
40. [URL: www.tcet.unt.edu/~chrisl/cufon/mcdon3.htm]

41 These documents were given to me by Dr Philip Mantle
42 *Sightings* magazine November 1997..
43 *X-Factor* November 1998
44 Cited in Bayanov, D *In Search of the Russian Snowman* (Moscow, 1996)

XIII

1 *Transactions of the Devonshire Association* 1898
2 ibid
3 ibid
4 ibid
5 *Domesday Book*
6 West Buckland School
7 Delderfield op cit.
8 URL: www.dartmoor-npa.gov.uk/tourism/pages/woodbury/castle.html
9 Nigel Wright pers comm
10 Delderfield op cit.
11 Downes (1999) op cit
12 ibid
13 Downes (1998) op cit.
14 ibid

XIV

1 A proposition suggested by Nick Pope
2 See the eponymous story by Robert A Heinlein presently available in *The Past Through Tomorrow* (NEL, London, 1974)
3 Are they fuck?
4 ibid
5 David-Neel, A, *Magic and Mystery in Tibet* (Picador ed., London, 1976)
6 Taken from a PD Internet version of the book.
7 Richard Freeman pers comm
8 *Goblin Universe* 7
9 As if any proof were needed.
10 McEwan op cit.
11 Gerry Connelly pers comm
12 McEwan op cit.
13 ibid
14 David-Neel op cit.

15 St Mary's Hospital, Axminster - now demolished.
16 In the CFZ files.
17 Nigel Wright pers comm
18 [URL: www.crown.net/X/Stories/HospitalGhost.html]
19 [URL: www.ghosts.org/stories/tales/nurse-stories.html]
20 The main mental handicapped hospital for South Devon.
21 I lived there intermittently between 1982 and 1985.
22 Trish Lovelock pers comm
23 Originally published in *Alien Encounters*, August 1997.
24 Hoban, R., *Turtle Diary* (Picador, London, 1976)
25 The quasi-religious aspects of the use of psychotropic substances, at least those within a broadly Christian context, will be the subject of another book.
26 [URL: www.csp.org/nicholas/shamanismTOC.html]
27 [URL: diseyes.lycaeum.org/fresh/discar.htm
28 "Terence McKenna is an anthropologist and ethnobotanist, specializing in shamanism. His works in recent years have revolved around a numeric system found in the hexigrams of the I Ching that he claims charts the
ebb and flow of the novel and habitual in history (termed as Novelty Theory)"
29 Carlos Castaneda (1925-1998) URL: headlines.yahoo.com/Full_Coverage/Entert...da__1925_1998_/
30 I do not presume to judge everyone's experiences by my own.

XV

1 This is one of Wilde's oft-quoted and most famous epigrams, but I have no idea when he first said it.
2 Too many people refuse to accept the fact that this is fiction.
3 W Petrovic pers comm
4 Various Internet Sources
5 Gerry Connelly pers comm
6 Ashe G "The Ancient Wisdom" cited by W Petrovic
7 Evans-Wertz cited on Mystical www
8 Beresford-Ellis,P., *The Druids* (HarperCollins, London, 1994)
9 David-neel op cit.
10 McEwan op cit.
11 This is an exercise which according to some of my collegues who are conversant with the theory and practice of ritual magic has been carried out on a number of occasions. Indeed, I have observed such a ritual.
12 David-Neel op cit.
13 Lovelock op cit.

14 Roerich N papers (archive unreferenced)
15 The trouble is with all of this stuff is that it came from an archive of photocopies bequeathed to me by a friend now dead and I don`t know the full references for all of it. This is, I belioeve, from Jung`s book on flying saucers
16 Shuker, Dr K. P. N., *CFZ Yearbook 1997.*
17 Di Francis (1993) op cit.
18 McClure K, *Abduction Watch* Issue 6
19 Hilary Evans pers comm
20 Debbie Jordan pers comm
21 ibid
22 ibid
23 ibid
24 ibid
25 *Transactions of the Devonshire Association* 1892
26 (FSR 41:3 Don Worley)
27 Downes J (1999) op cit.
28 Joyce Howarth pers comm
29 Downes J (1999) op cit.
30   McEwan op cit.
31 ibid.
32 Shuker, Dr K. P. N. (1997) op cit.
33 A theory upon which I expounded in *Sightings* magazine, May 1997.
34 *Exmouth Journal* 25 Jun 1998.
35 *Exmouth Journal* 2 Jul 1998
36 *Exmouth Journal* 9 Jul 1998
37 ibid
38. [URL: isur.com/articles/liverpool.html]
39. [URL: web.ukonline.co.uk/Members/ad.johnson/text/bl.htm]
40 Graham Inglis pers comm
41 "*as any fule kno*" (Geoffrey Molesworth c. 1951)

EPILOGUE

1 As I sit with Graham doing the references to this volume, a few days before Christmas 1998, I am still attending Wonford House on a weekly basis.

APPENDIX

An excerpt from *Dragons: More than a Myth?*
By Richard Freeman
courtesy the author and CFZ Press

British biologist Rupert Sheldrake infuriated adherents to academic dogma in 1981 when he published his revolutionary theories in a book entitled *A New Science of Life*. In this book Sheldrake raised the question of how - if every DNA molecule contained the coded information to make a specific creature - did the body know just what went where. For example, how did it know to grow skin-cells, and not - say - muscle-cells in the right areas. Also, many animals (like some lizards), can regrow lost-limbs, whilst others - such as echinoderms - can be totally destroyed, (for example by putting them in a liquidizer), but each piece will regrow into a fully-formed adult.

Sheldrake realised that - contained within the DNA - must be something akin to a 'blueprint' for each species - a life-shaping field *unique* to each life-form, that orders the DNA. He called his hypothetical 'blueprints' morphogenic-fields - or m-fields for short. The m-field theory might also explain how subjective information like emotions and memories are retained. The cells in our bodies are constantly dying and being replaced, and this includes brain-tissue. Yet we retain our memories and personalities – except under conditions of severe or maximum brain-damage, (even minimal to moderate brain-damage is self-repairable) - ergo *something* must be making the new atoms follow the exact patterns of their forbears.

This m-field template may be the key to understanding other biological mysteries such as migration. Darwin believed that this kind of information was passed on in the genetic-characteristics of the parents, but some startling experiments have challenged this view.

In the USA a series of experiments were carried out on rats. The rats had to learn how to escape from a pool of water without following the most logical course - as this had been rigged to give them an electric-shock. The first generation took a number of attempts to learn this. The young of these rats took less time to work out the problem. This seemed to be supporting the Darwinian idea, but identical experiments were being carried out in another country with rats that had no genetic relationship to the ones in America. These rats took even less time to solve the puzzle than the second generation of rats in the American labs.

Sheldrake believed that this was because of a *shared* m-field. He hypothesised the m-fields of all individuals of a species were linked to a huge gestalt m-field. He proposed that evolutionary changes, behavioural patterns, and information were shared at a subconscious level between the whole species. When individuals pick up advantageous new behavioural traits, it is incorporated into the gestalt. He believed this was passed on by resonance, rather like the way that the energy wave from a plucked string on an instrument can resonate onto another string on the same instrument that has not been plucked. This works because part of the unplucked string has the potential to resonate at frequencies in common with the vibrating string, and thus can resonate in harmony. In music this is called harmonic resonance. Sheldrake called his biological analogue, morphic resonance.

Of course the inverse of this also occurred, wherein the individual's behaviour is altered by the m-field of the species. Animals with fewer turnovers of generations - those with longer life spans - would have m-fields that work more slowly. But they work nonetheless. Some Einstein of the sheep-world worked out how to cross cattlegrids in Britain. The sheep curled up in a ball, and *rolled* across the grid! Initially only a few did this trick, but within weeks sheep all over the world were making P.O.W style escapes from farms.

This would seem to be the ideal was for gigantic "racial thought forms" to occur. Perhaps we should seek the origin of dragons and other monsters, in the jungles of our own minds, and in the fossil memories handed down to us in our genes from our remote ancestors.

Several million years ago, on the plains of East Africa, our remote ancestors were struggling to survive. Australopithecus had an existence fraught with peril. In moving down from the trees, and onto the grassland to exploit untapped food-sources, he faced new and deadly enemies. The crocodile was - and is - the biggest killer of mankind. The rock-python would also have found our ancestors easy prey. Australopithecus was small enough to have fallen victim to large raptors, and fossil evidence from South Africa supports this. Lions and leopards would have certainly preyed on our ancestors, and hunting-dogs may have also given them sleepless nights. Australopithecus and its descendents would have been in direct competition with other primate species. Some were smaller than itself - other, including the horrific giant baboon *Dinopithecus* - were larger.

Think about it. Here we have the genesis of mankind's monsters, the beginning of our species' bugbears. The dragon, the giant bird, the mystery big-cat, the phantom dog, the little people, and the hairy giant.

Sheldrake himself seems to support this notion.

In the early stages of a form's history, the morphogenetic field will be relatively ill-defined and significantly influenced by individual variants. But as time goes on, the cumulative influence of countless previous systems will confer an ever-

increasing stability on the field; the more probable the average type becomes, the more likely that it will be repeated in the future.

Perhaps our fossil memories can be triggered by certain things in our surroundings. Maybe some kinds of electromagnetic-interference coupled with the right person, with the right brain chemistry, in the right place, at the right time, can create a monster. If the brain - an electro-chemical computer - is "shorted" it "reboots" like an mechanical computer, and for a while switches to its most primitive "operating-system" In this condition, our m-field kicks in, and together with our fossil-memories, creates a defence mechanism - the primal fear, 'flight or fight', taken to its extreme in the creation of something visible and (for a time at least), tangible.

But we have ignored some of the most important archetypes of the 20th century, ones that are pertinent to our search for the nature of dragons - the UFO and the "reptoid".

Strange lights have always been seen in our skies. They are recorded in ancient manuscripts from China and India, and are mentioned in The Bible. Their interpretation has differed through the ages. In the early part of the 20th century "waves" of sighting of what were then called "mystery airships" were reported from all over the world. In Britain some believed that they were the spearhead of an invasion fleet sent by Kaiser Wilhelm. In the Second World War, they were referred to as "foo-fighters". Both The Allies *and* The Axis Forces saw them, and each believed them to be new enemy technology. It was not until the post-war era that the idea that these phenomena may be alien spacecraft appeared. The phenomenon has "updated" itself, in keeping with the mindset of the era that it appears in. It is hence unsurprising that in an age dominated by technology, 'they' manifest as a technophoic nightmare.

In a more primitive age, one of mankind's greatest fears would have been of devouring predators. Maybe the UFO phenomenon - as viewed by our ancestors - were dragons. There are links between the two.

- Both dragons and UFOs seem to have an affinity with water, often appearing in or around lakes, seas and other bodies of water.

- Both seem far above the powers of mankind - the dragon, an unkillable monster of god-like power (in the early legends). The UFO a machine made by technology so advanced it seems god-like.

- Both appear suddenly, often causing panic, and then just as quickly disappear. Some myths state that as well as breathing fire dragons clutched fiery balls in their claws or pursued pearl like objects (pearls of wisdom in the orient).

Appearances by UFO "occupants" are another facet to this phenomenon. Early reports of "aliens" usually portrayed them as looking like very beautiful human-beings. They were usually tall, fair haired, and pale skinned. They first raised their heads in the post-war years and one has only to think of Hitler's putative super-race to explain their Aryan looks. "Contactees" such as George Adamski claimed to have met such beautiful space-people in the deserts of the American south-west. They span wild yarns of being taken to planets in our solar system - such as Venus - that were lush utopias. In such early cases, the "extraterrestrials" generally had some kind of warning for mankind to mend its ways, or suffer global catastrophe. The link to a post-war mind-set is obvious.

We now know that Venus is incapable of supporting life as we understand it, and that aliens are highly unlikely to resemble human-beings. This persistence of humanoid-aliens is one of my main reasons for rejecting the extraterrestrial hypothesis (ETH). It seems to be a kind of narcissus complex in the collective mind of mankind. Many of our past monsters have been humanoid too - trolls, elves, giants, angels, mermaids, vampires, werewolves, and satyrs to name but a few. I call this humanoid obsession 'The *Star Trek* effect'. One only has to watch a couple of episodes of this series to see the lack of imagination in the design of the alien races. Most of them look perfectly human, except for pointed ears or wrinkled foreheads. The chances of evolution on another biosphere being so like the chance-events on earth that spawned us, to result in a human-like lifeform are astronomical. To get a better idea of what something from another world might look, like I would suggest watching some classic *Doctor Who*. With far greater imagination, the costume-designers at the BBC produced some genuinely *alien* looking aliens.

As if growing directly with our knowledge, and perhaps liked directly to our minds, the UFO phenomenon has changed. Now the "aliens" look less human, and claim to come from other solar systems - such as Zeta Reticuli. The commonest alien type reported today is 'The Grey'. These are small in stature, with grey skin, lipless-mouths, flat noses and huge, dark eyes. In some ways they resemble the goblins of ancient legend. But the resemblance does not end there.

Beginning in the 1960s, a new facet to the UFO phenomenon emerged - the abduction. These scenarios involve the apparent kidnap of people, (sometimes several at once), by "aliens" who take them on board their vessel, and conduct medical-experiments on them - sometimes of a sexual nature. Often the abductee has no memory of the event, but finds they have "lost" several hours of time. The memories may come back during hypnotic-regression, or naturally bit-by-bit. They sometimes claim to have been "implanted" with small probe-like devices, although these have never been confirmed by scientists. Some female abductees claim that eggs have been taken from their wombs, or even that they have been implanted with human/alien hybrid-foetuses that are harvested later.

Students of folklore reading this, may find it all rather familiar - and with good reason. None of it is new. All the above have been claimed to be the work of fairies in times past. People abducted by 'The Fair Folk', were said to be spirited away to Faerieland. These victims often had little memory of their sojourn, but experienced lost-time. Time was said to be non-existent in Faerieland, so what seemed like a short stay there could account for days, weeks, or even years, in our world. The abductees were often returned with magickal silver-pins inserted into them - in some cases to render them mute. Most tellingly, fairies were supposed to be a waning race who wished to interbreed with humans to strengthen their racial stock. They would steal babies and leave sickly offspring of their own - known as changelings - in their place. There are many tales of fairies seducing mortal men and women, and mating with them to produce hybrid-children. The alien-abductee scenario is merely a high-tech update of this age-old story.

A fine example of this is recounted in historian Robert Hunt's book, *Popular Romances of the West of England*. The story concerns Ann Jeffries - a teenaged girl from Cornwall. One day in 1647 she was in her employer's garden, when she felt a whirling, floating sensation. She was approached by two small beings and then passed out. She came-to in Faerieland. Ann describes this place as colourful, flower-filled, and populated by strange creatures. The fairies seemed intensely interested in human sexual-reproduction. When returned, Ann heard a loud buzzing-noise and experienced the same floating sensation and blackout. After the encounter, she stopped eating certain types of food, and became a renowned psychic and healer. The relationship to modern abduction cases is startling.

Now the fairies are aliens, and the dragons may well be UFOs. But dragon-like creatures are still seen today - as the "Encounters with Modern Dragons" section of this book shows. The dragon-image refuses to be vanquished, and it may even have a new form from the ranks of the so called alien sightings.

INDEX

Abductions - 56, 87, 266, 323, 324
Airships / UFOs - 210, 214, 215, 216, 217, 236, 375
Anning, Mary (1799-1847: naturalist) - 240, 241, 242, 369
Animal deaths - see chicken. Elliston - 15, 18, 48, 54, 55, 56, 57, 58, 59, 60, 61, 79, 80, 81, 82, 83, 85, 86, 87, 128, 162, 163, 164, 183, 186, 249, 256, 268, 314, 315, 332
Ball lightning - 340, 341
Ball, Martin: merfolk, 101, 102, 105, 107, 115, 116, 277
Baring-Gould, Rev. Sabine, 146, 147, 204
Bearne, A (auctioneer & witness) - 218, 219
Berry Head (Brixham) - 65, 66, 67
BHM (Bigfoot, Yeti) -14, 118, 119,249, 256, 257, 258, 259, 320
Black Dog - 14, 50, 51, 171
Boleskine House - 260, 261, 262, 263
Branksome, Dorset (thylacine?) - 244
Branson, J (witness) - 221
Brighton - 113, 114, 115, 261, 285
Brittany mutilated dolphins - 85
Brixham coastguards - 66, 67, 69
Budleigh Salterton - 40, 53, 54, 81, 88, 125, 139, 147, 224
Cadejo (El Salvador) - 51
Cats, big - 78, 136, 151, 161,162,165, 166, 167, 168, 169, 170, 171,172, 220, 228, 230, 231, 236, 294
Canvin, Jerome (witness) - 17
Centre for Fortean Zoology, The (CFZ) - 11, 34, 70, 119, 161, 379
Chicken deaths - 38
Chicken Giant, Dorset - 102
Conspiracies/cover-ups - 14,15, 25, 26, 52,132, 199, 200,205, 207, 266, 271, 272
CIA - 67, 68, 69
Clyst St Mary mystery sounds - see Weird Warbling Whatsit
Crop Circle(s) - 14, 17, 18, 23, 24, 25, 26, 27, 28, 49, 55, 124, 171, 274,

332, 335, 336, 337, 338, 339, 346
Crowley, Aleister - 15, 259, 260, 261, 262, 263
Cullompton - 43
Cuvier's beaked whale - see whale
Dartmouth - 28
Dawlish - 42, 54, 186, 225, 237
Dartmoor - 43, 165, 204, 266
Devil's Footprints - 186, 187, 188, 240, 275
Dorset - 29, 51, 101, 107, 116, 118, 239, 242, 244, 258, 276, 277, 336
Dorchester, Dorset - 28, 29, 85
Dragons - 12, 48, 107, 117, 118, 176, 177, 178, 179, 180, 181, 182, 242, 249, 259, 277, 373, 374, 375, 377
Dr. Who - 273
East Budleigh - 35, 47, 48, 53, 65, 124, 144, 145, 146, 286, 338
Electromagnetism - 154, 156, 172, 174, 249, 314, 321, 376
Elliston. Jon "Operation Mutilation" - 86
Exeter Strange Phenomena Research Group (ESP) - 22, 34, 35, 42, 44, 53, 65, 70, 74, 78, 157, 337
Exeter - 11,17, 21, 22, 25, 28, 31, 34, 35, 37, 39, 42, 43, 44, 46, 52, 53, 65, 66, 70, 71, 74, 75, 78, 80, 83, 85, 87, 138, 141, 143, 145, 157, 180, 184, 200, 223, 225, 237, 254, 266, 273, 284, 300, 301, 337, 338
Exeter Airport - 43, 46, 66, 223
Exmouth - 17, 34, 35, 39, 40, 41, 42, 43, 45, 46, 53, 54, 65, 66, 69, 78, 80, 81, 83, 87, 88, 94, 95, 96, 113 124, 125, 126, 138, 139 , 146 ,147, 149, 158, 159, 161, 163, 164, 165, 166, 170, 182, 184, 185, 200, 202 ,203, 205 206, 206, 207, 209, 210, 214, 217, 218 221, 222, 223, 224, 225, 226, 227, 232, 233, 234, 236, 237, 240, 254, 256, 259, 267, 271, 283, 284, 285, 286, 287, 336
Fairy Rings - 26, 27, 246
Falls (Fafrotskies) - 60, 174, 182, 183, 184
Florida - 82, 168
Frazer-Jennings. William (witness) - 54
Freeman. Richard (CFZ zoologist) - 12, 34, 119, 178, 180, 293, 295, 338, 373
Geology - 123, 276
Ghosts - 21, 39, 72, 141, 142, 142, 146, 148, 149, 151, 154, 157, 158, 159, 171, 231, 247, 248, 249, 258, 270, 300, 301, 303, 317, 321, 332
Glastonbury, Pete - 22, 24, 25
Gulf of Mexico - 82
Hairy wallpaper - see hallucinations
Haldon Hill UFOs (Exeter) - 36, 44, 47, 65, 224, 232
hallucinations - 103, 104, 105, 176, 215, 301, 311
Hawkwind - 105
helicopter(s) - 32, 40, 55, 66, 67, 87, 88, 249

Heuvelmans, Bernard - 83, 85, 257
Holiday, Ted - 48, 117, 244, 245
Hopkins, Dave (ornithologist & researcher) - 72
Hospital ghosts - 300, 301,302, 303, 326
Inglis, Graham - 18, 21, 22, 24, 38, 34, 35, 37, 38, 39, 44, 45, 52, 70, 73, 104, 134, 311, 324, 336, 343,
Isle of Lewis. Scotland (crash debris) - 32, 33, 34, 268
Johnston,Phil (Psychic detective) - 134, 135, 136
Jordan, Debbie (researcher & writer) - 324, 329
Kelowana, B.C. - 90
Kingston, David (CSETI group) - 29
KGB - 279
Lake Mjosa (Norway) - 89
Led Zeppelin - 261, 311
Littleham - 46, 95, 113, 138, 139, 141,142, 145, 146, 147, 148, 149, 151, 157, 158, 159, 184, 250, 255, 256, 265, 269, 270, 283, 284, 285, 286, 287, 316, 322
Lizards - 240, 277, 373
LSD / magic mushrooms - 104, 311
Lulworth Cove butterflies - 239,
Lyme Bay - 43, 46, 47, 50, 51, 52, 80, 85, 87, 88, 95, 97, 101, 102, 239, 240, 241, 242, 250, 269, 270, 276, 277, 282, 322
Lympstone - 94, 95, 185, 222
Lynx - 117, 161, 163, 169, 231
Magnetic effects - see electromagnctism
Maiden Castle Hillfort, Dorset - 28, 29, 30
Marriage breakup - 11, 12, 21, 28, 39, 75
Meller, Steve - 30
Mermaids / merfolk - 15, 97, 101, 105, 106, 107, 108, 109, 110, 111, 376
Mesoplodons - 84, 85
mental block (witness inhibition) - 48
Mexico - 249, 273, 287, 332
Men in Black (MIB) - 217, 218, 217
Minnesota Iceman - 107
Mutilations, Animal - 14, 18, 49, 55, 56, 57, 58, 59, 60, 61, 81, 86, 87, 256, 268, 332
Mutilations, Cattle - 79, 80,249
Mutilations, Deer - 86
Mutilations, Human - 332
Mutilations, Whale - 14, 78, 81, 85,
Namibian flying snake - 109,181
Ogopogo - 92, 93, 94
Olcott. Frances (author) - 245
Oliver's Castle UFO video - 23, 24, 25, 28, 274, 335

Otter Cove - 14, 78, 79, 80, 81, 83, 85, 96, 269
Ottery St. Mary - 35, 39, 339
Owlman of Mawnan - 49, 99,106, 115, 154, 237, 249, 253, 254, 256, 257, 263, 288, 333
Poltergeist - 72, 113, 151, 154, 156, 157, 228
Portland, Dorset - 29, 66, 101, 102, 103, 104, 105, 115, 116, 117, 277
RAF Cosford - 235
Redfern, Nick - 11, 13, 207
Rendlesham Forest - 39
Roswell - 11, 15, 40, 52, 180, 199, 209
Sandys, Duncan (UK Govt minister) - 206, 208, 271
Satanism - 87, 126, 127, 128, 129, 261, 271, 315
Scarff, Martin 'Jan' (ESP researcher) - 45, 46, 70
Shiels, Tony 'Doc' (artist & fortean facilitator) - 26, 113, 232
Shuker, Dr. K. P. N - 111, 172, 176, 177, 231, 320
Sky creatures - 172, 176, 177
Skywatch - 29, 45, 46,
Space animals - see sky creatures
Spider invocation - 293, 294
Spoor, David - 176
Stealth technology - 95
Steller's Sea cow - 97, 98, 99, 100
Tasmanian wolf / Tasmanian tiger - 242, 243, 244
Tate, Genette - 125, 133, 134, 137, 138, 222, 265, 266, 323
Texas - 82, 176,202, 287
Thylacine - see Tasmanian wolf / Tasmanian tiger
Tin mines - 248
Toby (CFZ Dog) - 15 , 37, 44, 71, 74, 135, 343
Topsham - 44, 52, 97, 101, 184, 185, 186, 236, 267
Torquay - 41, 45, 221, 338
Triangular craft - 29, 30, 55, 235, 249, 339
Tulpa - 291, 292, 293, 294, 295, 297, 300, 315, 316, 318, 320, 323
Veasta, Chesil Beach Monster - 101, 102, 105, 107, 116, 117, 267
Virginid meteors - 69
Walker, Scott (singer) - 71,
Weymouth, Dorset - 115, 116, 221, 240, 285
Wilson, Tracey (witness) - 42, 53
Window areas - 232, 248, 249, 313
Witchcraft - 21, 26, 127, 128, 129, 130, 131, 132, 204, 205, 228, 246, 248, 356
Weird about the West (radio show) - 35, 70
Weird Warbling Whatsit - 70, 73, 74, 75, 76
Westcountry TV - 21, 25, 265
Woodbury Common - 35, 40, 41, 43, 44, 45, 46, 50, 51, 52, 53, 75, 123,

124, 126, 133, 135, 139, 163, 164, 166, 170, 206, 227, 237, 250, 256, 265, 266, 271, 273, 275, 286, 287, 316, 322, 323, 334, 336, 338, 343
Wright Family - 228, 229, 230, 231, 232
Ziphiidae (beaked) whales - 82, 83, 84, 85
Zooform phenomena - 99, 118, 199, 256, 257, 259, 270
Zoologica (exhibition in Sussex) - 31

ABOUT THE AUTHORS

Jonathan Downes was born in Portsmouth in 1959, and spent much of his childhood in Hong Kong where, surrounded by age-old Chinese superstitions and a dazzlingly diverse range of exotic wildlife, he soon became infected with the twin passions for exotic zoology and the paranormal which were to define his adult life. He spent some years as a nurse for the mentally handicapped but began writing professionally in the late 1980s. He has now written seventeen books. He is also a musician and songwriter who has made a number of critically acclaimed but commercially unsuccessful albums.

In 1992 he founded The Centre for Fortean Zoology, with the aim of coordinating research into mystery animals, bizarre and aberrant animal behaviour and his own particular love of zooform phenomena (paranormal entities which only appear to be animals!)

Nigel Wright was born in Yeovil in 1957. He has had a life long interest in the unexplained, especially UFOlogy and folklore. He is a well known researcher and author who co wrote "The Rising of the Moon" with Jon Downes in 1998. His writings have appeared in UFO Magazine, Parascience, Animals & Men, Caravan Magazine and for some years he had a column in the Exmouth Journal.

He met Jon Downes and the rest of the CFZ Crew in 1997 since when he has been a lone voice of sanity in an increasingly weird universe. He lives in Exmouth with his wife Sue and their two daughters

Jon and Nigel in early 1998

Also available from Xiphos Books....

Ronan Coghlan *A Dictionary of Cryptozoology*

An alphabetical guide to animals not recognised by science or from the realm of myth.

Large format. 273pp. Paperbound. £14.99/$29.95

Ronan Coghlan *Cryptosup*

Supplement to the above, containing many truly obscure mystery animals and creatures.

Large format paperbound booklet. 61pp. £7.99/$11.25

Ronan Coghlan *The Robin Hood Companion*

An A-Z guide to the legend and literature of the famous outlaw.

Paperbound. 207pp. £7.99/$11.25

INFORMATION ON NEW AND UPCOMING
TITLES ARE AVAILABLE BY CONTACTING
THE ADDRESS BELOW

XIPHOS BOOKS
1, HILLSIDE GARDENS, BANGOR
NORTHERN IRELAND
BT19 6SJ

THE CENTRE FOR FORTEAN ZOOLOGY

The Centre for Fortean Zoology is the world's only professional and scientific organisation dedicated to research into unknown animals. Although we work all over the world, we carry out regular work in the United Kingdom and abroad, investigating accounts of strange creatures.

THAILAND 2000
An expedition to investigate the legendary creature known as the Naga

SUMATRA 2003
'Project Kerinci'
In search of the bi-pedal ape Orang Pendek

MONGOLIA 2005
'Operation Death Worm'
An expedition to track the fabled 'Allghoi Khorkhoi' or Death Worm

Led by scientists, the CFZ is staffed by volunteers and is always looking for new members.

To apply for a <u>FREE</u> information pack about the organisation and details of how to join, plus information on current and future projects, expeditions and events.

Send a stamp addressed envelope to:

THE CENTRE FOR FORTEAN ZOOLOGY
MYRTLE COTTAGE, WOOLSERY,
BIDEFORD, DEVON, EX39 5QR.

or alternatively visit our website at: w w w . c f z . o r g . u k

www.ingramcontent.com/pod-product-compliance
Ingram Content Group UK Ltd.
Pitfield, Milton Keynes, MK11 3LW, UK
UKHW021316180426
11947UKWH00015B/1266